LEAP YEARS

BY IAN BENNETT

CANDLE LIGHT PRESS
WWW.CANDLELIGHTPRESS.COM

FRESHMAN YEAR

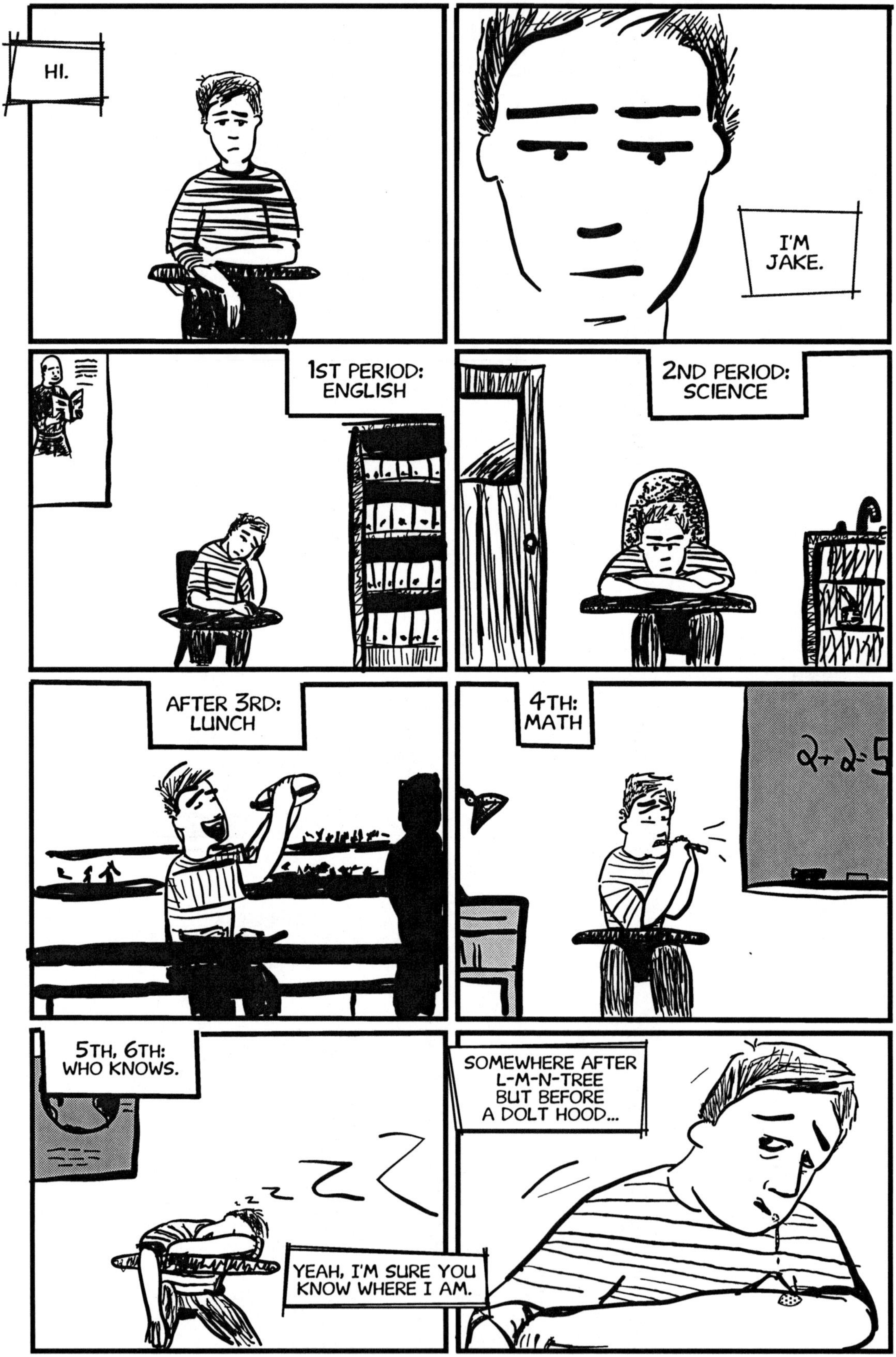
HI.
I'M JAKE.
1ST PERIOD: ENGLISH
2ND PERIOD: SCIENCE
AFTER 3RD: LUNCH
4TH: MATH
2+2=5
5TH, 6TH: WHO KNOWS.
YEAH, I'M SURE YOU KNOW WHERE I AM.
SOMEWHERE AFTER L-M-N-TREE BUT BEFORE A DOLT HOOD...

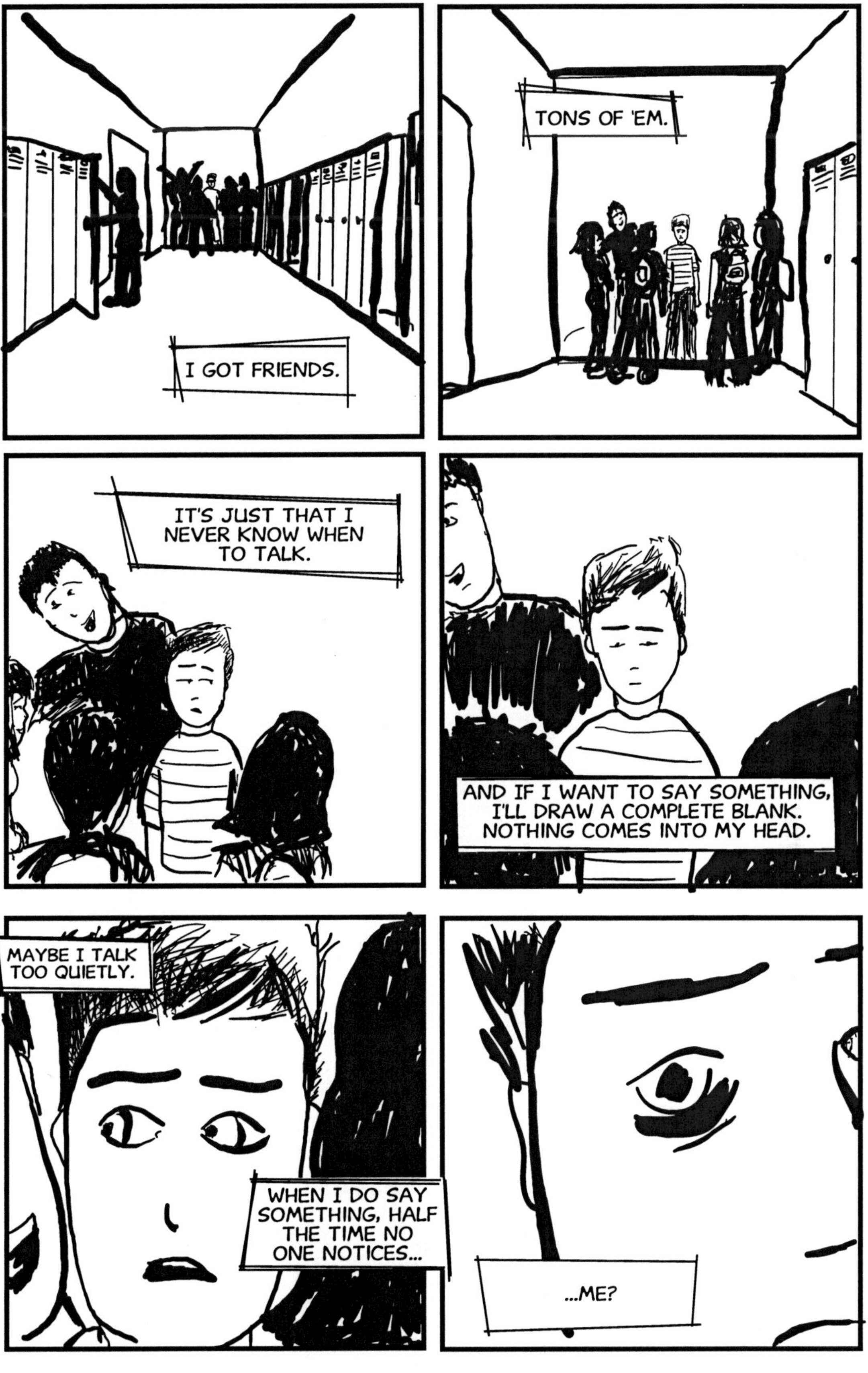
I GOT FRIENDS.
TONS OF 'EM.
IT'S JUST THAT I NEVER KNOW WHEN TO TALK.
AND IF I WANT TO SAY SOMETHING, I'LL DRAW A COMPLETE BLANK. NOTHING COMES INTO MY HEAD.
MAYBE I TALK TOO QUIETLY.
WHEN I DO SAY SOMETHING, HALF THE TIME NO ONE NOTICES...
...ME?

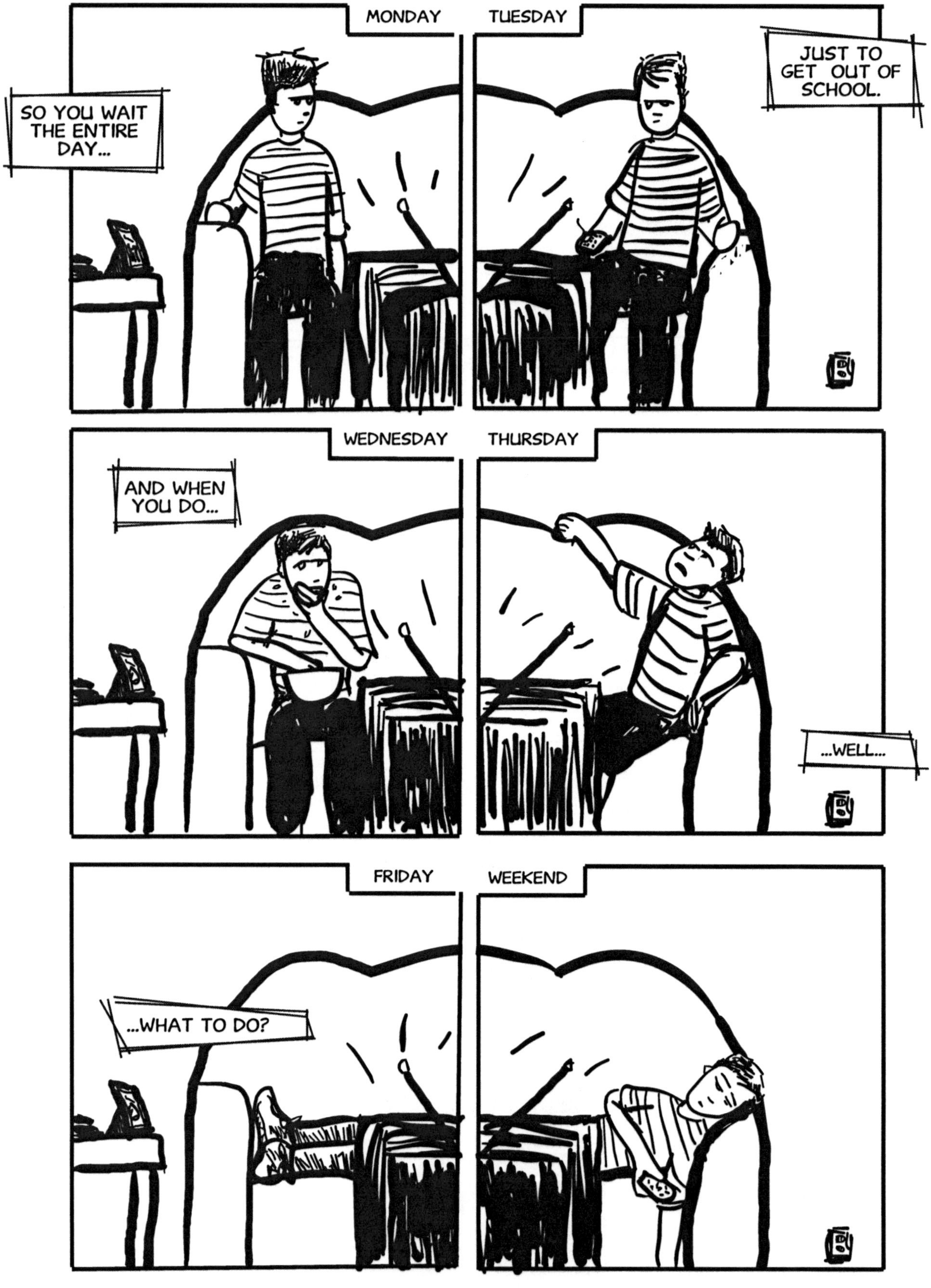
MONDAY
SO YOU WAIT THE ENTIRE DAY...
TUESDAY
JUST TO GET OUT OF SCHOOL.
WEDNESDAY
AND WHEN YOU DO...
THURSDAY
...WELL...
FRIDAY
...WHAT TO DO?
WEEKEND

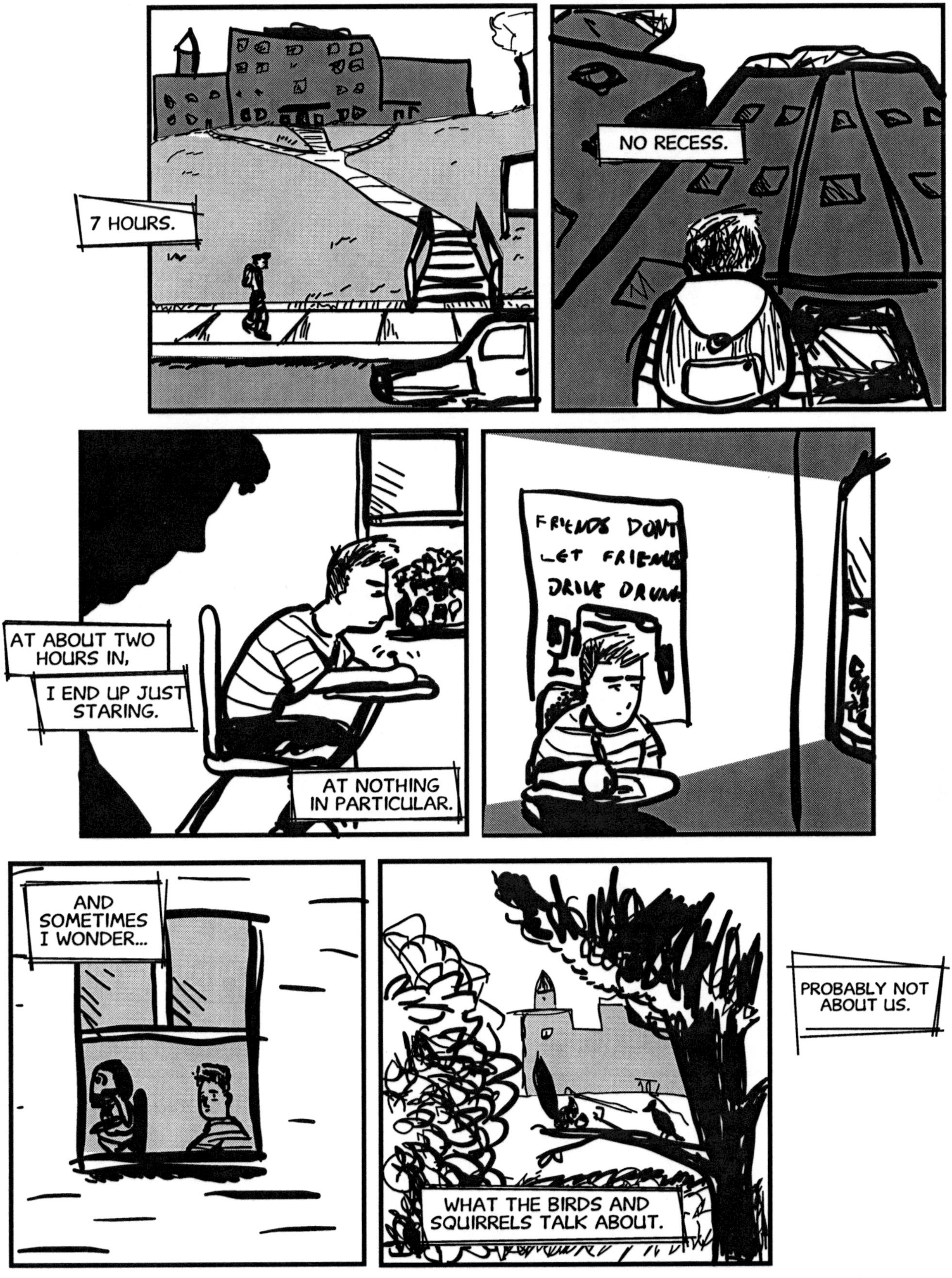
7 HOURS.
NO RECESS.
AT ABOUT TWO HOURS IN,
I END UP JUST STARING.
AT NOTHING IN PARTICULAR.
FRIENDS DON'T LET FRIENDS DRIVE DRUNK
AND SOMETIMES I WONDER...
WHAT THE BIRDS AND SQUIRRELS TALK ABOUT.
PROBABLY NOT ABOUT US.

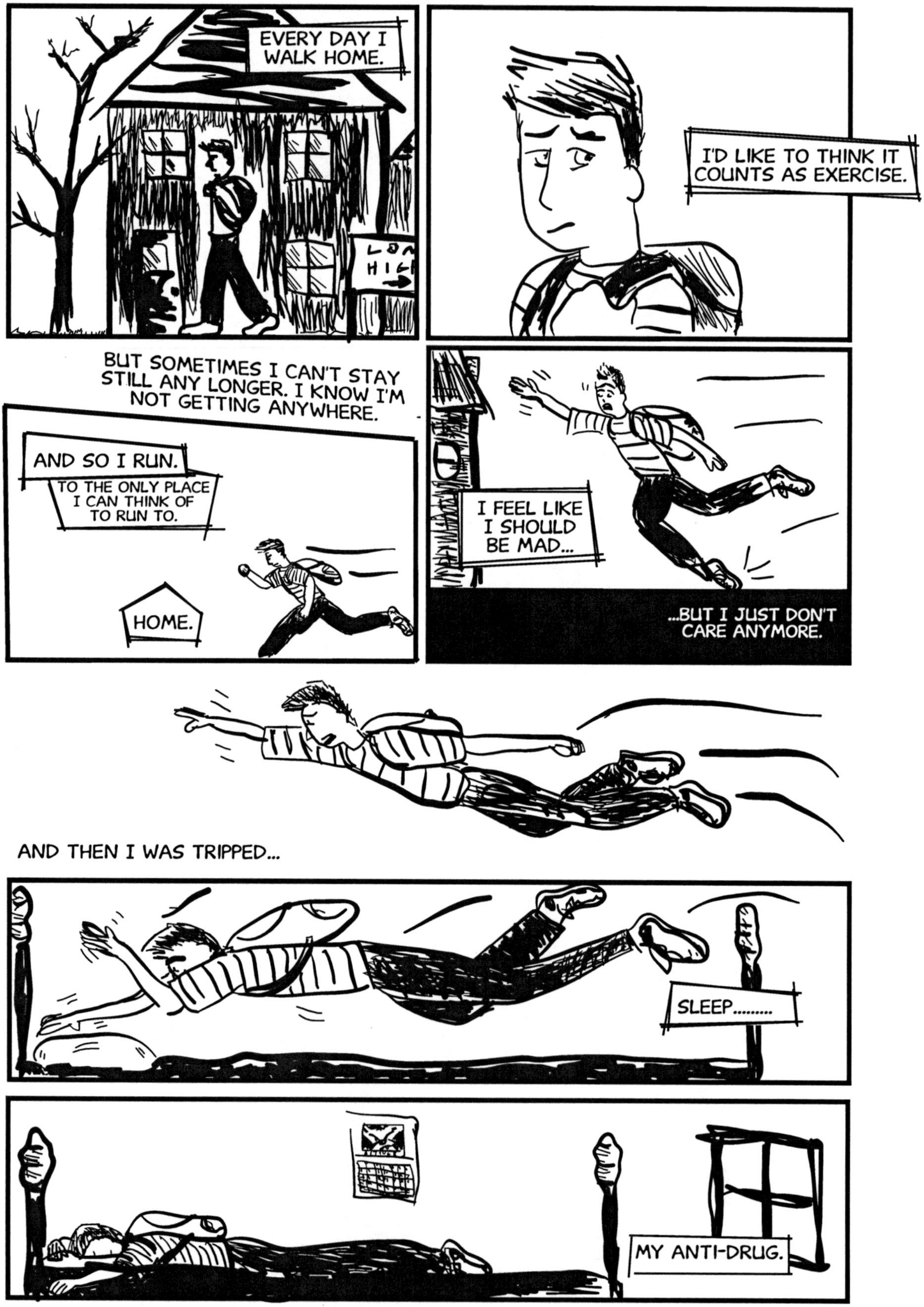
EVERY DAY I WALK HOME.
I'D LIKE TO THINK IT COUNTS AS EXERCISE.
BUT SOMETIMES I CAN'T STAY STILL ANY LONGER. I KNOW I'M NOT GETTING ANYWHERE.
AND SO I RUN.
TO THE ONLY PLACE I CAN THINK OF TO RUN TO.
HOME.
I FEEL LIKE I SHOULD BE MAD...
...BUT I JUST DON'T CARE ANYMORE.
AND THEN I WAS TRIPPED...
SLEEP.........
MY ANTI-DRUG.

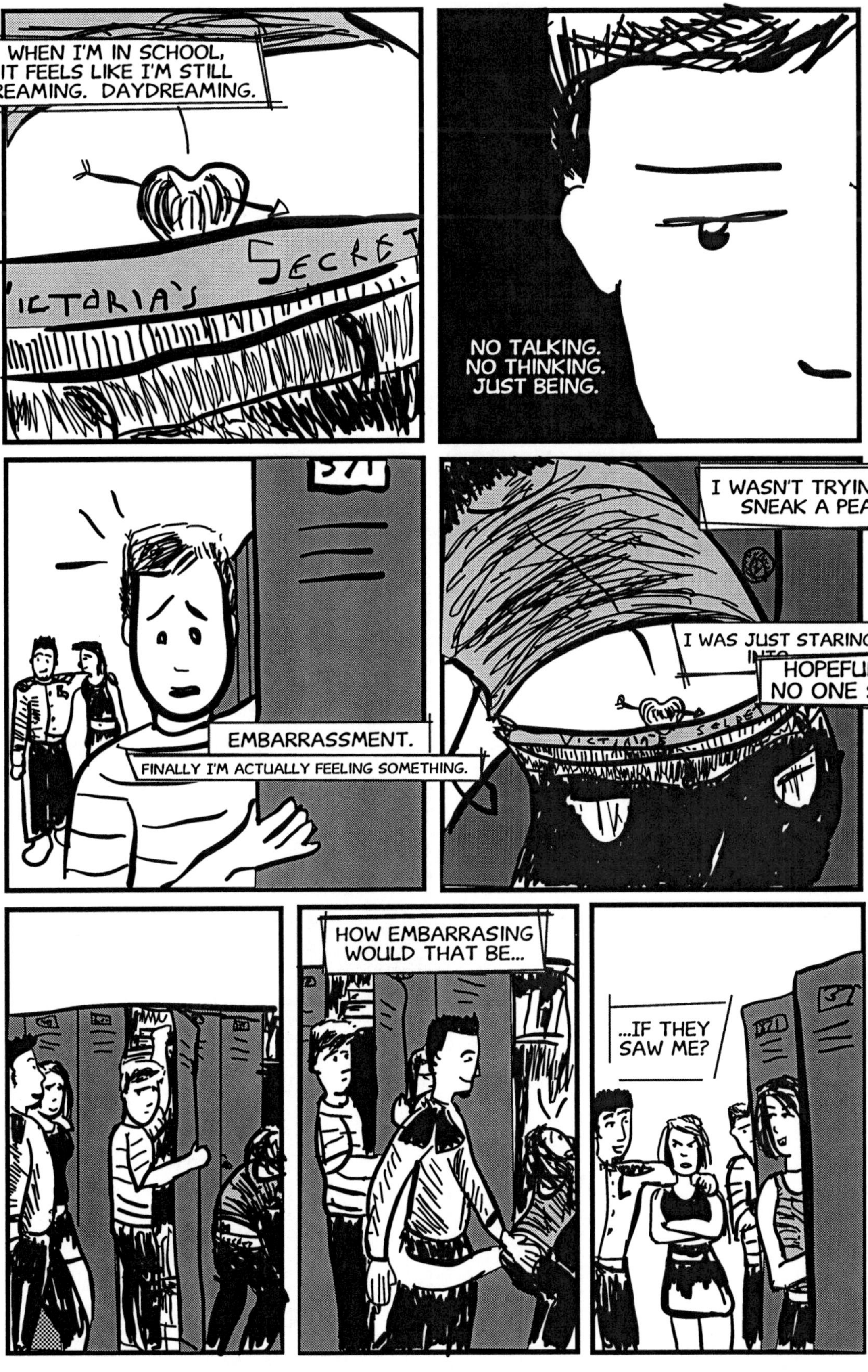
WHEN I'M IN SCHOOL, IT FEELS LIKE I'M STILL DREAMING. DAYDREAMING.
NO TALKING. NO THINKING. JUST BEING.
EMBARRASSMENT.
FINALLY I'M ACTUALLY FEELING SOMETHING.
I WASN'T TRYING TO SNEAK A PEAK.
I WAS JUST STARING
HOPEFULLY NO ONE SAW.
HOW EMBARRASING WOULD THAT BE...
...IF THEY SAW ME?

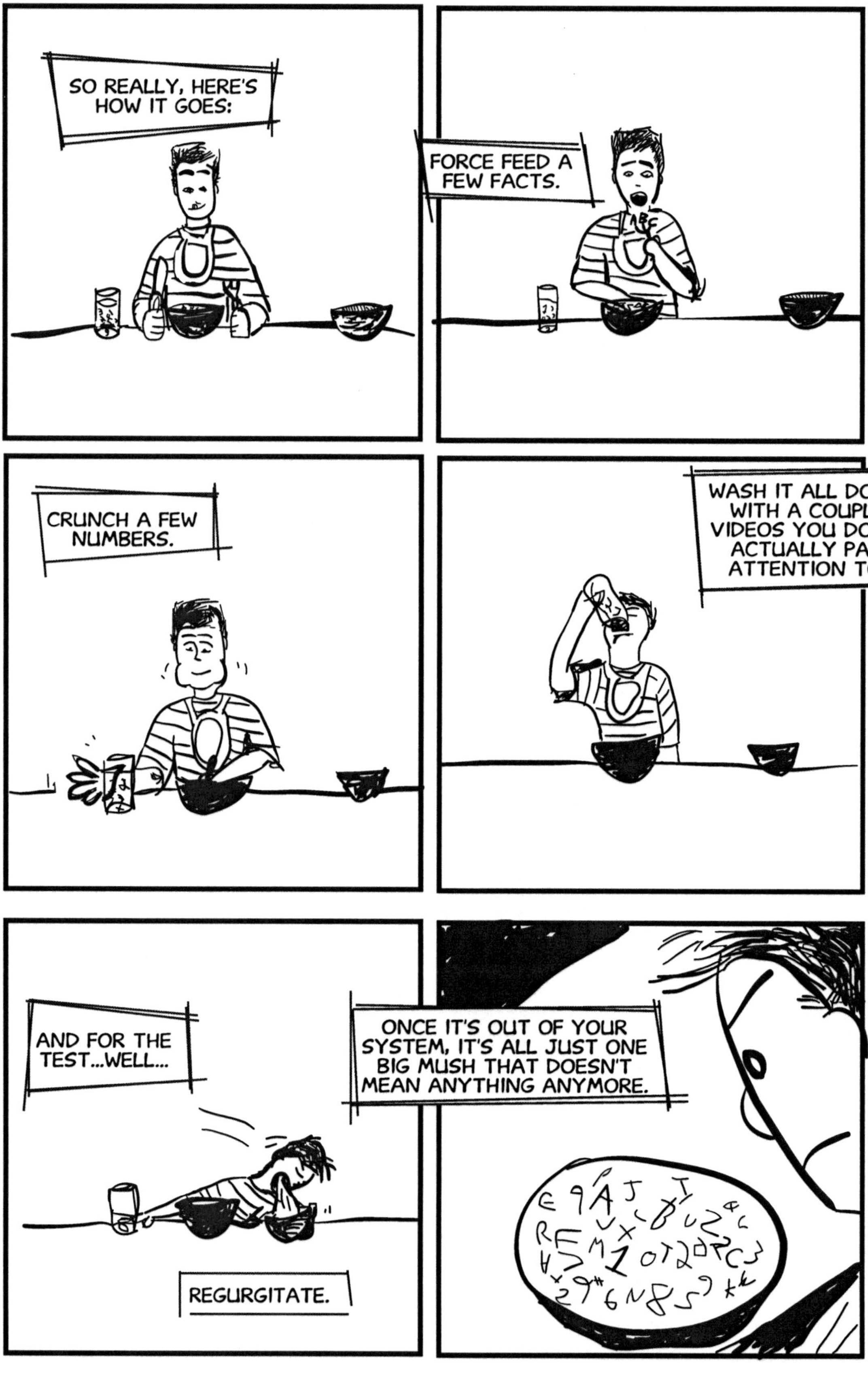
SO REALLY, HERE'S HOW IT GOES:
FORCE FEED A FEW FACTS.
CRUNCH A FEW NUMBERS.
WASH IT ALL DOWN WITH A COUPLE VIDEOS YOU DON'T ACTUALLY PAY ATTENTION TO.
AND FOR THE TEST...WELL...
REGURGITATE.
ONCE IT'S OUT OF YOUR SYSTEM, IT'S ALL JUST ONE BIG MUSH THAT DOESN'T MEAN ANYTHING ANYMORE.

SO THERE I WAS. MINDING MY OWN BUSINESS, CERTAINLY NO ONE ELSE WAS MINDING MINE...

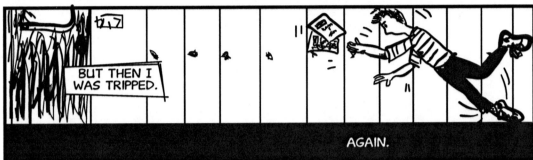

BUT THEN I WAS TRIPPED.

AGAIN.

AND WHEN I SAY TRIPPED, I DON'T MEAN I FELL. SOMETHING TRIPPED ME.

I DON'T KNOW WHAT IT WAS, BUT I FELT IT. SOMETHING ATTACKED ME.

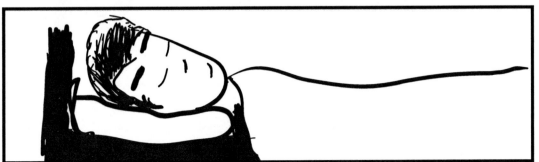

SUMMER

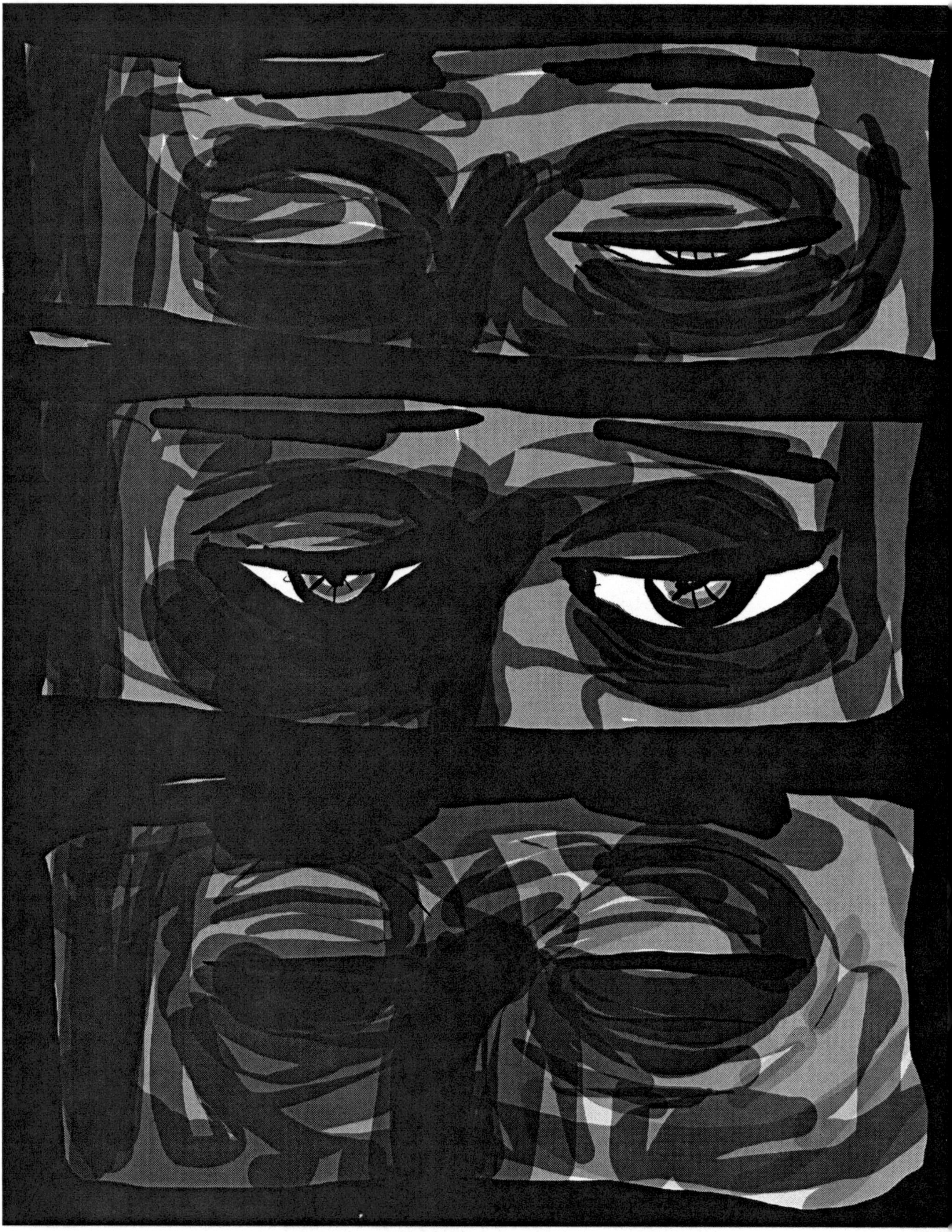

SOPHOMORE YEAR

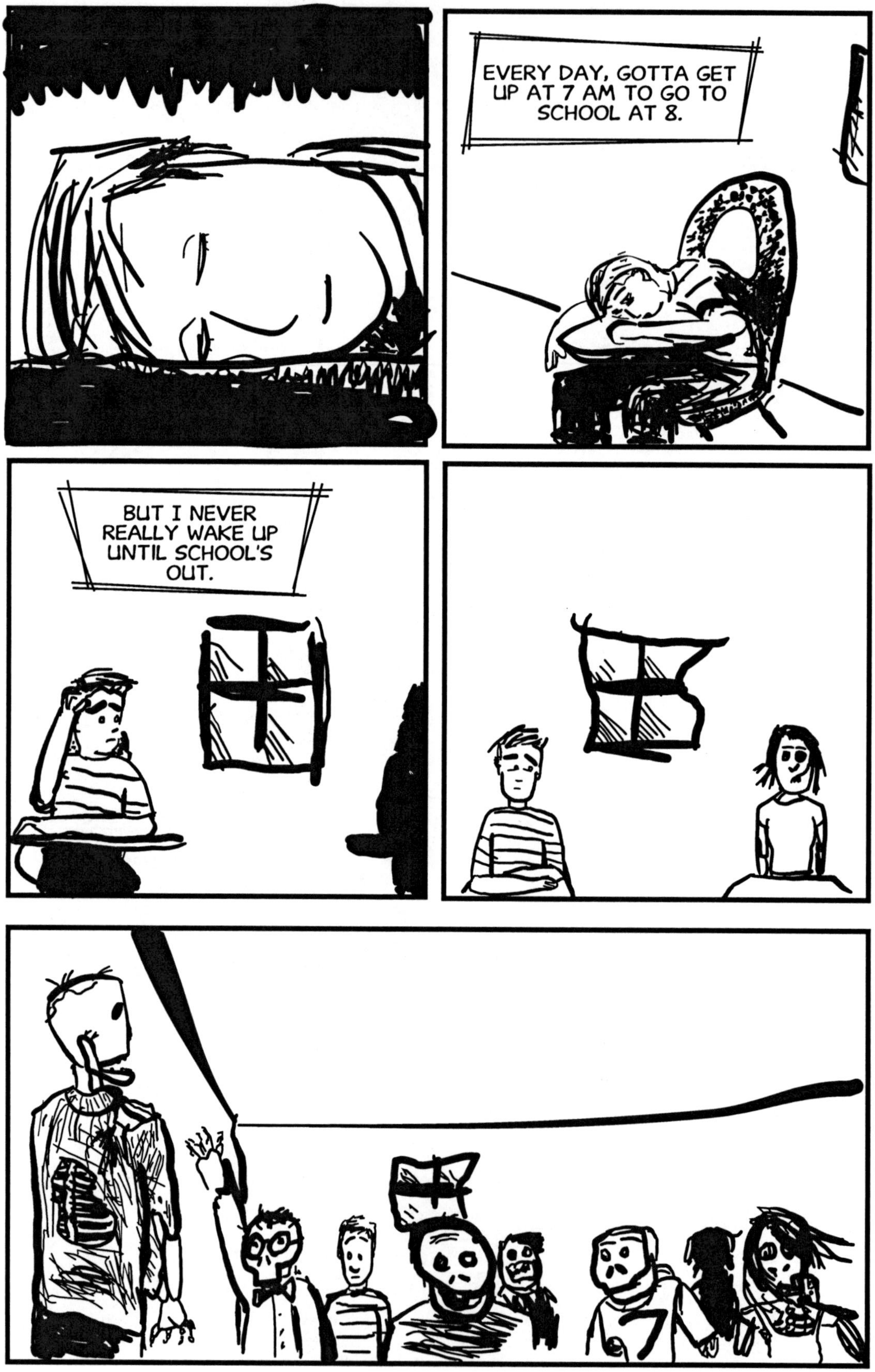
EVERY DAY, GOTTA GET UP AT 7 AM TO GO TO SCHOOL AT 8.
BUT I NEVER REALLY WAKE UP UNTIL SCHOOL'S OUT.

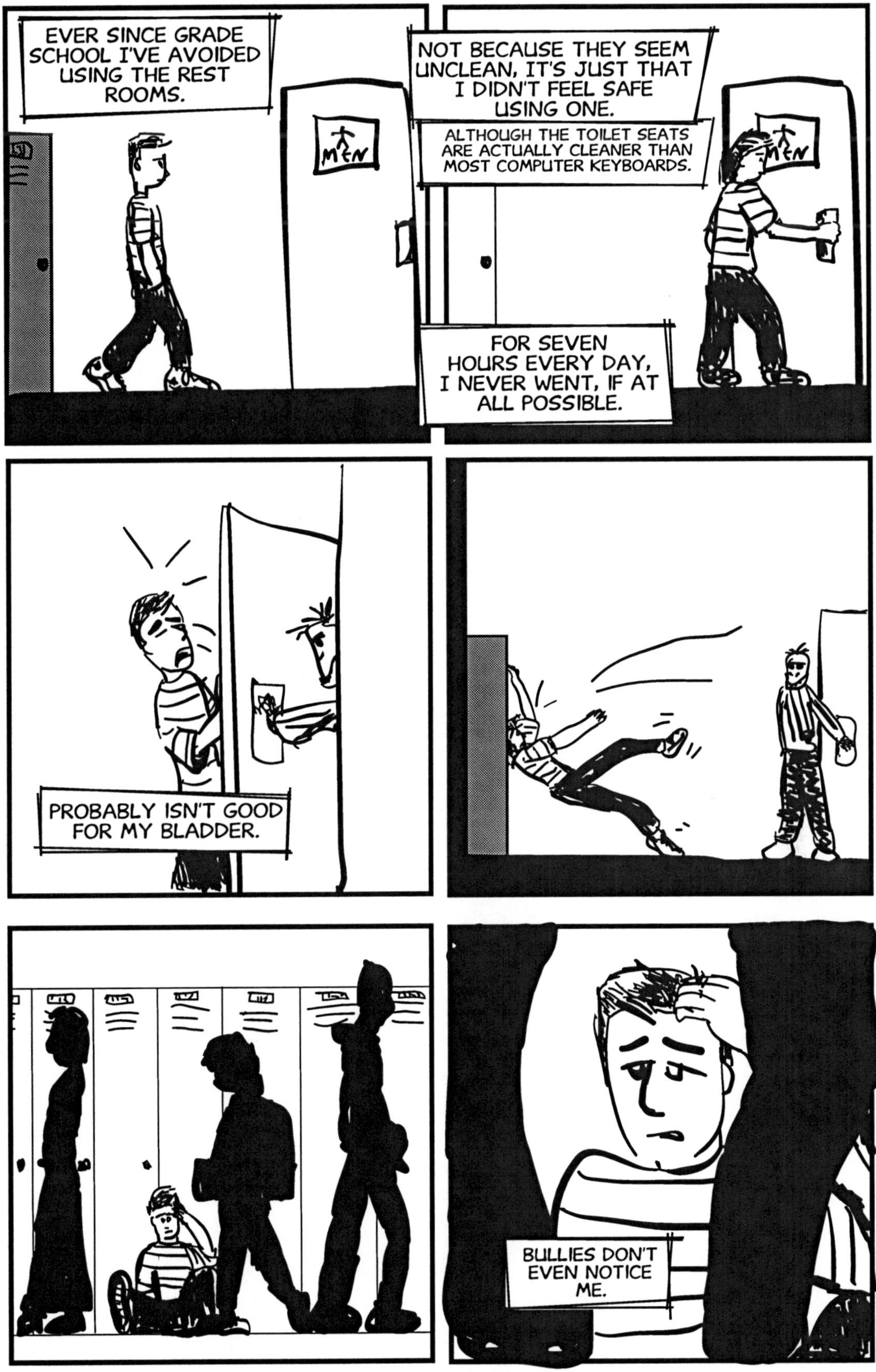
EVER SINCE GRADE SCHOOL I'VE AVOIDED USING THE REST ROOMS.
MEN
NOT BECAUSE THEY SEEM UNCLEAN, IT'S JUST THAT I DIDN'T FEEL SAFE USING ONE.
ALTHOUGH THE TOILET SEATS ARE ACTUALLY CLEANER THAN MOST COMPUTER KEYBOARDS.
MEN
FOR SEVEN HOURS EVERY DAY, I NEVER WENT, IF AT ALL POSSIBLE.
PROBABLY ISN'T GOOD FOR MY BLADDER.
BULLIES DON'T EVEN NOTICE ME.

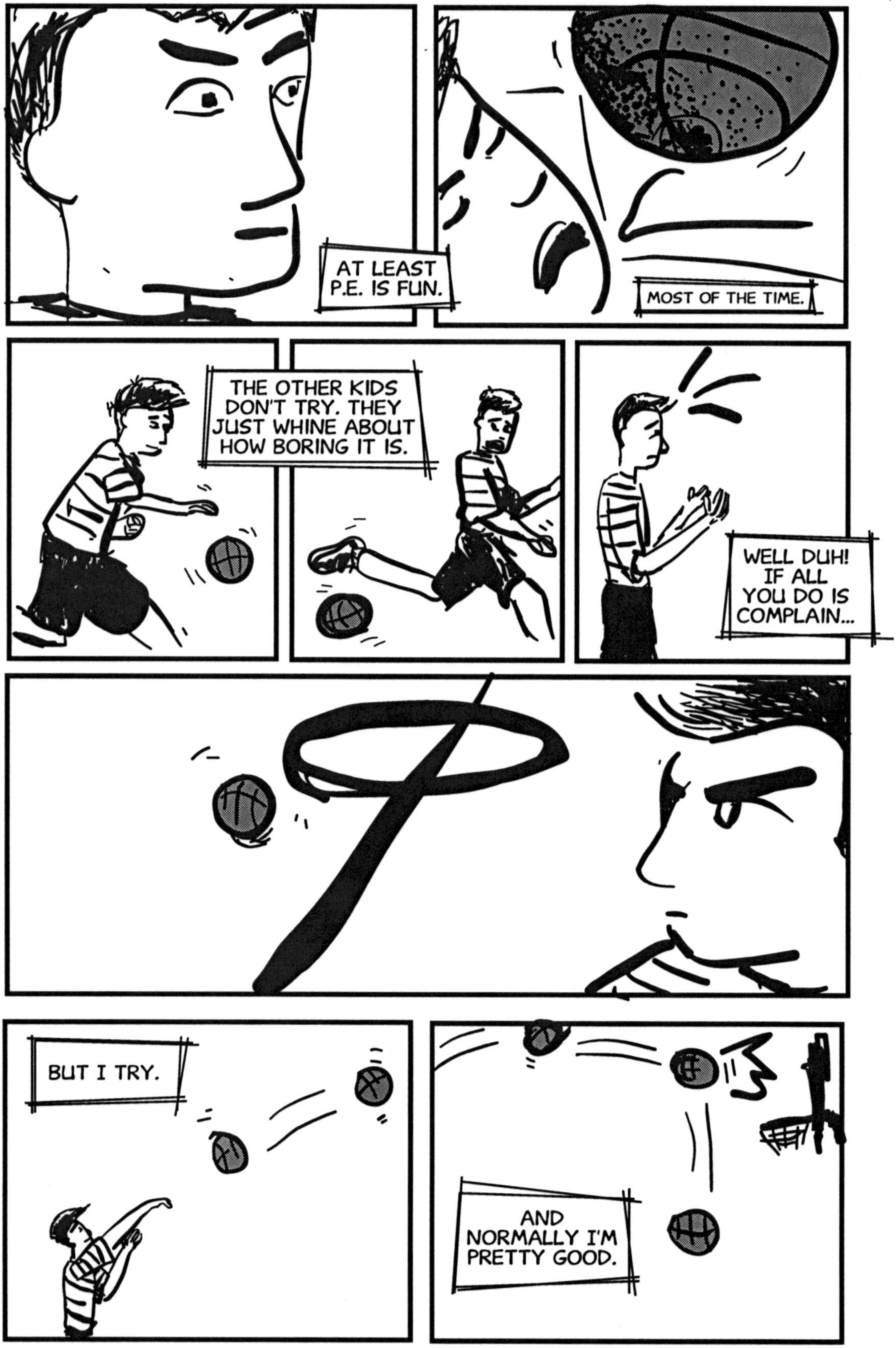
AT LEAST P.E. IS FUN.
MOST OF THE TIME.
THE OTHER KIDS DON'T TRY. THEY JUST WHINE ABOUT HOW BORING IT IS.
WELL DUH! IF ALL YOU DO IS COMPLAIN...
BUT I TRY.
AND NORMALLY I'M PRETTY GOOD.

APPARENTLY THE CHAIR DOESN'T THINK MY BUTT IS GOOD ENOUGH TO SIT ON IT.

MY PENCIL HAS OSTEOPEROSIS. BRITTLE LIKE OLD BONES.

SNAP

THE PENCIL SHARPENER MUST BE HUNGRY.

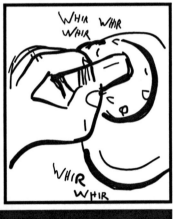

WHIR

WHIR

WHIR WHIR WHIR

WHIR

WHIR

NOTHING LIKES ME THESE DAYS.

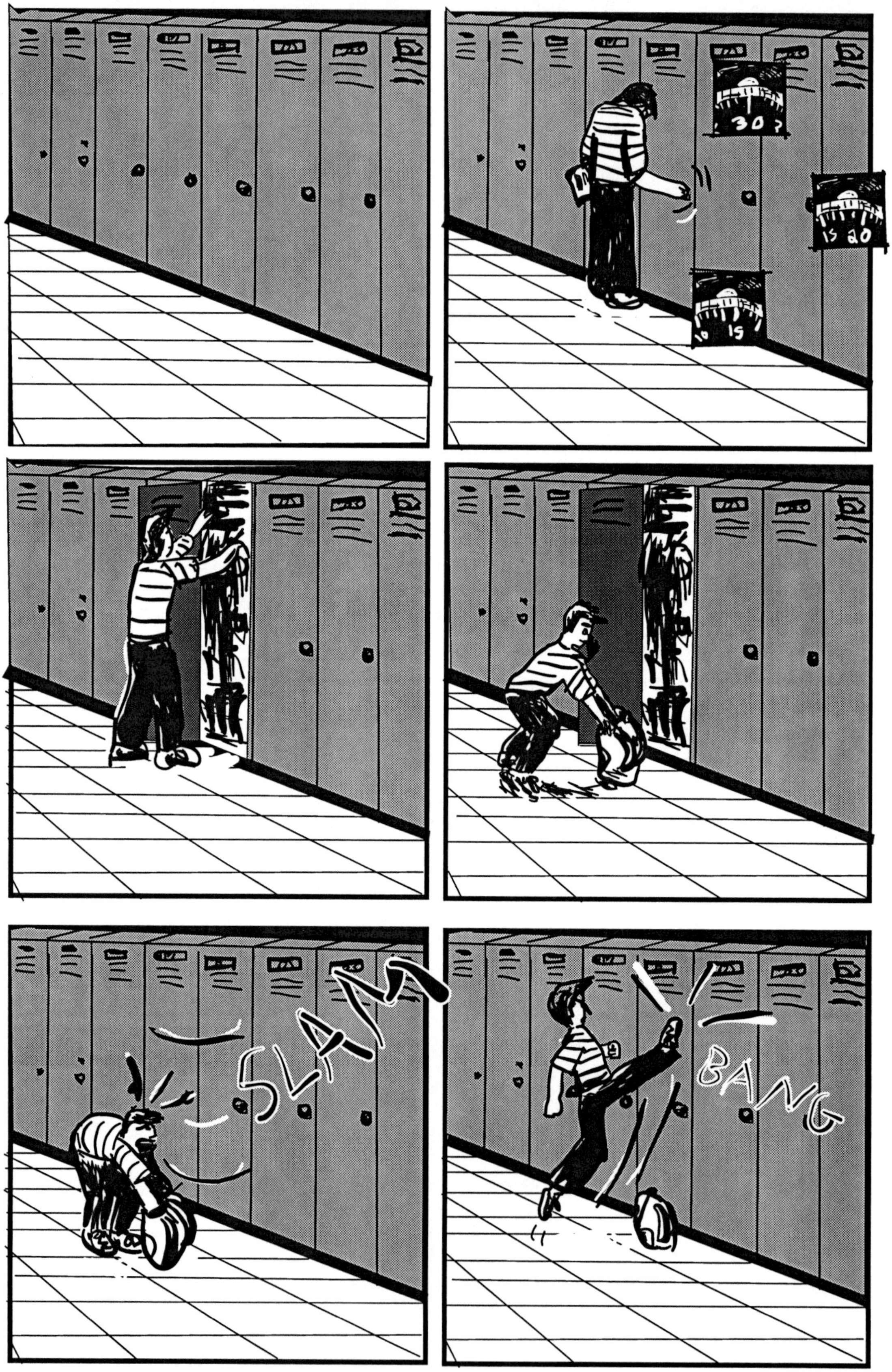
30
15 20
10 15
SLAM
BANG

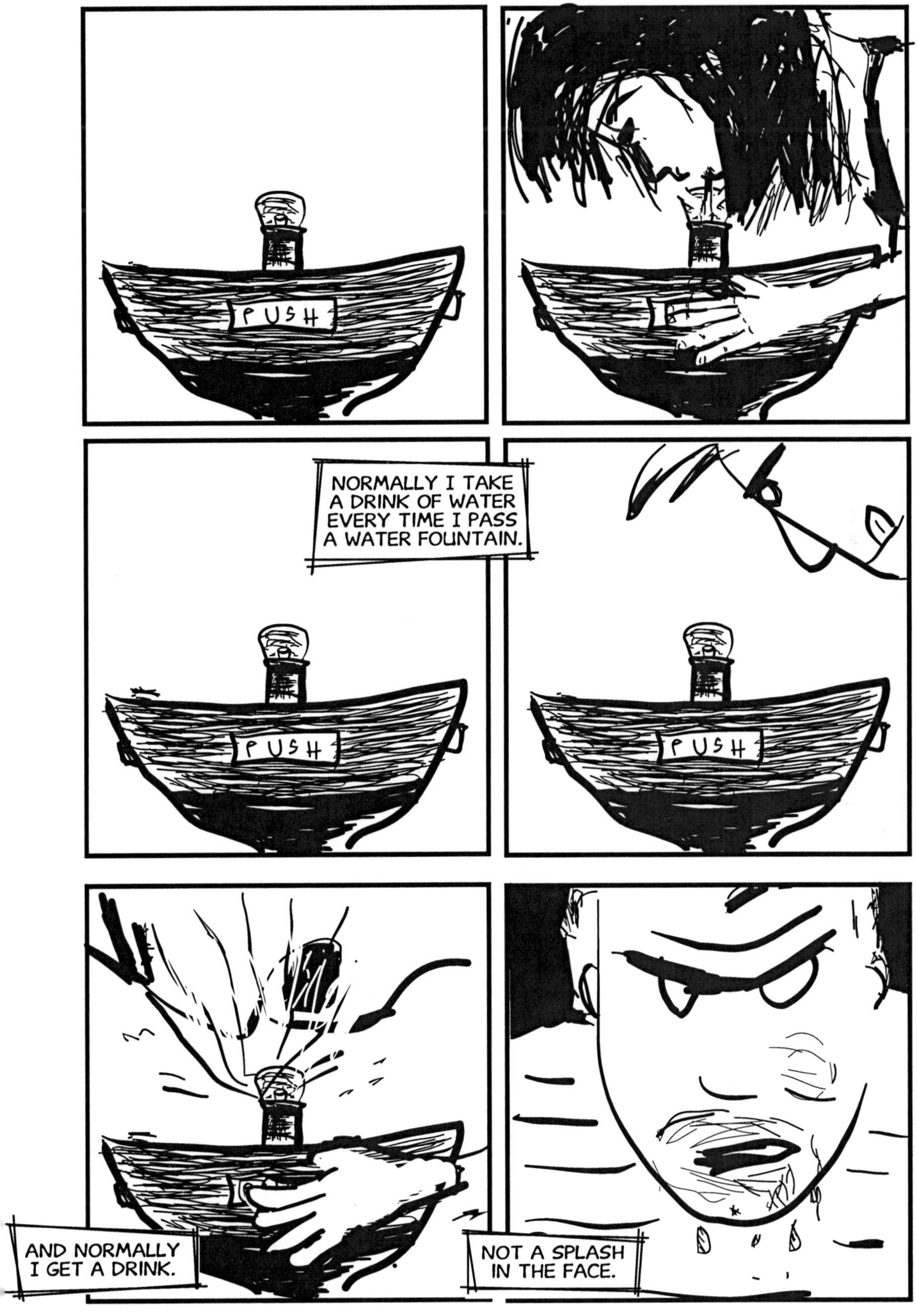
PUSH
NORMALLY I TAKE A DRINK OF WATER EVERY TIME I PASS A WATER FOUNTAIN.
PUSH
PUSH
AND NORMALLY I GET A DRINK.
NOT A SPLASH IN THE FACE.

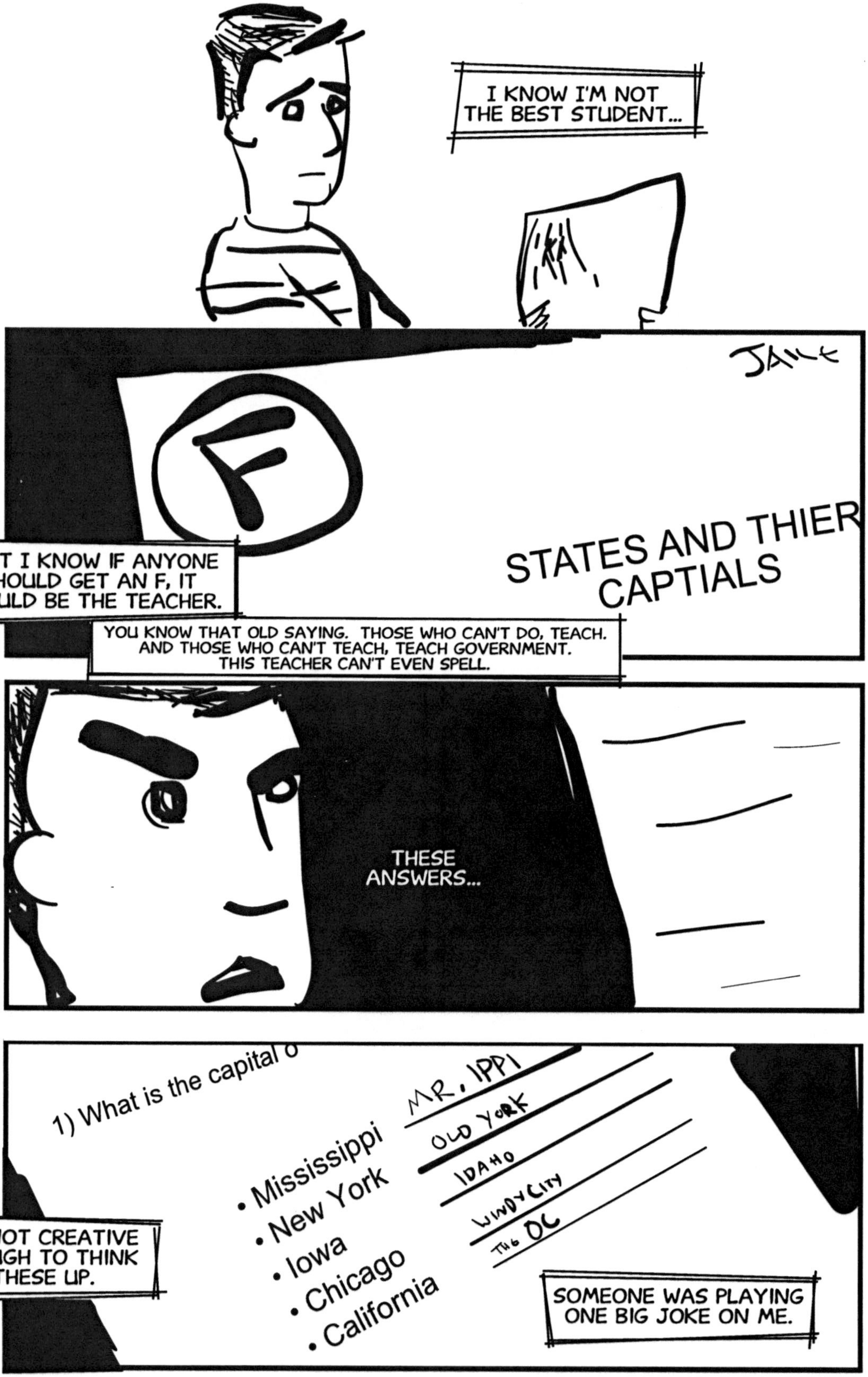
I KNOW I'M NOT THE BEST STUDENT...
JAKE
STATES AND THIER CAPTIALS
...BUT I KNOW IF ANYONE SHOULD GET AN F, IT SHOULD BE THE TEACHER.
YOU KNOW THAT OLD SAYING. THOSE WHO CAN'T DO, TEACH. AND THOSE WHO CAN'T TEACH, TEACH GOVERNMENT. THIS TEACHER CAN'T EVEN SPELL.
THESE ANSWERS...
1) What is the capital o
• Mississippi MR. IPPI
• New York OLD YORK
• Iowa IDAHO
• Chicago WINDY CITY
• California THE OC
I'M NOT CREATIVE EHOUGH TO THINK THESE UP.
SOMEONE WAS PLAYING ONE BIG JOKE ON ME.

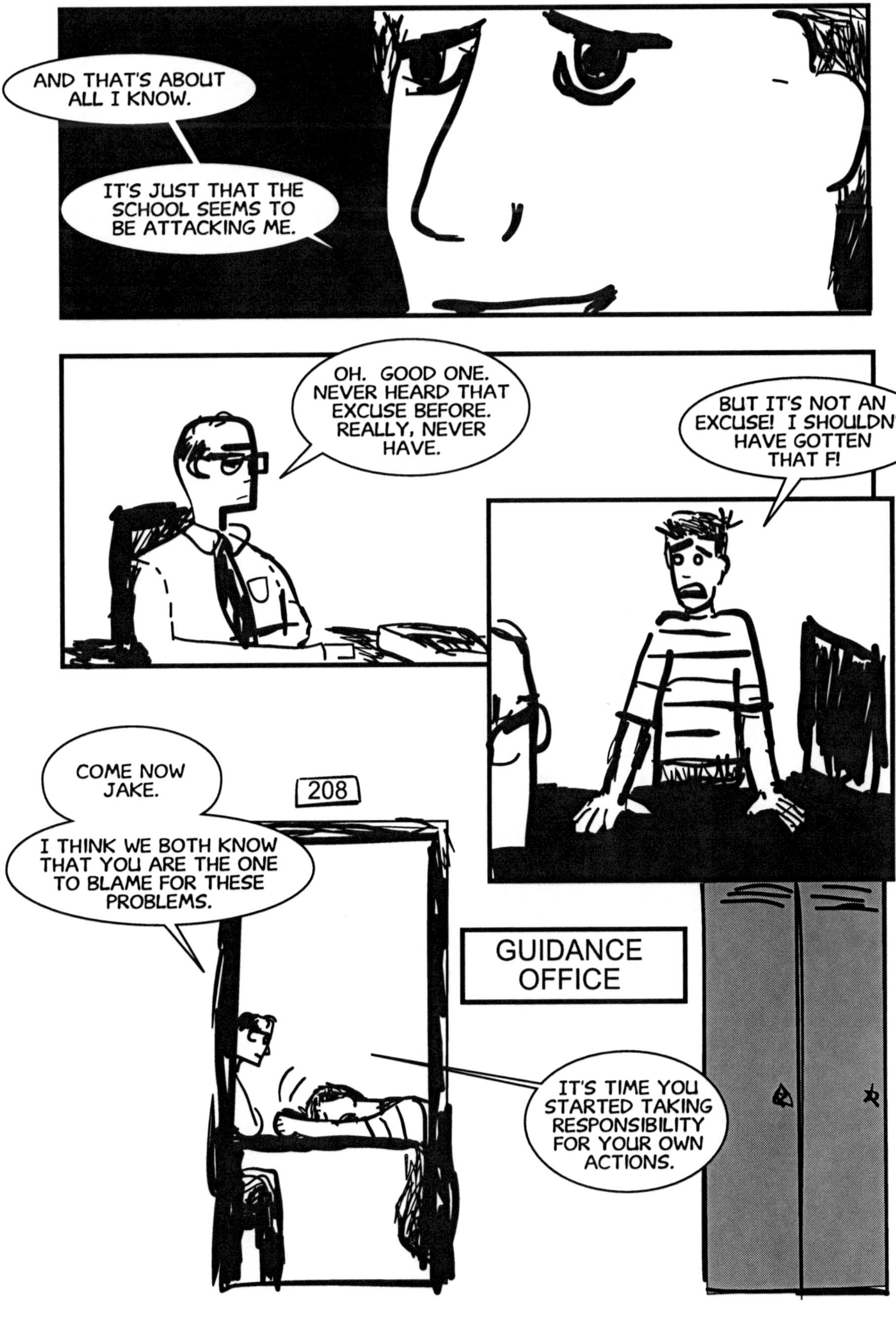
AND THAT'S ABOUT ALL I KNOW.
IT'S JUST THAT THE SCHOOL SEEMS TO BE ATTACKING ME.
OH. GOOD ONE. NEVER HEARD THAT EXCUSE BEFORE. REALLY, NEVER HAVE.
BUT IT'S NOT AN EXCUSE! I SHOULDN'T HAVE GOTTEN THAT F!
COME NOW JAKE.
208
I THINK WE BOTH KNOW THAT YOU ARE THE ONE TO BLAME FOR THESE PROBLEMS.
GUIDANCE OFFICE
IT'S TIME YOU STARTED TAKING RESPONSIBILITY FOR YOUR OWN ACTIONS.

ANY MOMENT I MIGHT BE TRIPPED

BUT THE WEIRDEST THING IS

NO ONE IS EVER AROUND TO HAVE DONE IT.

LET ALONE NOTICE IT.

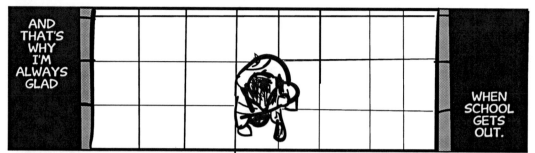

AND THAT'S WHY I'M ALWAYS GLAD

WHEN SCHOOL GETS OUT.

EVEN WHEN I'M TRIPPED...

AHHHHHHH!

I'VE BEEN TRIPPED!

I ALWAYS LAND IN THE ONE SAFE PLACE SCHOOL CAN NEVER REACH ME.

AND THEN

SOMETHING THREW ME

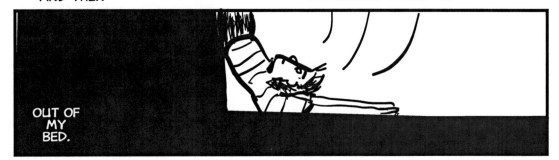

OUT OF
MY
BED.

WELL
THAT'S
IT.

SCHOOL, YOU'VE
GONE TOO FAR.

IT'S
TIME
FOR
BATTLE!

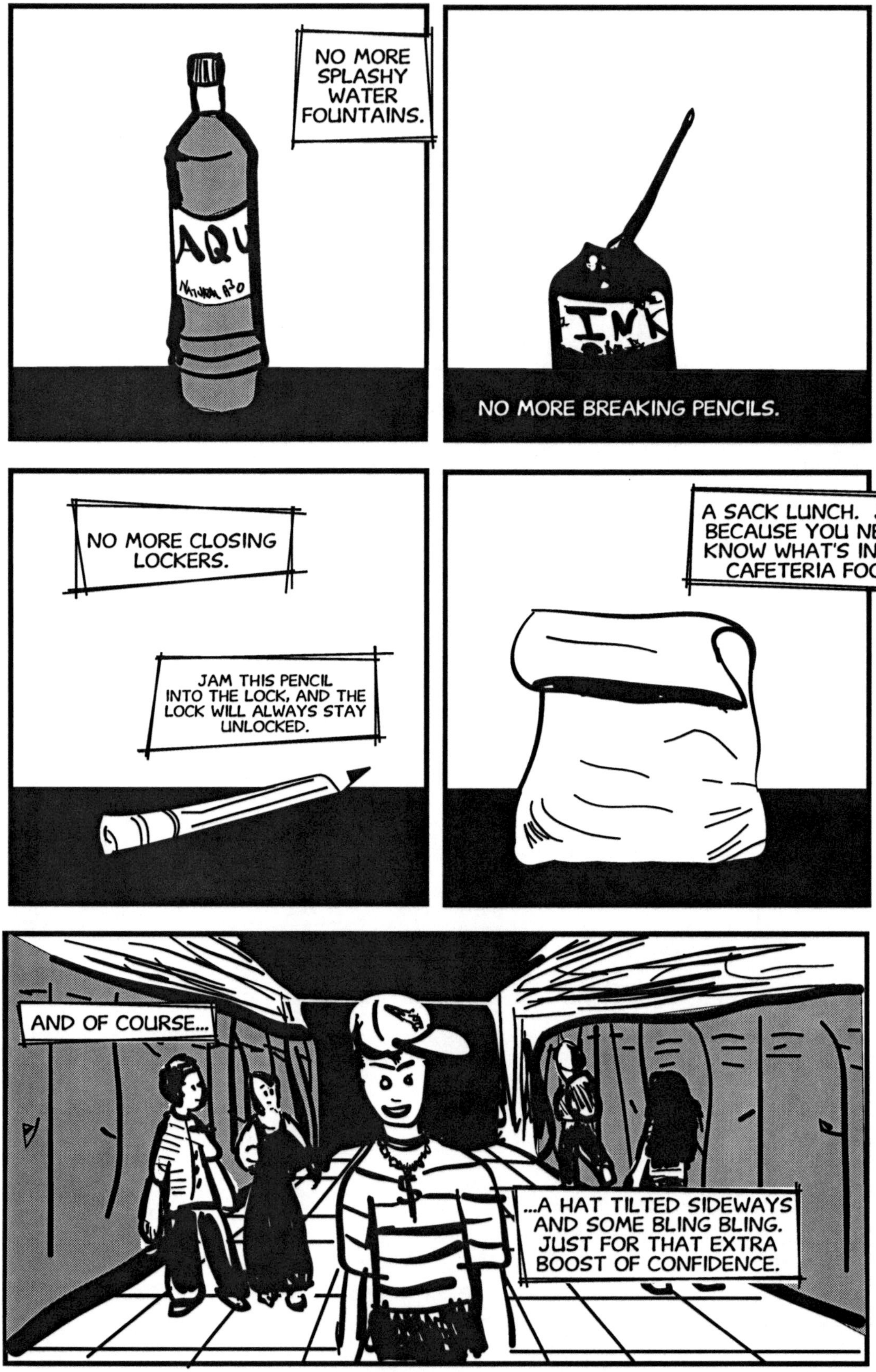
NO MORE SPLASHY WATER FOUNTAINS.
AQU
NATURAL H2O
INK
NO MORE BREAKING PENCILS.
NO MORE CLOSING LOCKERS.
JAM THIS PENCIL INTO THE LOCK, AND THE LOCK WILL ALWAYS STAY UNLOCKED.
A SACK LUNCH. JUST BECAUSE YOU NEVER KNOW WHAT'S IN THE CAFETERIA FOOD.
AND OF COURSE...
...A HAT TILTED SIDEWAYS AND SOME BLING BLING. JUST FOR THAT EXTRA BOOST OF CONFIDENCE.

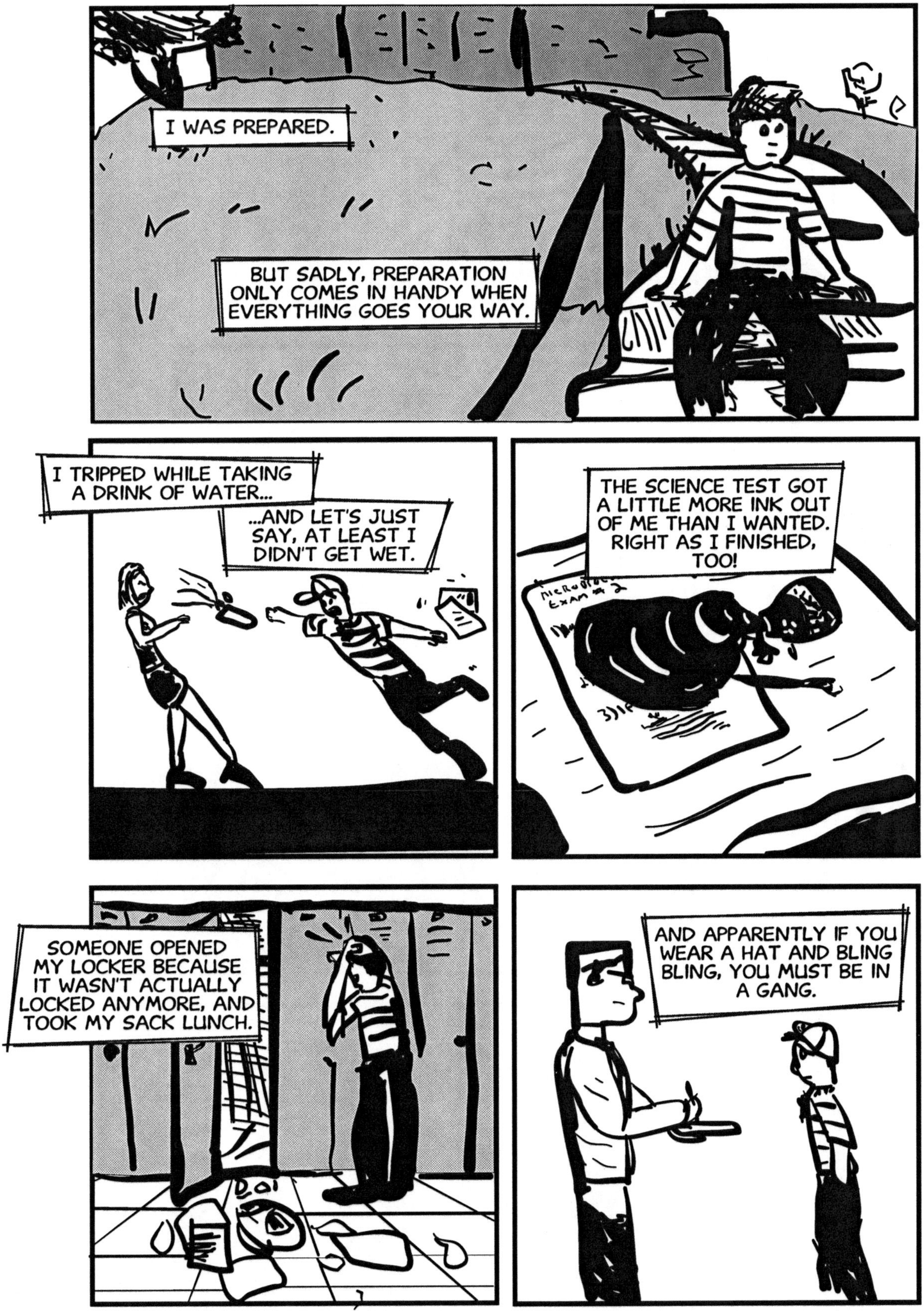
I WAS PREPARED.
BUT SADLY, PREPARATION ONLY COMES IN HANDY WHEN EVERYTHING GOES YOUR WAY.
I TRIPPED WHILE TAKING A DRINK OF WATER...
...AND LET'S JUST SAY, AT LEAST I DIDN'T GET WET.
THE SCIENCE TEST GOT A LITTLE MORE INK OUT OF ME THAN I WANTED. RIGHT AS I FINISHED, TOO!
SOMEONE OPENED MY LOCKER BECAUSE IT WASN'T ACTUALLY LOCKED ANYMORE, AND TOOK MY SACK LUNCH.
AND APPARENTLY IF YOU WEAR A HAT AND BLING BLING, YOU MUST BE IN A GANG.

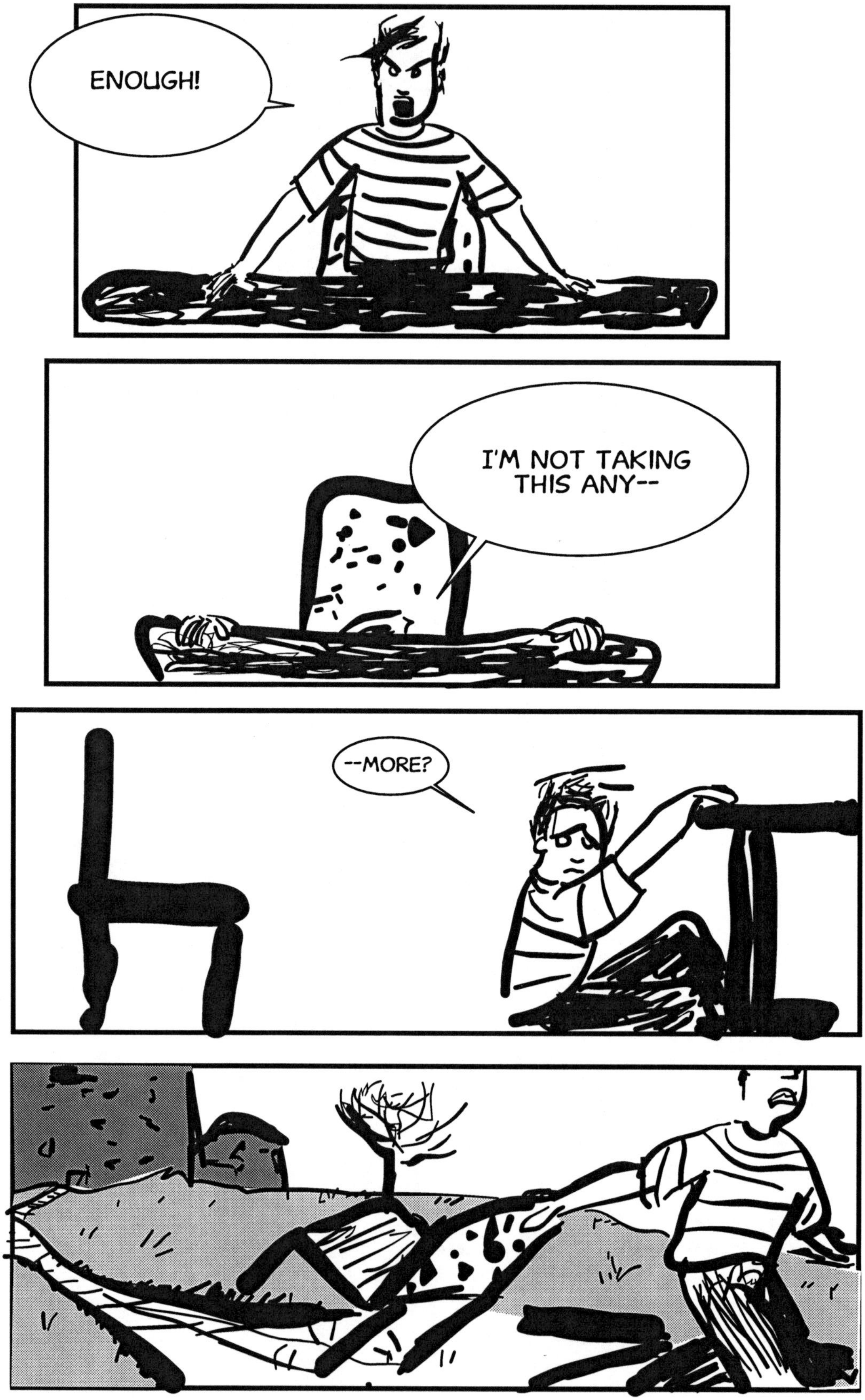
ENOUGH!
I'M NOT TAKING THIS ANY--
--MORE?

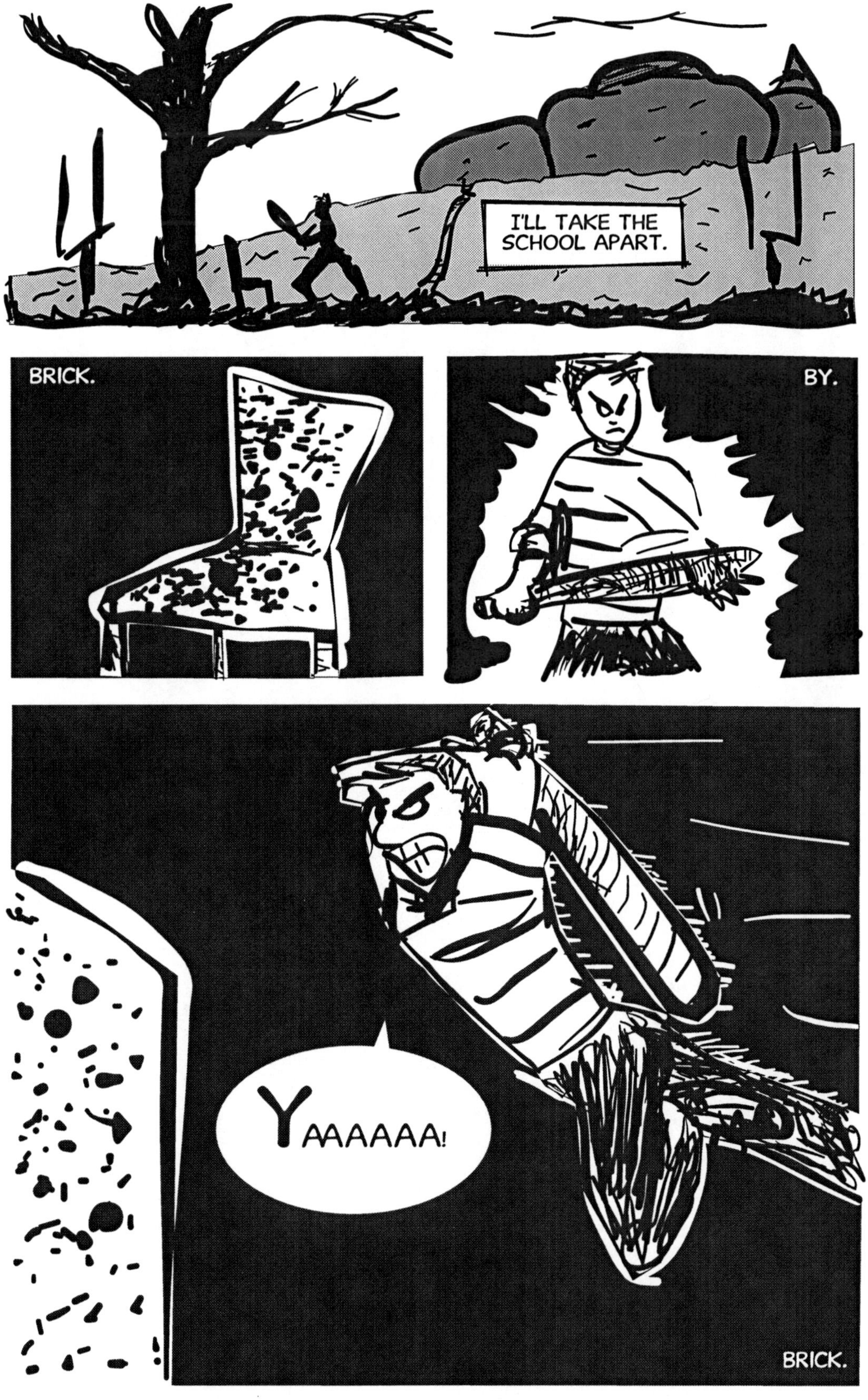
I'LL TAKE THE SCHOOL APART.
BRICK.
BY.
YAAAAAA!
BRICK.

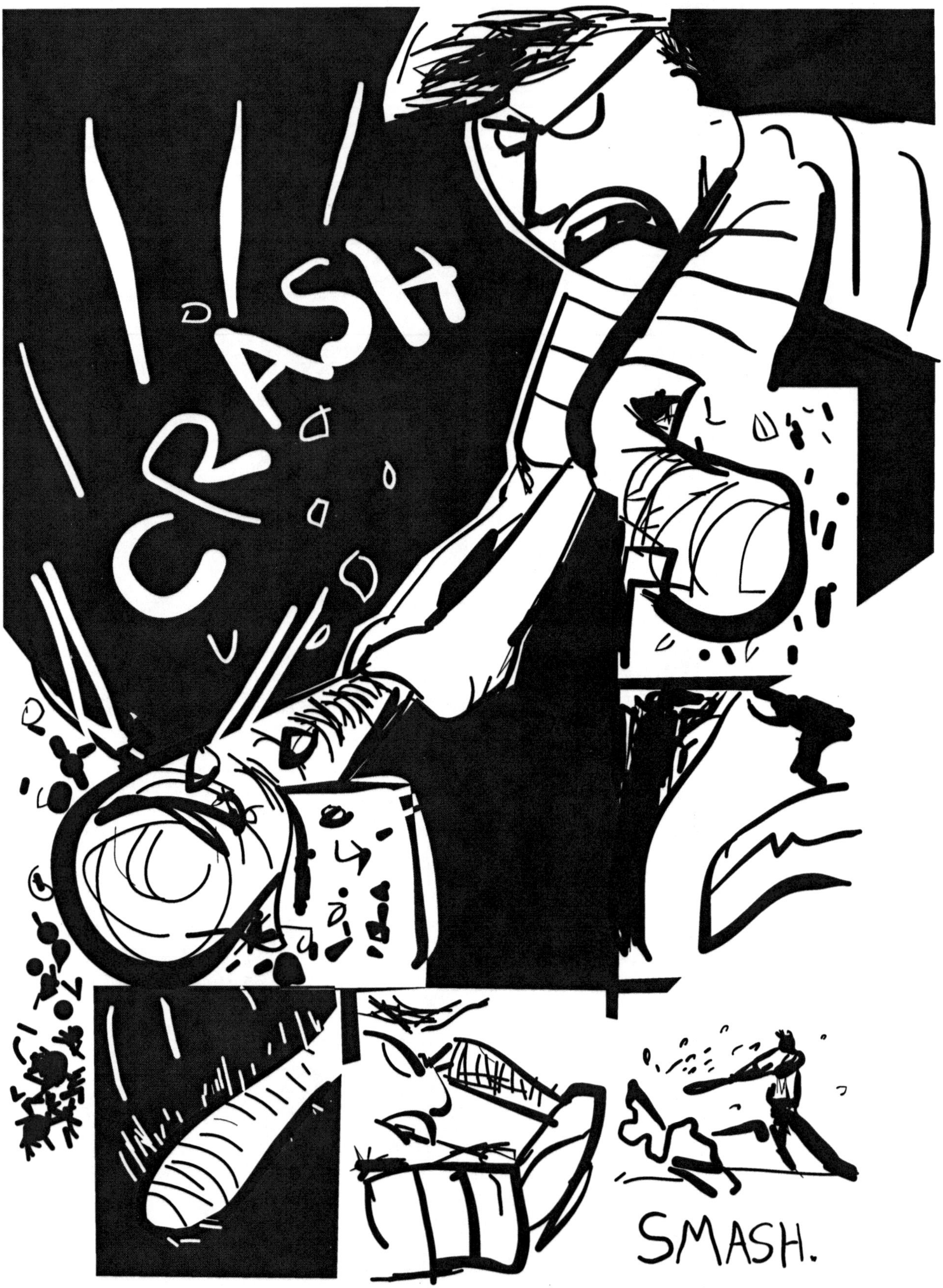
CRASH
SMASH.

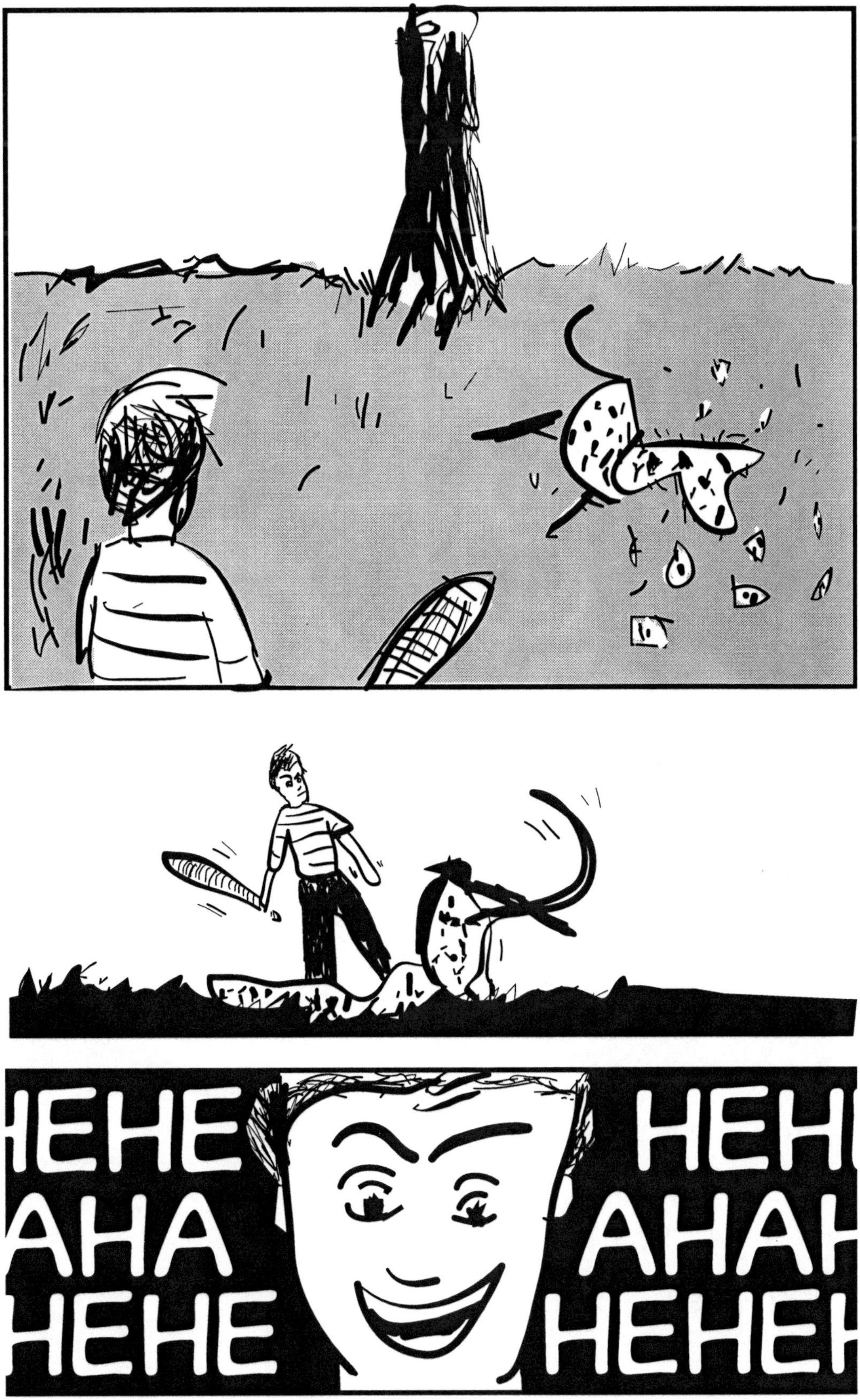
HEHE
AHA
HEHE
HEH
AHAH
HEHEH

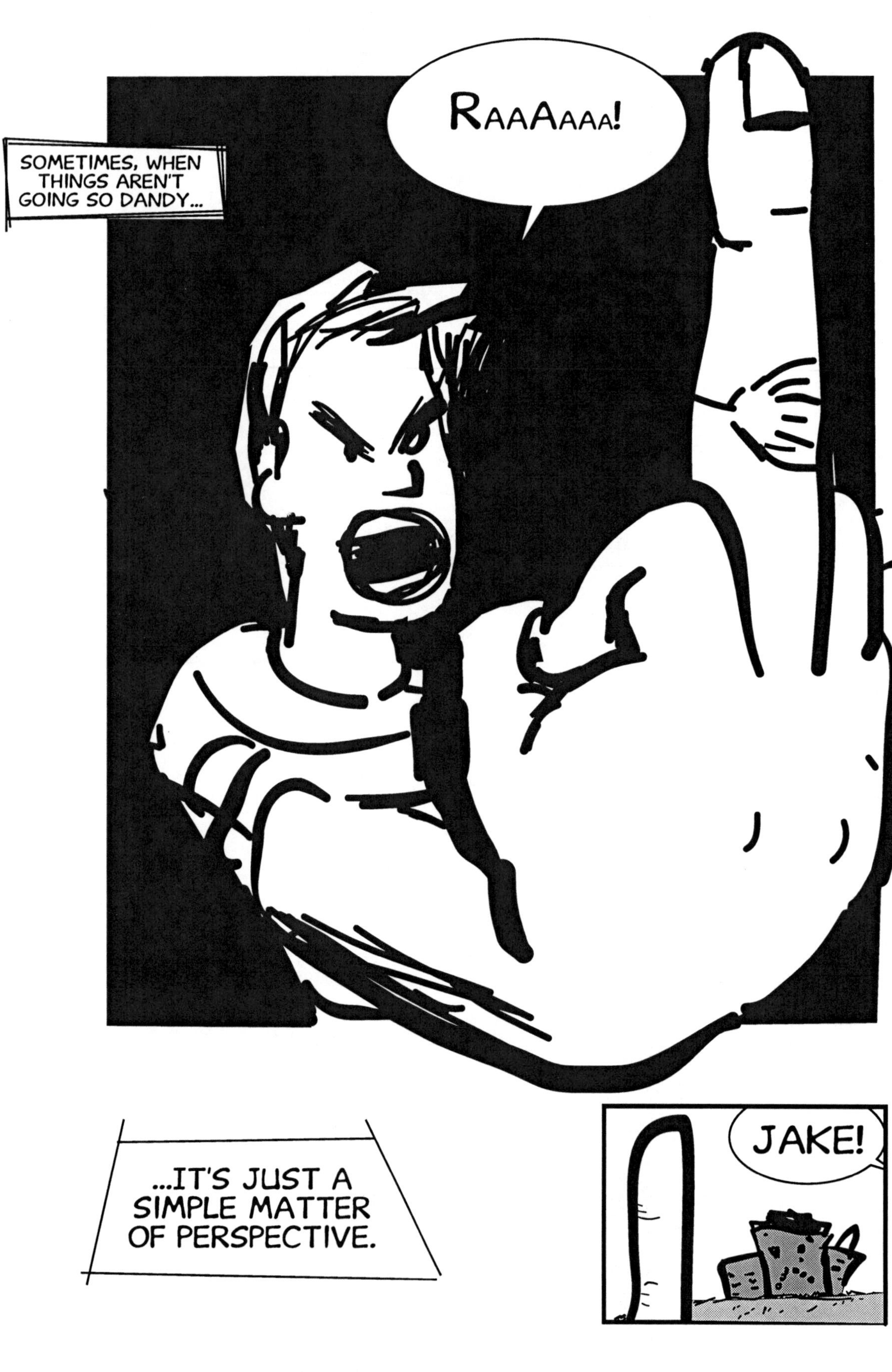
SOMETIMES, WHEN THINGS AREN'T GOING SO DANDY...
RAAAAAA!
...IT'S JUST A SIMPLE MATTER OF PERSPECTIVE.
JAKE!

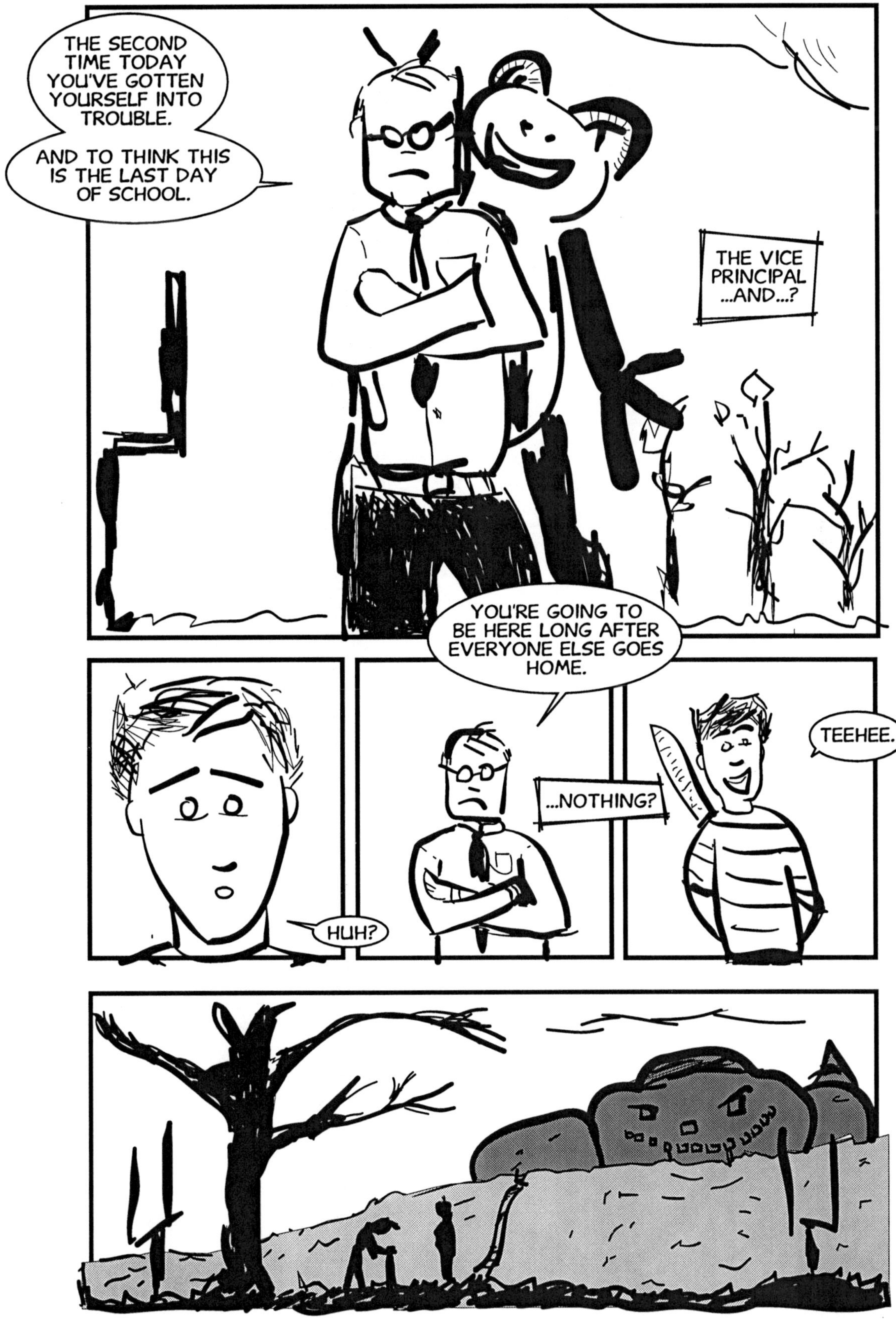
THE SECOND TIME TODAY YOU'VE GOTTEN YOURSELF INTO TROUBLE.
AND TO THINK THIS IS THE LAST DAY OF SCHOOL.
THE VICE PRINCIPAL ...AND...?
YOU'RE GOING TO BE HERE LONG AFTER EVERYONE ELSE GOES HOME.
HUH?
...NOTHING?
TEEHEE.

LAST DAY OF SOPHOMORE YEAR.

SCHOOL'S OUT.

HOORAY.

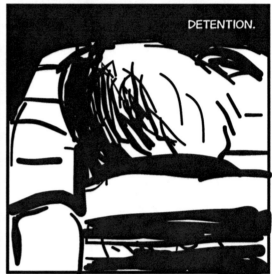

DETENTION.

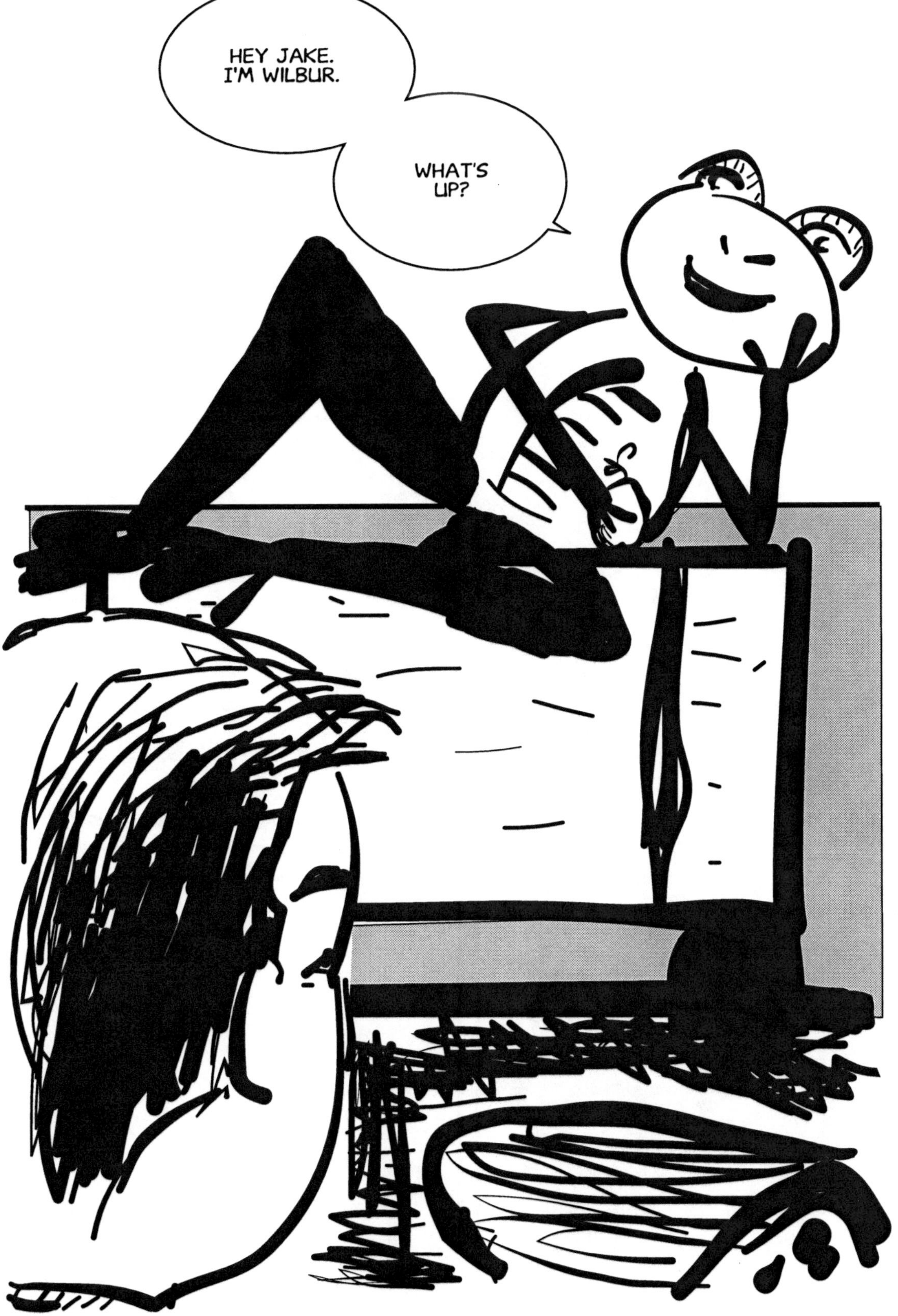
HEY JAKE.
I'M WILBUR.
WHAT'S
UP?

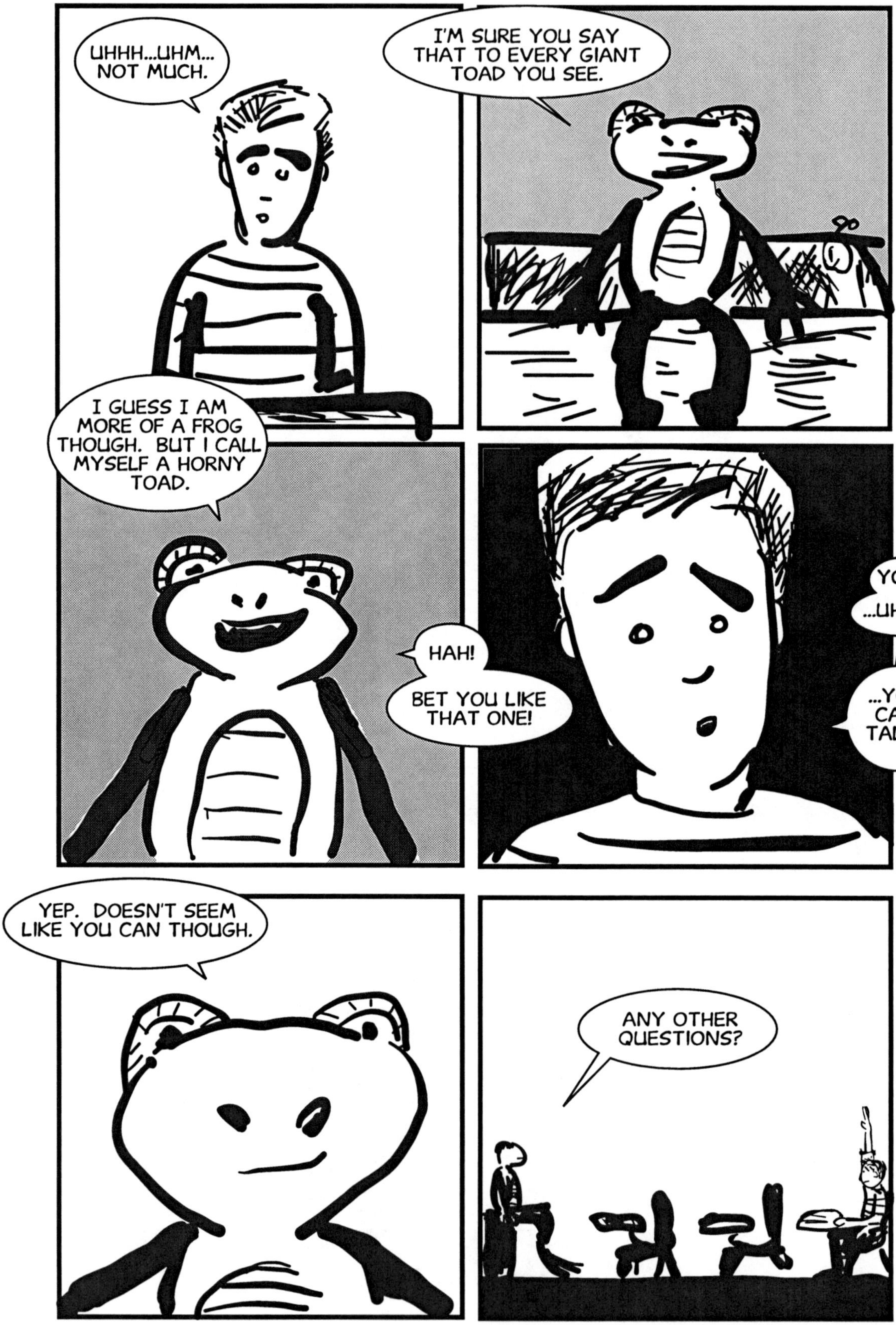
UHHH...UHM... NOT MUCH.
I'M SURE YOU SAY THAT TO EVERY GIANT TOAD YOU SEE.
I GUESS I AM MORE OF A FROG THOUGH. BUT I CALL MYSELF A HORNY TOAD.
HAH!
BET YOU LIKE THAT ONE!
YOU...
...UHHH...
...YOU CAN TALK?
YEP. DOESN'T SEEM LIKE YOU CAN THOUGH.
ANY OTHER QUESTIONS?

SUMMER

YEAH, I KNOW. UNBELIEVABLE.

EXCEPT AT THIS POINT, NOTHING SURPRISED ME ANYMORE.

BUT THIS FELT MORE THAN SURPRISING.

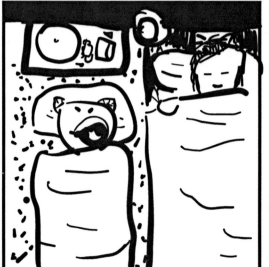

IT FELT RIGHT.

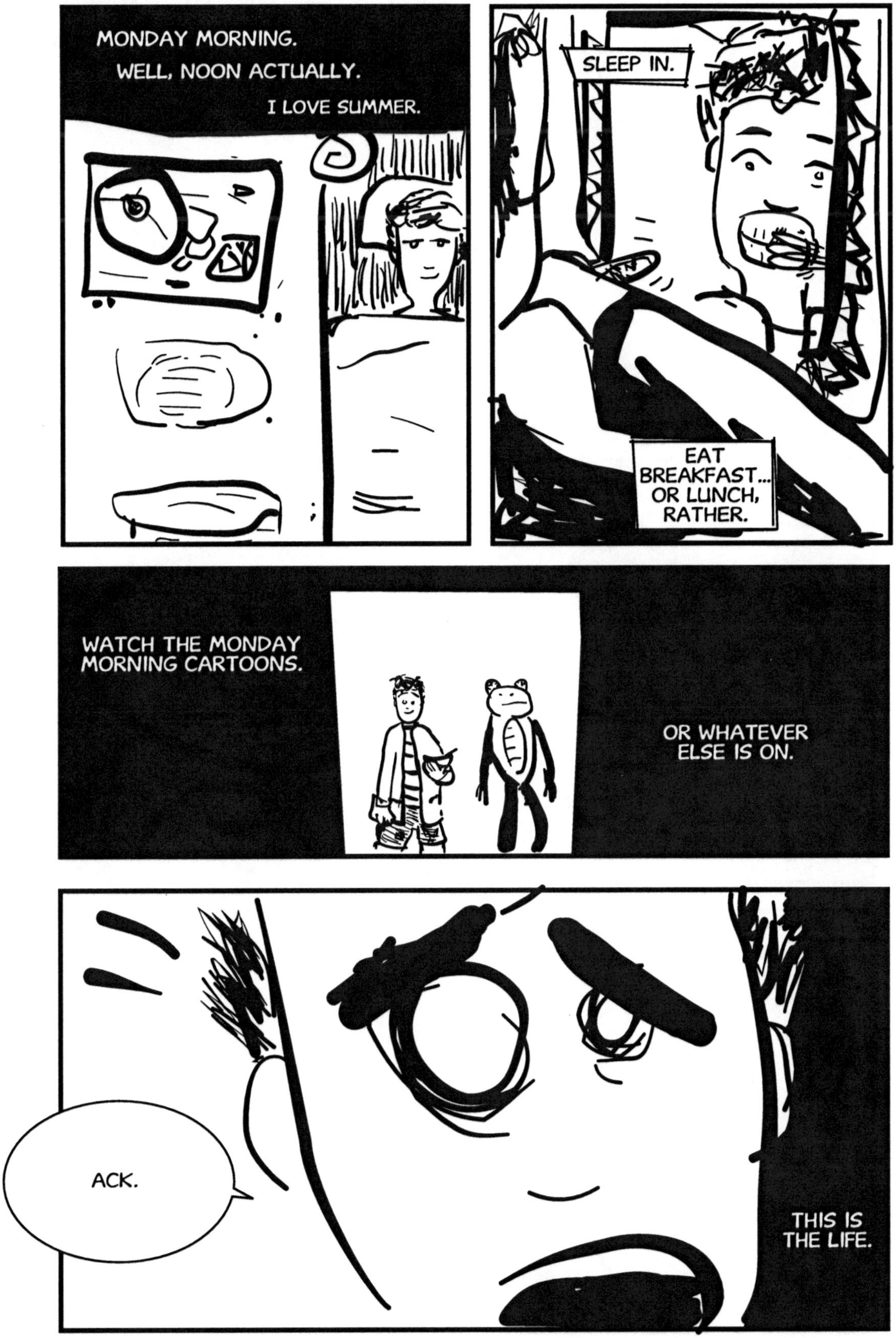
MONDAY MORNING.
WELL, NOON ACTUALLY.
I LOVE SUMMER.
SLEEP IN.
EAT BREAKFAST... OR LUNCH, RATHER.
WATCH THE MONDAY MORNING CARTOONS.
OR WHATEVER ELSE IS ON.
ACK.
THIS IS THE LIFE.

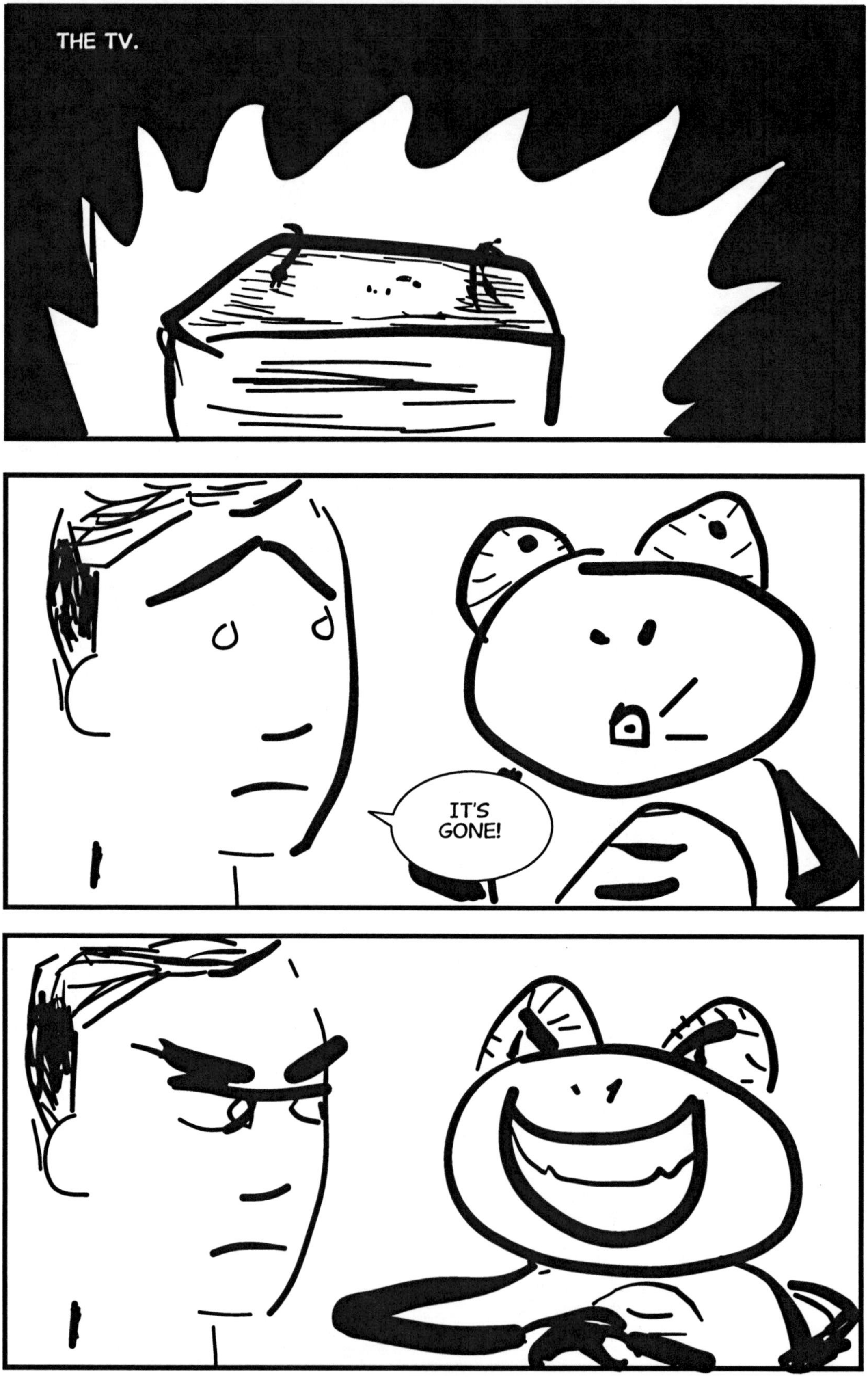
THE TV.
IT'S GONE!

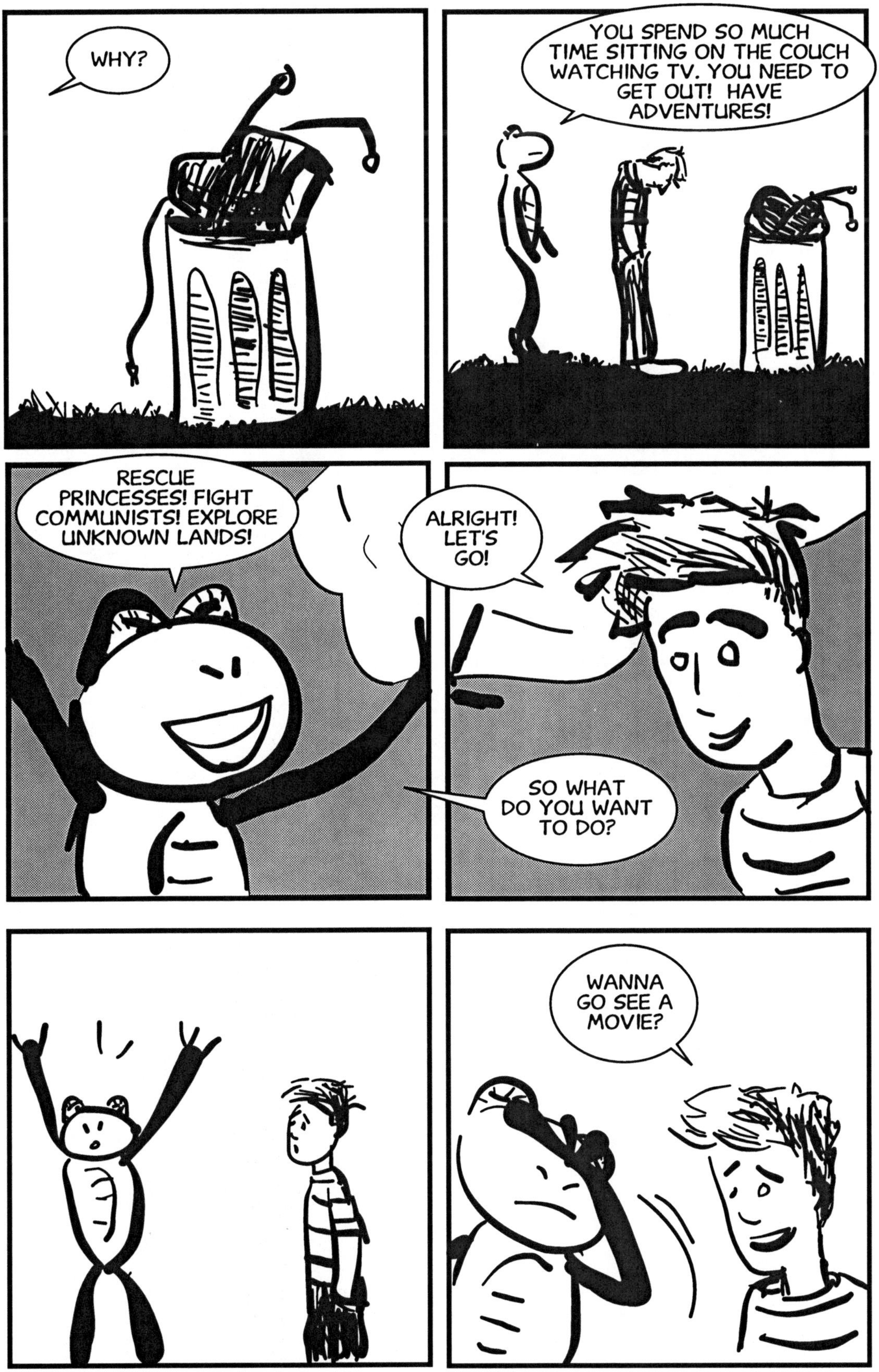
WHY?
YOU SPEND SO MUCH TIME SITTING ON THE COUCH WATCHING TV. YOU NEED TO GET OUT! HAVE ADVENTURES!
RESCUE PRINCESSES! FIGHT COMMUNISTS! EXPLORE UNKNOWN LANDS!
ALRIGHT! LET'S GO!
SO WHAT DO YOU WANT TO DO?
WANNA GO SEE A MOVIE?

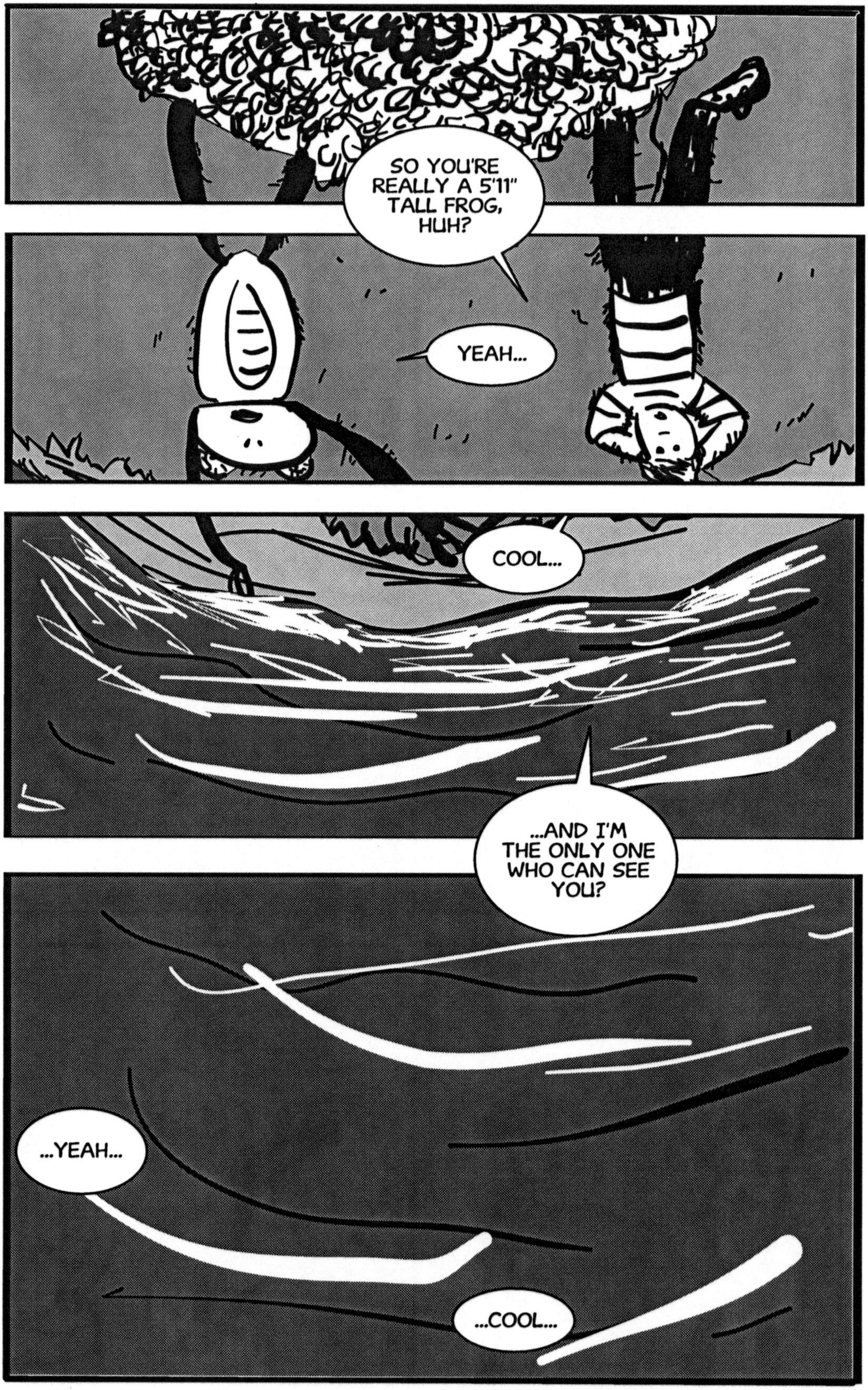
SO YOU'RE REALLY A 5'11" TALL FROG, HUH?
YEAH...
COOL...
...AND I'M THE ONLY ONE WHO CAN SEE YOU?
...YEAH...
...COOL...

JUNIOR YEAR

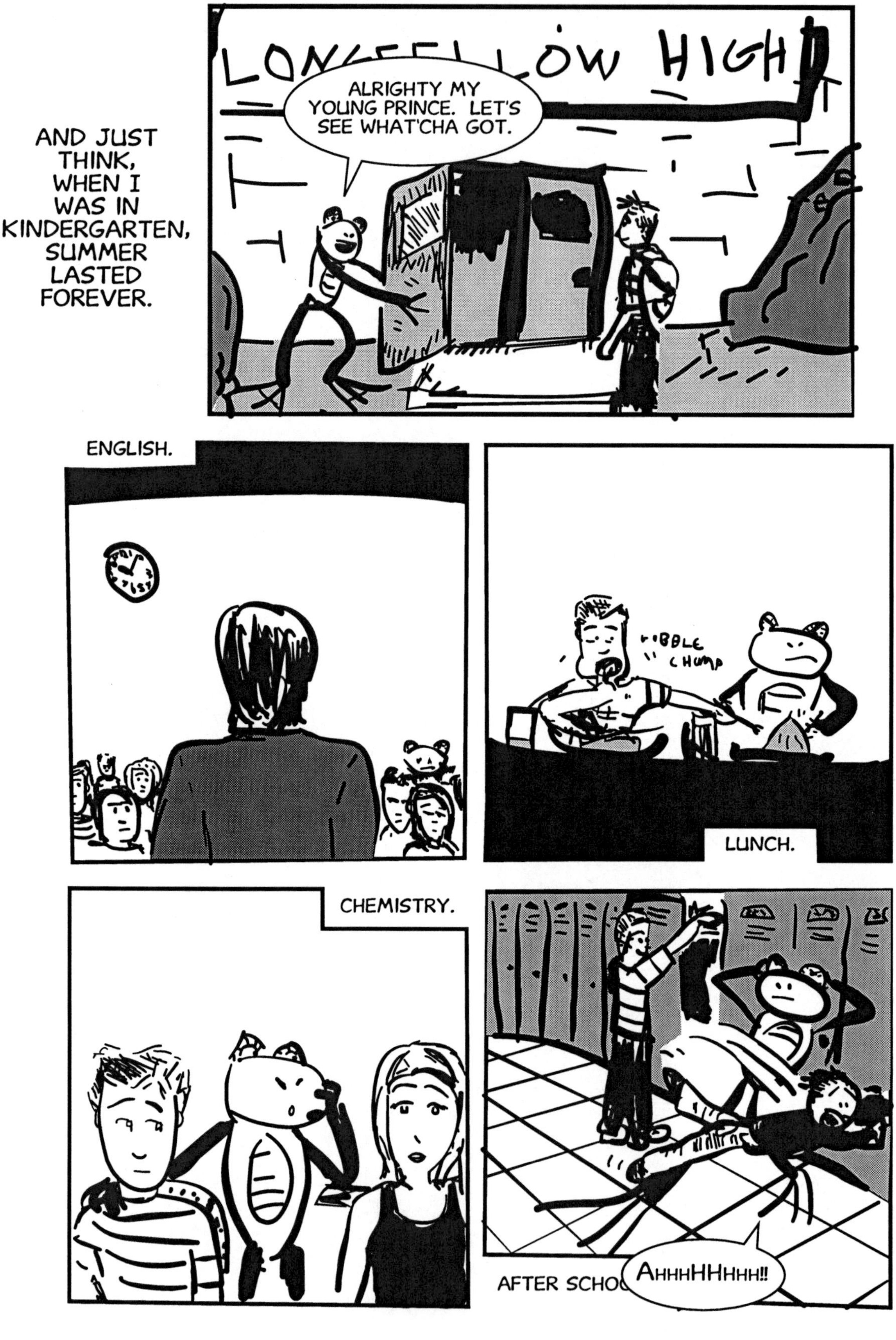
AND JUST THINK, WHEN I WAS IN KINDERGARTEN, SUMMER LASTED FOREVER.
LONGFELLOW HIGH
ALRIGHTY MY YOUNG PRINCE. LET'S SEE WHAT'CHA GOT.
ENGLISH.
LUNCH.
CHEMISTRY.
AFTER SCHOO
AhhhHHhhh!!

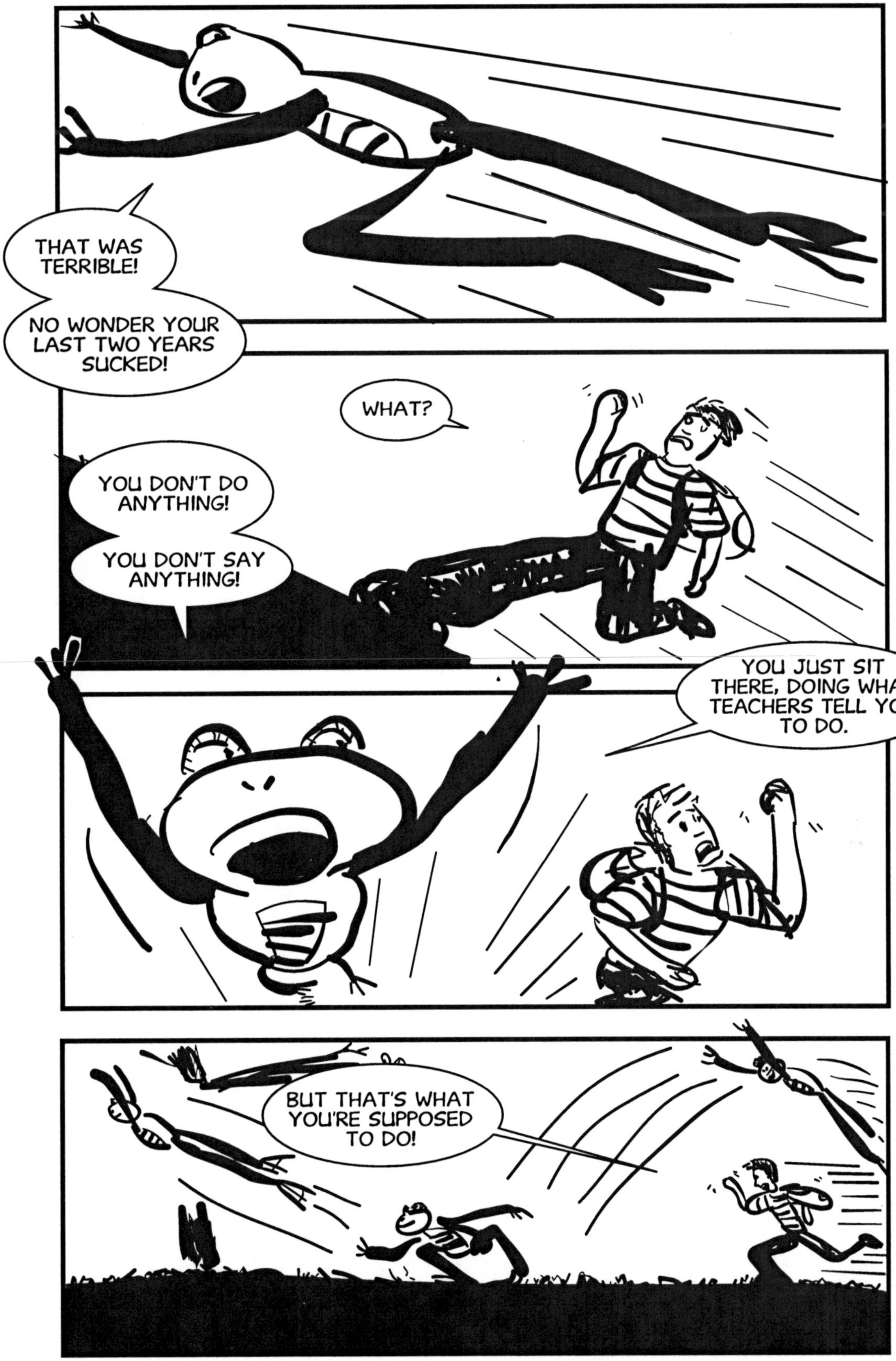
THAT WAS TERRIBLE!
NO WONDER YOUR LAST TWO YEARS SUCKED!
WHAT?
YOU DON'T DO ANYTHING!
YOU DON'T SAY ANYTHING!
YOU JUST SIT THERE, DOING WHAT TEACHERS TELL YOU TO DO.
BUT THAT'S WHAT YOU'RE SUPPOSED TO DO!

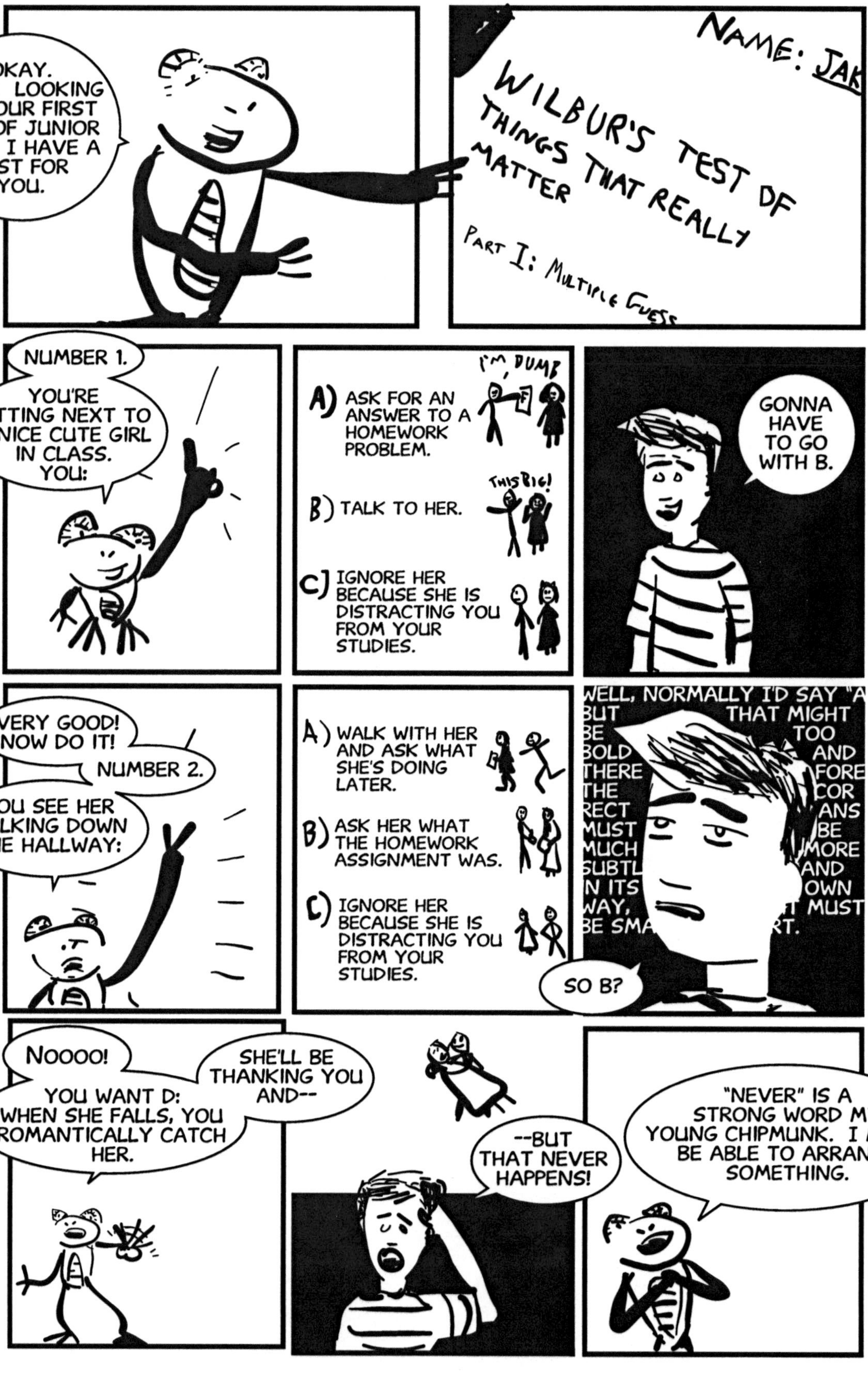
OKAY. AFTER LOOKING AT YOUR FIRST DAY OF JUNIOR YEAR, I HAVE A TEST FOR YOU.
NAME: JAK
WILBUR'S TEST OF THINGS THAT REALLY MATTER
PART I: MULTIPLE GUESS
NUMBER 1.
YOU'RE SITTING NEXT TO A NICE CUTE GIRL IN CLASS. YOU:
A) ASK FOR AN ANSWER TO A HOMEWORK PROBLEM.
I'M DUMB
B) TALK TO HER.
THIS BIG!
C) IGNORE HER BECAUSE SHE IS DISTRACTING YOU FROM YOUR STUDIES.
GONNA HAVE TO GO WITH B.
VERY GOOD! NOW DO IT!
NUMBER 2.
YOU SEE HER WALKING DOWN THE HALLWAY:
A) WALK WITH HER AND ASK WHAT SHE'S DOING LATER.
B) ASK HER WHAT THE HOMEWORK ASSIGNMENT WAS.
C) IGNORE HER BECAUSE SHE IS DISTRACTING YOU FROM YOUR STUDIES.
SO B?
NOOOO!
YOU WANT D: WHEN SHE FALLS, YOU ROMANTICALLY CATCH HER.
SHE'LL BE THANKING YOU AND--
--BUT THAT NEVER HAPPENS!
"NEVER" IS A STRONG WORD MY YOUNG CHIPMUNK. I MIGHT BE ABLE TO ARRANGE SOMETHING.

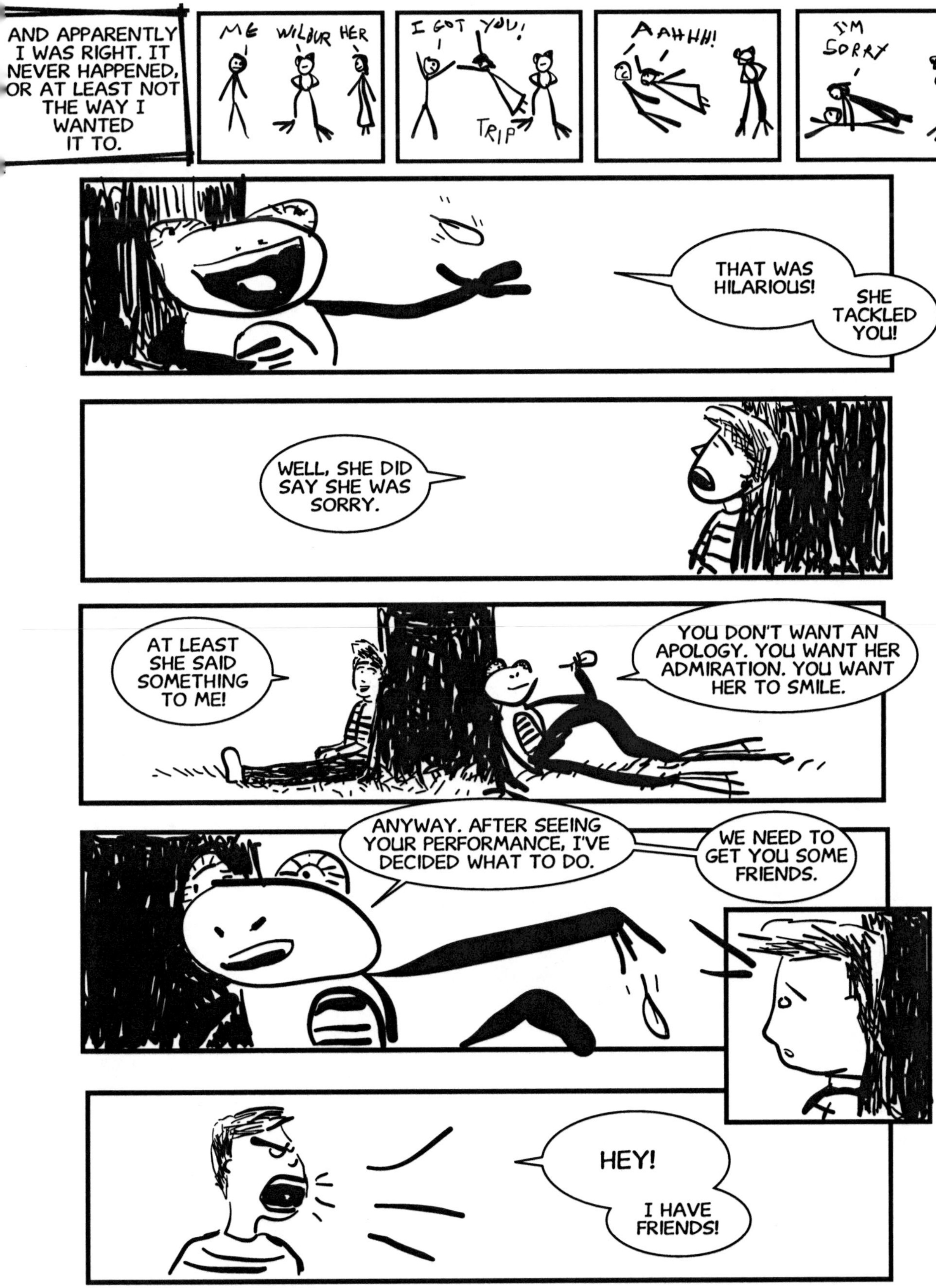
AND APPARENTLY I WAS RIGHT. IT NEVER HAPPENED, OR AT LEAST NOT THE WAY I WANTED IT TO.
ME
WILBUR
HER
I GOT YOU!
TRIP
AAHHH!
I'M SORRY
THAT WAS HILARIOUS!
SHE TACKLED YOU!
WELL, SHE DID SAY SHE WAS SORRY.
AT LEAST SHE SAID SOMETHING TO ME!
YOU DON'T WANT AN APOLOGY. YOU WANT HER ADMIRATION. YOU WANT HER TO SMILE.
ANYWAY. AFTER SEEING YOUR PERFORMANCE, I'VE DECIDED WHAT TO DO.
WE NEED TO GET YOU SOME FRIENDS.
HEY!
I HAVE FRIENDS!

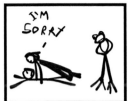

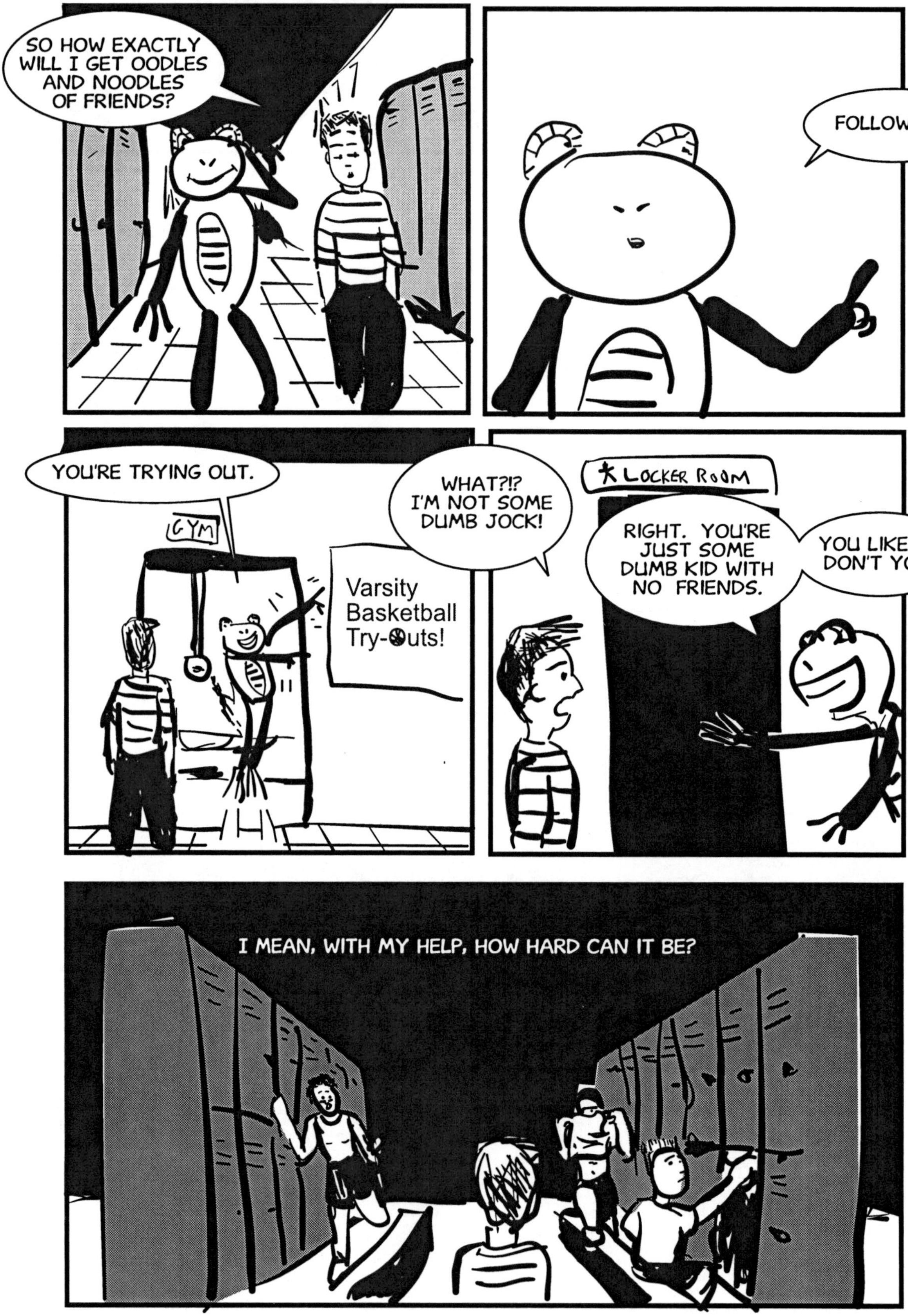
SO HOW EXACTLY WILL I GET OODLES AND NOODLES OF FRIENDS?
FOLLOW ME.
YOU'RE TRYING OUT.
CYM
Varsity Basketball Try-Outs!
WHAT?!? I'M NOT SOME DUMB JOCK!
LOCKER ROOM
RIGHT. YOU'RE JUST SOME DUMB KID WITH NO FRIENDS.
YOU LIKE P.E. DON'T YOU?
I MEAN, WITH MY HELP, HOW HARD CAN IT BE?

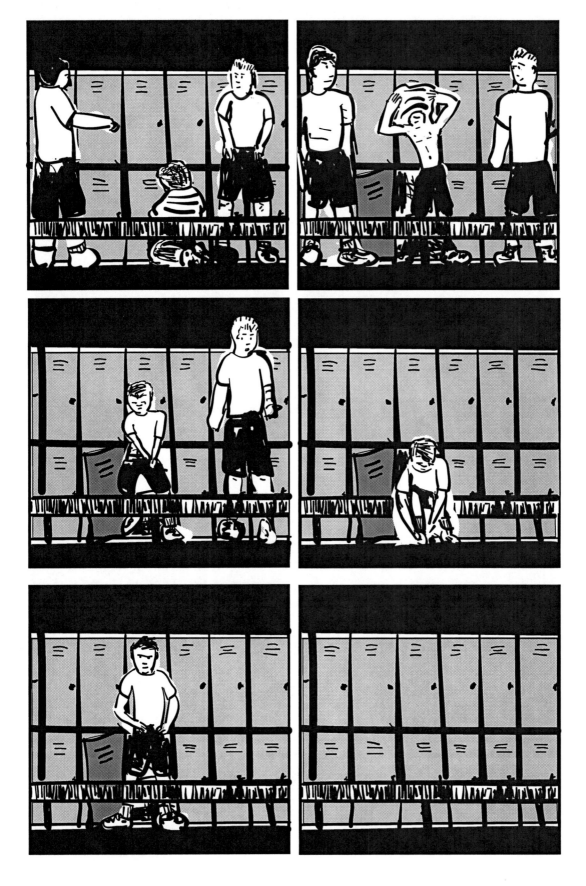

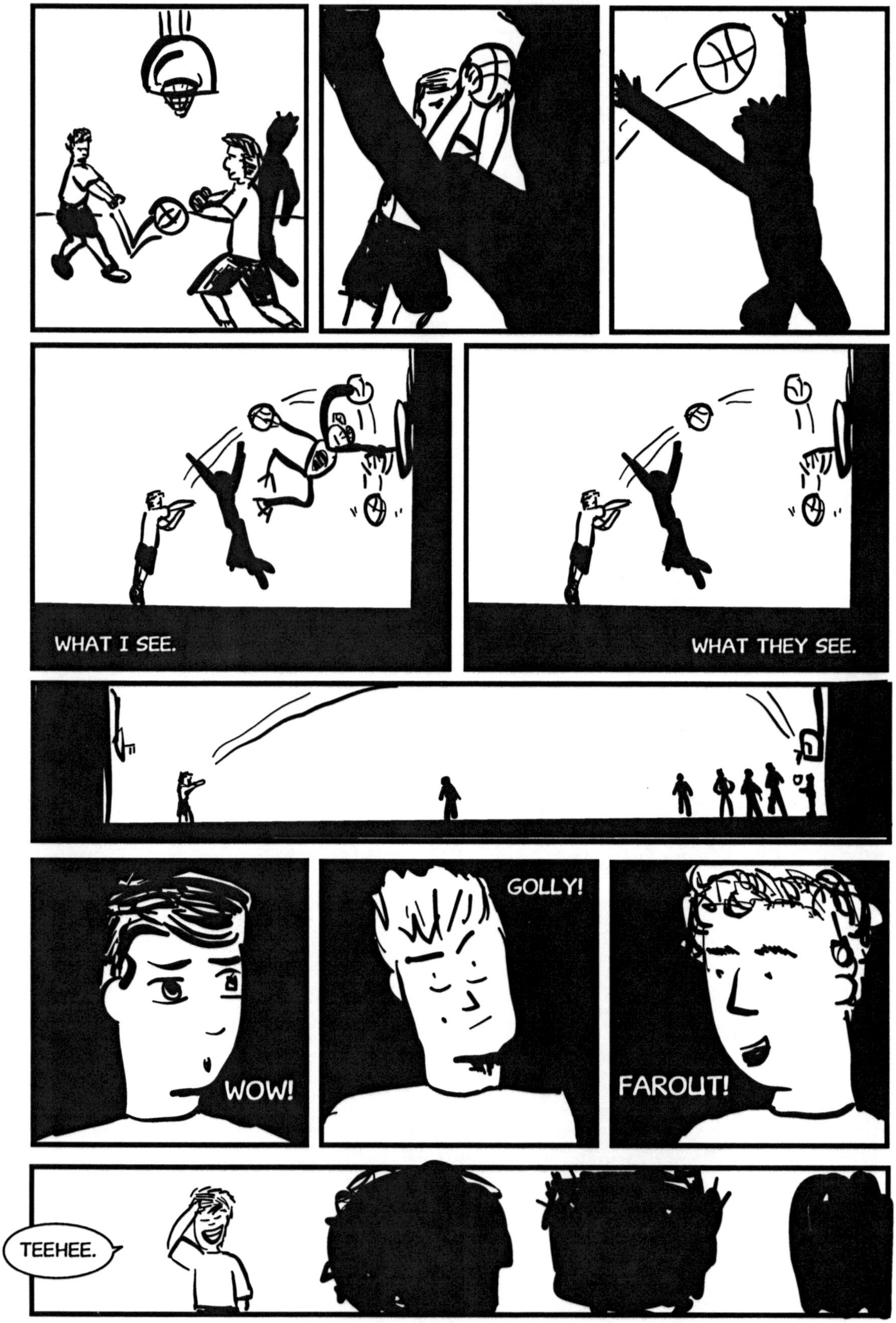
WHAT I SEE.
WHAT THEY SEE.
WOW!
GOLLY!
FAROUT!
TEEHEE.

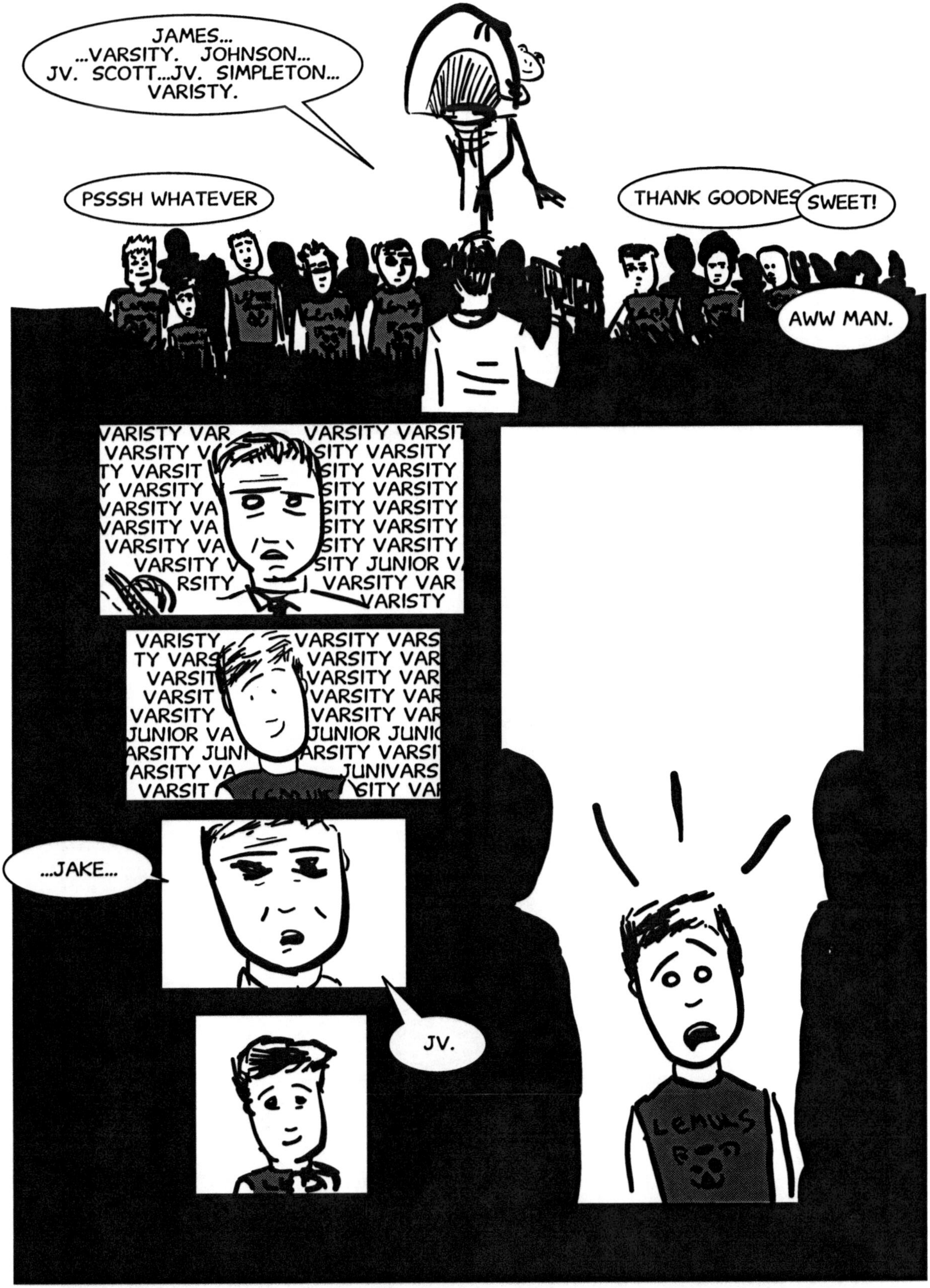
JAMES... ...VARSITY. JOHNSON... JV. SCOTT...JV. SIMPLETON... VARISTY.
PSSSH WHATEVER
THANK GOODNES
SWEET!
AWW MAN.
...JAKE...
JV.

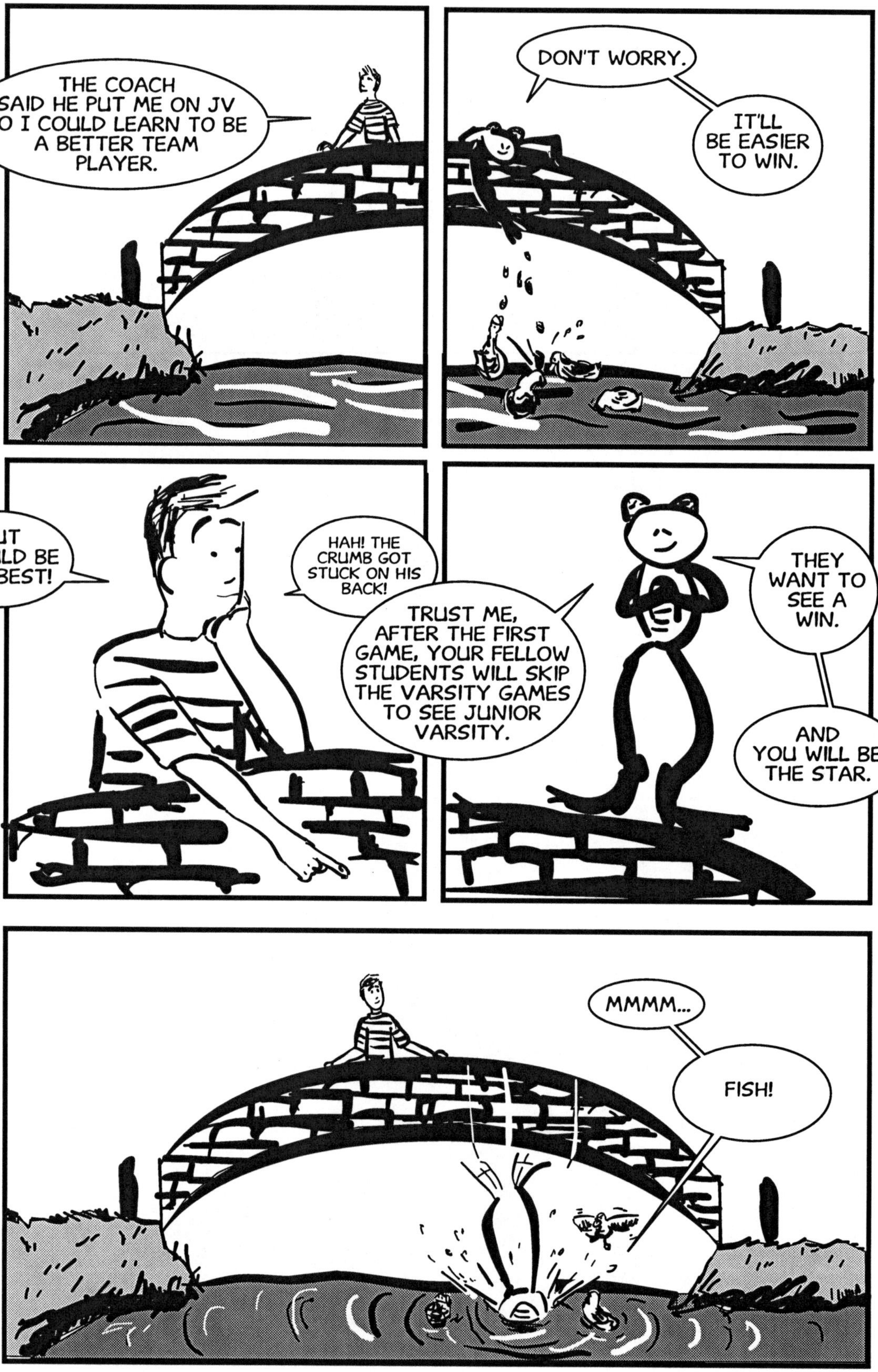
THE COACH SAID HE PUT ME ON JV SO I COULD LEARN TO BE A BETTER TEAM PLAYER.
DON'T WORRY.
IT'LL BE EASIER TO WIN.
BUT I COULD BE THE BEST!
HAH! THE CRUMB GOT STUCK ON HIS BACK!
TRUST ME, AFTER THE FIRST GAME, YOUR FELLOW STUDENTS WILL SKIP THE VARSITY GAMES TO SEE JUNIOR VARSITY.
THEY WANT TO SEE A WIN.
AND YOU WILL BE THE STAR.
MMMM...
FISH!

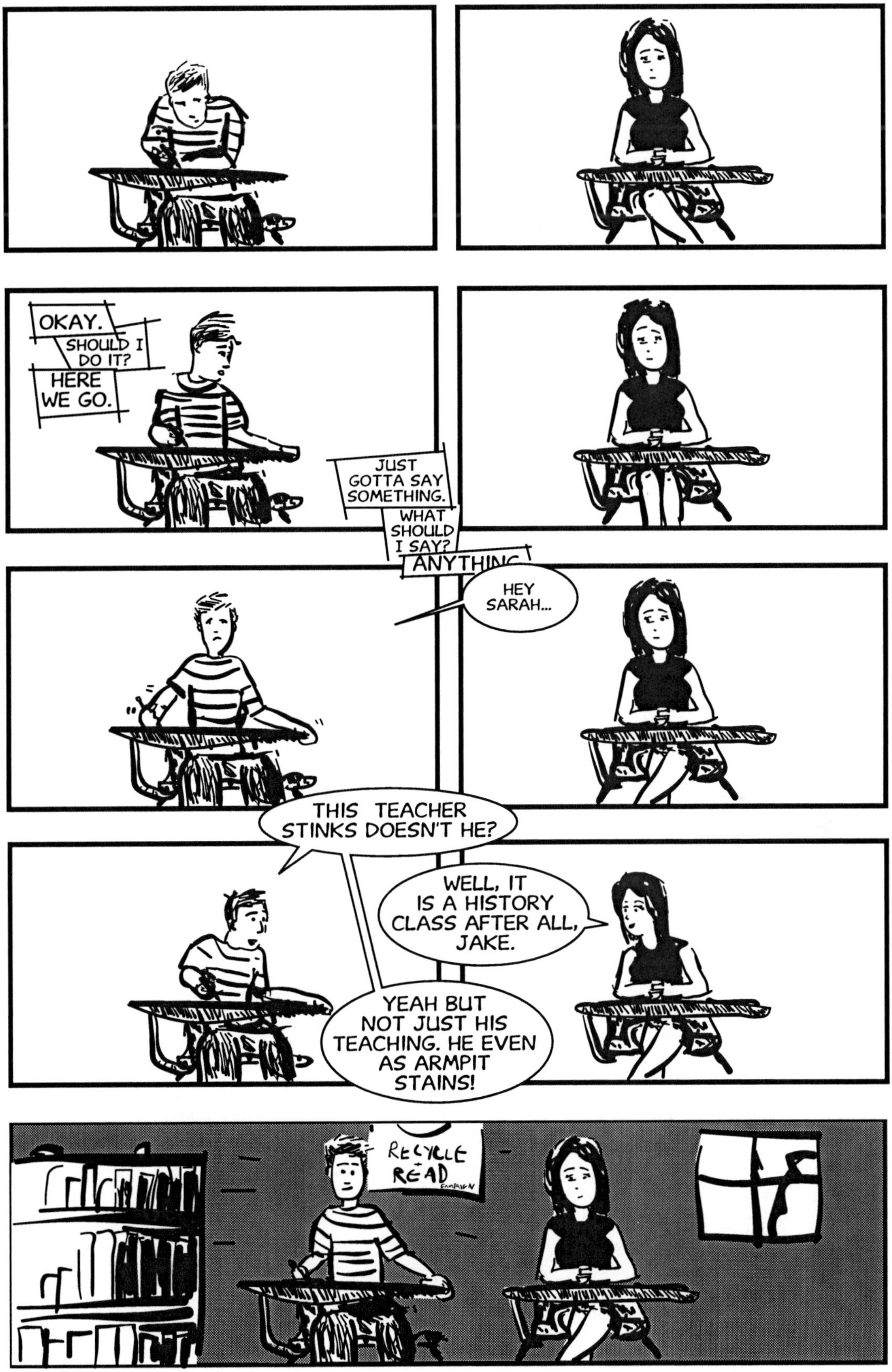
OKAY.
SHOULD I DO IT?
HERE WE GO.
JUST GOTTA SAY SOMETHING.
WHAT SHOULD I SAY?
ANYTHING.
HEY SARAH...
THIS TEACHER STINKS DOESN'T HE?
WELL, IT IS A HISTORY CLASS AFTER ALL, JAKE.
YEAH BUT NOT JUST HIS TEACHING. HE EVEN AS ARMPIT STAINS!
RECYCLE + READ

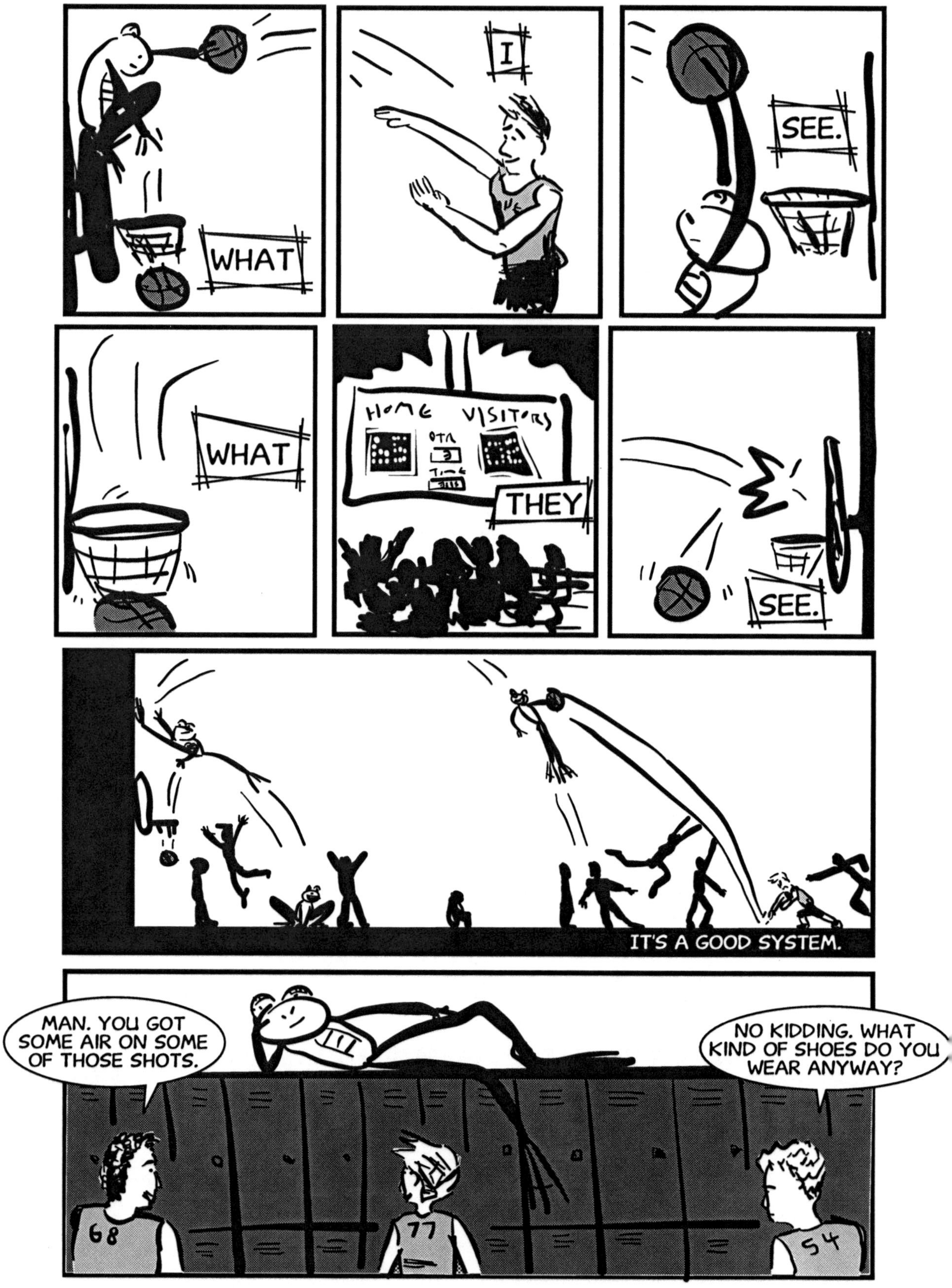
WHAT
I
SEE.
WHAT
HOME VISITORS
THEY
SEE.
IT'S A GOOD SYSTEM.
MAN. YOU GOT SOME AIR ON SOME OF THOSE SHOTS.
NO KIDDING. WHAT KIND OF SHOES DO YOU WEAR ANYWAY?
68
77
54

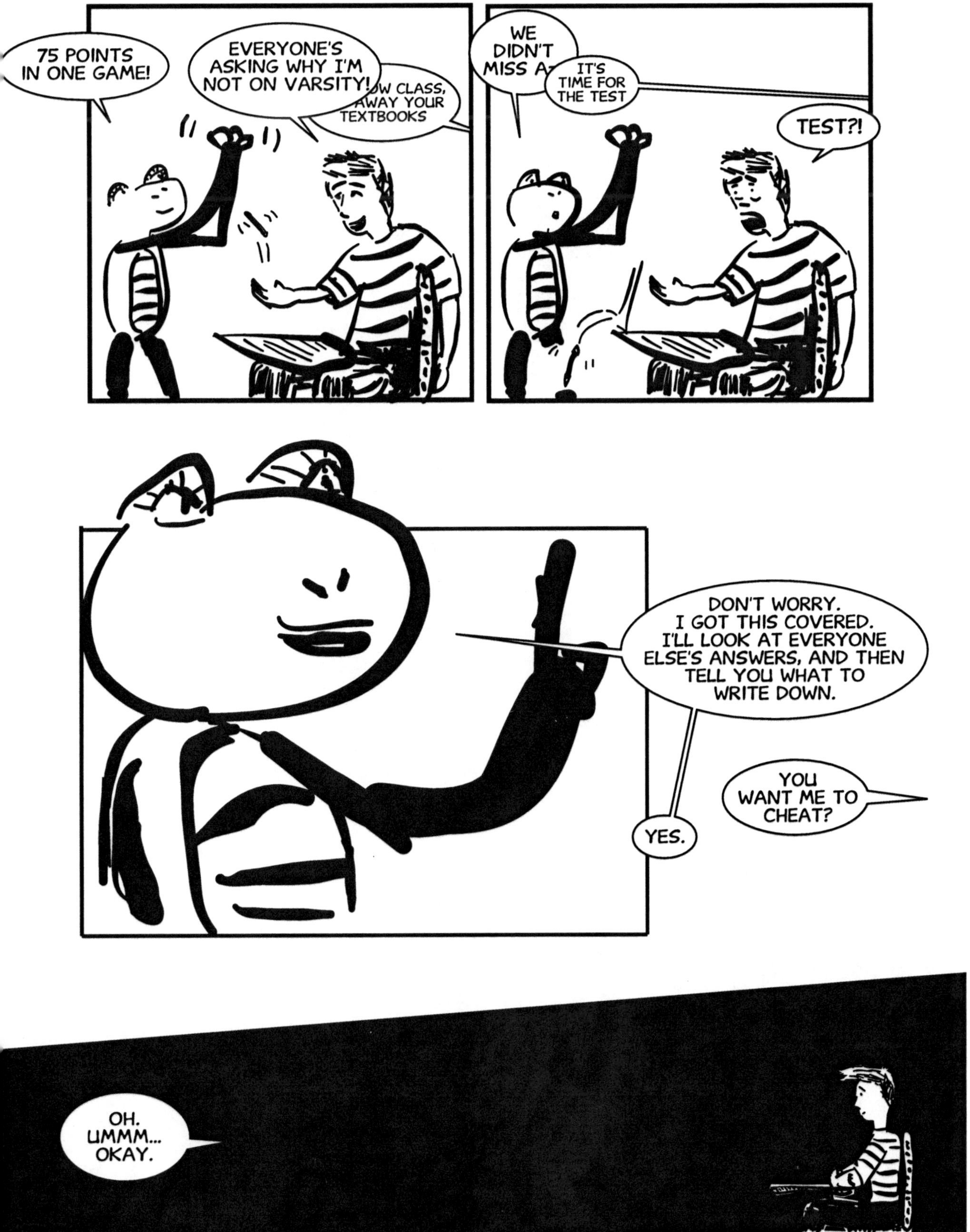
75 POINTS IN ONE GAME!
EVERYONE'S ASKING WHY I'M NOT ON VARSITY!
OW CLASS, AWAY YOUR TEXTBOOKS
WE DIDN'T MISS A–
IT'S TIME FOR THE TEST
TEST?!
DON'T WORRY. I GOT THIS COVERED. I'LL LOOK AT EVERYONE ELSE'S ANSWERS, AND THEN TELL YOU WHAT TO WRITE DOWN.
YOU WANT ME TO CHEAT?
YES.
OH. UMMM... OKAY.

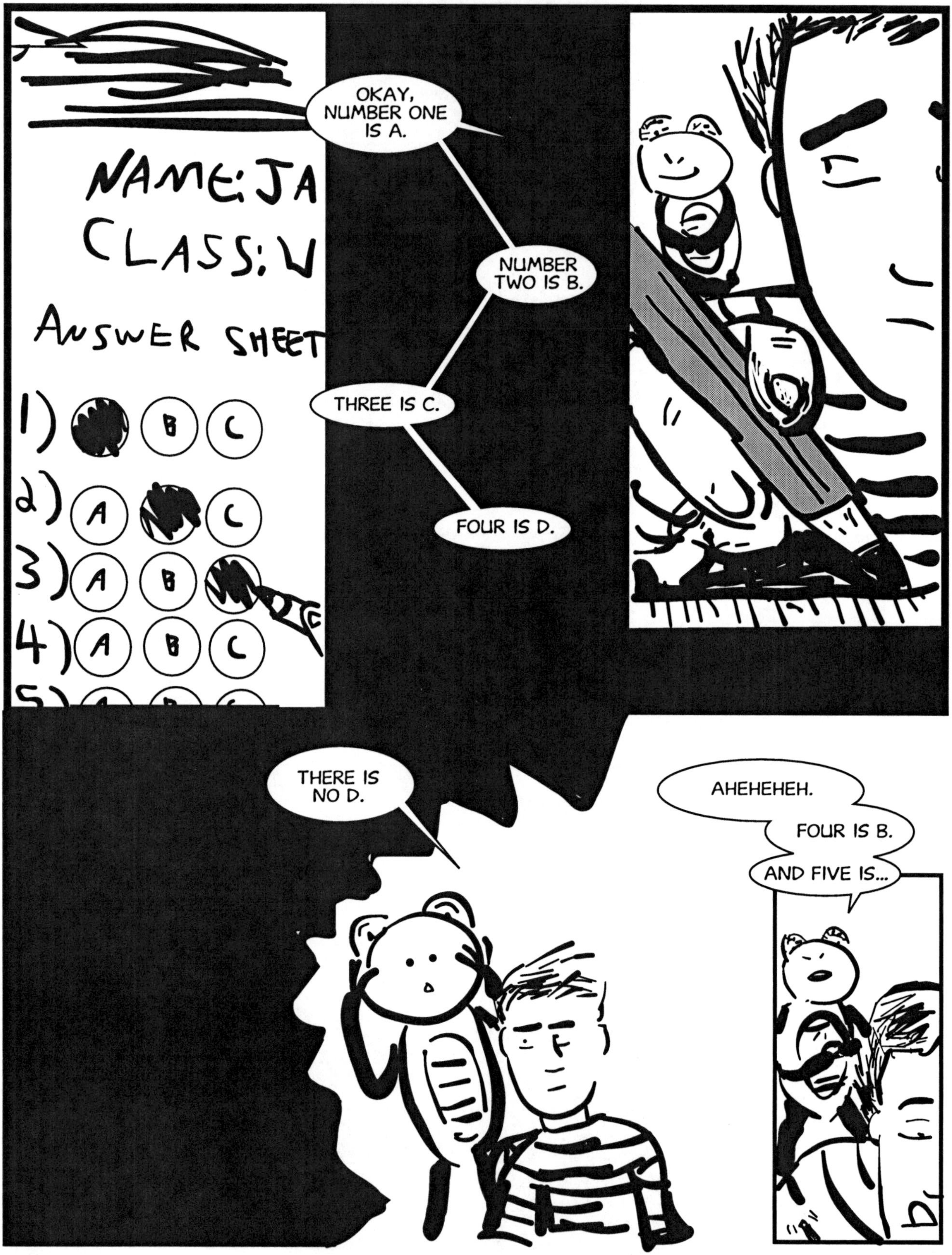
NAME:JA
CLASS:V
ANSWER SHEET
OKAY, NUMBER ONE IS A.
NUMBER TWO IS B.
THREE IS C.
FOUR IS D.
THERE IS NO D.
AHEHEHEH.
FOUR IS B.
AND FIVE IS...

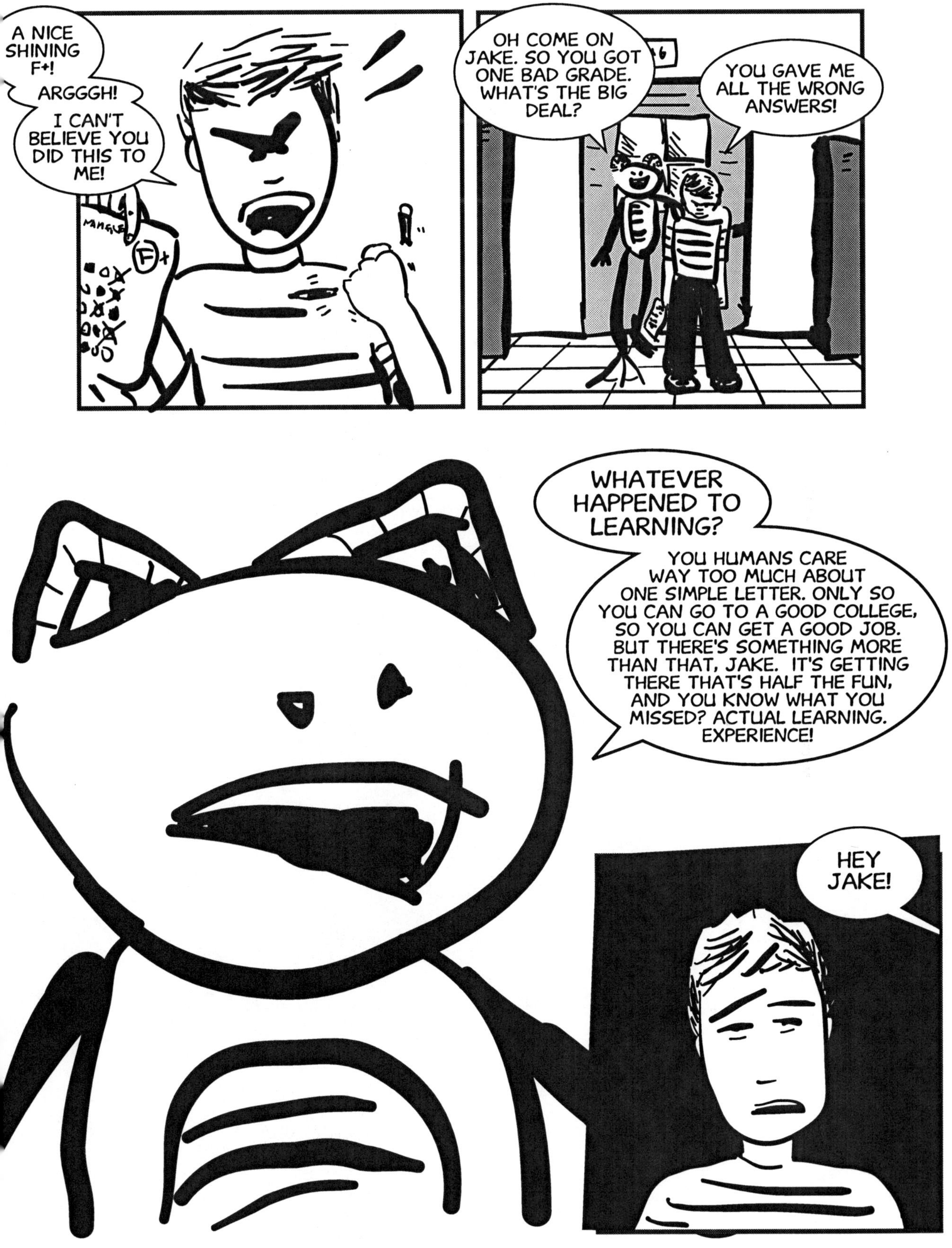
A NICE SHINING F+!
ARGGGH!
I CAN'T BELIEVE YOU DID THIS TO ME!
MANGLE
OH COME ON JAKE. SO YOU GOT ONE BAD GRADE. WHAT'S THE BIG DEAL?
YOU GAVE ME ALL THE WRONG ANSWERS!
WHATEVER HAPPENED TO LEARNING?
YOU HUMANS CARE WAY TOO MUCH ABOUT ONE SIMPLE LETTER. ONLY SO YOU CAN GO TO A GOOD COLLEGE, SO YOU CAN GET A GOOD JOB. BUT THERE'S SOMETHING MORE THAN THAT, JAKE. IT'S GETTING THERE THAT'S HALF THE FUN, AND YOU KNOW WHAT YOU MISSED? ACTUAL LEARNING. EXPERIENCE!
HEY JAKE!

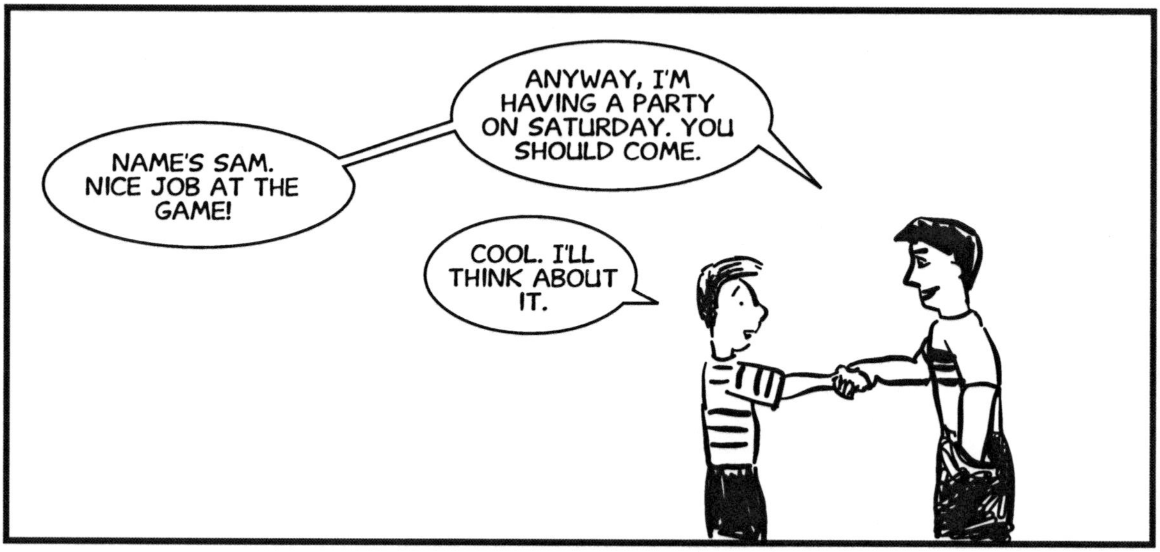
NAME'S SAM. NICE JOB AT THE GAME!
ANYWAY, I'M HAVING A PARTY ON SATURDAY. YOU SHOULD COME.
COOL. I'LL THINK ABOUT IT.

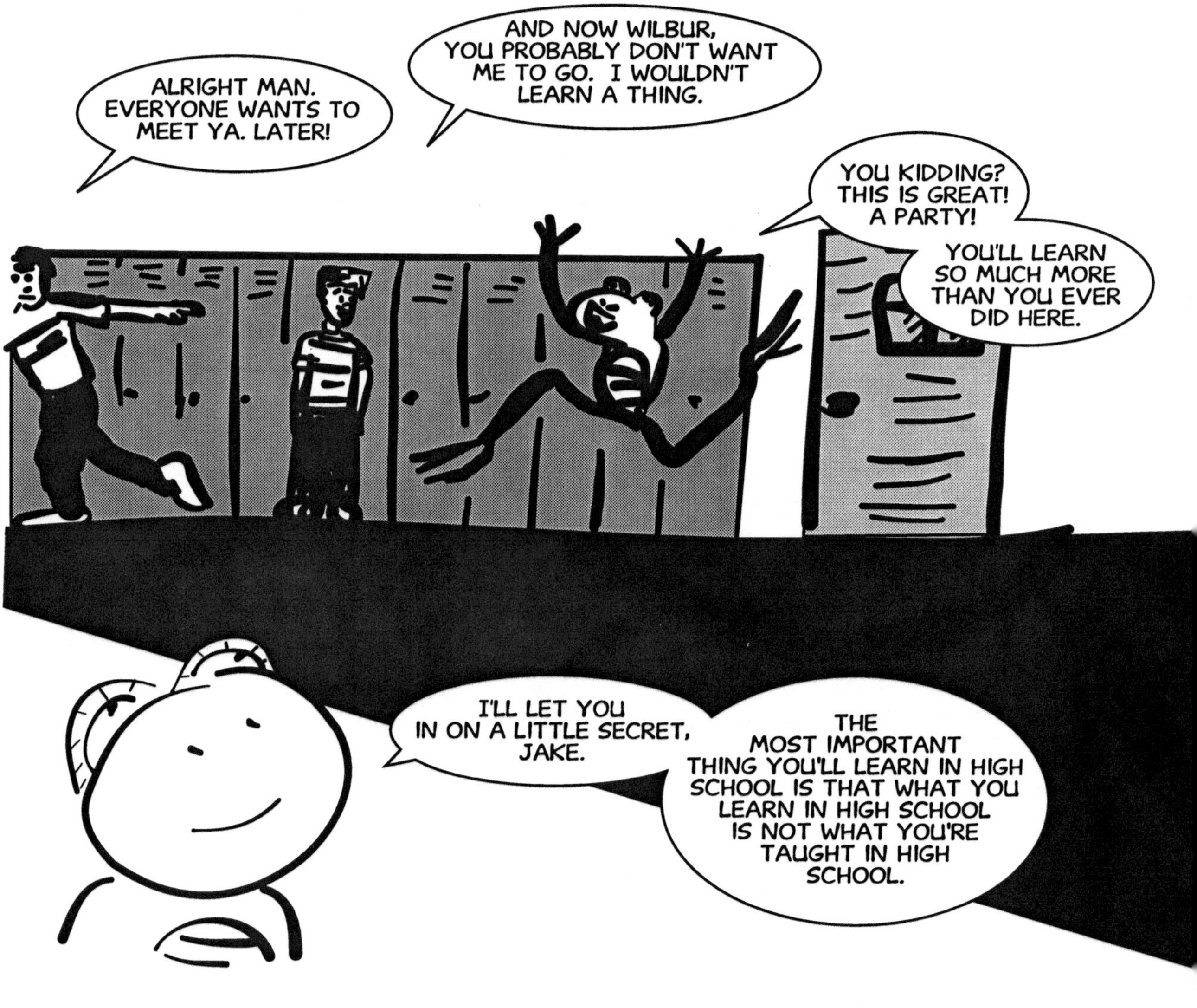
ALRIGHT MAN. EVERYONE WANTS TO MEET YA. LATER!
AND NOW WILBUR, YOU PROBABLY DON'T WANT ME TO GO. I WOULDN'T LEARN A THING.
YOU KIDDING? THIS IS GREAT! A PARTY!
YOU'LL LEARN SO MUCH MORE THAN YOU EVER DID HERE.
I'LL LET YOU IN ON A LITTLE SECRET, JAKE.
THE MOST IMPORTANT THING YOU'LL LEARN IN HIGH SCHOOL IS THAT WHAT YOU LEARN IN HIGH SCHOOL IS NOT WHAT YOU'RE TAUGHT IN HIGH SCHOOL.

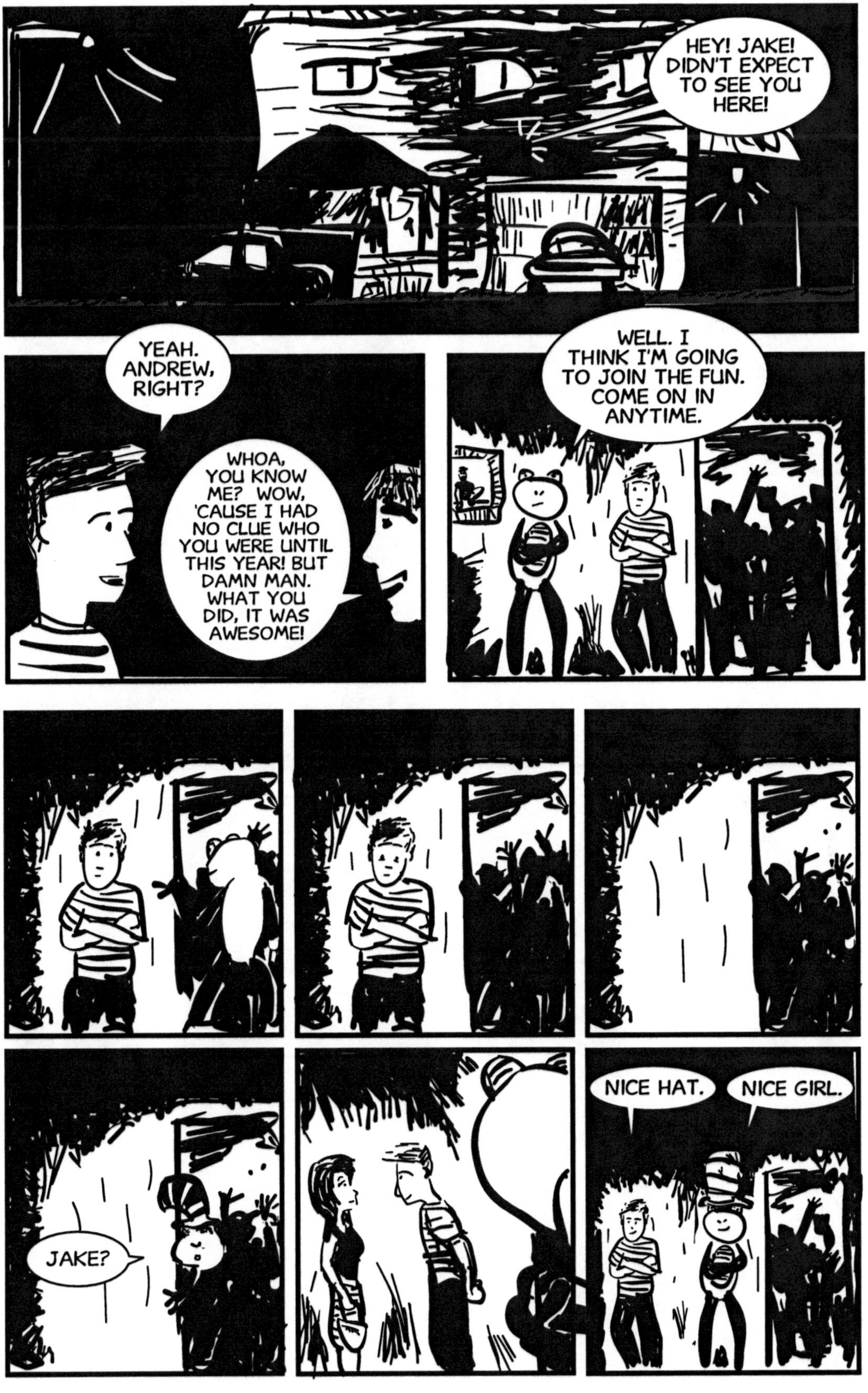
HEY! JAKE! DIDN'T EXPECT TO SEE YOU HERE!
YEAH. ANDREW, RIGHT?
WHOA, YOU KNOW ME? WOW, 'CAUSE I HAD NO CLUE WHO YOU WERE UNTIL THIS YEAR! BUT DAMN MAN. WHAT YOU DID, IT WAS AWESOME!
WELL. I THINK I'M GOING TO JOIN THE FUN. COME ON IN ANYTIME.
JAKE?
NICE HAT.
NICE GIRL.

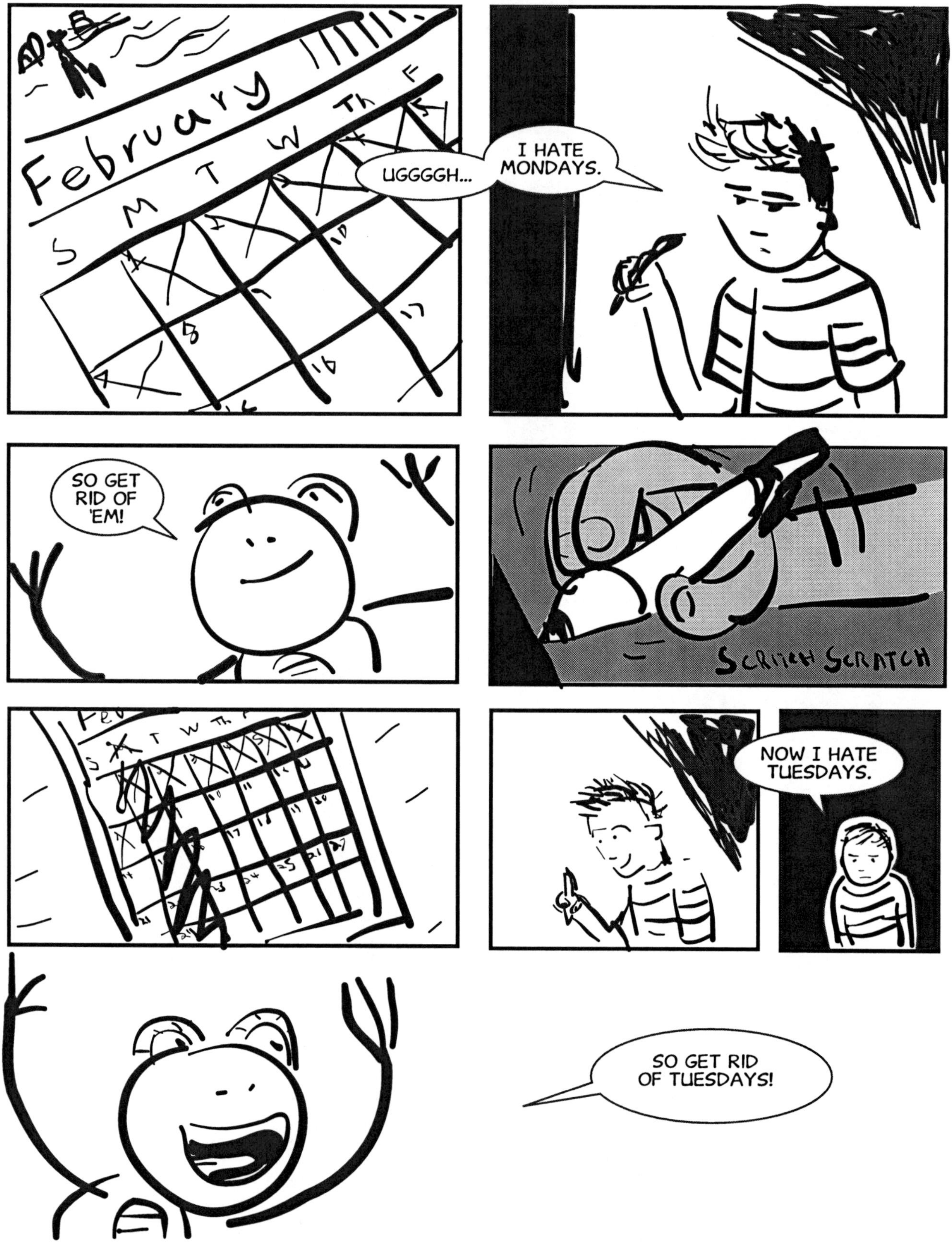
February
S M T W Th F
UGGGGH...
I HATE MONDAYS.
SO GET RID OF 'EM!
SCRITCH SCRATCH
NOW I HATE TUESDAYS.
SO GET RID OF TUESDAYS!

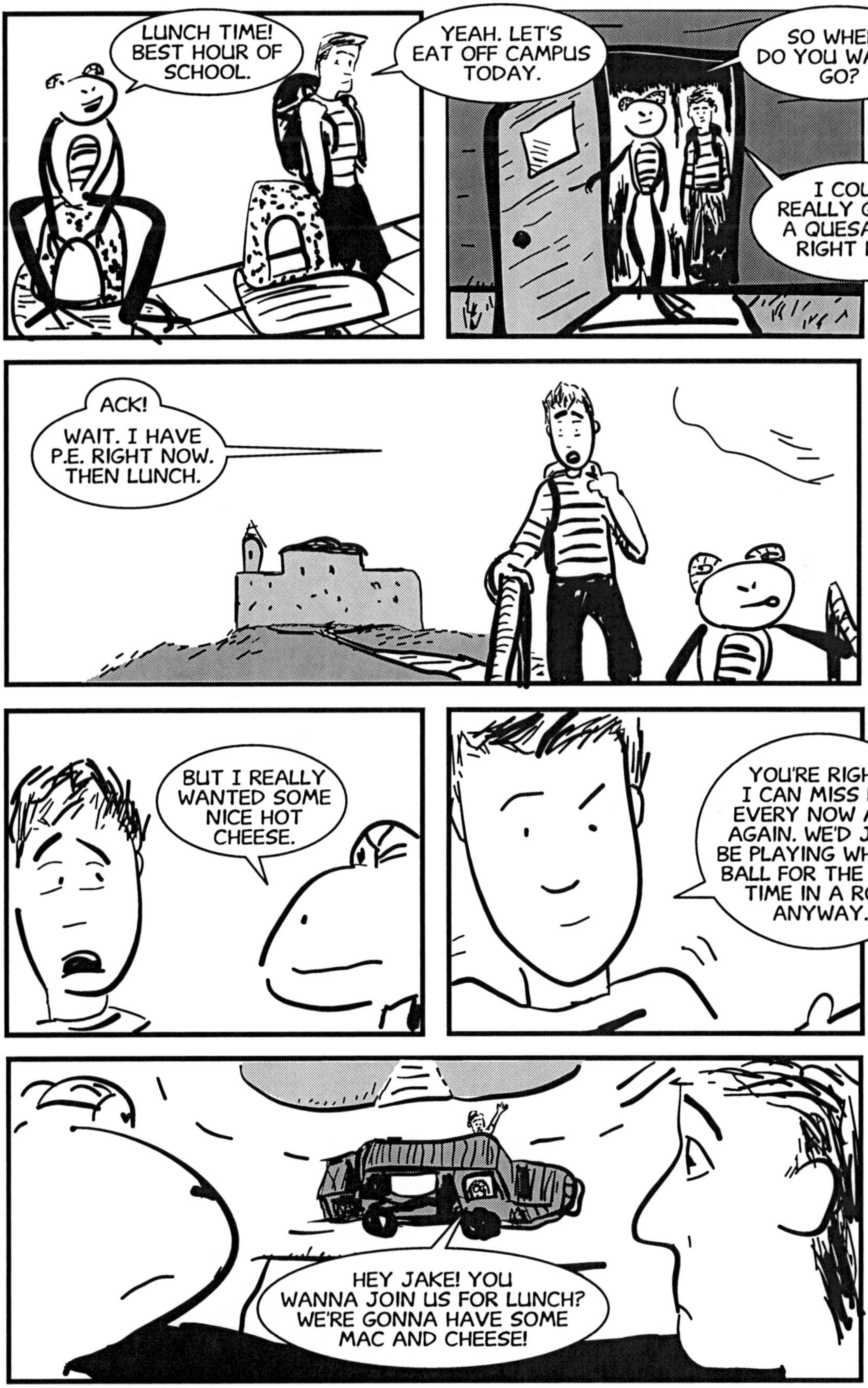
LUNCH TIME! BEST HOUR OF SCHOOL.
YEAH. LET'S EAT OFF CAMPUS TODAY.
SO WHERE DO YOU WANNA GO?
I COULD REALLY GO FOR A QUESADILLA RIGHT NOW.
ACK!
WAIT. I HAVE P.E. RIGHT NOW. THEN LUNCH.
BUT I REALLY WANTED SOME NICE HOT CHEESE.
YOU'RE RIGHT. I CAN MISS P.E. EVERY NOW AND AGAIN. WE'D JUST BE PLAYING WHIFFLE BALL FOR THE 14TH TIME IN A ROW ANYWAY.
HEY JAKE! YOU WANNA JOIN US FOR LUNCH? WE'RE GONNA HAVE SOME MAC AND CHEESE!

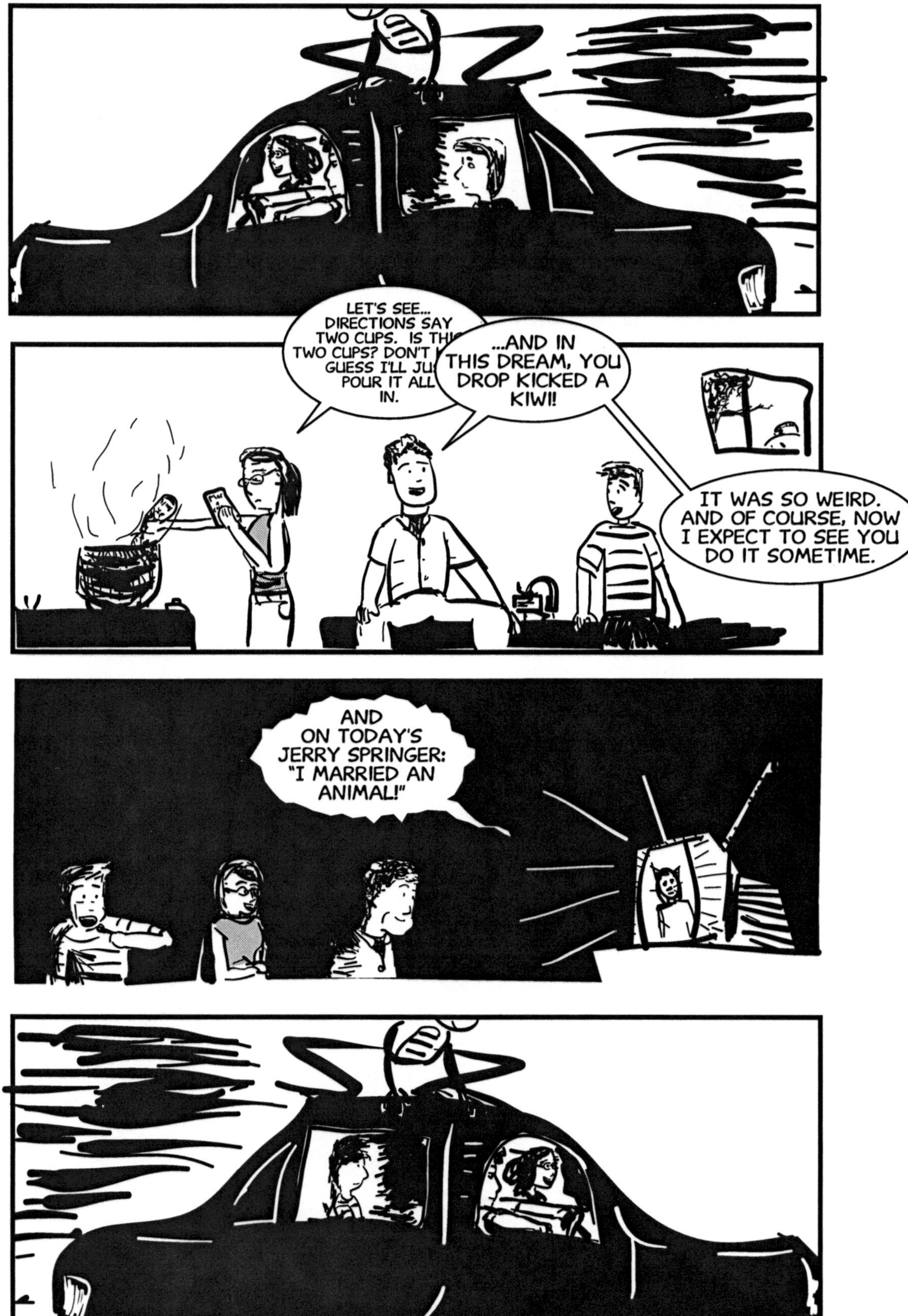
LET'S SEE... DIRECTIONS SAY TWO CUPS. IS THI TWO CUPS? DON'T GUESS I'LL JUS POUR IT ALL IN.
...AND IN THIS DREAM, YOU DROP KICKED A KIWI!
IT WAS SO WEIRD. AND OF COURSE, NOW I EXPECT TO SEE YOU DO IT SOMETIME.
AND ON TODAY'S JERRY SPRINGER: "I MARRIED AN ANIMAL!"

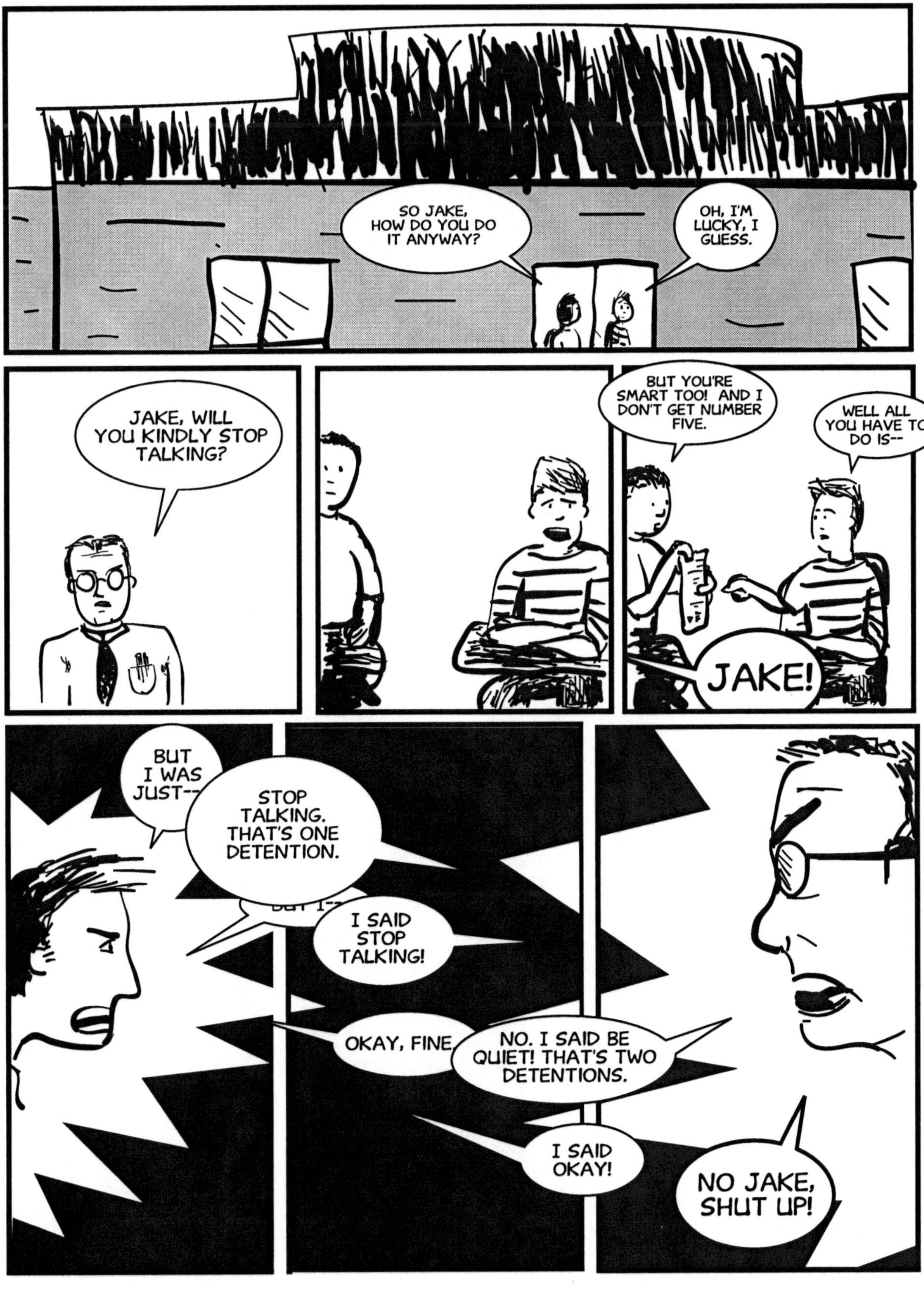
SO JAKE, HOW DO YOU DO IT ANYWAY?
OH, I'M LUCKY, I GUESS.
JAKE, WILL YOU KINDLY STOP TALKING?
BUT YOU'RE SMART TOO! AND I DON'T GET NUMBER FIVE.
WELL ALL YOU HAVE TO DO IS--
JAKE!
BUT I WAS JUST--
STOP TALKING. THAT'S ONE DETENTION.
BUT I--
I SAID STOP TALKING!
OKAY, FINE.
NO. I SAID BE QUIET! THAT'S TWO DETENTIONS.
I SAID OKAY!
NO JAKE, SHUT UP!

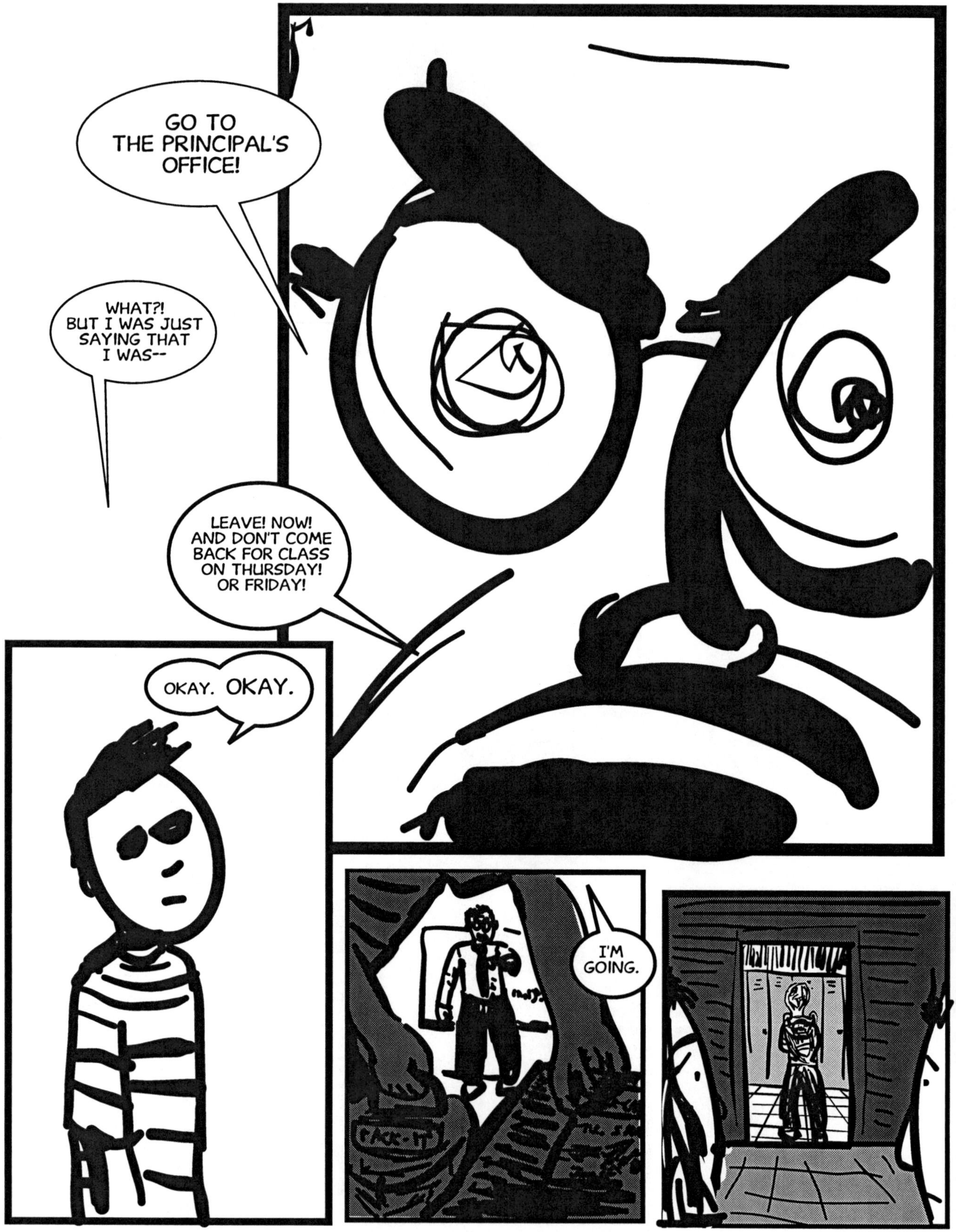
GO TO THE PRINCIPAL'S OFFICE!
WHAT?! BUT I WAS JUST SAYING THAT I WAS--
LEAVE! NOW! AND DON'T COME BACK FOR CLASS ON THURSDAY! OR FRIDAY!
OKAY. OKAY.
I'M GOING.

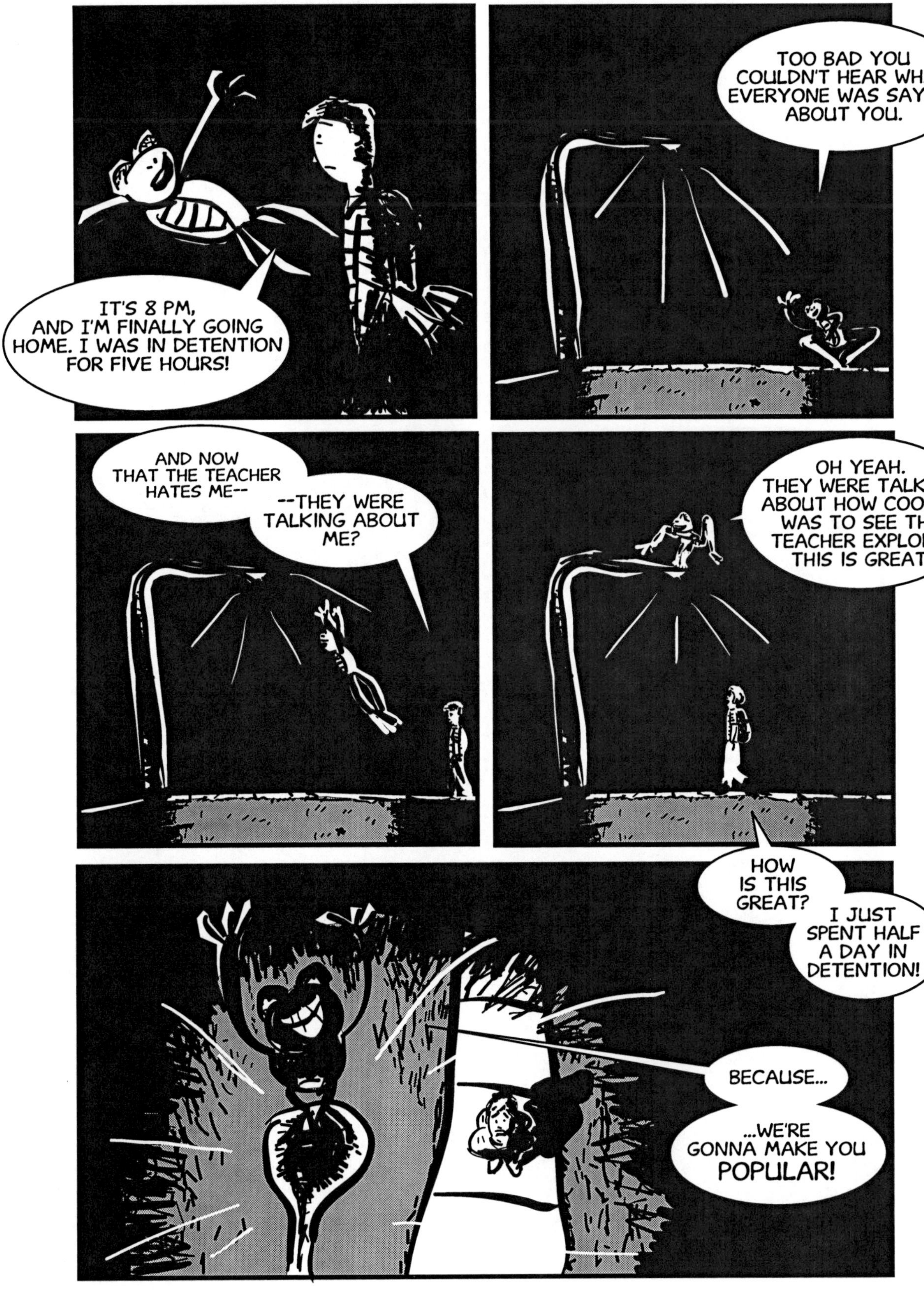
IT'S 8 PM, AND I'M FINALLY GOING HOME. I WAS IN DETENTION FOR FIVE HOURS!
TOO BAD YOU COULDN'T HEAR WHAT EVERYONE WAS SAYING ABOUT YOU.
AND NOW THAT THE TEACHER HATES ME--
--THEY WERE TALKING ABOUT ME?
OH YEAH. THEY WERE TALKING ABOUT HOW COOL IT WAS TO SEE THE TEACHER EXPLODE, THIS IS GREAT!
HOW IS THIS GREAT?
I JUST SPENT HALF A DAY IN DETENTION!
BECAUSE...
...WE'RE GONNA MAKE YOU POPULAR!

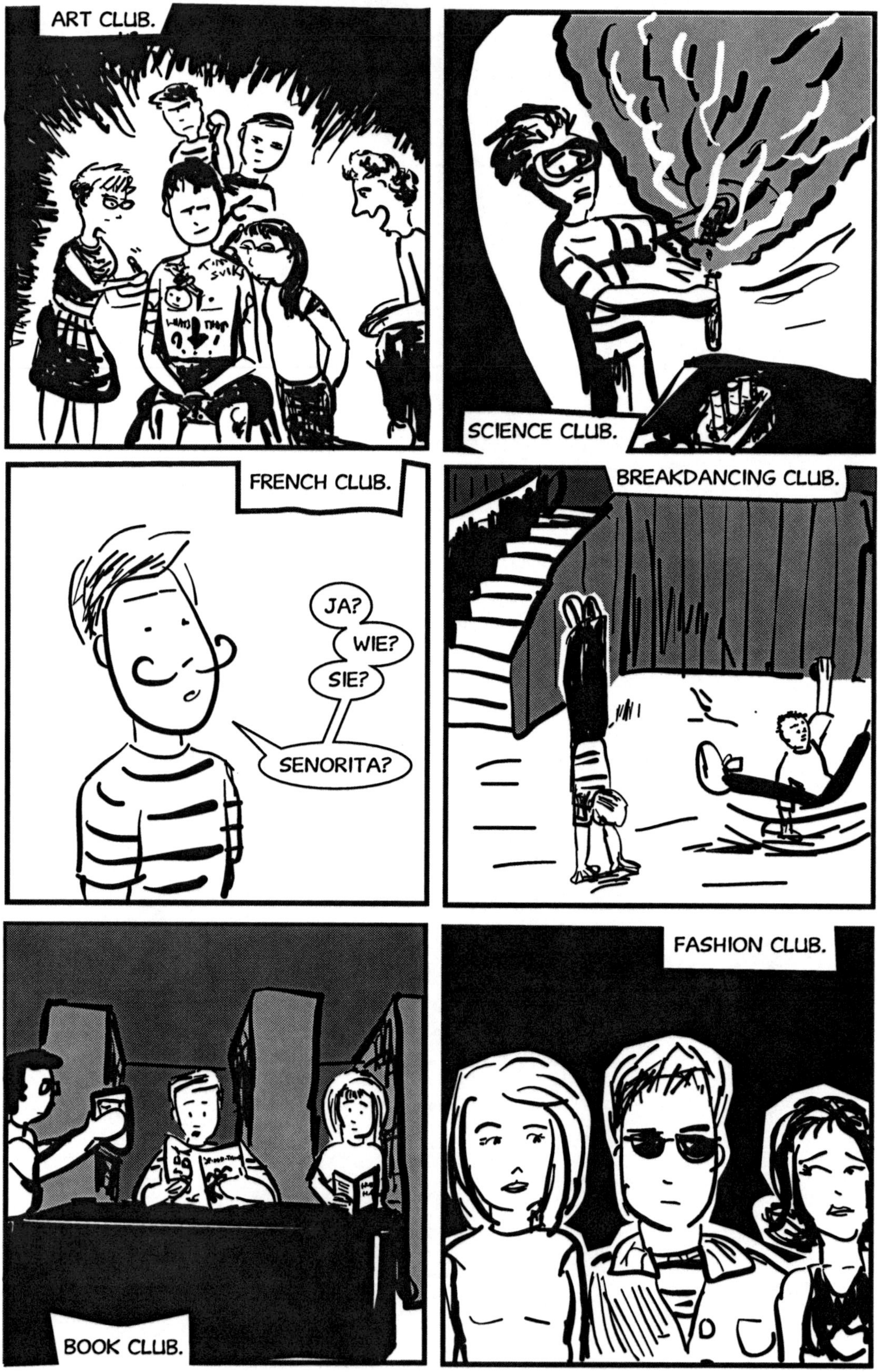
ART CLUB.
SCIENCE CLUB.
FRENCH CLUB.
JA?
WIE?
SIE?
SENORITA?
BREAKDANCING CLUB.
BOOK CLUB.
FASHION CLUB.

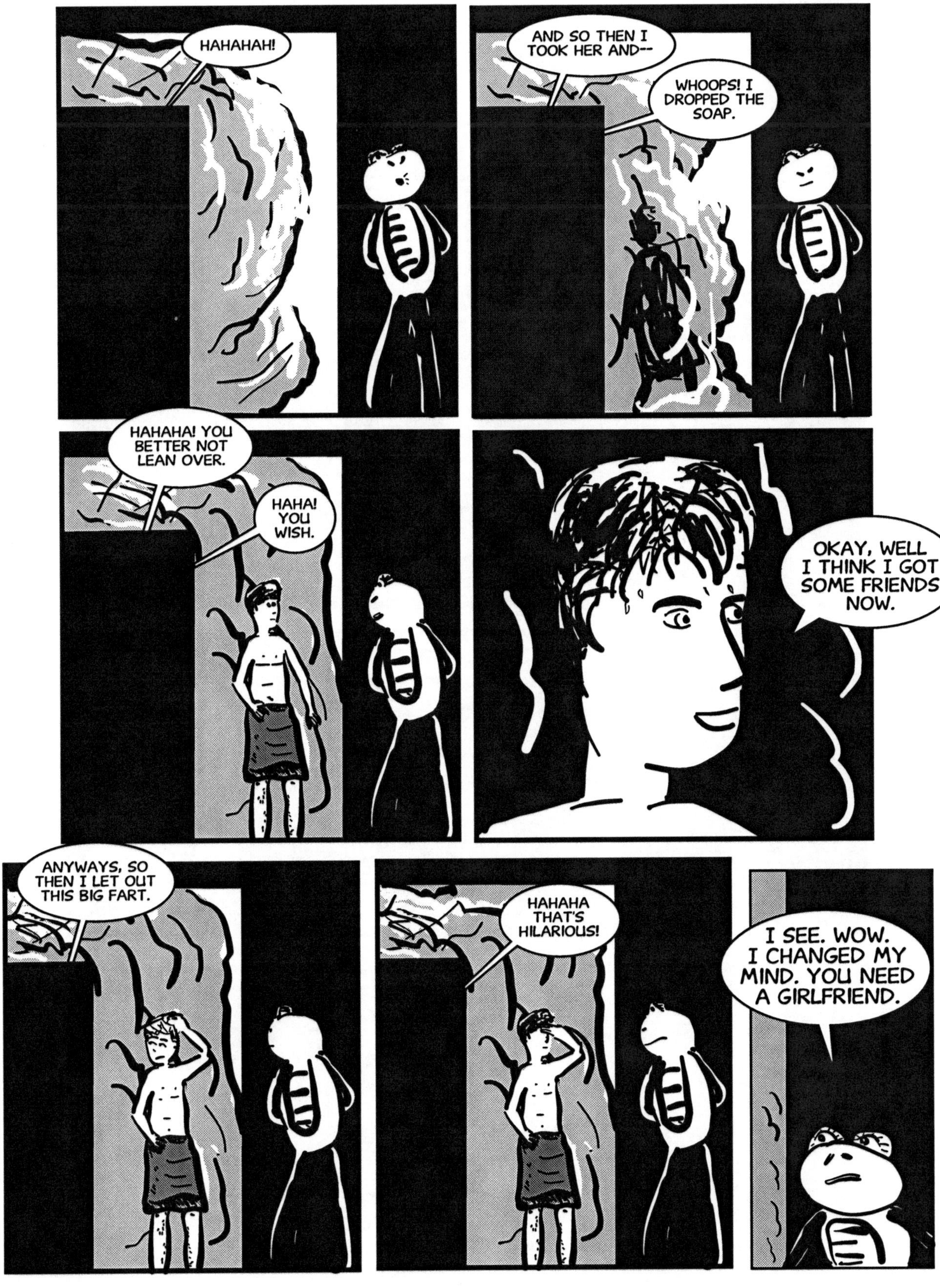
HAHAHAH!
AND SO THEN I TOOK HER AND--
WHOOPS! I DROPPED THE SOAP.
HAHAHA! YOU BETTER NOT LEAN OVER.
HAHA! YOU WISH.
OKAY, WELL I THINK I GOT SOME FRIENDS NOW.
ANYWAYS, SO THEN I LET OUT THIS BIG FART.
HAHAHA THAT'S HILARIOUS!
I SEE. WOW. I CHANGED MY MIND. YOU NEED A GIRLFRIEND.

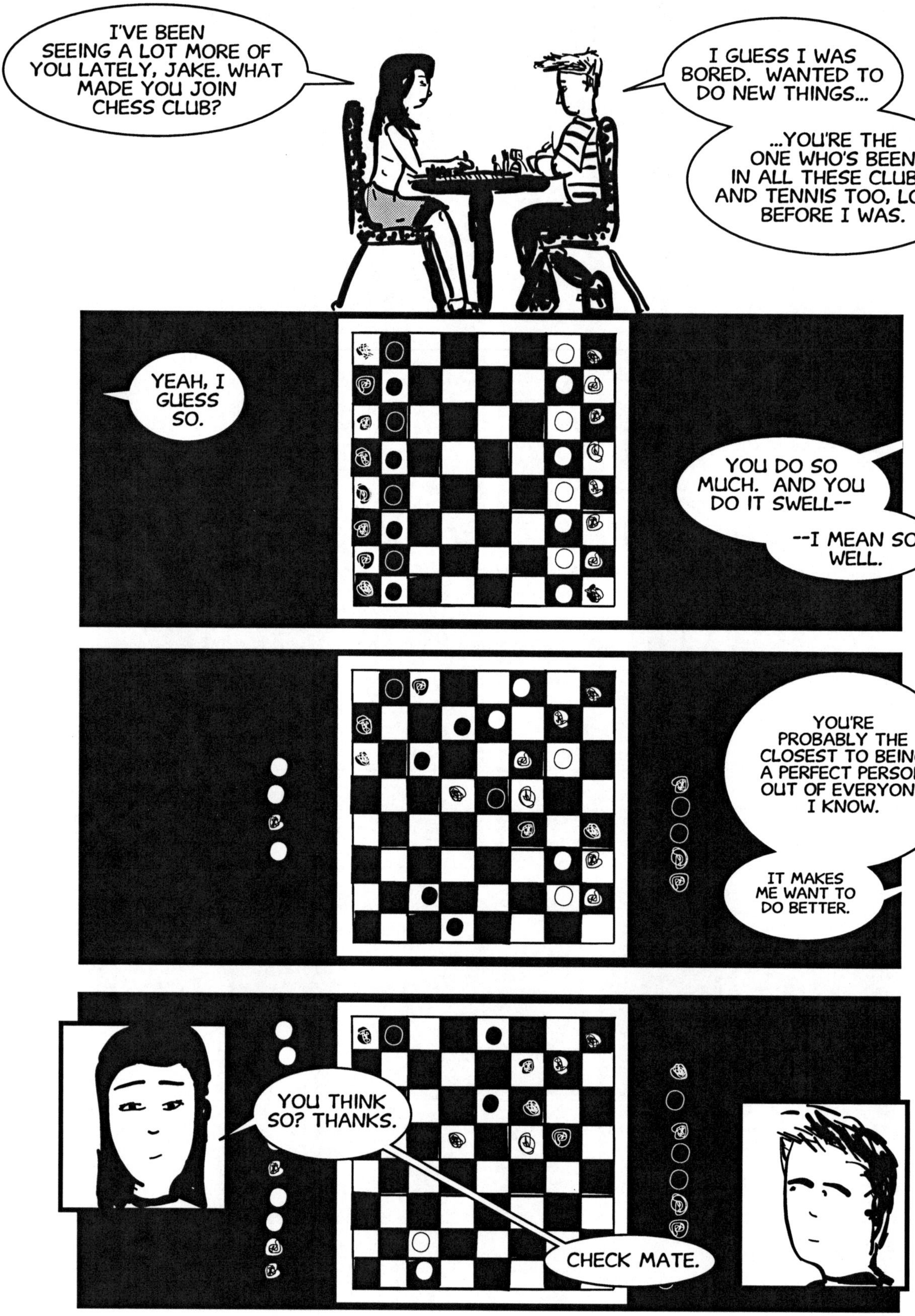
I'VE BEEN SEEING A LOT MORE OF YOU LATELY, JAKE. WHAT MADE YOU JOIN CHESS CLUB?
I GUESS I WAS BORED. WANTED TO DO NEW THINGS...
...YOU'RE THE ONE WHO'S BEEN IN ALL THESE CLUBS, AND TENNIS TOO, LONG BEFORE I WAS.
YEAH, I GUESS SO.
YOU DO SO MUCH. AND YOU DO IT SWELL--
--I MEAN SO WELL.
YOU'RE PROBABLY THE CLOSEST TO BEING A PERFECT PERSON OUT OF EVERYONE I KNOW.
IT MAKES ME WANT TO DO BETTER.
YOU THINK SO? THANKS.
CHECK MATE.

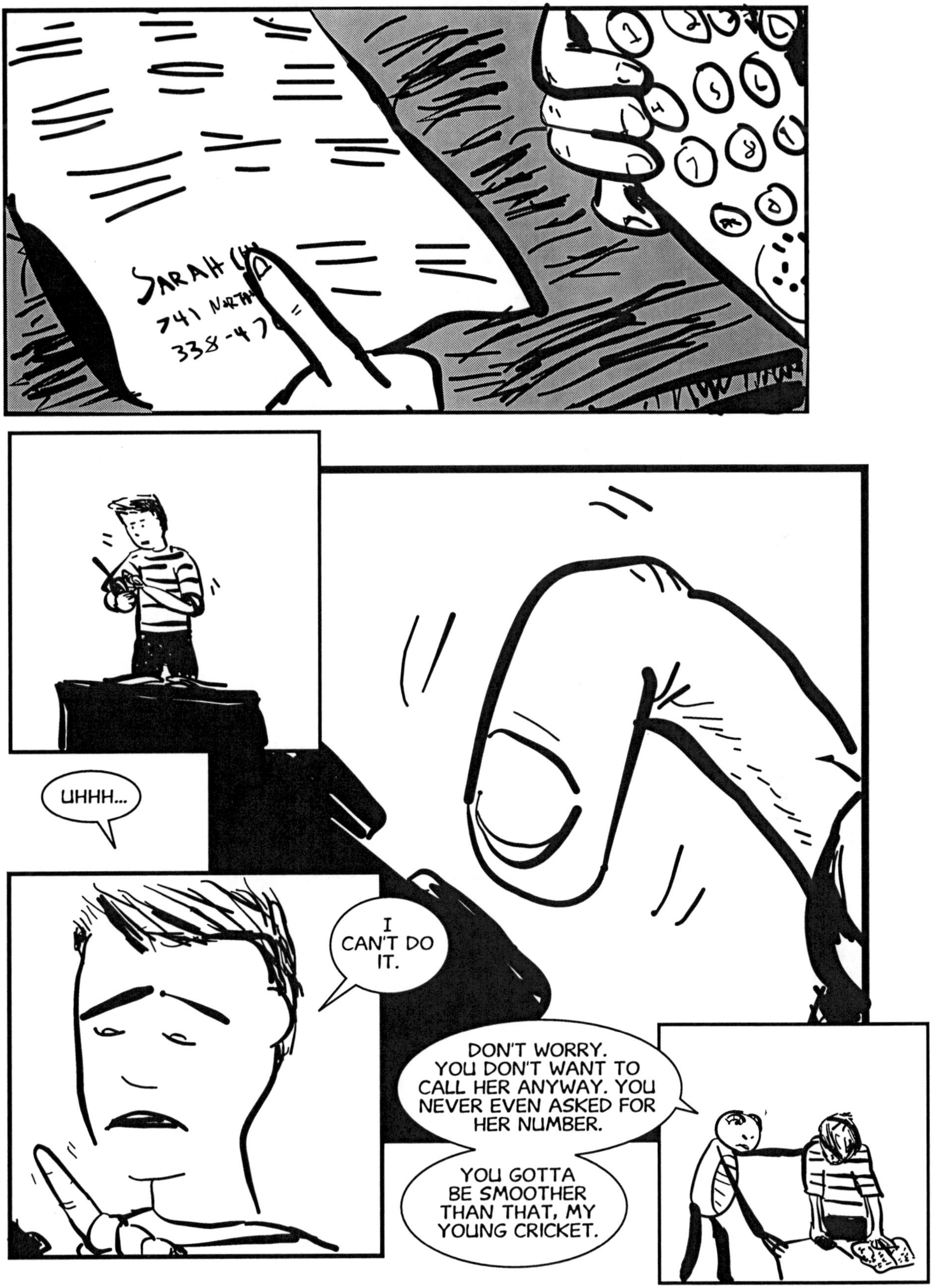
SARAH
741 NORTH
338-47
UHHH...
I CAN'T DO IT.
DON'T WORRY. YOU DON'T WANT TO CALL HER ANYWAY. YOU NEVER EVEN ASKED FOR HER NUMBER.
YOU GOTTA BE SMOOTHER THAN THAT, MY YOUNG CRICKET.

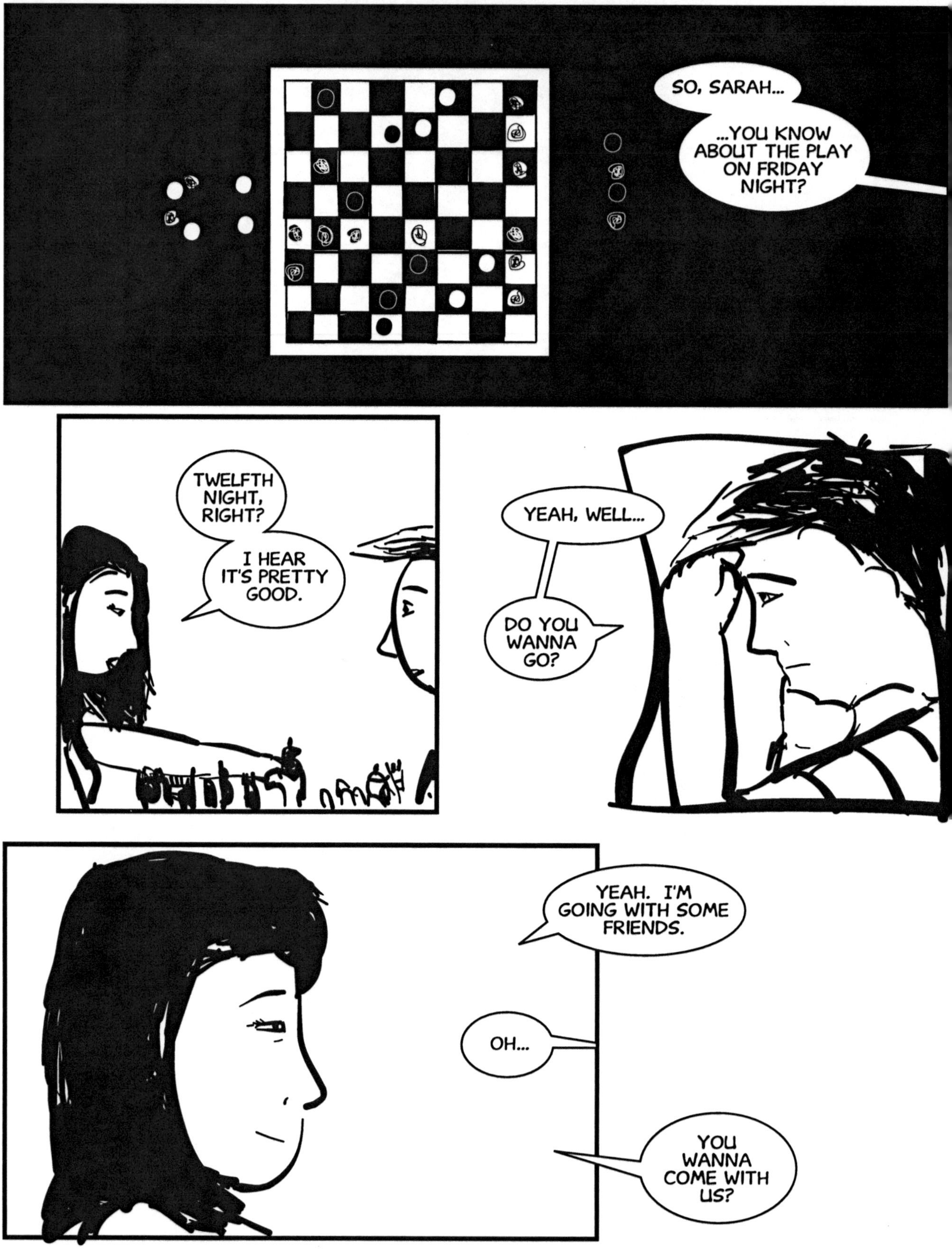
SO, SARAH...
...YOU KNOW ABOUT THE PLAY ON FRIDAY NIGHT?
TWELFTH NIGHT, RIGHT?
I HEAR IT'S PRETTY GOOD.
YEAH, WELL...
DO YOU WANNA GO?
YEAH. I'M GOING WITH SOME FRIENDS.
OH...
YOU WANNA COME WITH US?

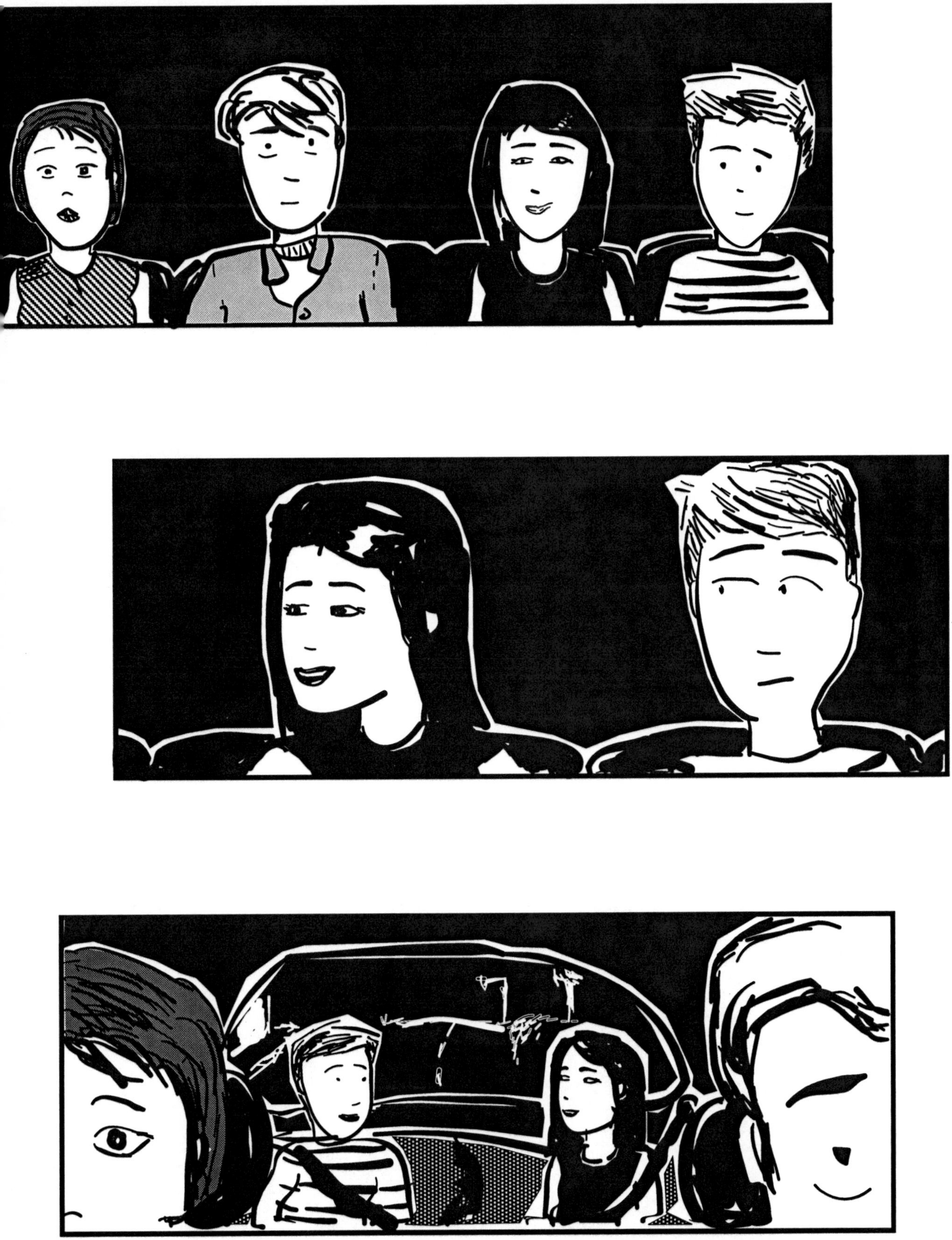

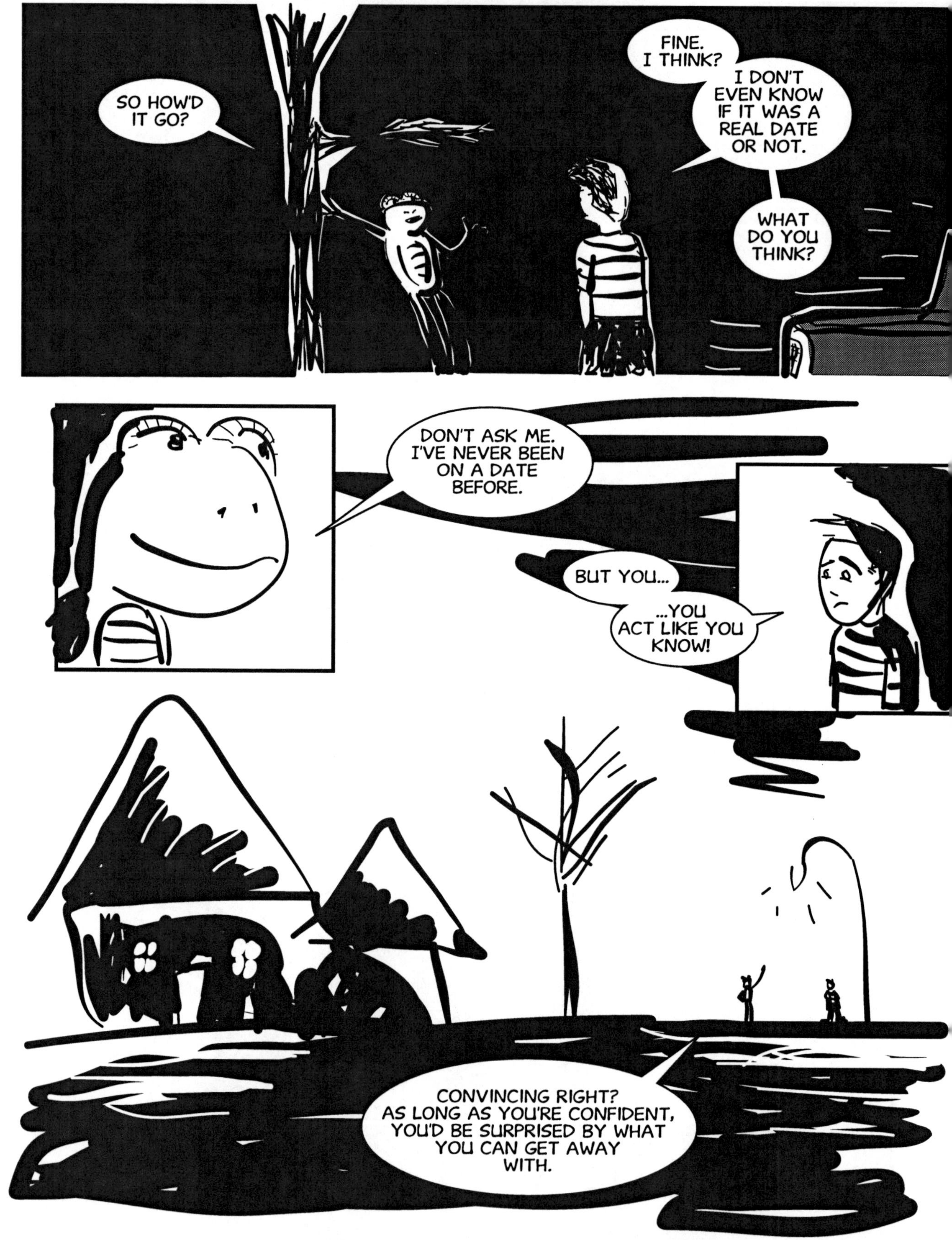
SO HOW'D IT GO?
FINE. I THINK?
I DON'T EVEN KNOW IF IT WAS A REAL DATE OR NOT.
WHAT DO YOU THINK?
DON'T ASK ME. I'VE NEVER BEEN ON A DATE BEFORE.
BUT YOU...
...YOU ACT LIKE YOU KNOW!
CONVINCING RIGHT? AS LONG AS YOU'RE CONFIDENT, YOU'D BE SURPRISED BY WHAT YOU CAN GET AWAY WITH.

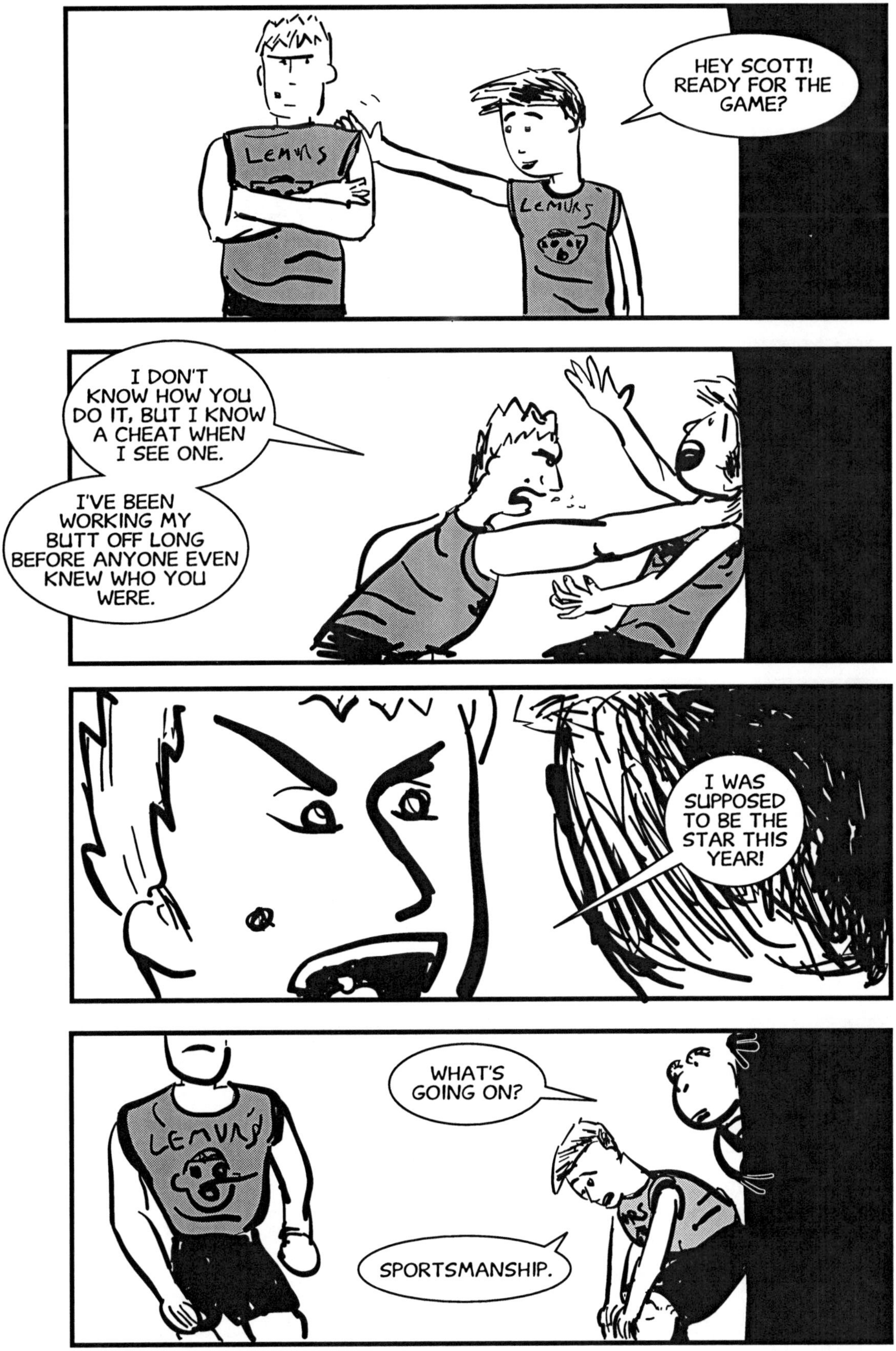
LEMURS
LEMURS
HEY SCOTT! READY FOR THE GAME?
I DON'T KNOW HOW YOU DO IT, BUT I KNOW A CHEAT WHEN I SEE ONE.
I'VE BEEN WORKING MY BUTT OFF LONG BEFORE ANYONE EVEN KNEW WHO YOU WERE.
I WAS SUPPOSED TO BE THE STAR THIS YEAR!
LEMURS
WHAT'S GOING ON?
SPORTSMANSHIP.

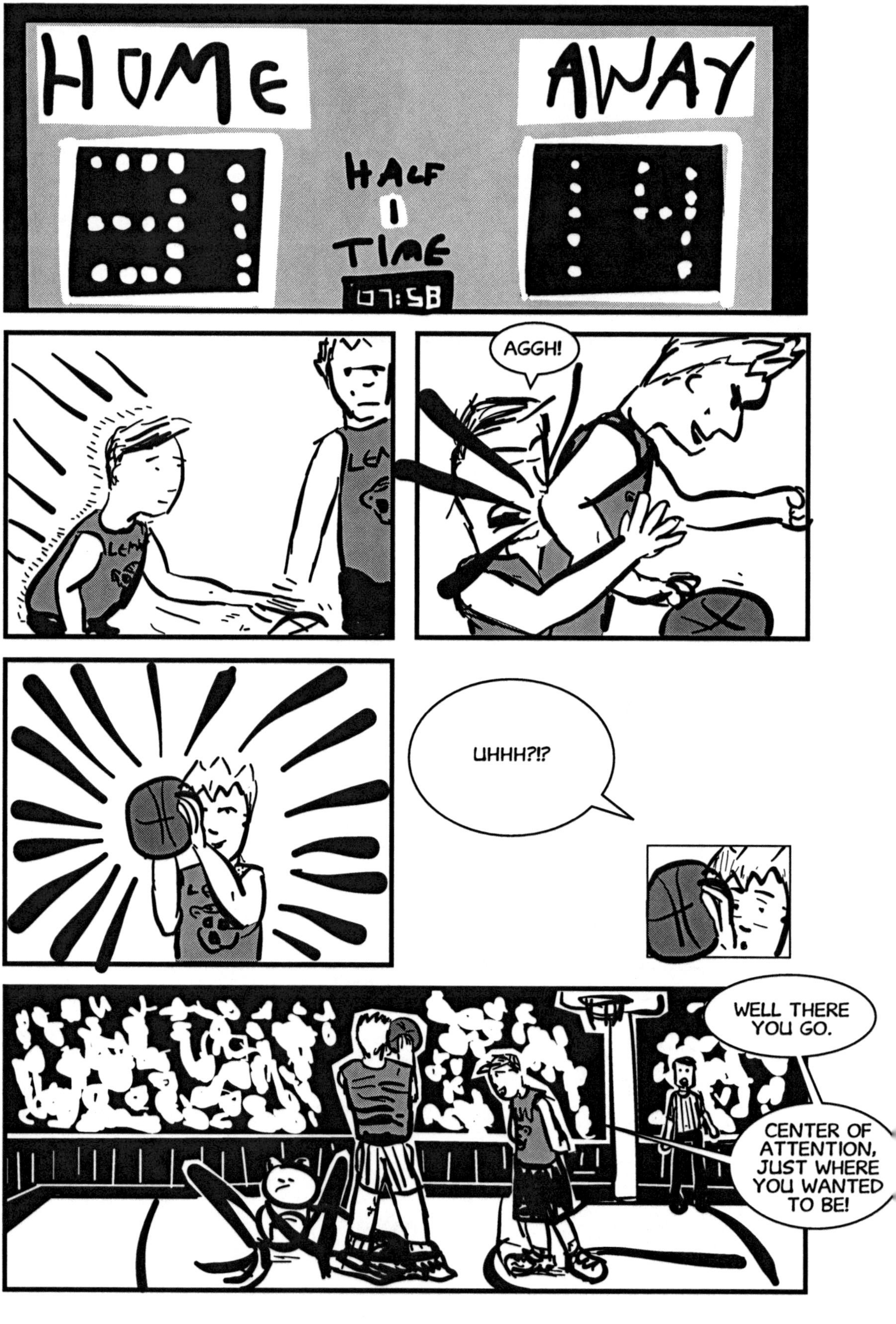
HOME
AWAY
HALF
1
TIME
07:58
AGGH!
UHHH?!?
WELL THERE YOU GO.
CENTER OF ATTENTION, JUST WHERE YOU WANTED TO BE!

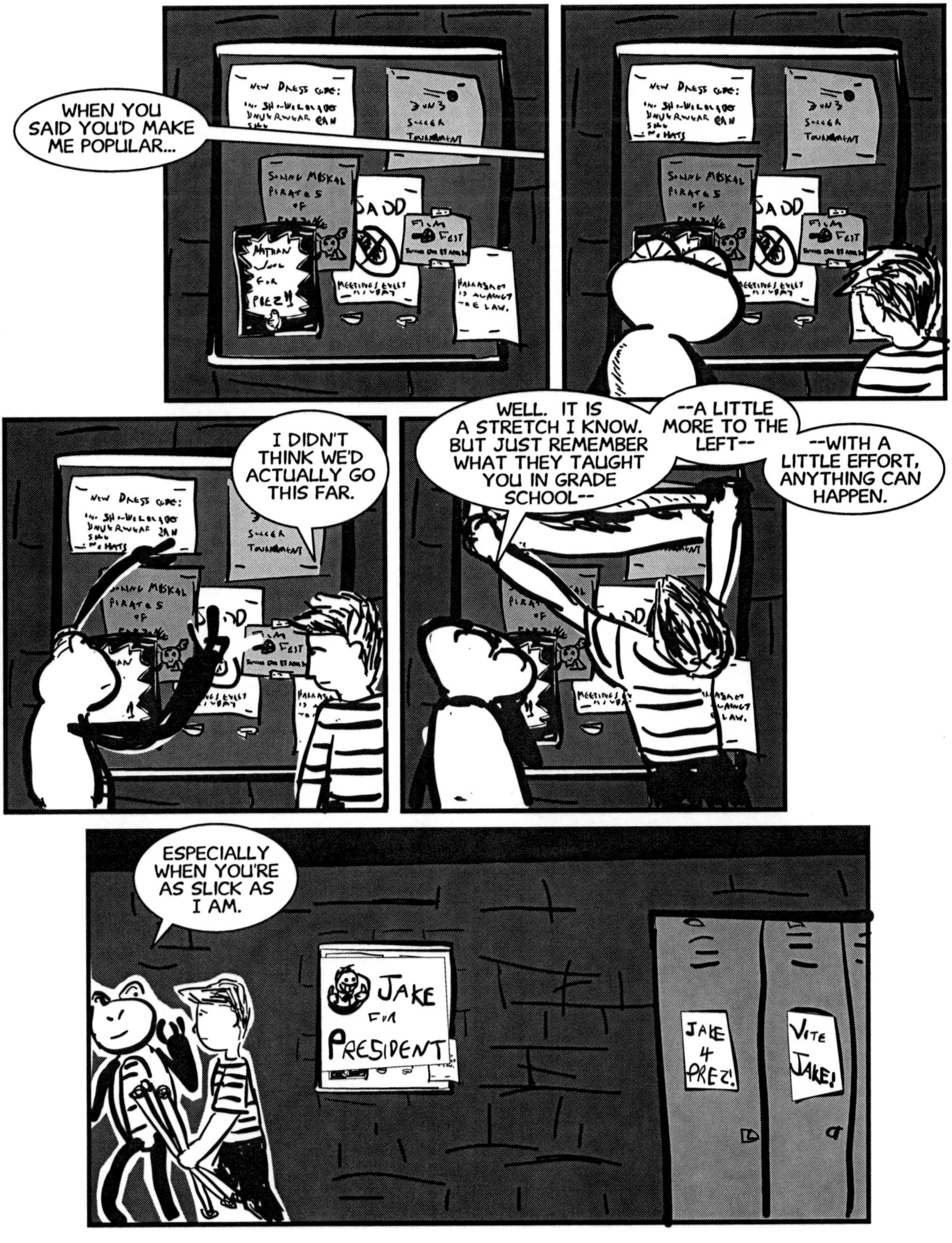
WHEN YOU SAID YOU'D MAKE ME POPULAR...
I DIDN'T THINK WE'D ACTUALLY GO THIS FAR.
WELL. IT IS A STRETCH I KNOW. BUT JUST REMEMBER WHAT THEY TAUGHT YOU IN GRADE SCHOOL--
--A LITTLE MORE TO THE LEFT--
--WITH A LITTLE EFFORT, ANYTHING CAN HAPPEN.
ESPECIALLY WHEN YOU'RE AS SLICK AS I AM.
JAKE FOR PRESIDENT
JAKE 4 PREZ!
VOTE JAKE!

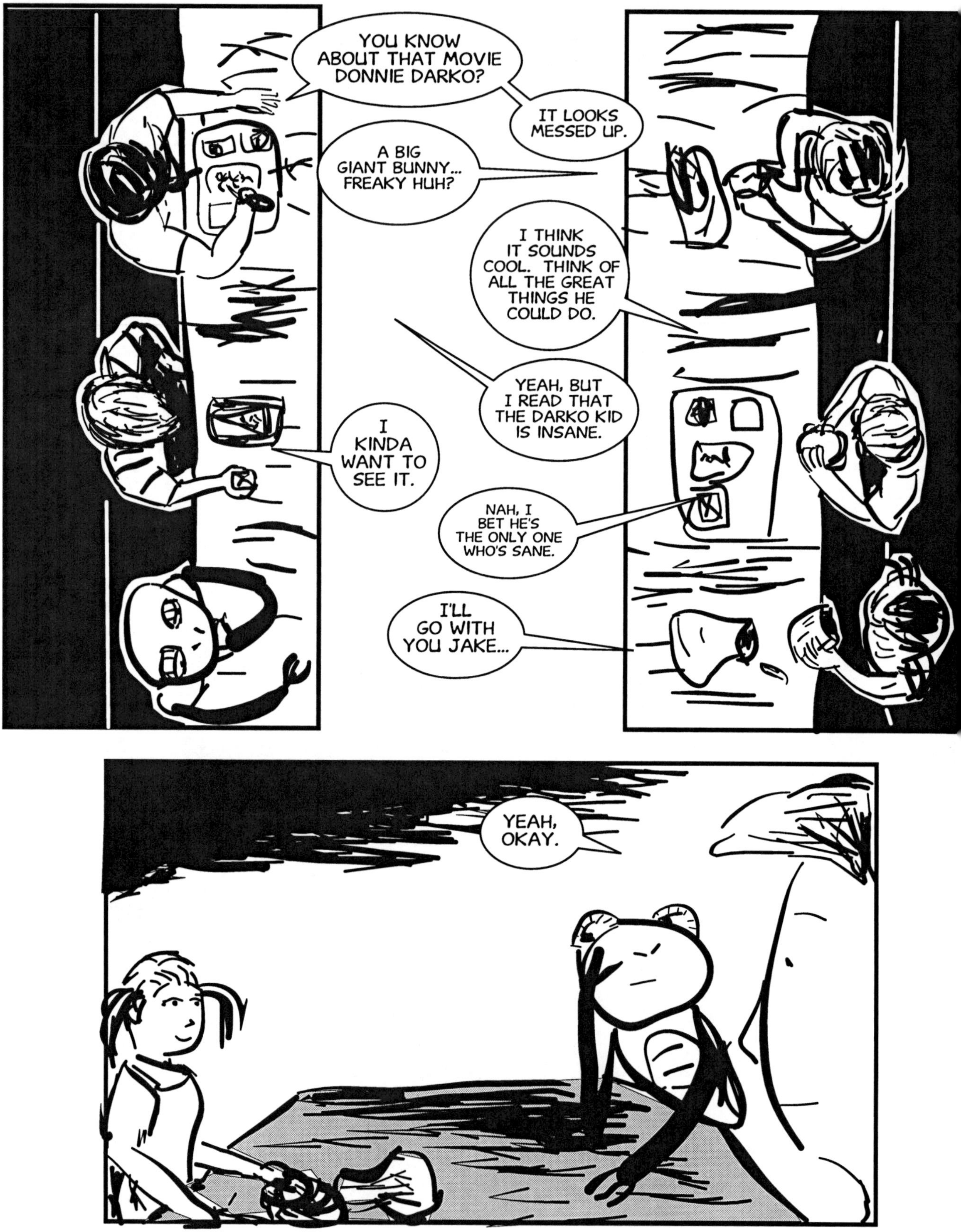
YOU KNOW ABOUT THAT MOVIE DONNIE DARKO?
IT LOOKS MESSED UP.
A BIG GIANT BUNNY... FREAKY HUH?
I THINK IT SOUNDS COOL. THINK OF ALL THE GREAT THINGS HE COULD DO.
YEAH, BUT I READ THAT THE DARKO KID IS INSANE.
I KINDA WANT TO SEE IT.
NAH, I BET HE'S THE ONLY ONE WHO'S SANE.
I'LL GO WITH YOU JAKE...
YEAH, OKAY.

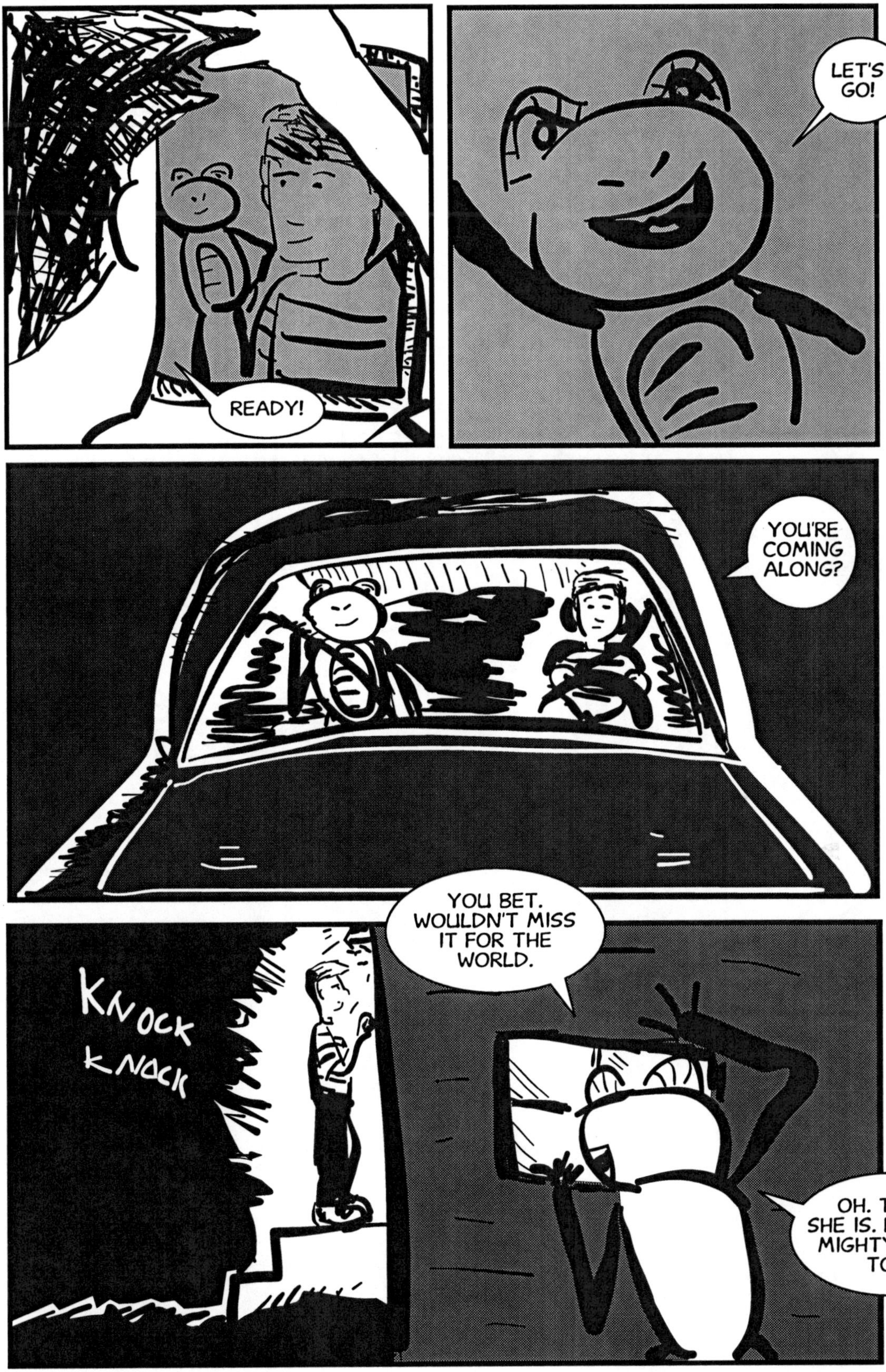
READY!
LET'S GO!
YOU'RE COMING ALONG?
YOU BET. WOULDN'T MISS IT FOR THE WORLD.
KNOCK KNOCK
OH. THERE SHE IS. LOOKING MIGHTY FOXY, TOO!

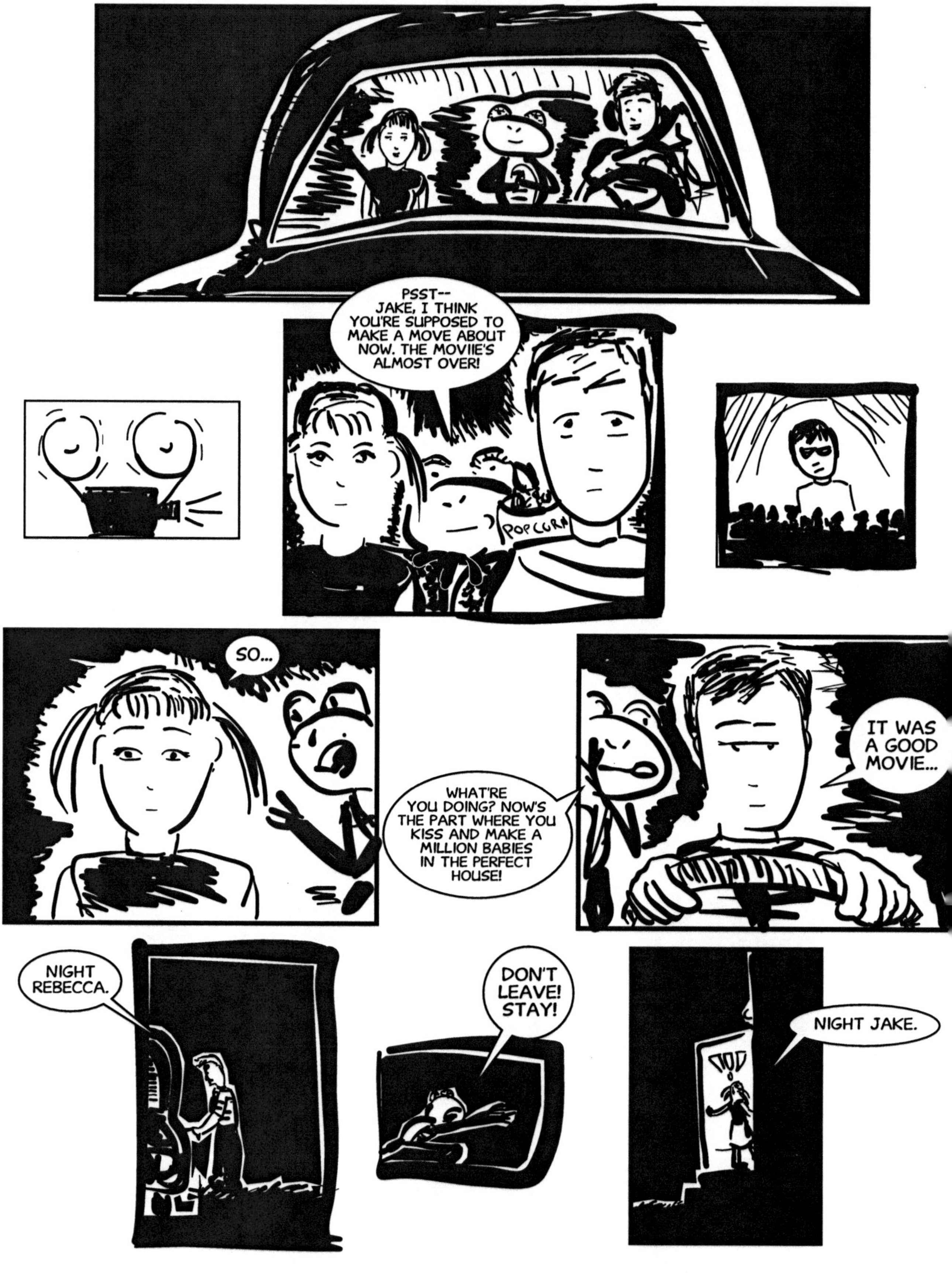
PSST--
JAKE, I THINK YOU'RE SUPPOSED TO MAKE A MOVE ABOUT NOW. THE MOVIIE'S ALMOST OVER!
POPCURN
SO...
WHAT'RE YOU DOING? NOW'S THE PART WHERE YOU KISS AND MAKE A MILLION BABIES IN THE PERFECT HOUSE!
IT WAS A GOOD MOVIE...
NIGHT REBECCA.
DON'T LEAVE! STAY!
NIGHT JAKE.

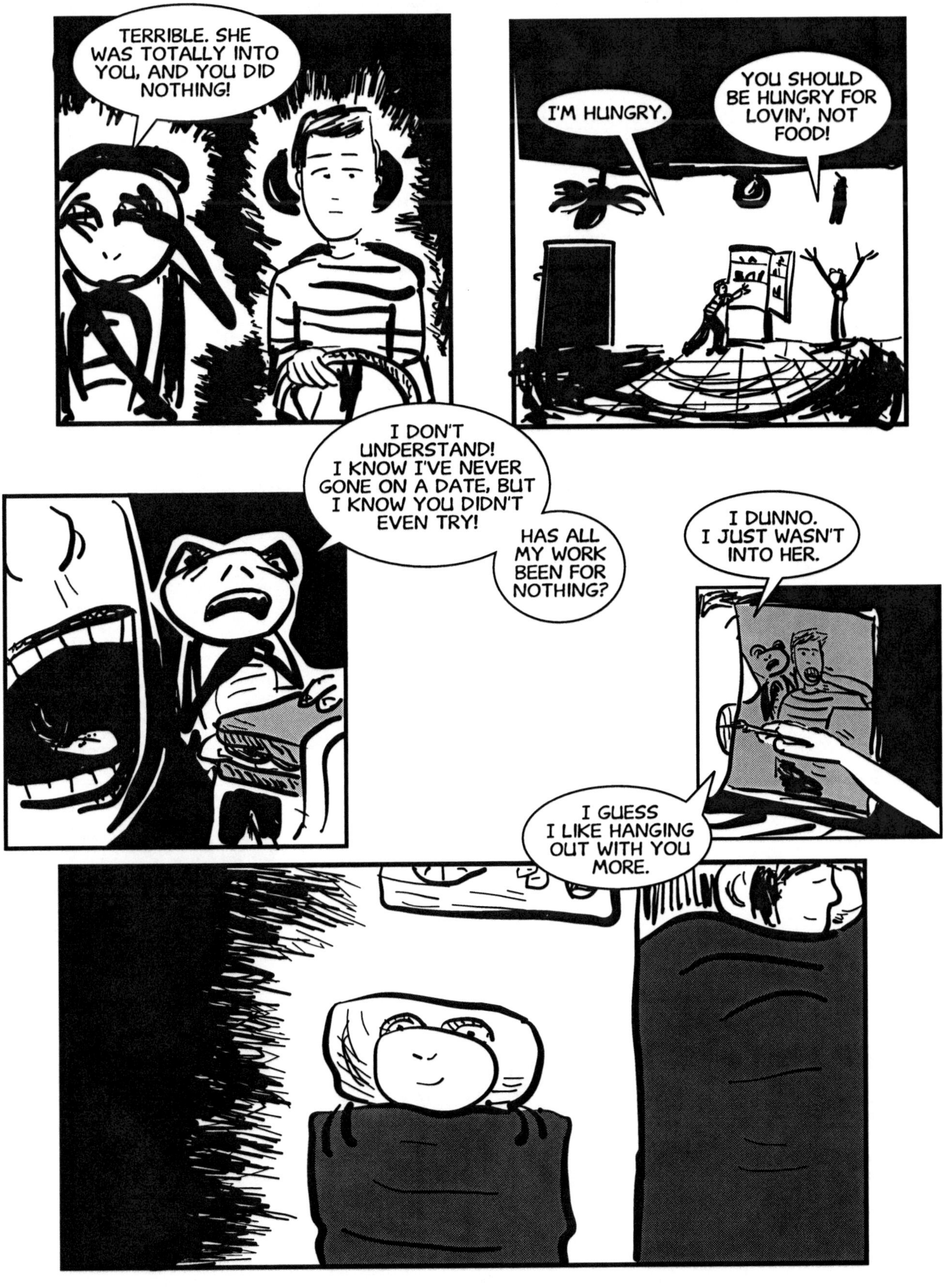
TERRIBLE. SHE WAS TOTALLY INTO YOU, AND YOU DID NOTHING!
I'M HUNGRY.
YOU SHOULD BE HUNGRY FOR LOVIN', NOT FOOD!
I DON'T UNDERSTAND! I KNOW I'VE NEVER GONE ON A DATE, BUT I KNOW YOU DIDN'T EVEN TRY!
HAS ALL MY WORK BEEN FOR NOTHING?
I DUNNO. I JUST WASN'T INTO HER.
I GUESS I LIKE HANGING OUT WITH YOU MORE.

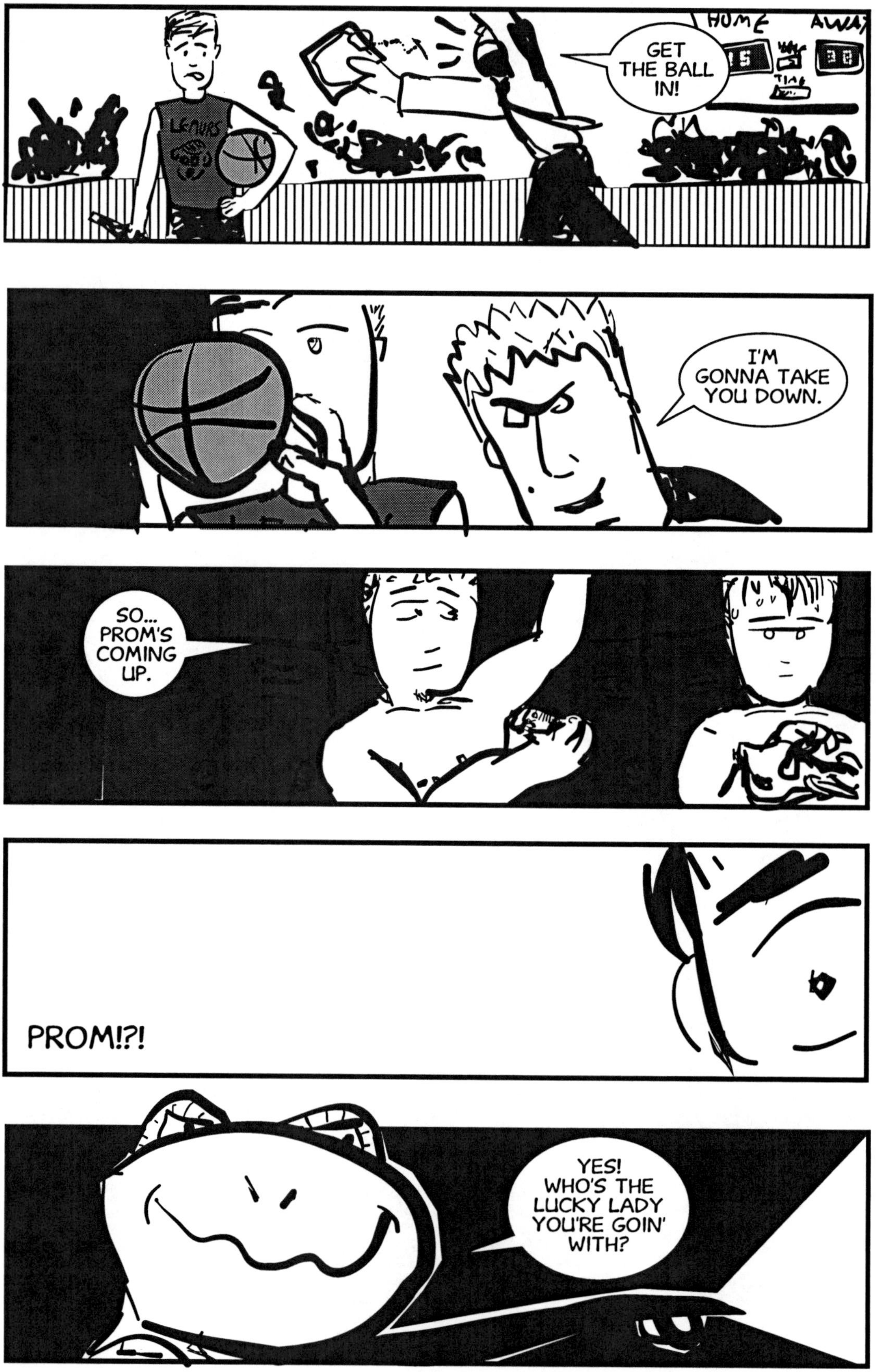
HOME
AWAY
GET THE BALL IN!
I'M GONNA TAKE YOU DOWN.
SO... PROM'S COMING UP.
PROM!?!
YES! WHO'S THE LUCKY LADY YOU'RE GOIN' WITH?

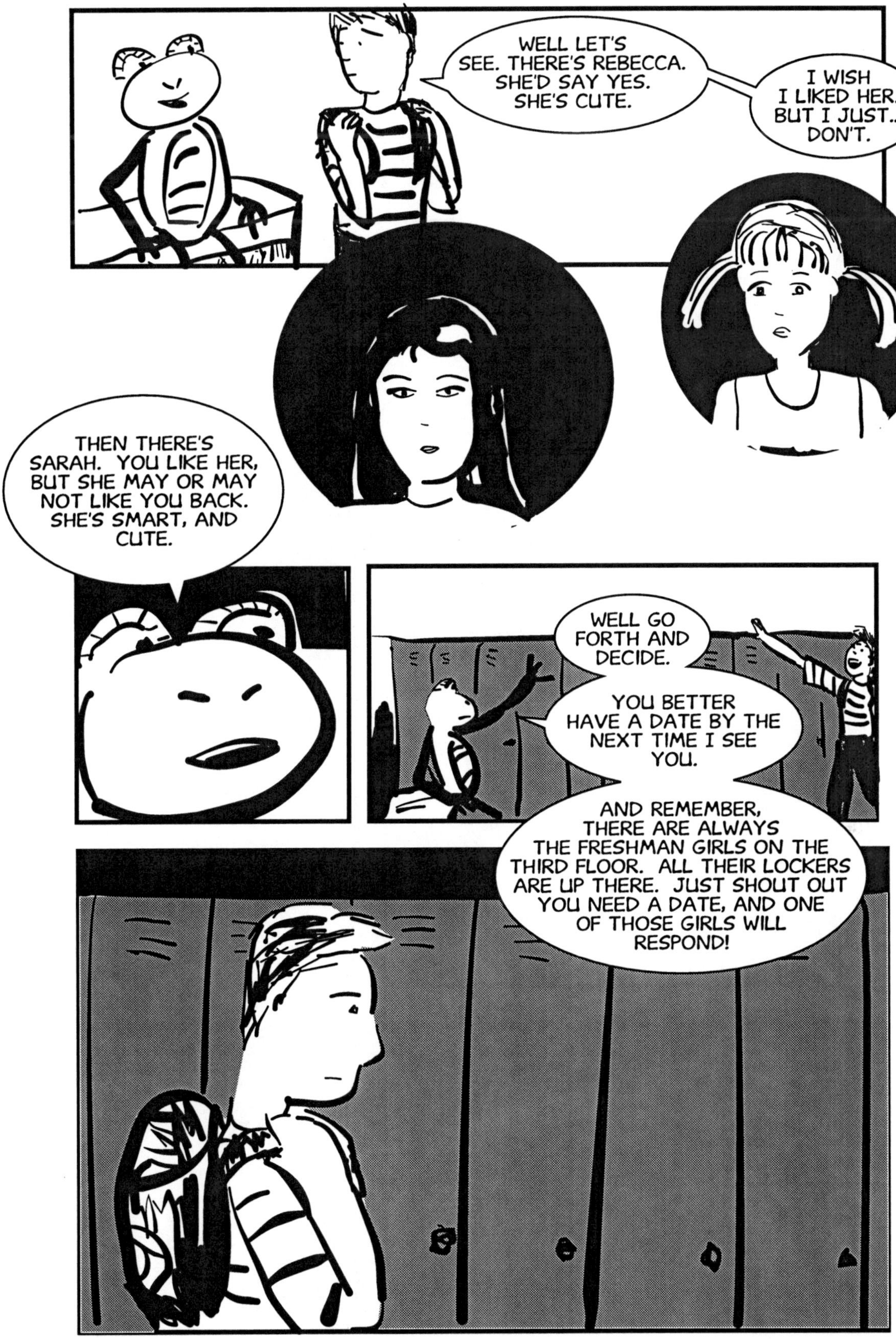
WELL LET'S SEE. THERE'S REBECCA. SHE'D SAY YES. SHE'S CUTE.
I WISH I LIKED HER. BUT I JUST... DON'T.
THEN THERE'S SARAH. YOU LIKE HER, BUT SHE MAY OR MAY NOT LIKE YOU BACK. SHE'S SMART, AND CUTE.
WELL GO FORTH AND DECIDE.
YOU BETTER HAVE A DATE BY THE NEXT TIME I SEE YOU.
AND REMEMBER, THERE ARE ALWAYS THE FRESHMAN GIRLS ON THE THIRD FLOOR. ALL THEIR LOCKERS ARE UP THERE. JUST SHOUT OUT YOU NEED A DATE, AND ONE OF THOSE GIRLS WILL RESPOND!

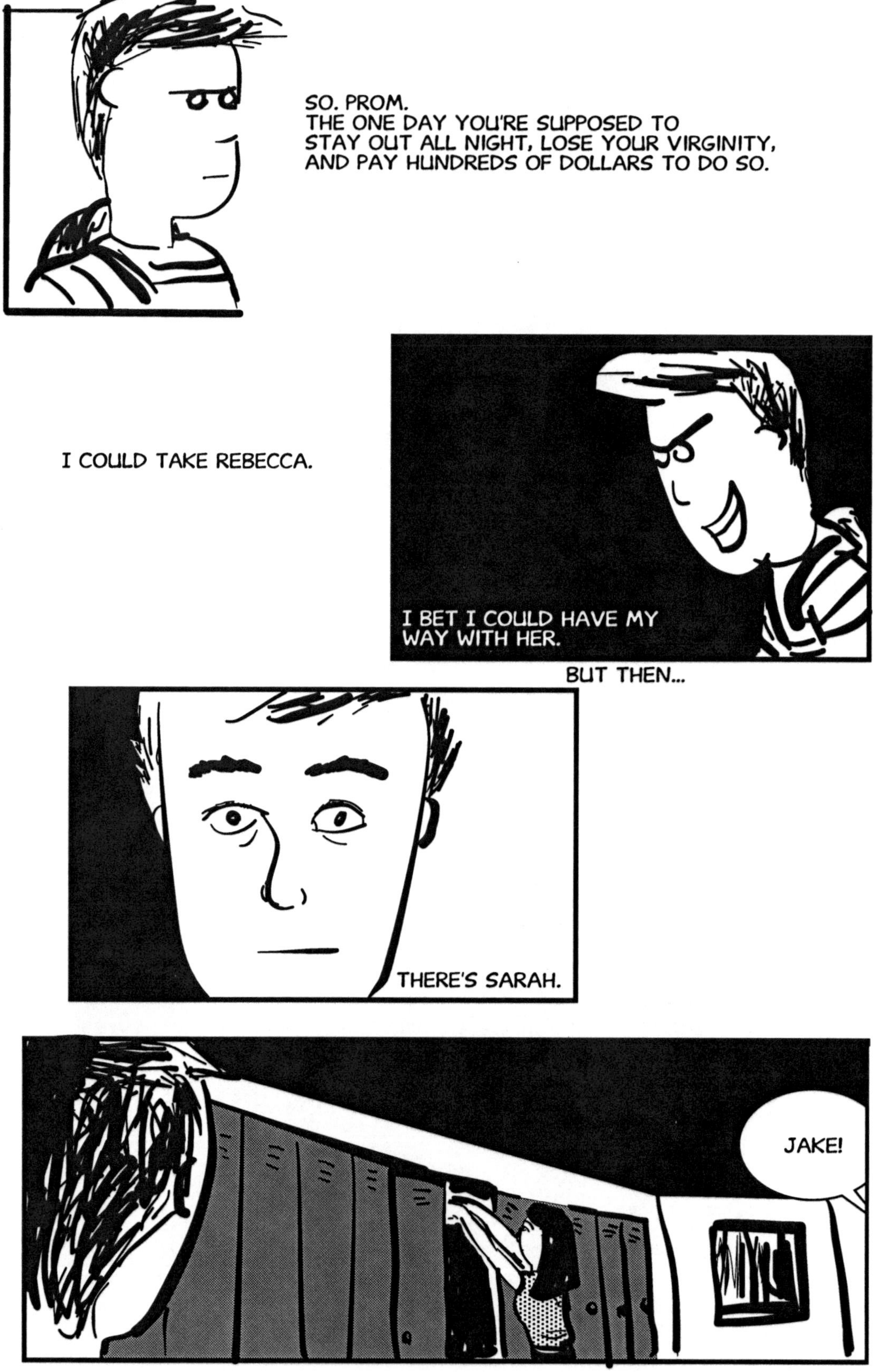
SO. PROM.
THE ONE DAY YOU'RE SUPPOSED TO STAY OUT ALL NIGHT, LOSE YOUR VIRGINITY, AND PAY HUNDREDS OF DOLLARS TO DO SO.
I COULD TAKE REBECCA.
I BET I COULD HAVE MY WAY WITH HER.
BUT THEN...
THERE'S SARAH.
JAKE!

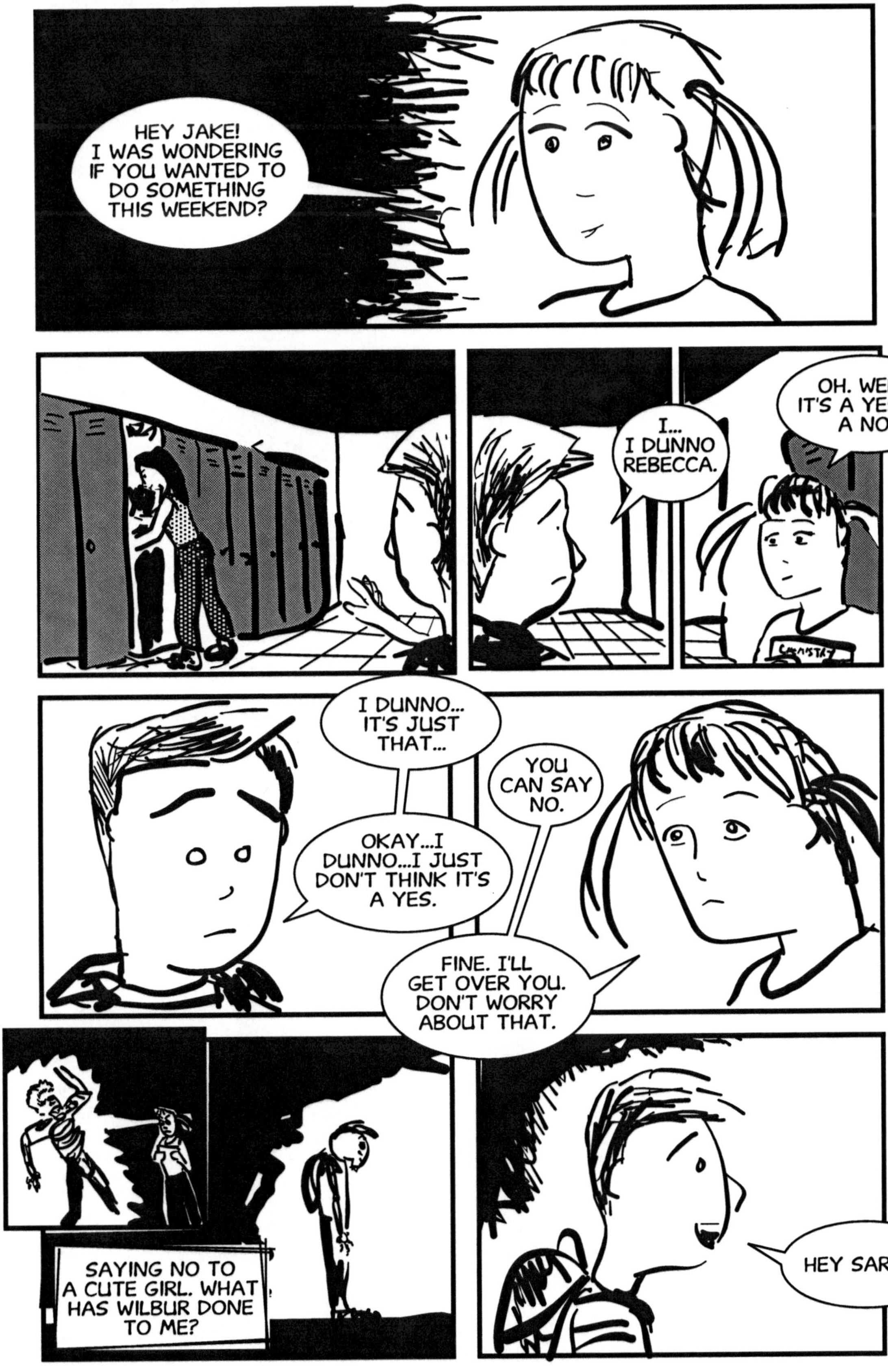
HEY JAKE! I WAS WONDERING IF YOU WANTED TO DO SOMETHING THIS WEEKEND?
I... I DUNNO REBECCA.
OH. WELL, IT'S A YES OR A NO.
I DUNNO... IT'S JUST THAT...
YOU CAN SAY NO.
OKAY...I DUNNO...I JUST DON'T THINK IT'S A YES.
FINE. I'LL GET OVER YOU. DON'T WORRY ABOUT THAT.
SAYING NO TO A CUTE GIRL. WHAT HAS WILBUR DONE TO ME?
HEY SARAH!

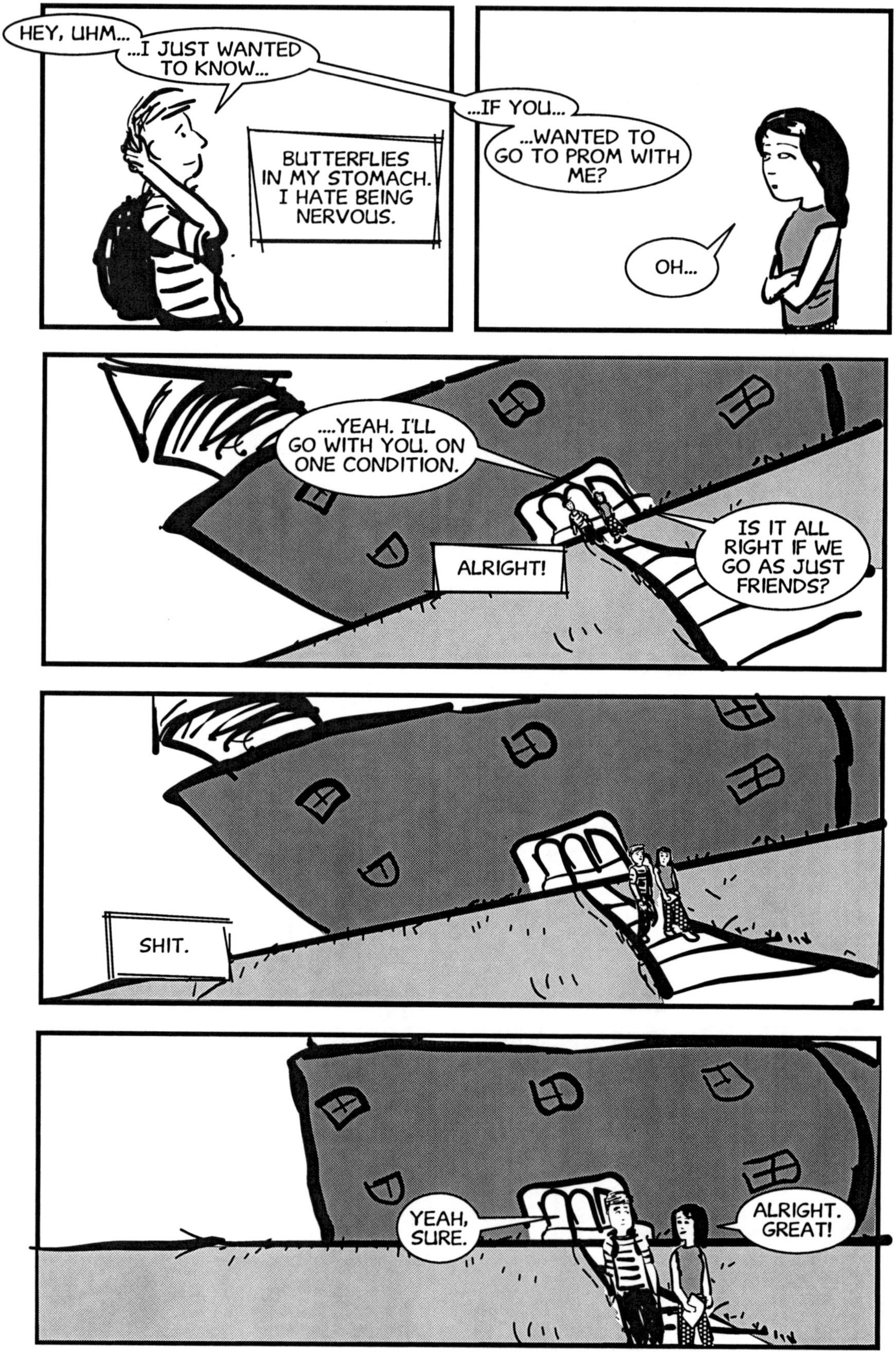
HEY, UHM...
...I JUST WANTED TO KNOW...
BUTTERFLIES IN MY STOMACH. I HATE BEING NERVOUS.
...IF YOU...
...WANTED TO GO TO PROM WITH ME?
OH...
....YEAH. I'LL GO WITH YOU. ON ONE CONDITION.
ALRIGHT!
IS IT ALL RIGHT IF WE GO AS JUST FRIENDS?
SHIT.
YEAH, SURE.
ALRIGHT. GREAT!

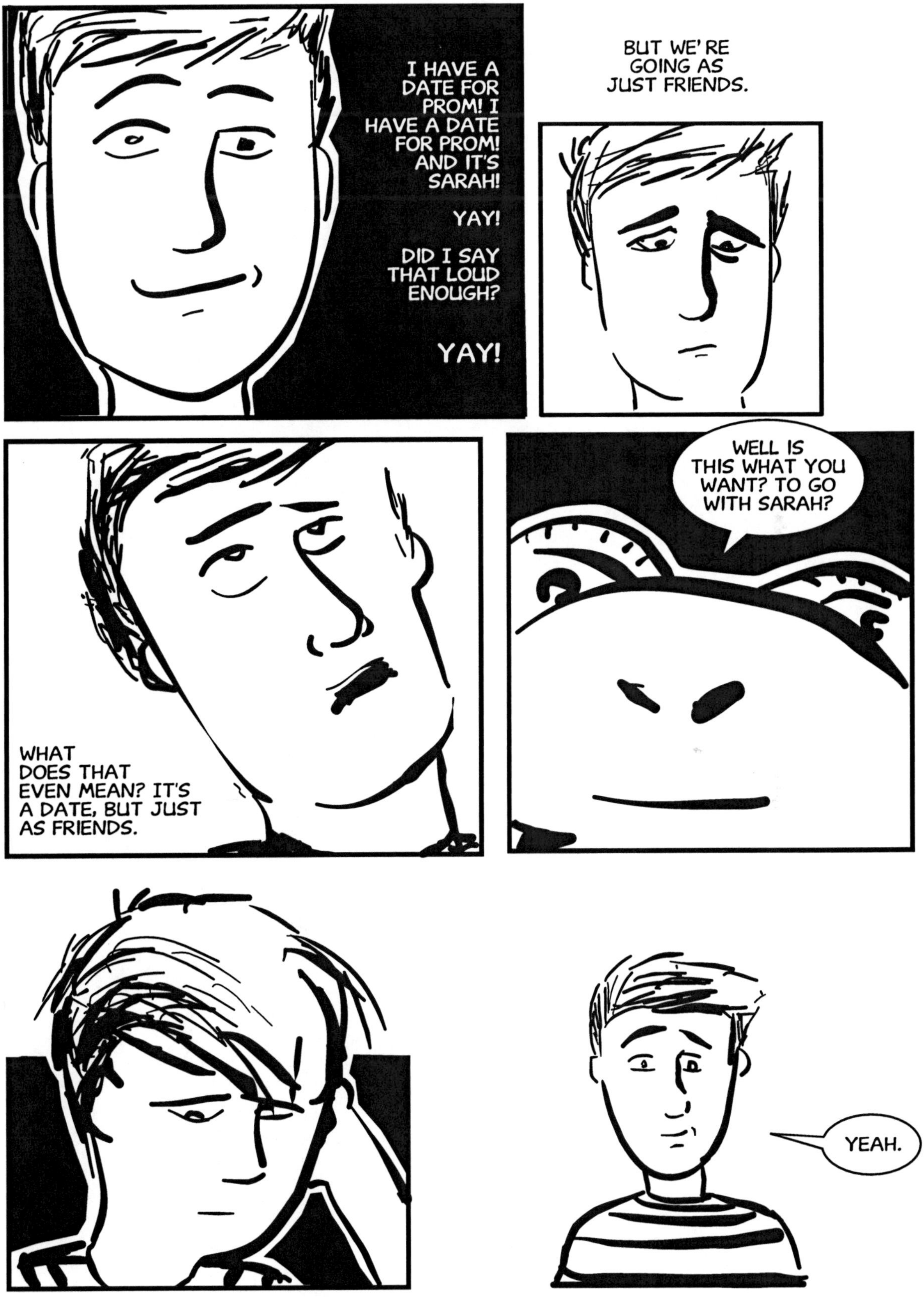
I HAVE A DATE FOR PROM! I HAVE A DATE FOR PROM! AND IT'S SARAH!
YAY!
DID I SAY THAT LOUD ENOUGH?
YAY!
BUT WE'RE GOING AS JUST FRIENDS.
WHAT DOES THAT EVEN MEAN? IT'S A DATE, BUT JUST AS FRIENDS.
WELL IS THIS WHAT YOU WANT? TO GO WITH SARAH?
YEAH.

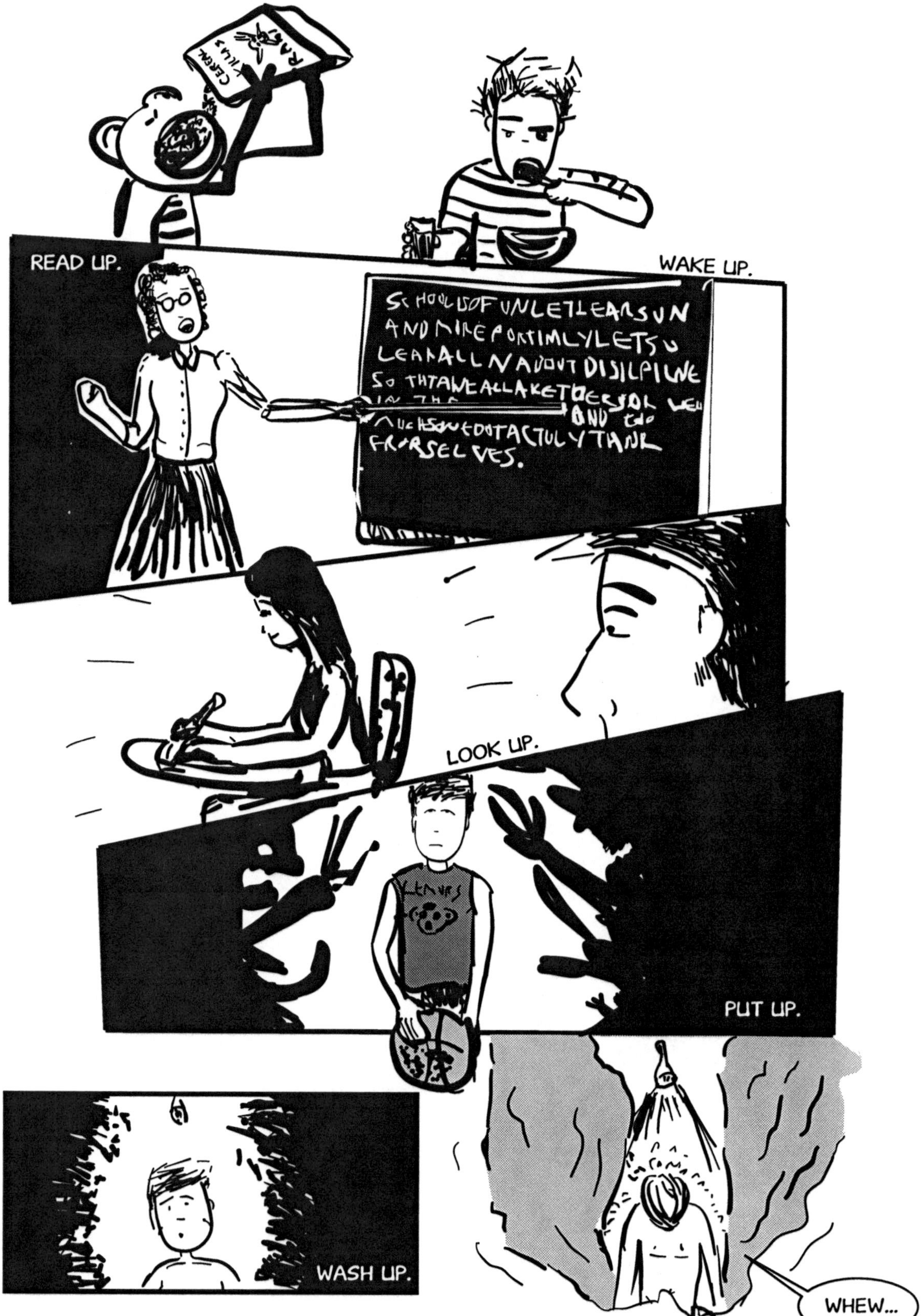
WAKE UP.
READ UP.
LOOK UP.
PUT UP.
WASH UP.
WHEW...

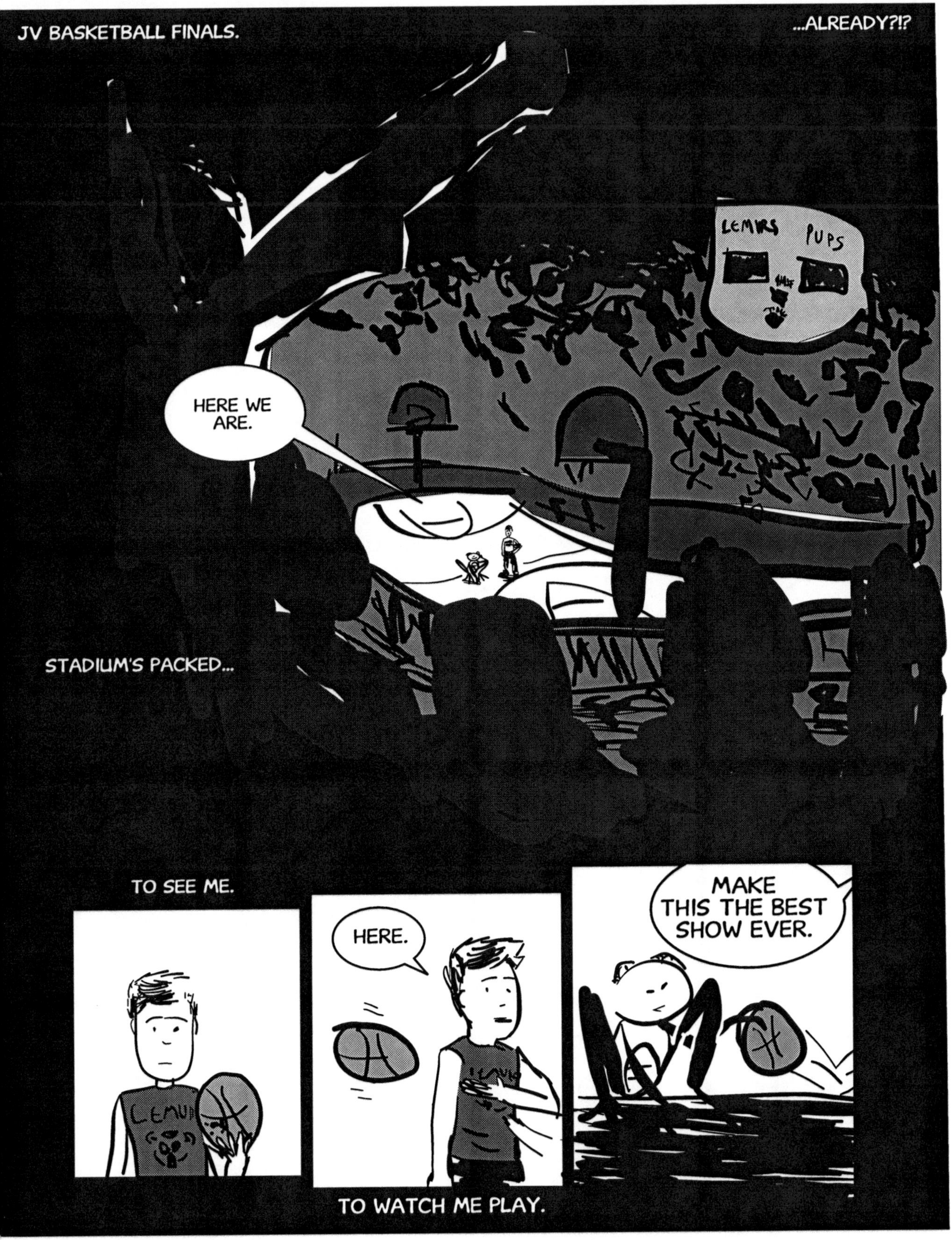
JV BASKETBALL FINALS.
...ALREADY?!?
LEMURS
PUPS
HERE WE ARE.
STADIUM'S PACKED...
TO SEE ME.
HERE.
MAKE THIS THE BEST SHOW EVER.
TO WATCH ME PLAY.

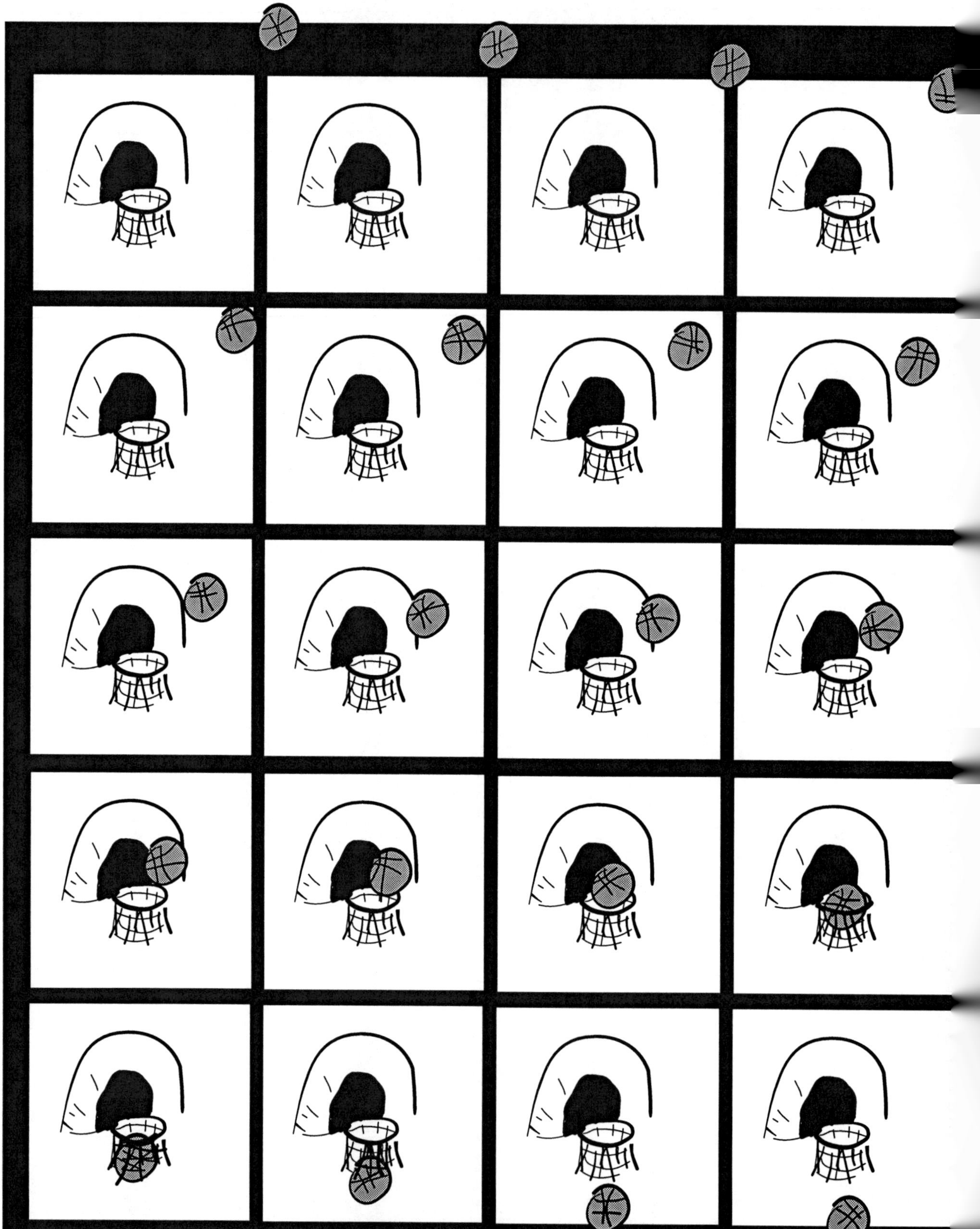

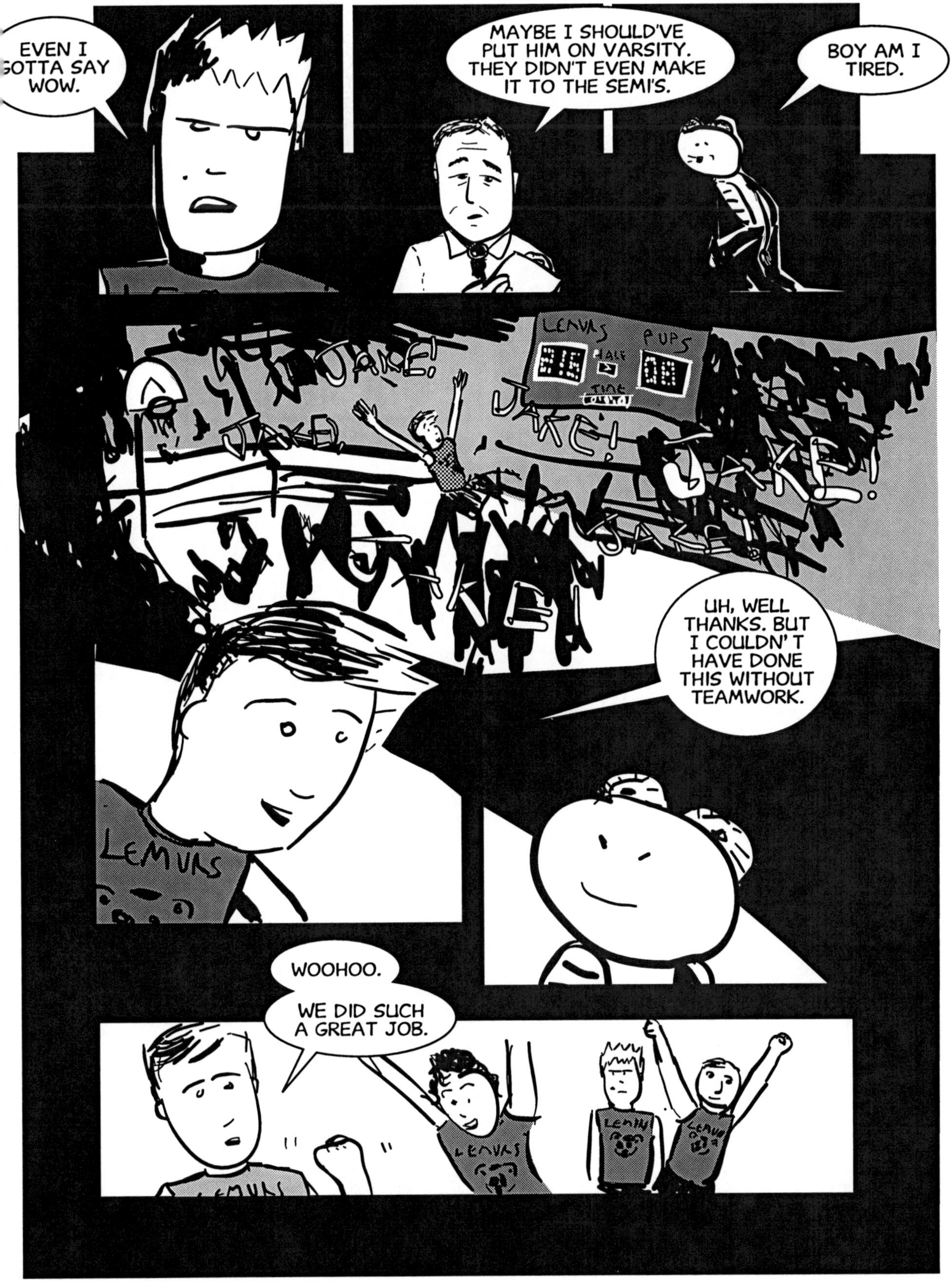
EVEN I GOTTA SAY WOW.
MAYBE I SHOULD'VE PUT HIM ON VARSITY. THEY DIDN'T EVEN MAKE IT TO THE SEMI'S.
BOY AM I TIRED.
UH, WELL THANKS. BUT I COULDN'T HAVE DONE THIS WITHOUT TEAMWORK.
WOOHOO.
WE DID SUCH A GREAT JOB.

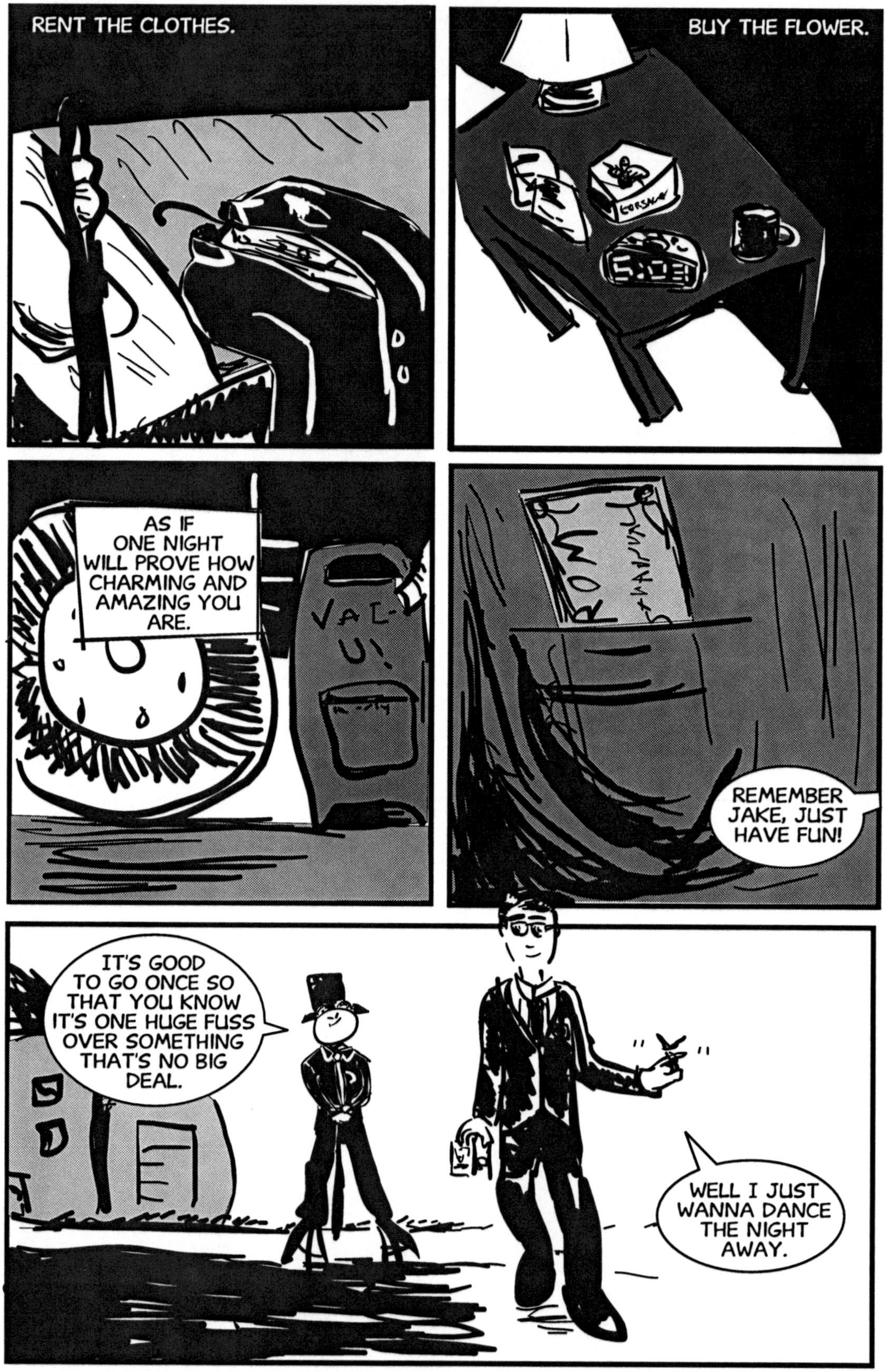
RENT THE CLOTHES.
BUY THE FLOWER.
AS IF ONE NIGHT WILL PROVE HOW CHARMING AND AMAZING YOU ARE.
REMEMBER JAKE, JUST HAVE FUN!
IT'S GOOD TO GO ONCE SO THAT YOU KNOW IT'S ONE HUGE FUSS OVER SOMETHING THAT'S NO BIG DEAL.
WELL I JUST WANNA DANCE THE NIGHT AWAY.

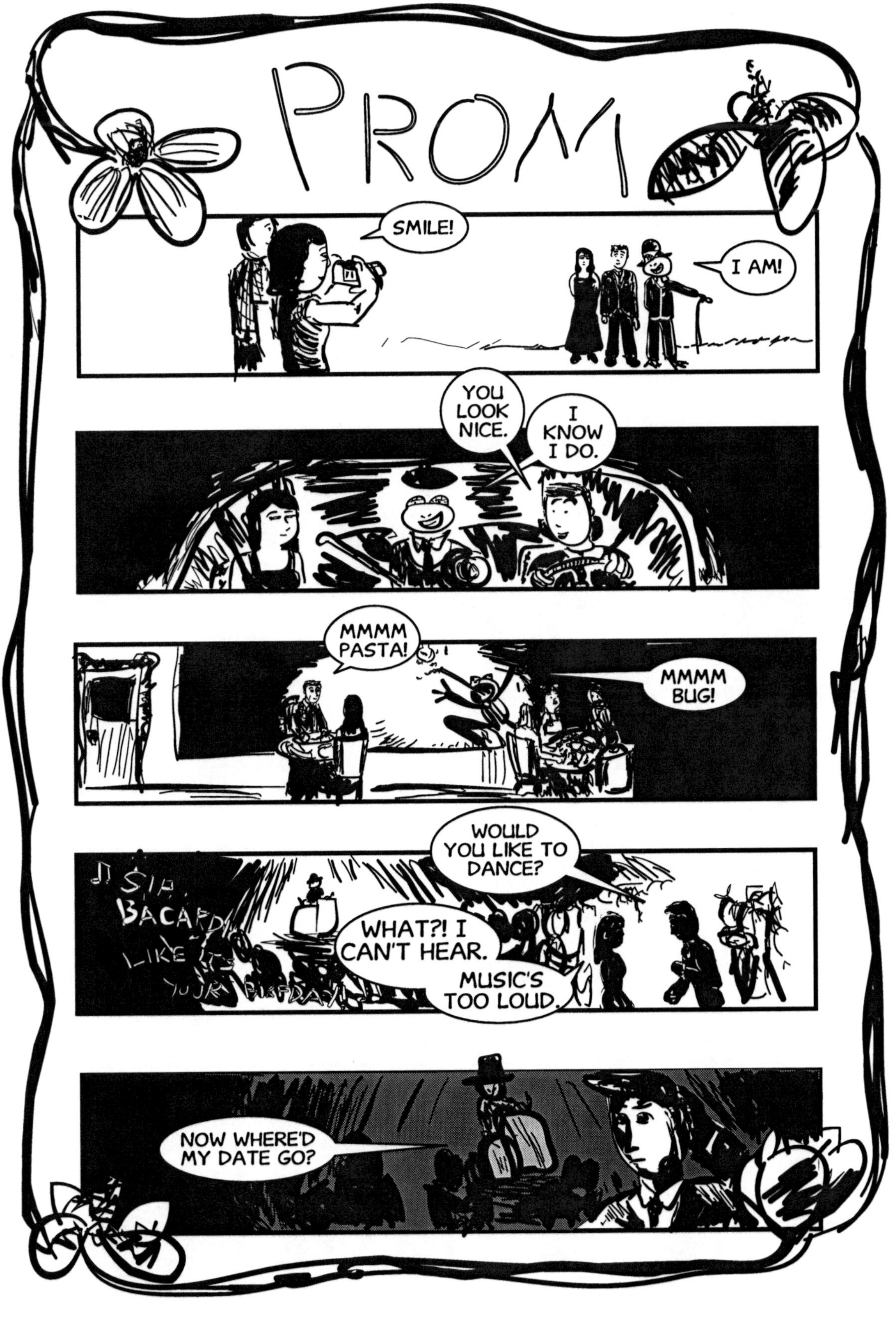
PROM
SMILE!
I AM!
YOU LOOK NICE.
I KNOW I DO.
MMMM PASTA!
MMMM BUG!
WOULD YOU LIKE TO DANCE?
SIP, BACARDI LIKE IT'S YOUR BIRFDAY!
WHAT?! I CAN'T HEAR.
MUSIC'S TOO LOUD.
NOW WHERE'D MY DATE GO?

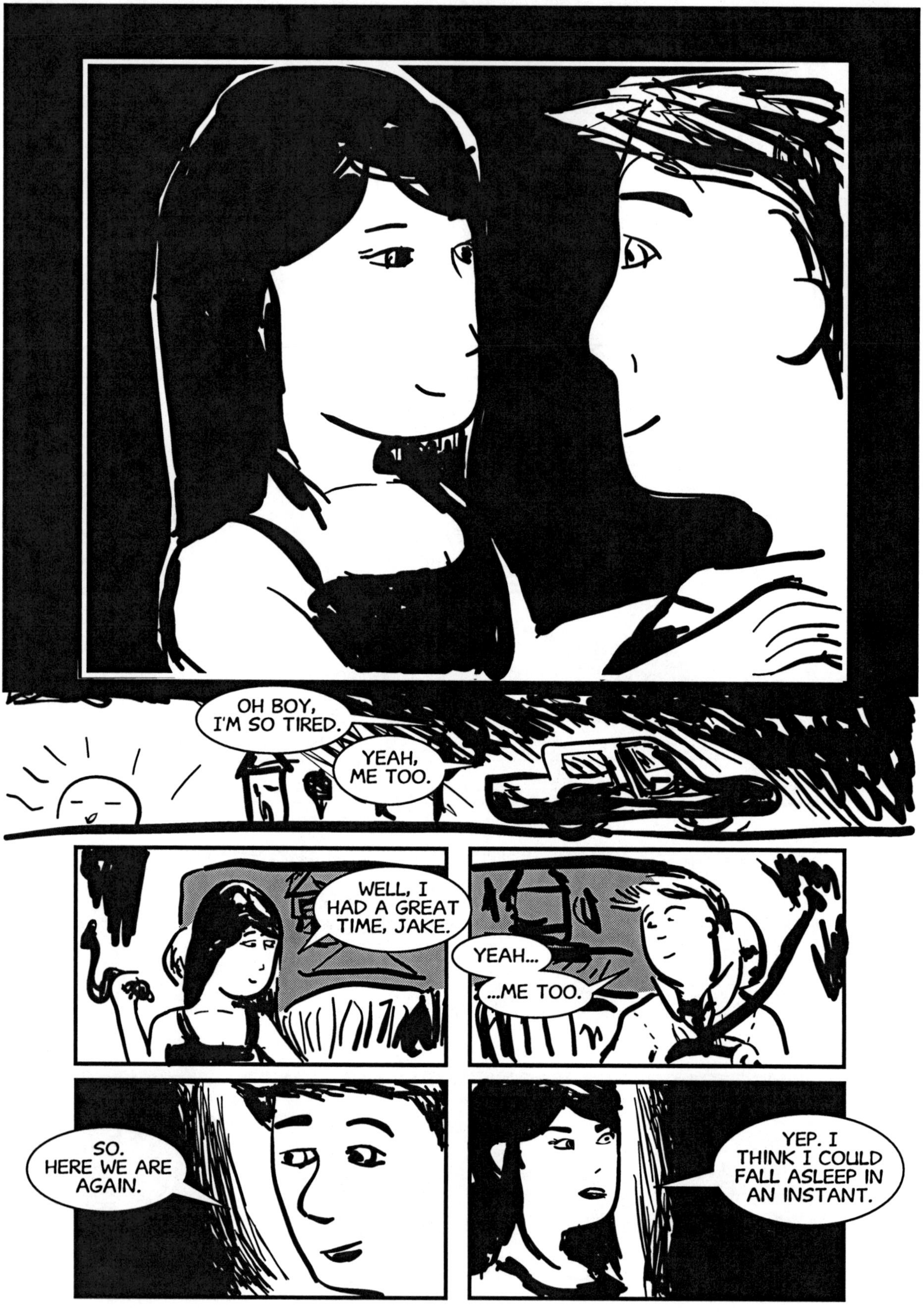
OH BOY, I'M SO TIRED.
YEAH, ME TOO.
WELL, I HAD A GREAT TIME, JAKE.
YEAH...
...ME TOO.
SO. HERE WE ARE AGAIN.
YEP. I THINK I COULD FALL ASLEEP IN AN INSTANT.

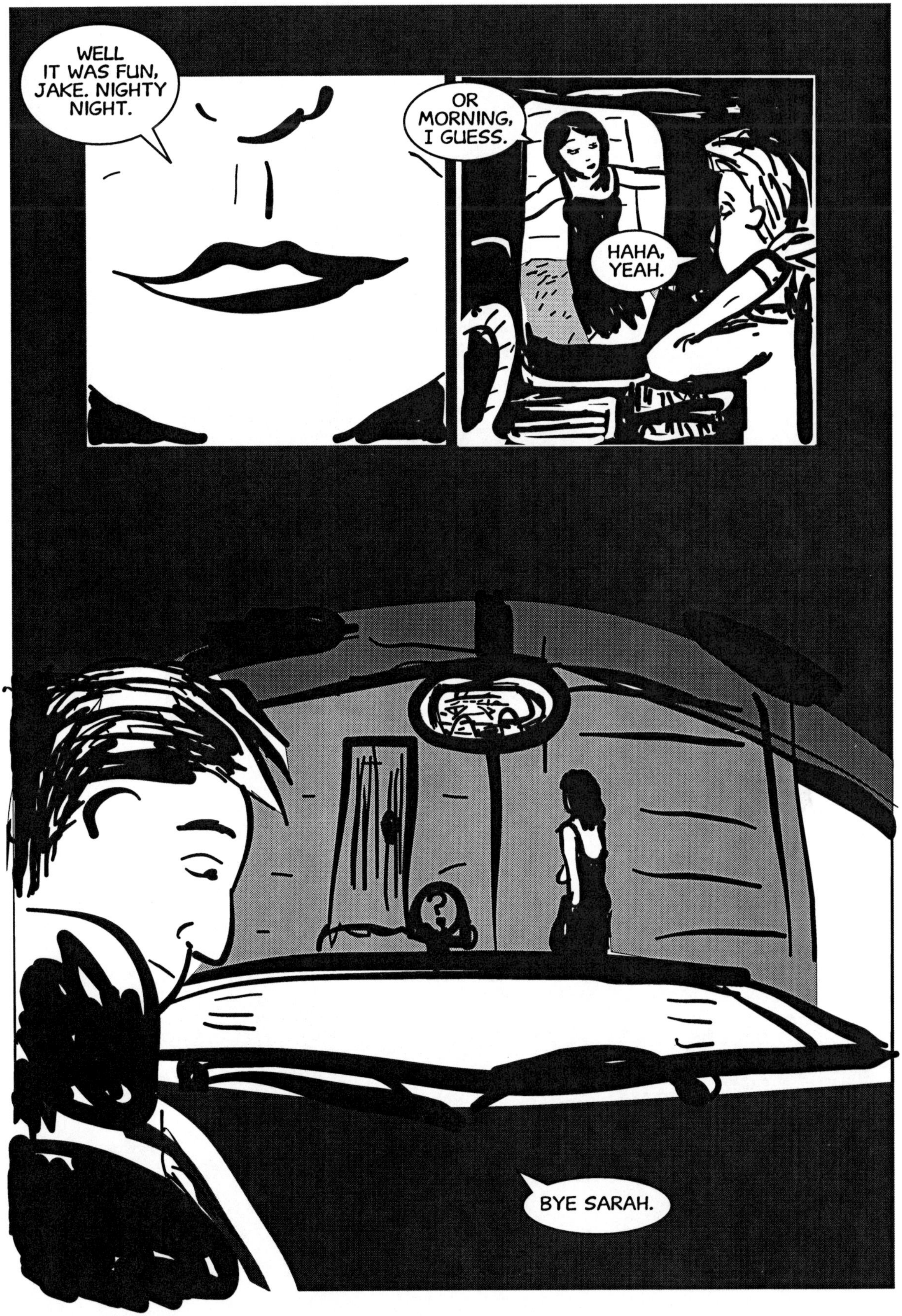
WELL IT WAS FUN, JAKE. NIGHTY NIGHT.
OR MORNING, I GUESS.
HAHA, YEAH.
BYE SARAH.

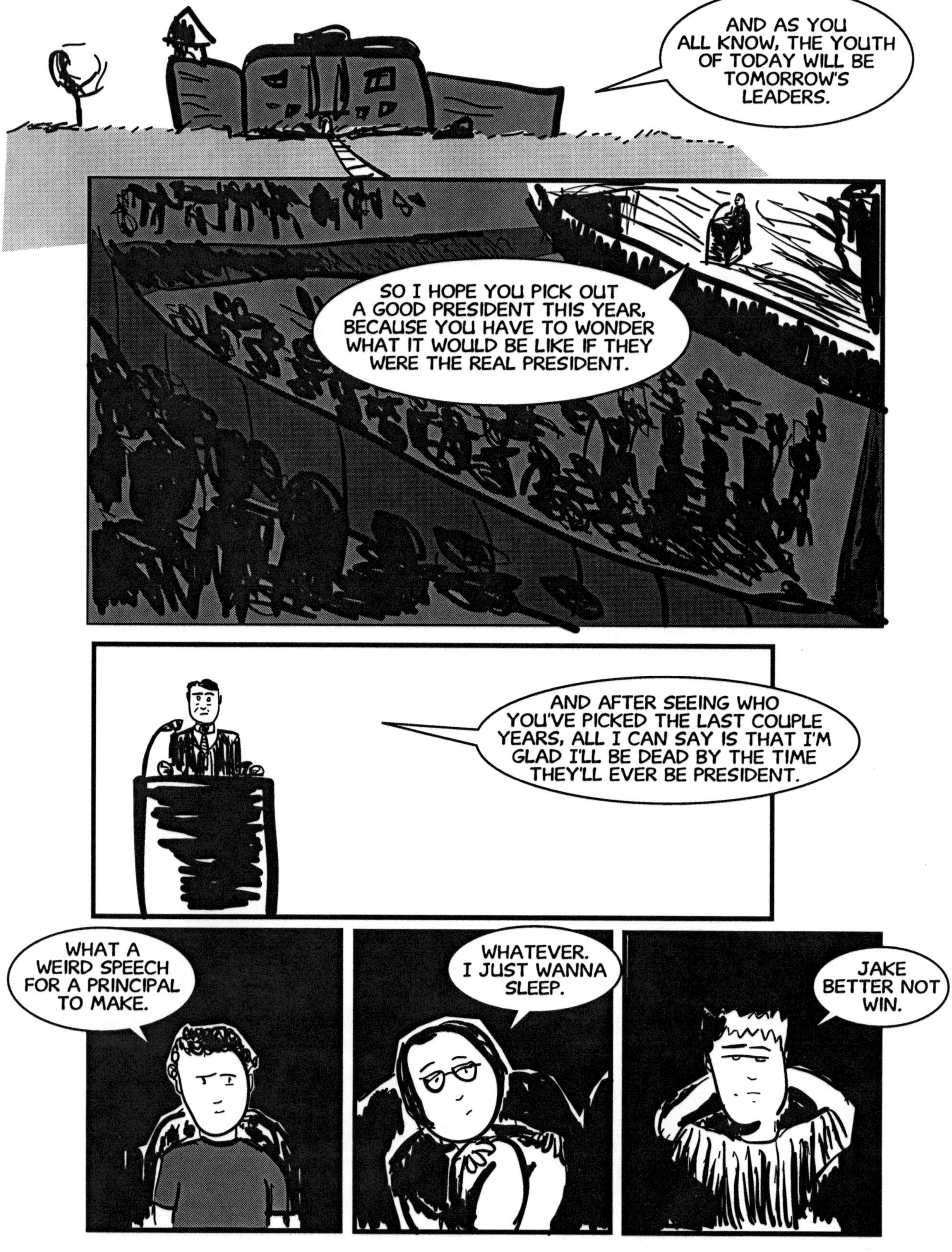
AND AS YOU ALL KNOW, THE YOUTH OF TODAY WILL BE TOMORROW'S LEADERS.
SO I HOPE YOU PICK OUT A GOOD PRESIDENT THIS YEAR, BECAUSE YOU HAVE TO WONDER WHAT IT WOULD BE LIKE IF THEY WERE THE REAL PRESIDENT.
AND AFTER SEEING WHO YOU'VE PICKED THE LAST COUPLE YEARS, ALL I CAN SAY IS THAT I'M GLAD I'LL BE DEAD BY THE TIME THEY'LL EVER BE PRESIDENT.
WHAT A WEIRD SPEECH FOR A PRINCIPAL TO MAKE.
WHATEVER. I JUST WANNA SLEEP.
JAKE BETTER NOT WIN.

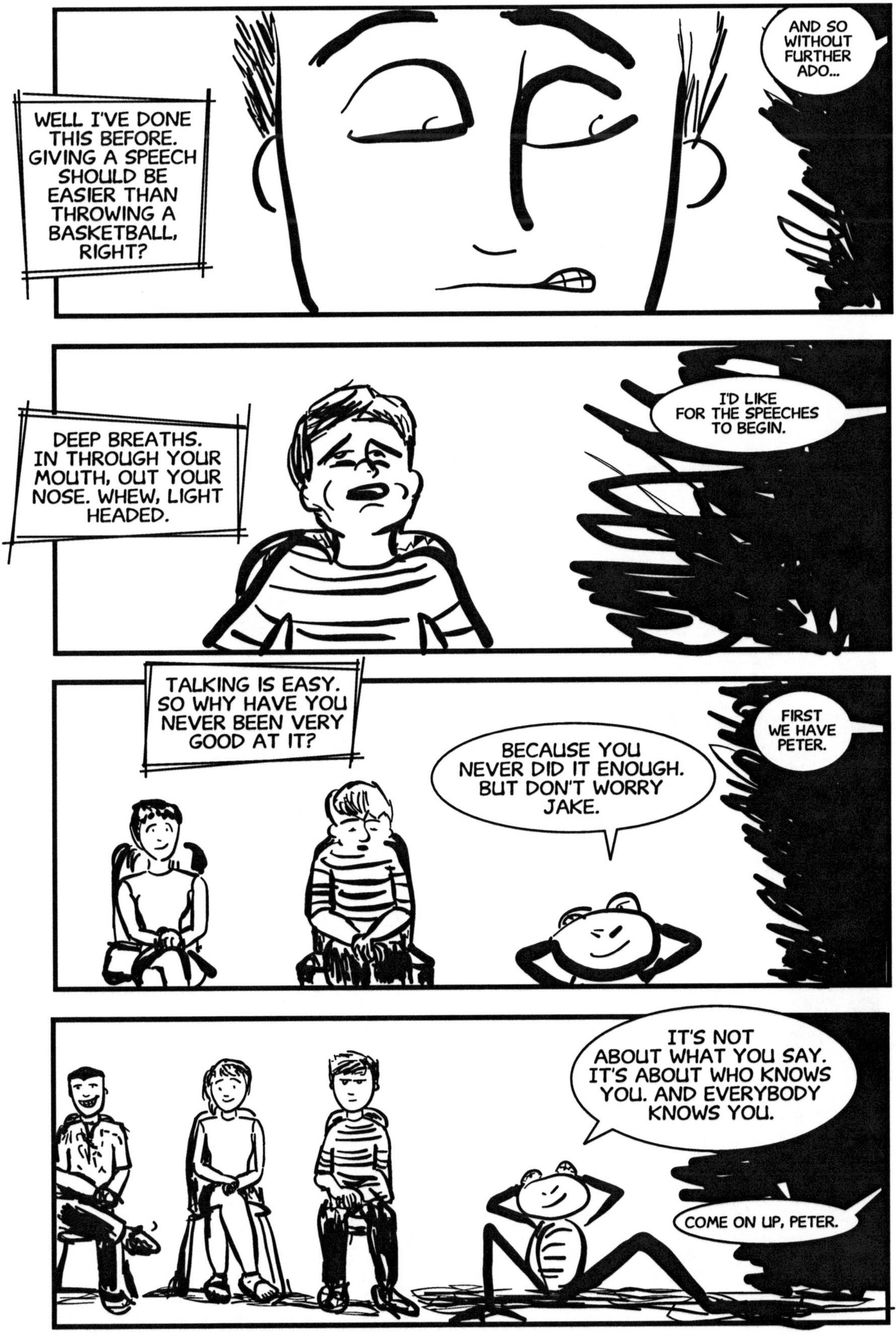

WELL I'VE DONE THIS BEFORE. GIVING A SPEECH SHOULD BE EASIER THAN THROWING A BASKETBALL, RIGHT?
AND SO WITHOUT FURTHER ADO...
DEEP BREATHS. IN THROUGH YOUR MOUTH, OUT YOUR NOSE. WHEW, LIGHT HEADED.
I'D LIKE FOR THE SPEECHES TO BEGIN.
TALKING IS EASY. SO WHY HAVE YOU NEVER BEEN VERY GOOD AT IT?
BECAUSE YOU NEVER DID IT ENOUGH. BUT DON'T WORRY JAKE.
FIRST WE HAVE PETER.
IT'S NOT ABOUT WHAT YOU SAY. IT'S ABOUT WHO KNOWS YOU. AND EVERYBODY KNOWS YOU.
COME ON UP, PETER.

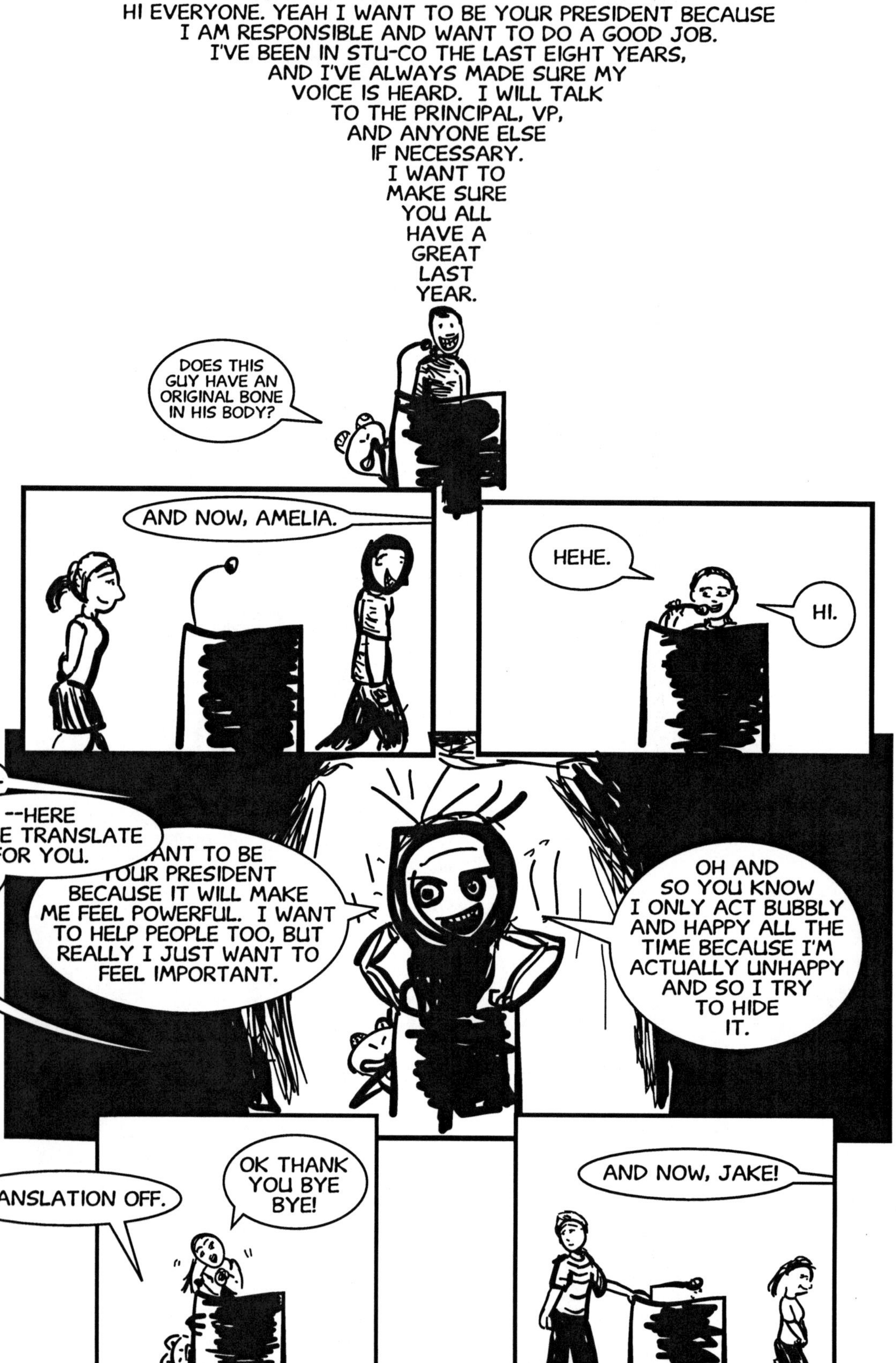
HI EVERYONE. YEAH I WANT TO BE YOUR PRESIDENT BECAUSE I AM RESPONSIBLE AND WANT TO DO A GOOD JOB. I'VE BEEN IN STU-CO THE LAST EIGHT YEARS, AND I'VE ALWAYS MADE SURE MY VOICE IS HEARD. I WILL TALK TO THE PRINCIPAL, VP, AND ANYONE ELSE IF NECESSARY. I WANT TO MAKE SURE YOU ALL HAVE A GREAT LAST YEAR.
DOES THIS GUY HAVE AN ORIGINAL BONE IN HIS BODY?
AND NOW, AMELIA.
HEHE.
HI.
I--
--HERE LET ME TRANSLATE FOR YOU.
ANT TO BE YOUR PRESIDENT BECAUSE IT WILL MAKE ME FEEL POWERFUL. I WANT TO HELP PEOPLE TOO, BUT REALLY I JUST WANT TO FEEL IMPORTANT.
OH AND SO YOU KNOW I ONLY ACT BUBBLY AND HAPPY ALL THE TIME BECAUSE I'M ACTUALLY UNHAPPY AND SO I TRY TO HIDE IT.
OK THANK YOU BYE BYE!
TRANSLATION OFF.
AND NOW, JAKE!

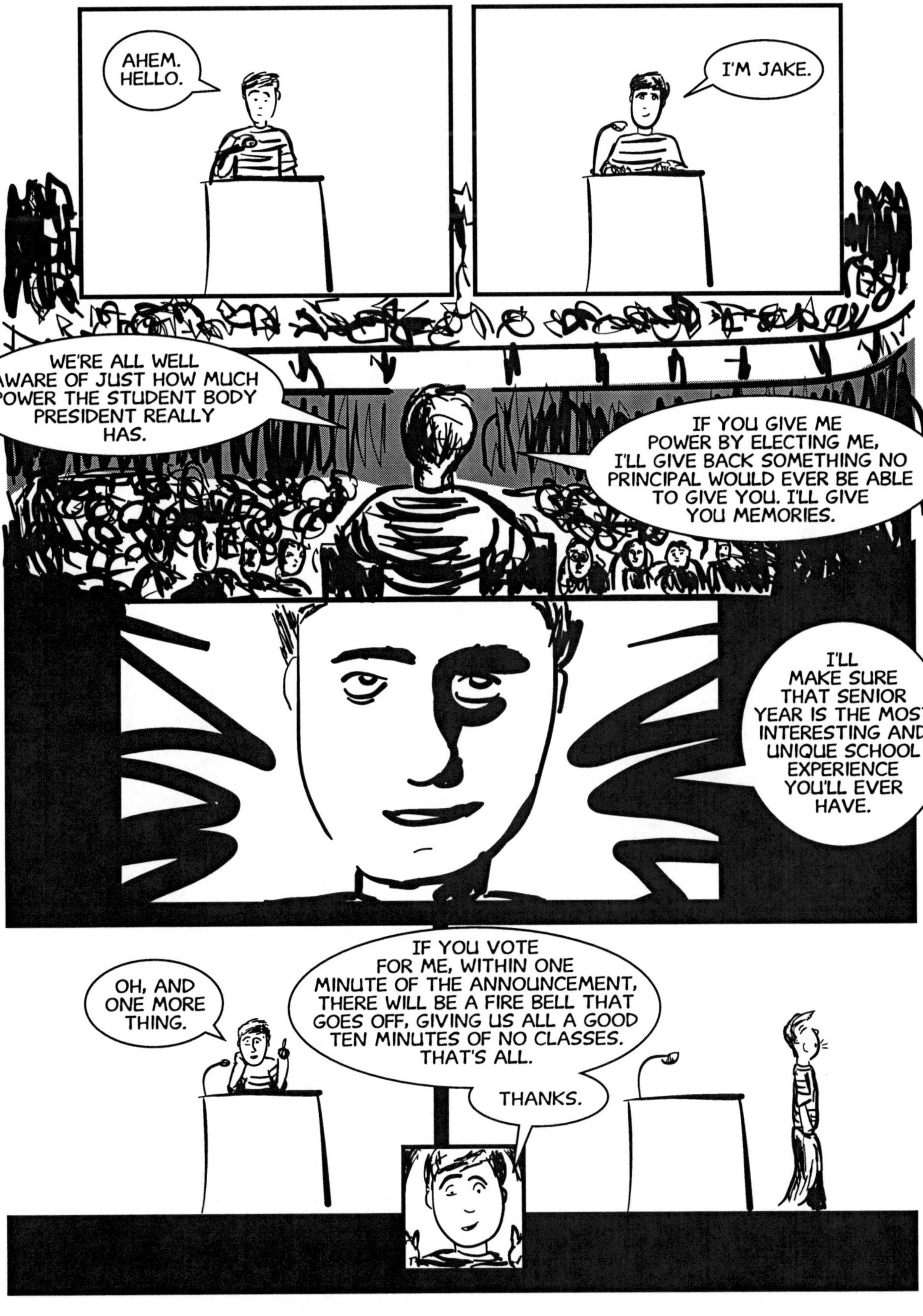
AHEM. HELLO.
I'M JAKE.
WE'RE ALL WELL AWARE OF JUST HOW MUCH POWER THE STUDENT BODY PRESIDENT REALLY HAS.
IF YOU GIVE ME POWER BY ELECTING ME, I'LL GIVE BACK SOMETHING NO PRINCIPAL WOULD EVER BE ABLE TO GIVE YOU. I'LL GIVE YOU MEMORIES.
I'LL MAKE SURE THAT SENIOR YEAR IS THE MOST INTERESTING AND UNIQUE SCHOOL EXPERIENCE YOU'LL EVER HAVE.
OH, AND ONE MORE THING.
IF YOU VOTE FOR ME, WITHIN ONE MINUTE OF THE ANNOUNCEMENT, THERE WILL BE A FIRE BELL THAT GOES OFF, GIVING US ALL A GOOD TEN MINUTES OF NO CLASSES. THAT'S ALL.
THANKS.

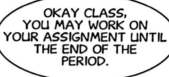

OKAY CLASS, YOU MAY WORK ON YOUR ASSIGNMENT UNTIL THE END OF THE PERIOD.

ON, HOW inTRISTING..

YES, YES. FASCINATING.

WHY COULDN'T THE TEACHER HAVE GIVEN US SOMETHING OTHER THAN TIME.

AHEM. THE RESULTS ARE IN.

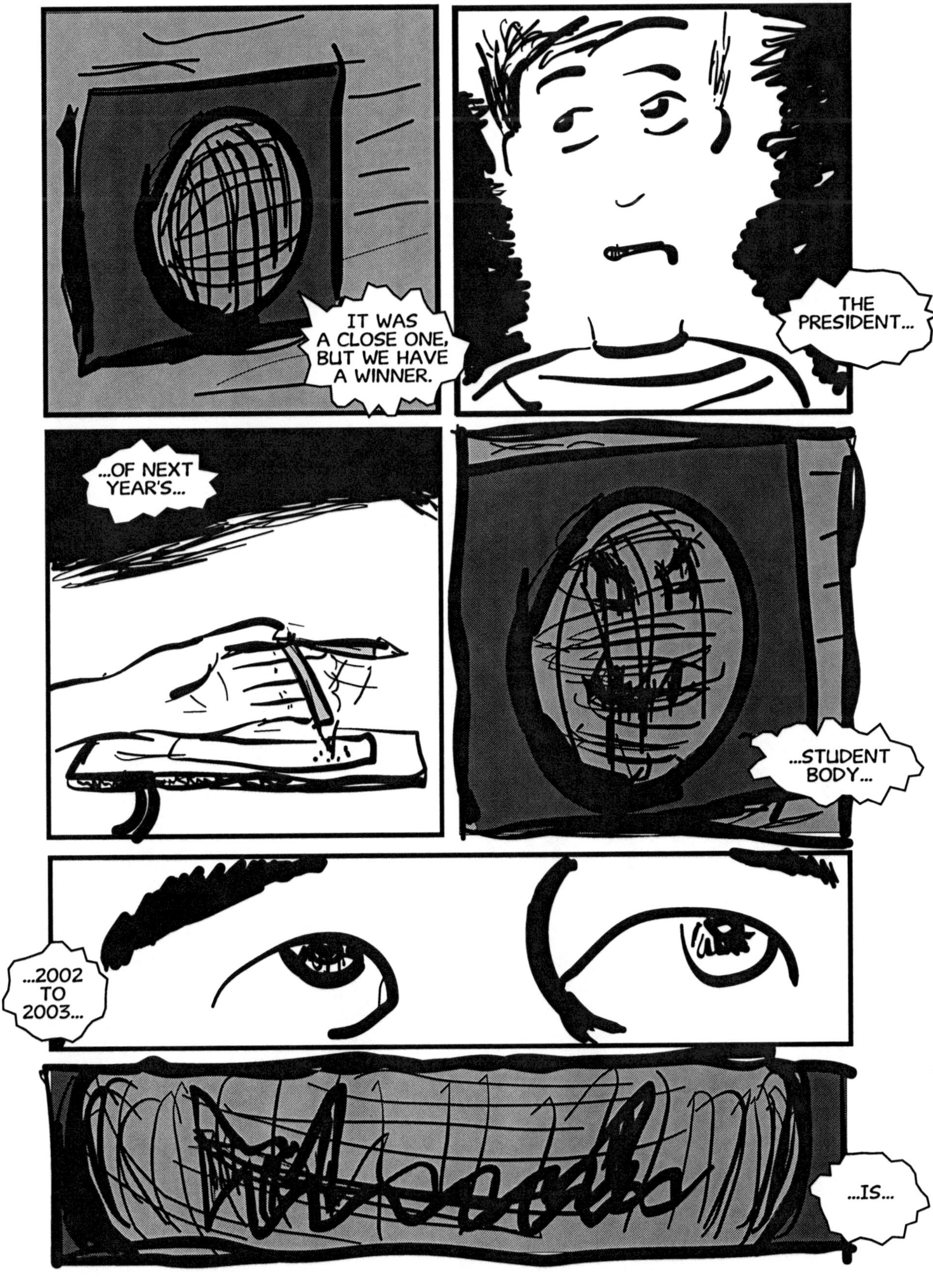

IT WAS A CLOSE ONE, BUT WE HAVE A WINNER.
THE PRESIDENT...
...OF NEXT YEAR'S...
...STUDENT BODY...
...2002 TO 2003...
...IS...

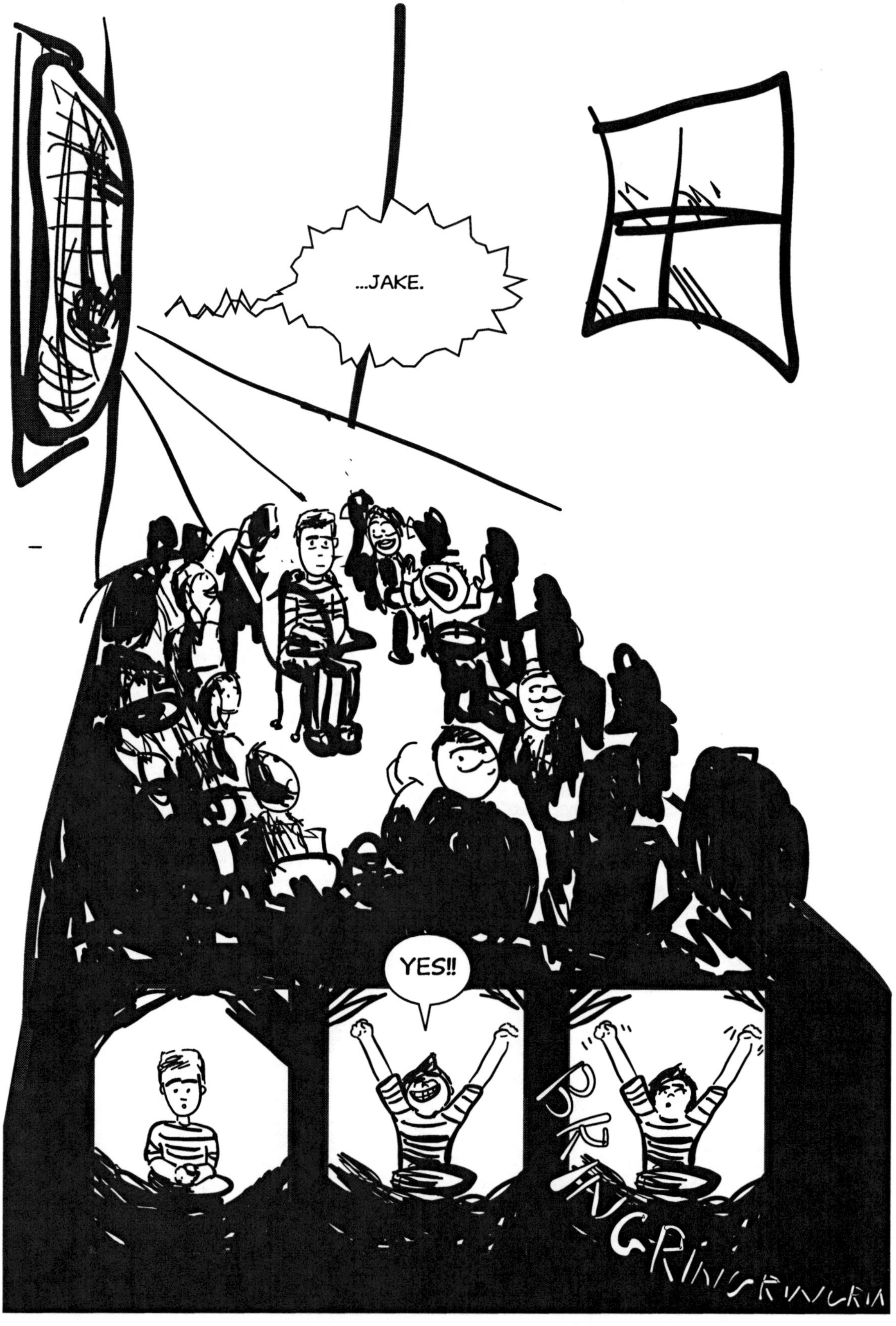
...JAKE.
YES!!

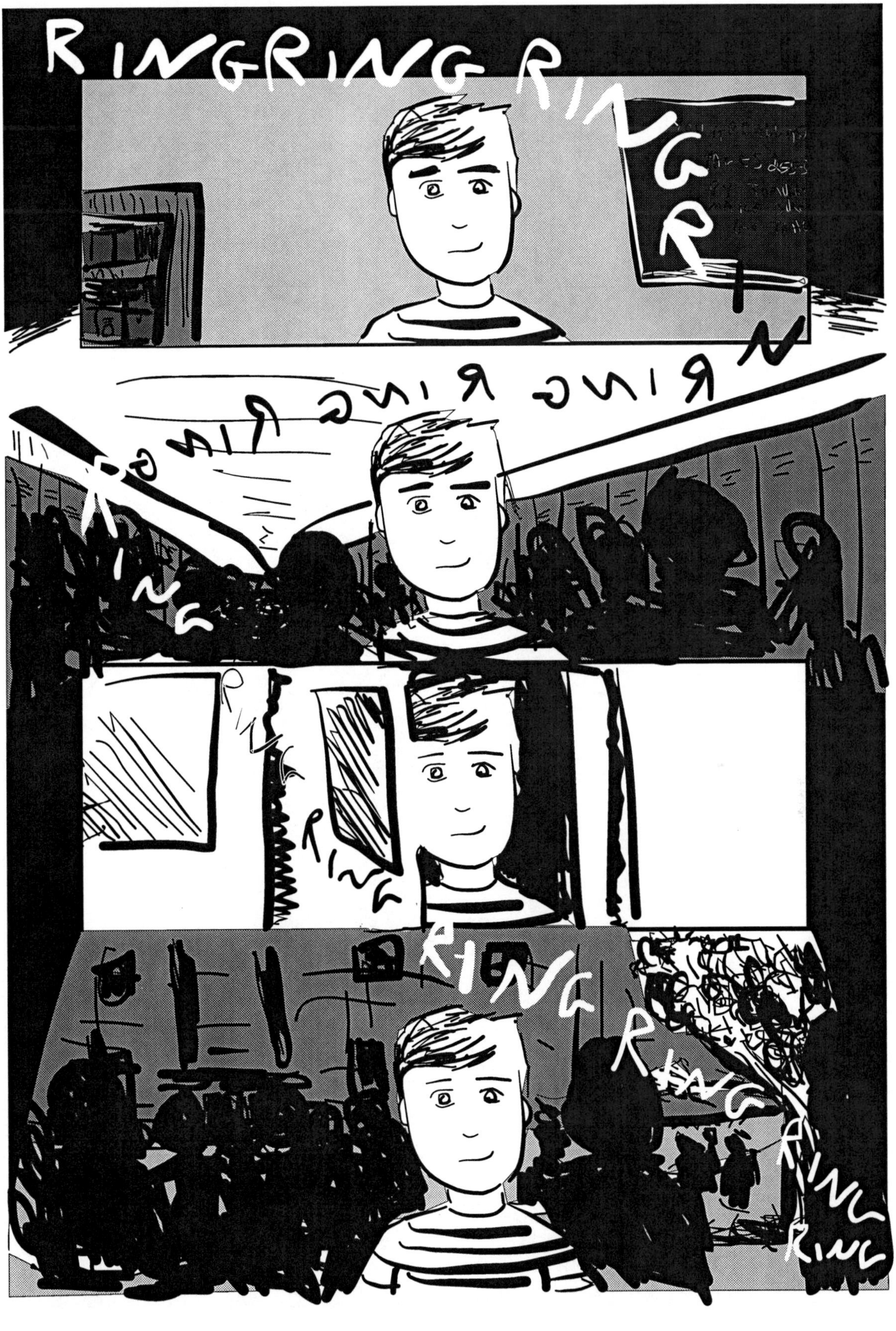
RINGRINGRINGRIN
RING RING RING RING
RING
RING RING RING RING

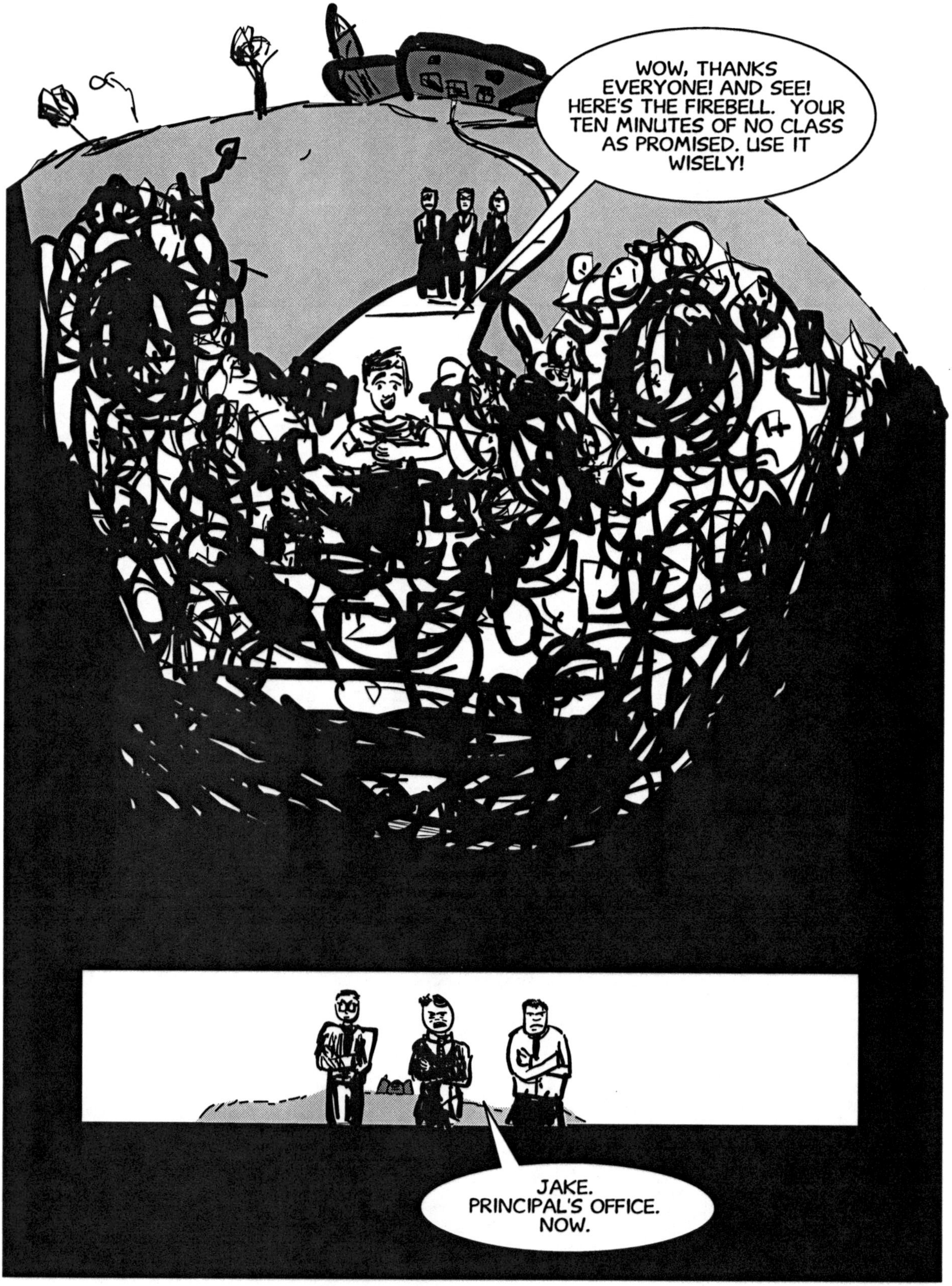
WOW, THANKS EVERYONE! AND SEE! HERE'S THE FIREBELL. YOUR TEN MINUTES OF NO CLASS AS PROMISED. USE IT WISELY!
JAKE. PRINCIPAL'S OFFICE. NOW.

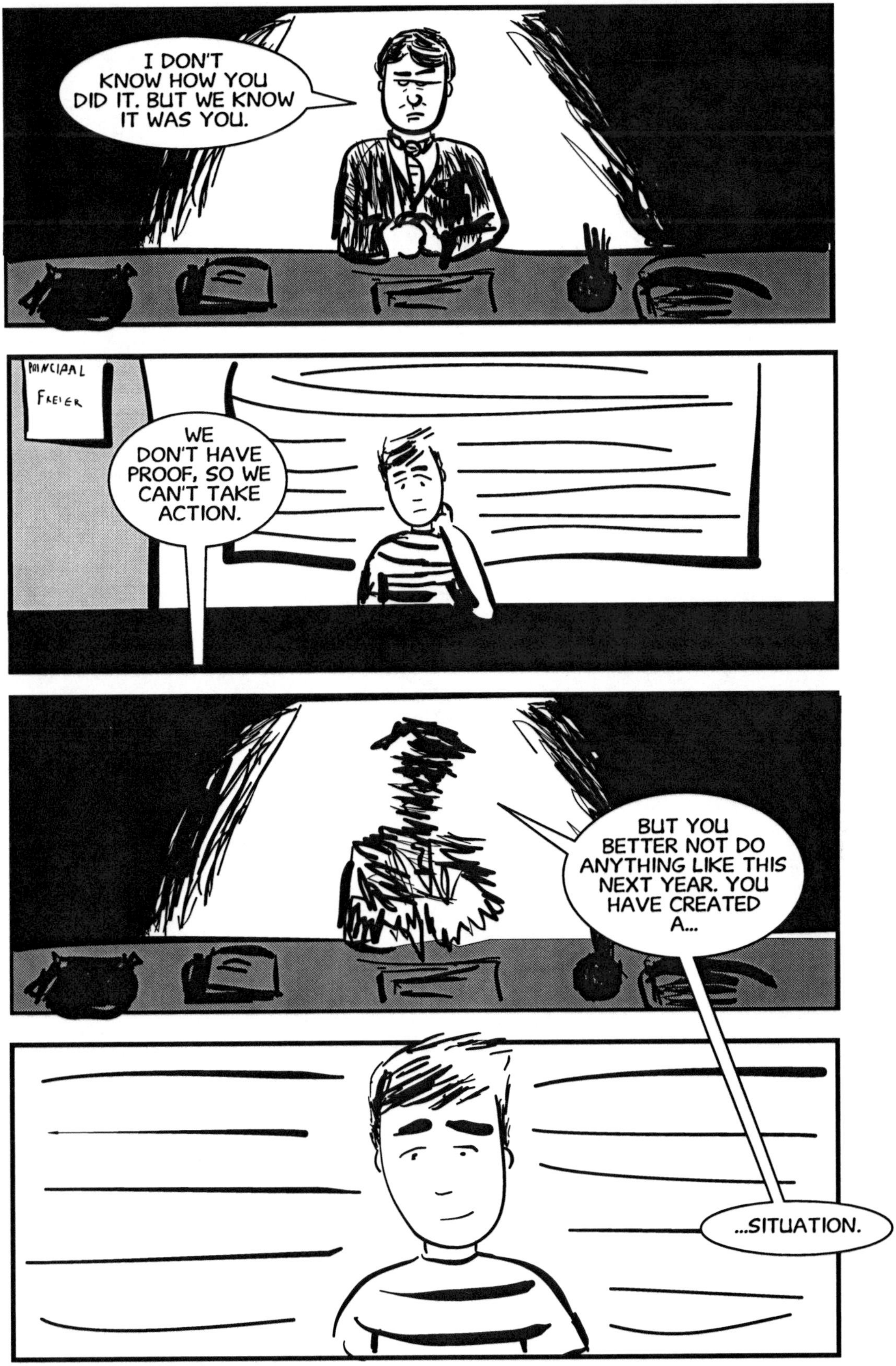
I DON'T KNOW HOW YOU DID IT. BUT WE KNOW IT WAS YOU.
PRINCIPAL FREIER
WE DON'T HAVE PROOF, SO WE CAN'T TAKE ACTION.
BUT YOU BETTER NOT DO ANYTHING LIKE THIS NEXT YEAR. YOU HAVE CREATED A...
...SITUATION.

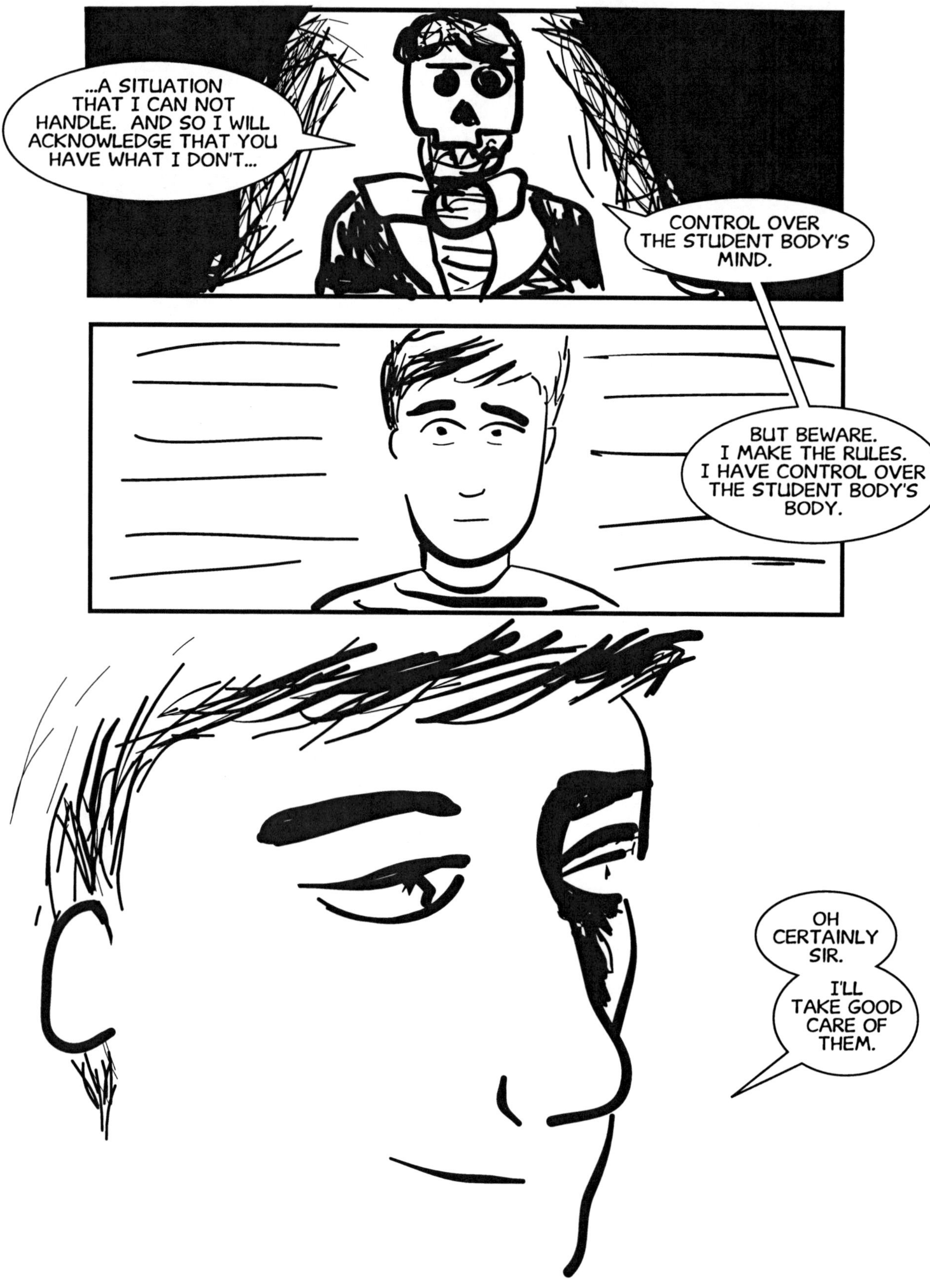
...A SITUATION THAT I CAN NOT HANDLE. AND SO I WILL ACKNOWLEDGE THAT YOU HAVE WHAT I DON'T...
CONTROL OVER THE STUDENT BODY'S MIND.
BUT BEWARE. I MAKE THE RULES. I HAVE CONTROL OVER THE STUDENT BODY'S BODY.
OH CERTAINLY SIR.
I'LL TAKE GOOD CARE OF THEM.

SUMMER

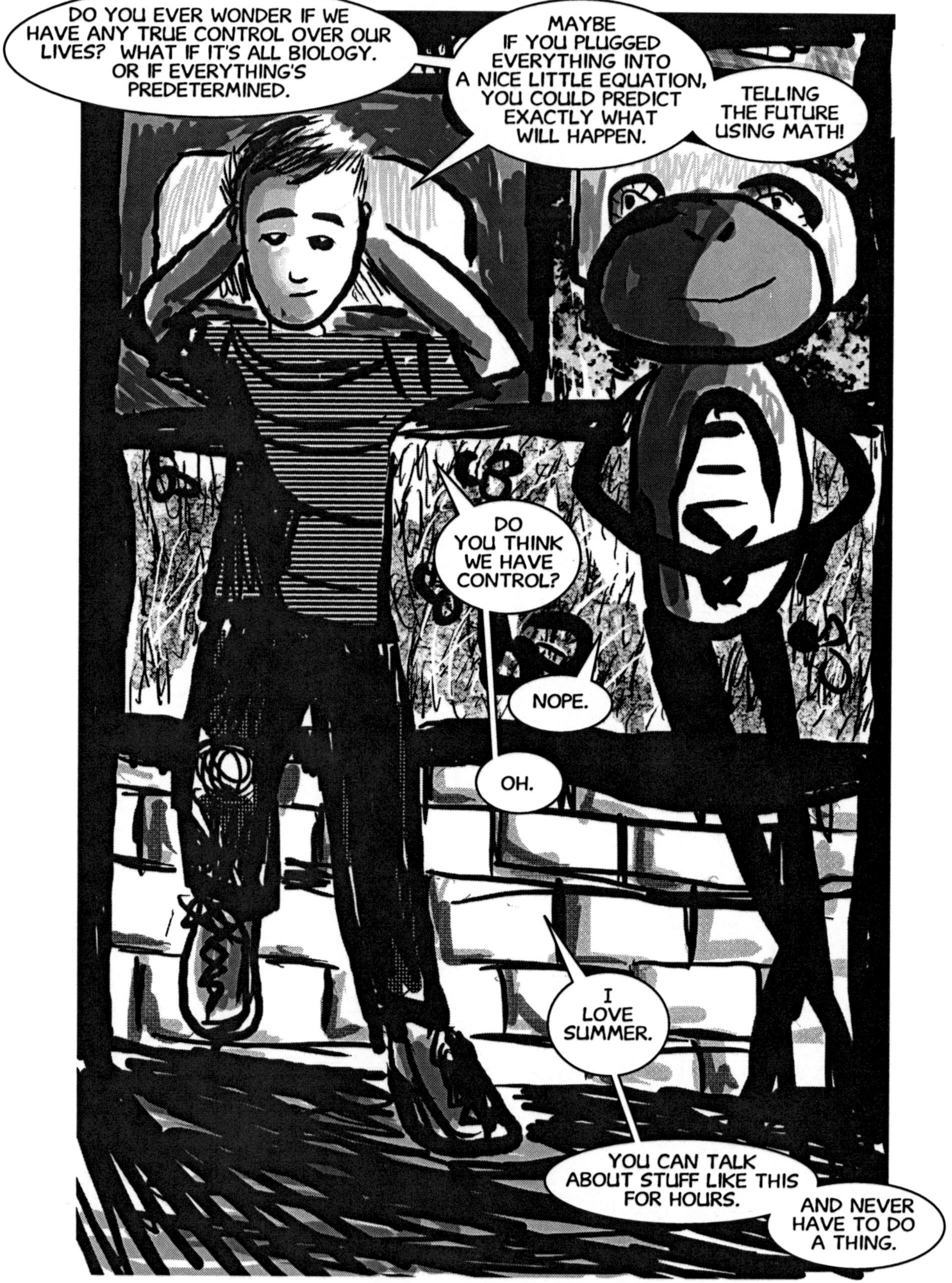
DO YOU EVER WONDER IF WE HAVE ANY TRUE CONTROL OVER OUR LIVES? WHAT IF IT'S ALL BIOLOGY. OR IF EVERYTHING'S PREDETERMINED.
MAYBE IF YOU PLUGGED EVERYTHING INTO A NICE LITTLE EQUATION, YOU COULD PREDICT EXACTLY WHAT WILL HAPPEN.
TELLING THE FUTURE USING MATH!
DO YOU THINK WE HAVE CONTROL?
NOPE.
OH.
I LOVE SUMMER.
YOU CAN TALK ABOUT STUFF LIKE THIS FOR HOURS.
AND NEVER HAVE TO DO A THING.

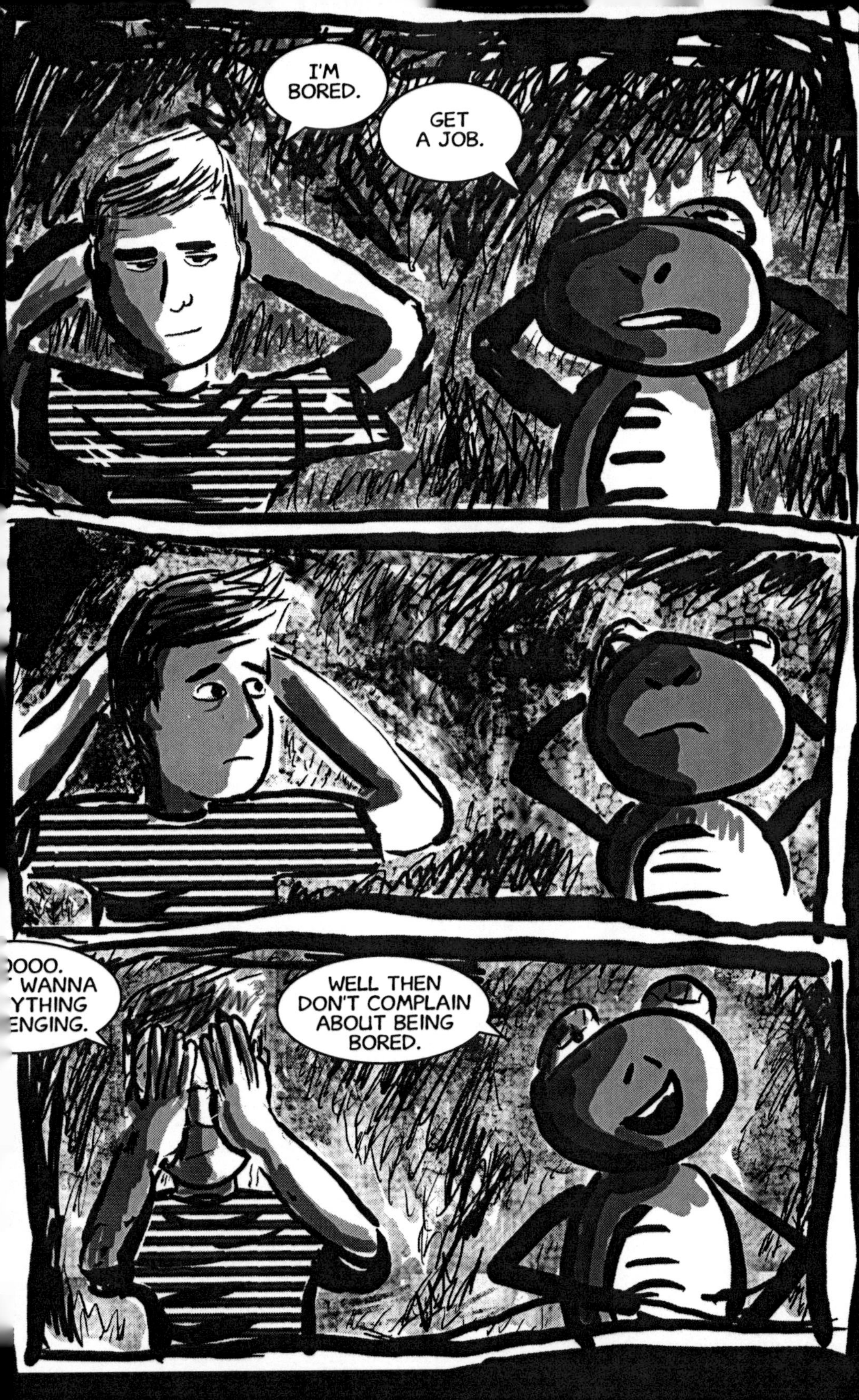
I'M BORED.
GET A JOB.
OOOO. WANNA YTHING ENGING.
WELL THEN DON'T COMPLAIN ABOUT BEING BORED.

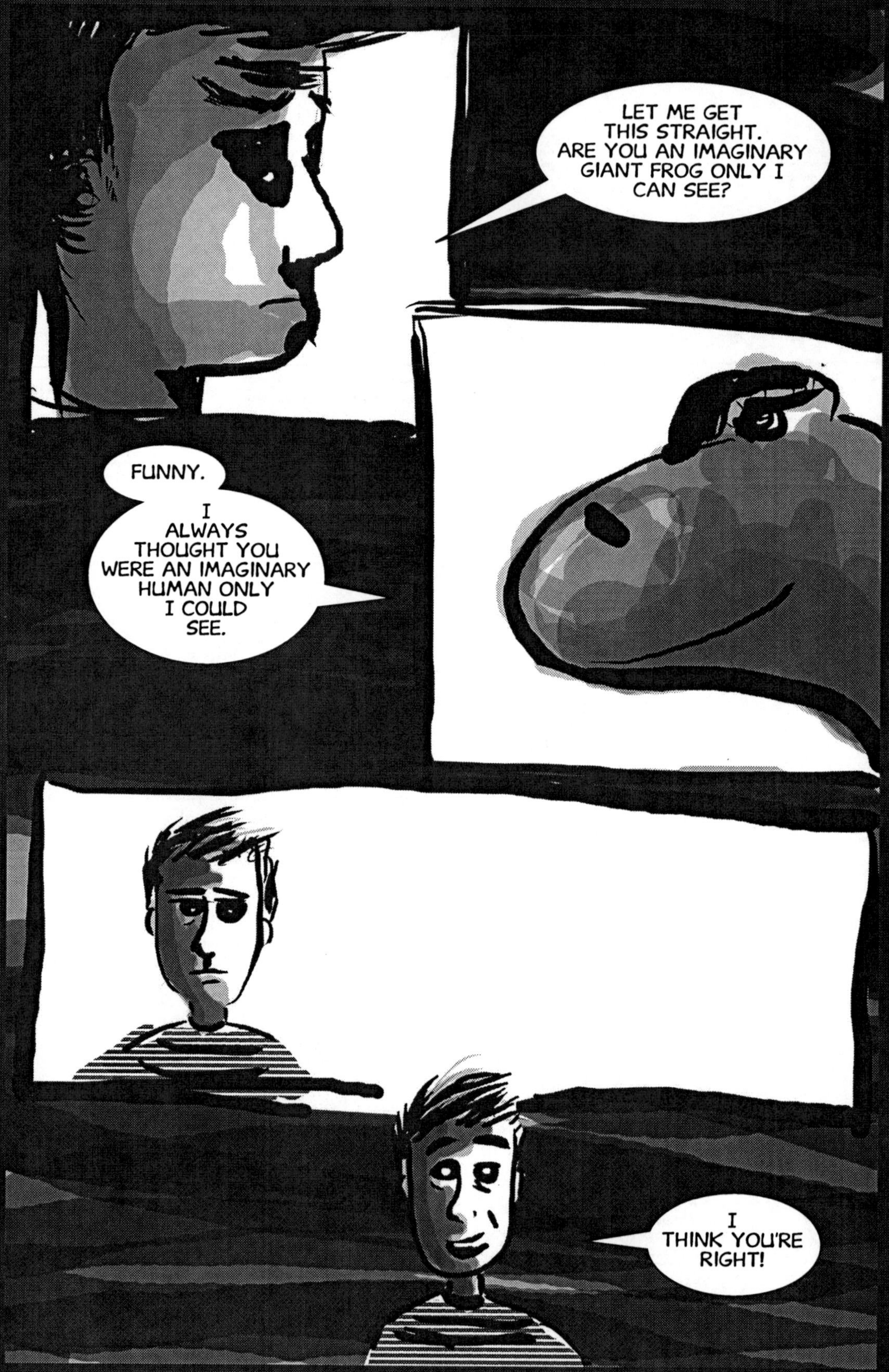
LET ME GET THIS STRAIGHT. ARE YOU AN IMAGINARY GIANT FROG ONLY I CAN SEE?
FUNNY.
I ALWAYS THOUGHT YOU WERE AN IMAGINARY HUMAN ONLY I COULD SEE.
I THINK YOU'RE RIGHT!

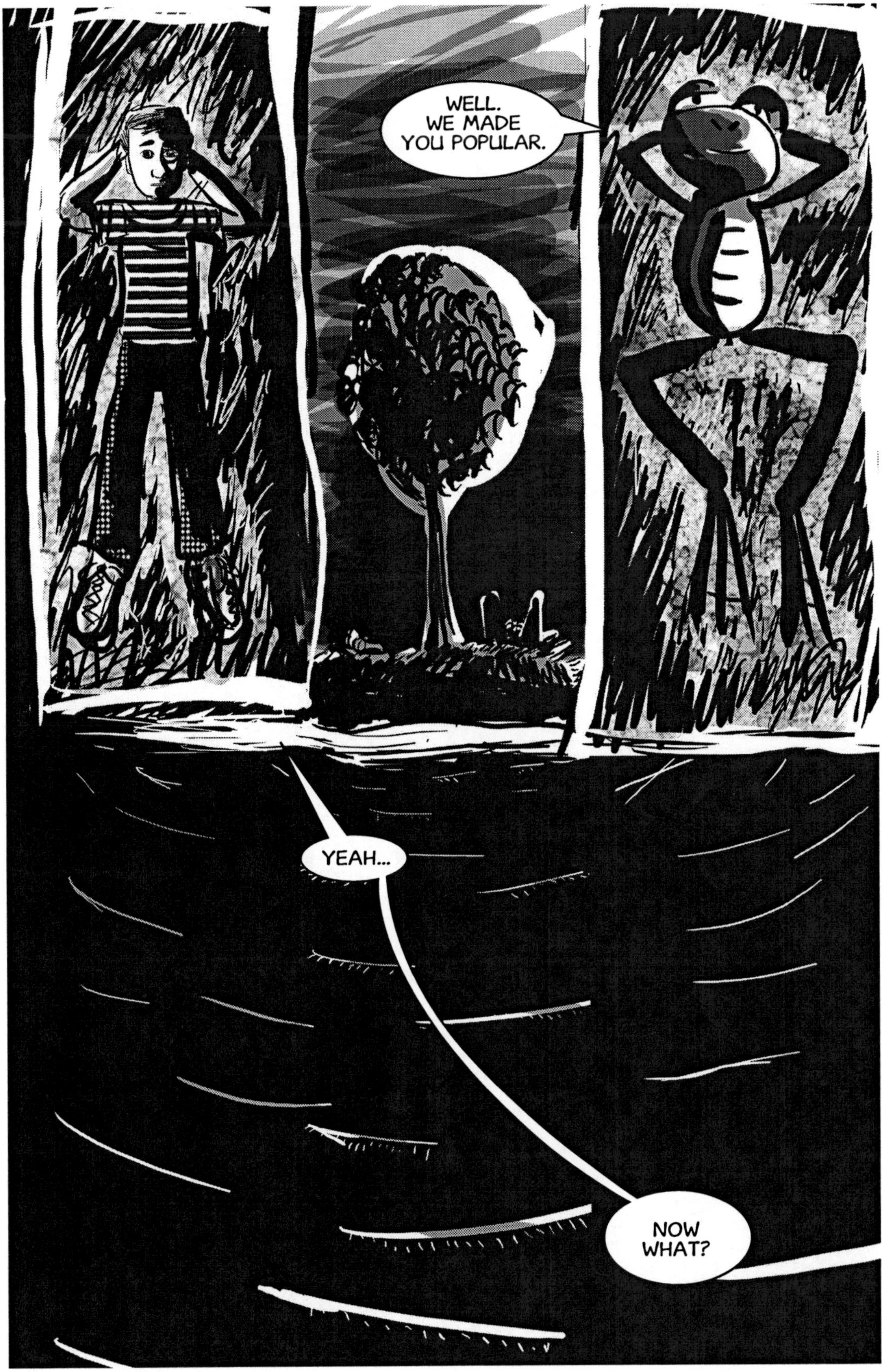
WELL. WE MADE YOU POPULAR.
YEAH...
NOW WHAT?

SENIOR YEAR

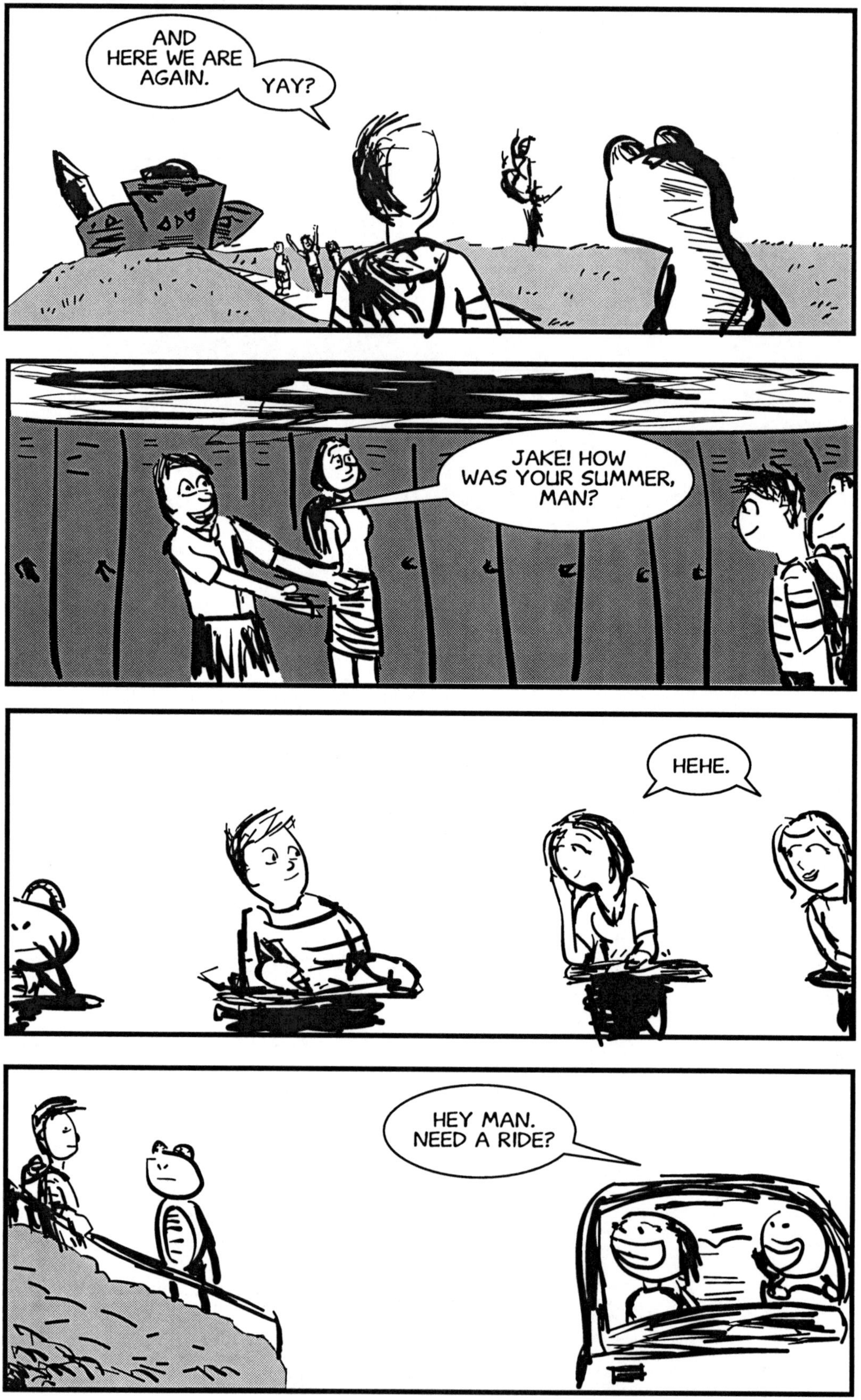
AND HERE WE ARE AGAIN.
YAY?
JAKE! HOW WAS YOUR SUMMER, MAN?
HEHE.
HEY MAN. NEED A RIDE?

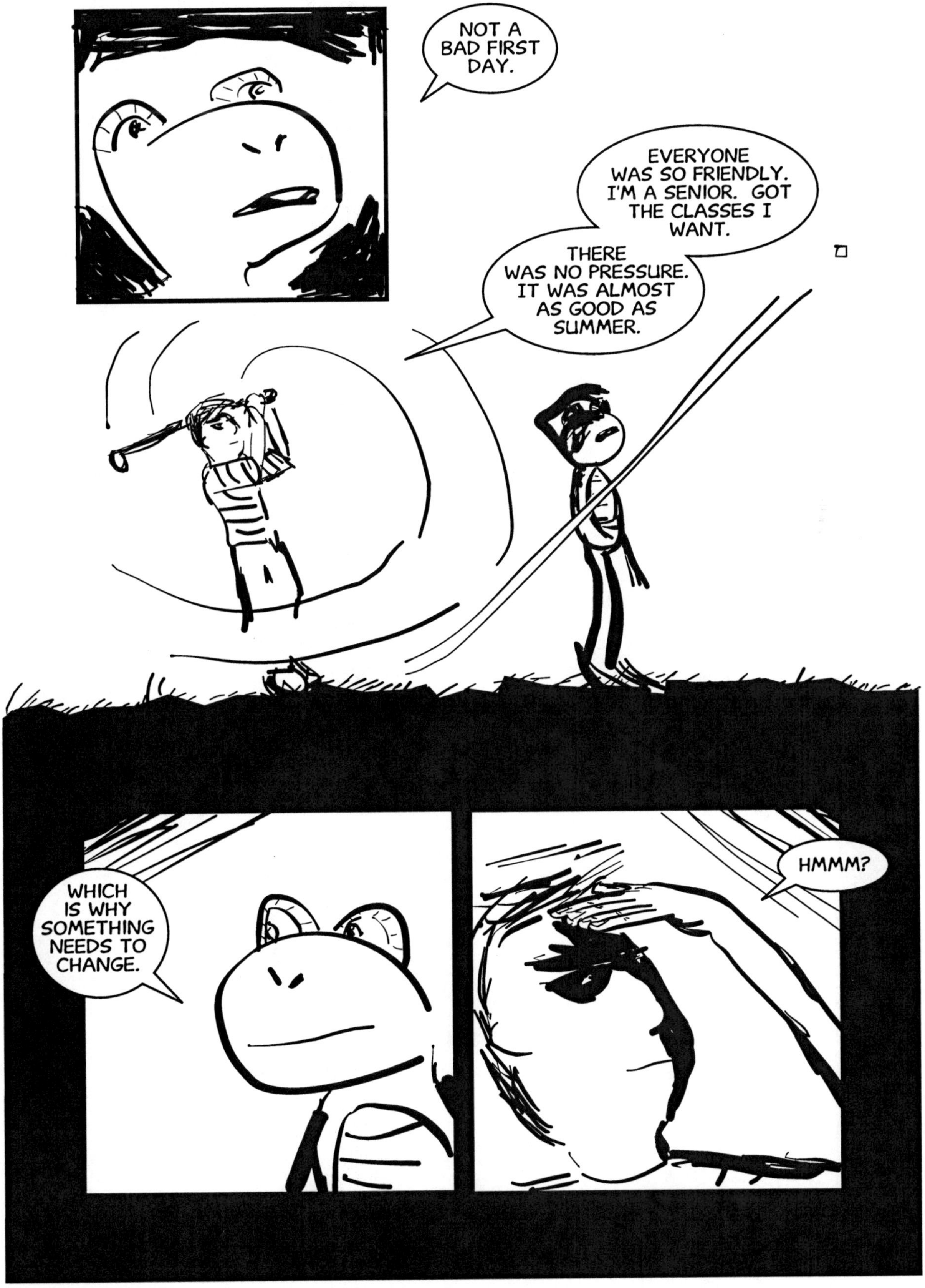
NOT A BAD FIRST DAY.
EVERYONE WAS SO FRIENDLY. I'M A SENIOR. GOT THE CLASSES I WANT.
THERE WAS NO PRESSURE. IT WAS ALMOST AS GOOD AS SUMMER.
WHICH IS WHY SOMETHING NEEDS TO CHANGE.
HMMM?

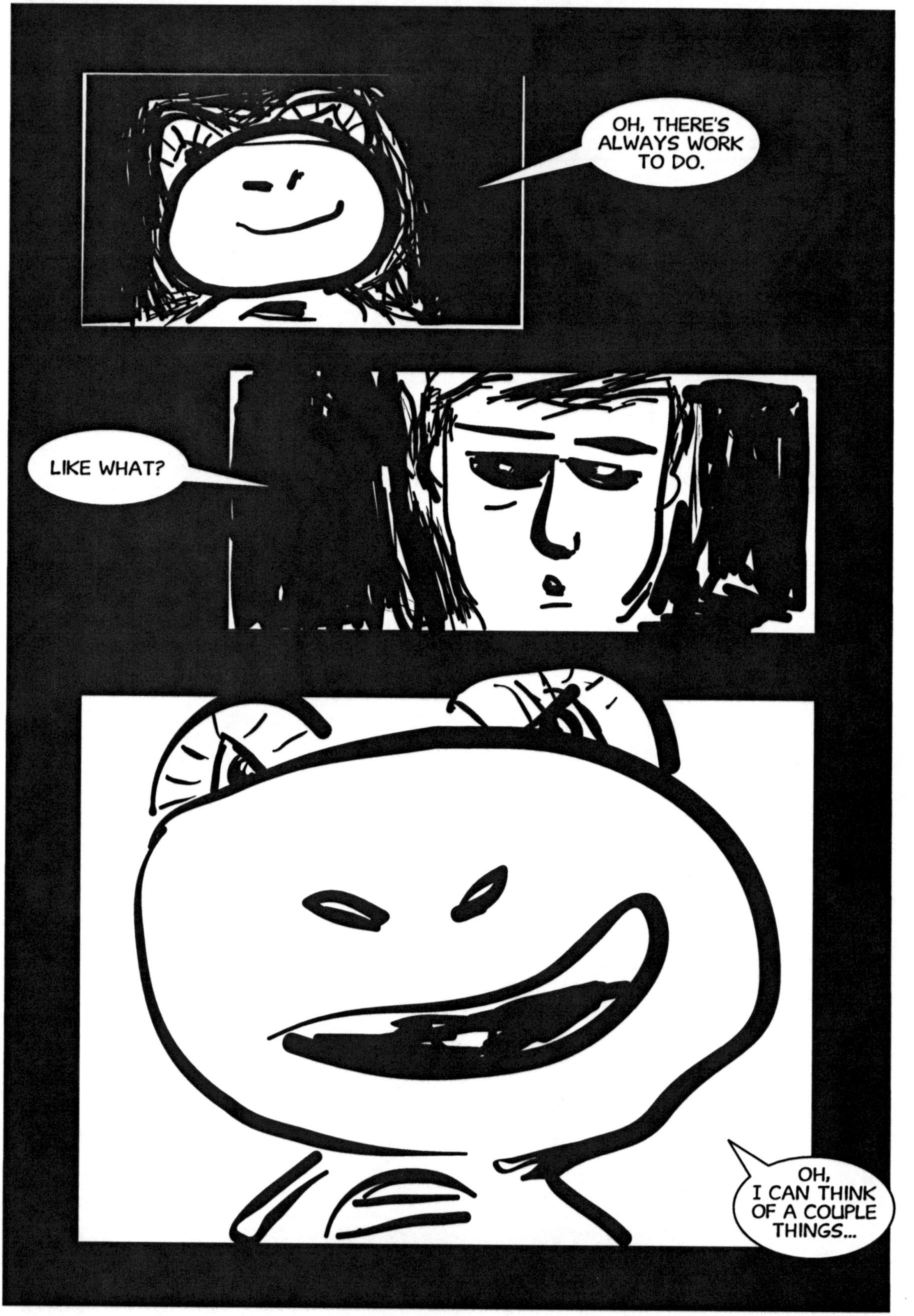
OH, THERE'S ALWAYS WORK TO DO.
LIKE WHAT?
OH, I CAN THINK OF A COUPLE THINGS...

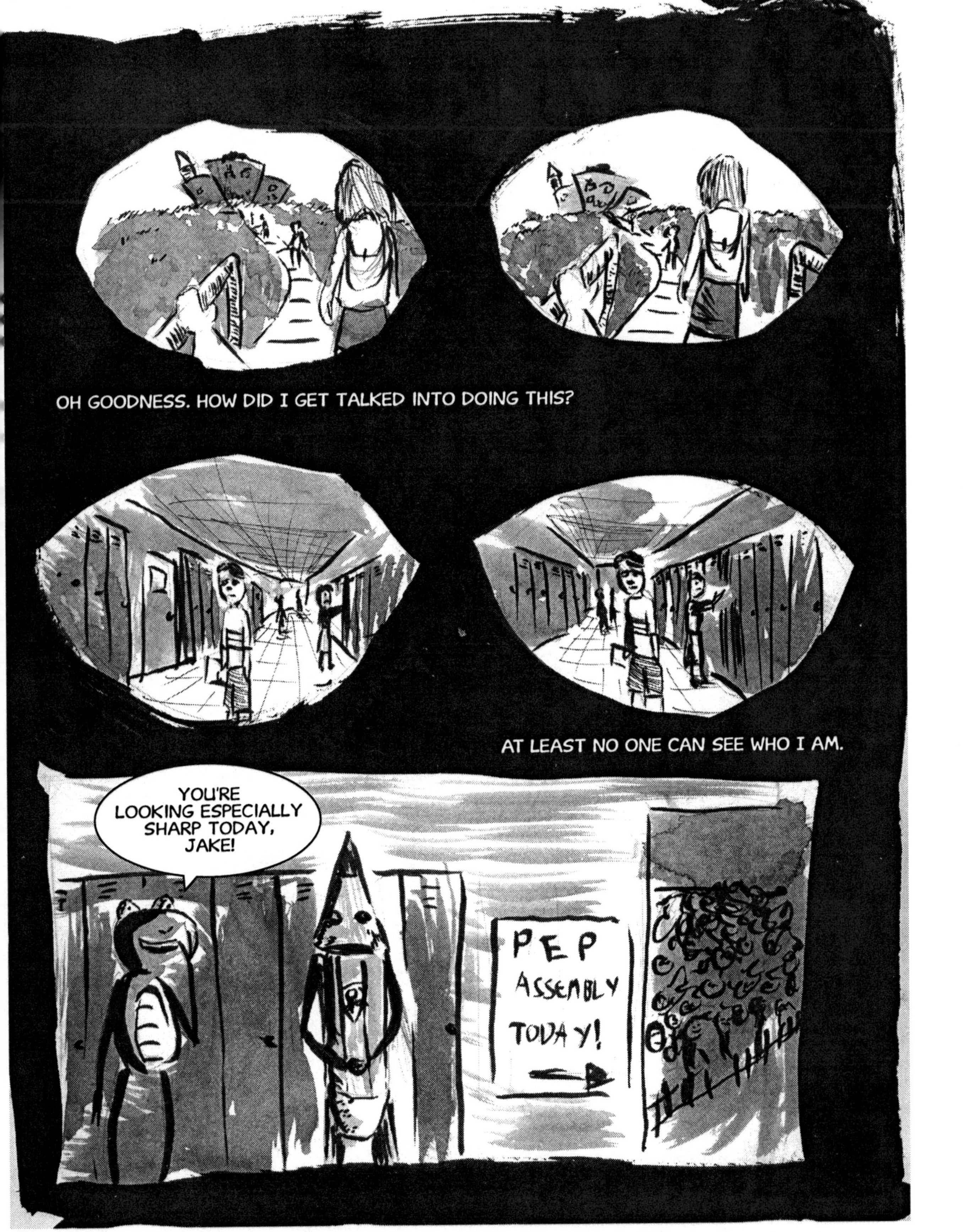
OH GOODNESS. HOW DID I GET TALKED INTO DOING THIS?
AT LEAST NO ONE CAN SEE WHO I AM.
YOU'RE LOOKING ESPECIALLY SHARP TODAY, JAKE!
PEP ASSEMBLY TODAY!

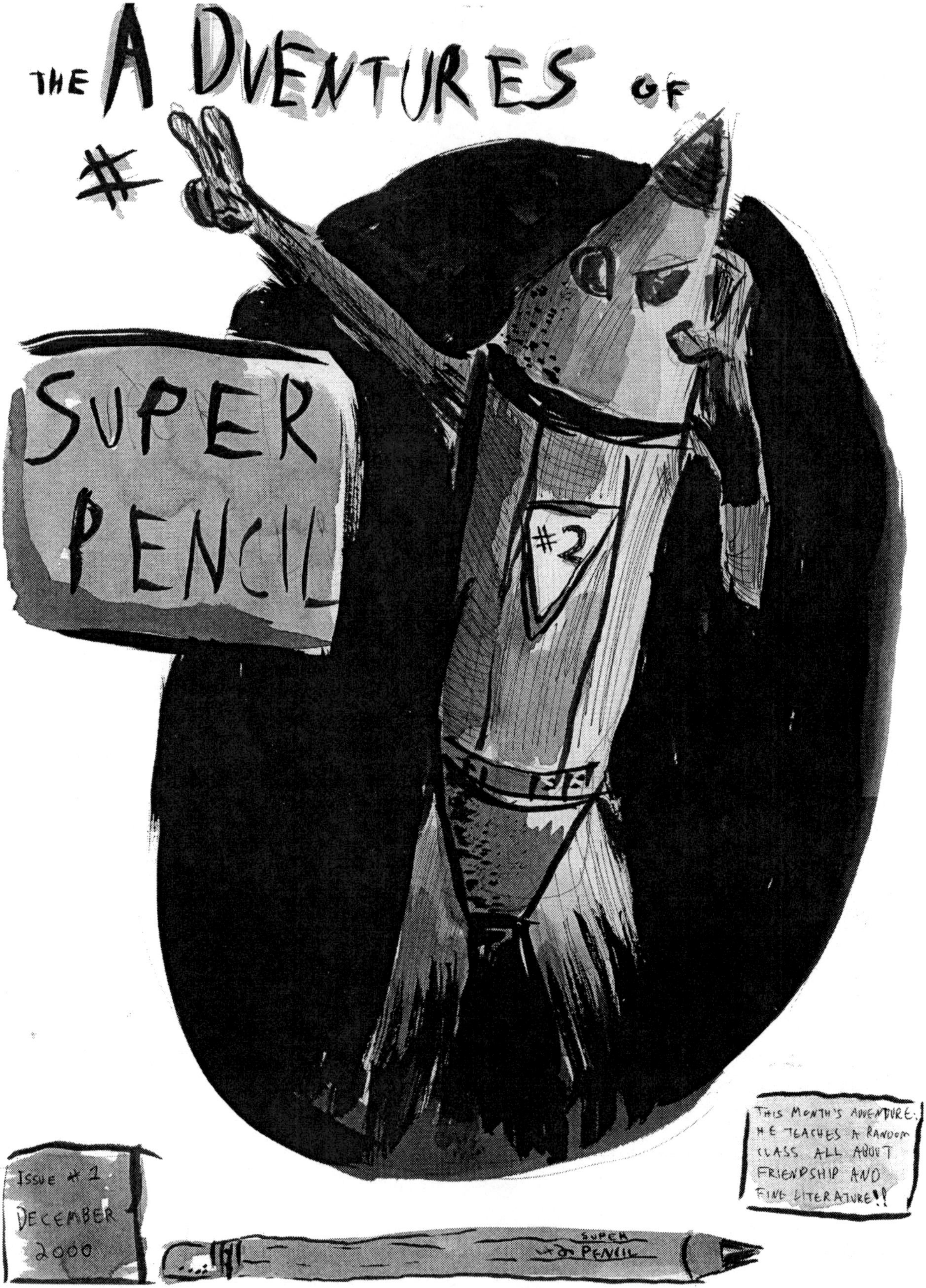
THE ADVENTURES OF #2
SUPER PENCIL
#2
SP
THIS MONTH'S ADVENTURE: HE TEACHES A RANDOM CLASS ALL ABOUT FRIENDSHIP AND FINE LITERATURE!!
ISSUE #1
DECEMBER 2000
SUPER PENCIL

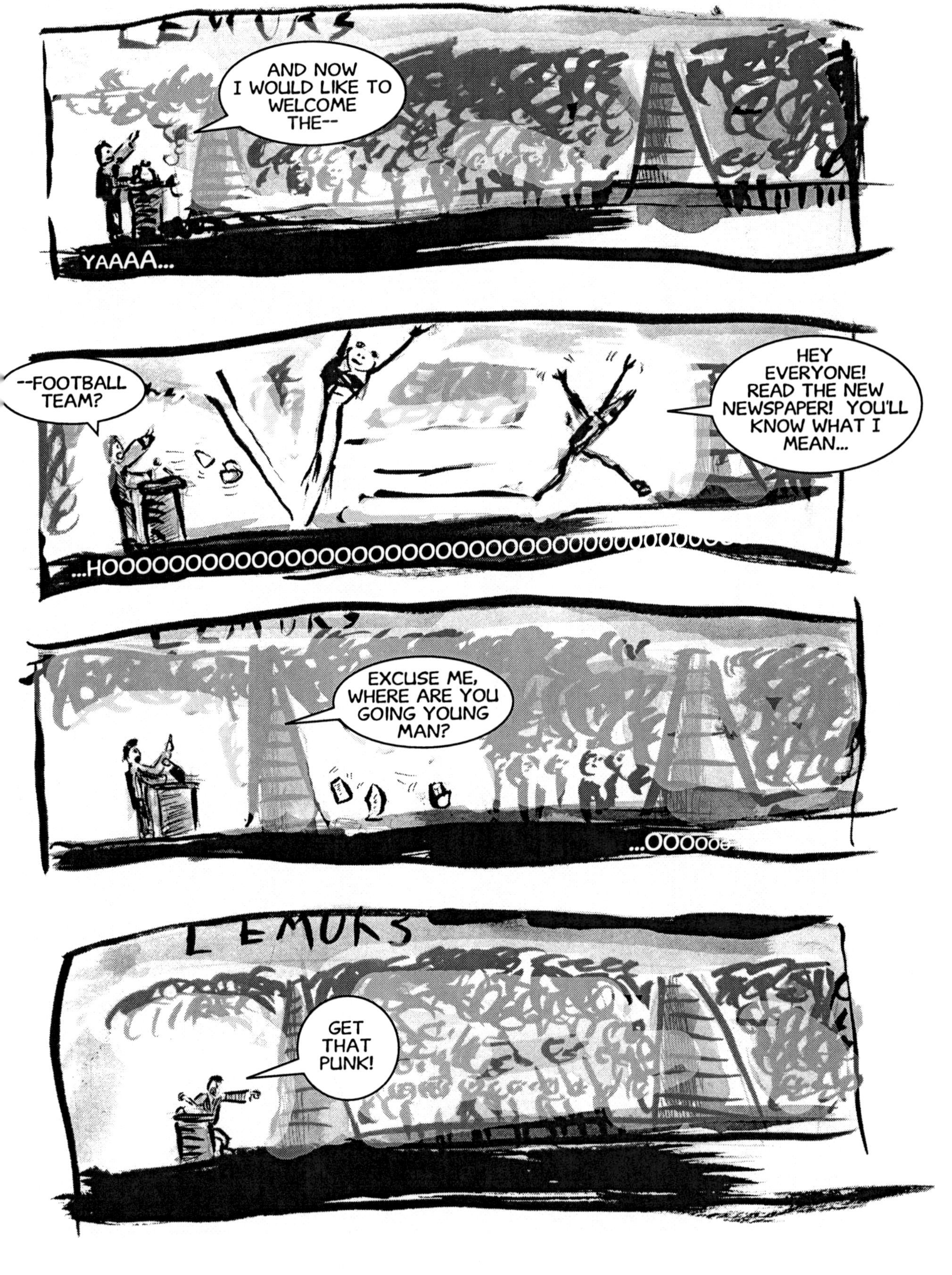

AND NOW I WOULD LIKE TO WELCOME THE--
YAAAA...
--FOOTBALL TEAM?
HEY EVERYONE! READ THE NEW NEWSPAPER! YOU'LL KNOW WHAT I MEAN...
...HOOOOOOOOOOOOOOOOOOOOOOOOOOOOOOOOOOOOOOOOOOOOO
EXCUSE ME, WHERE ARE YOU GOING YOUNG MAN?
...OOOOOO
GET THAT PUNK!

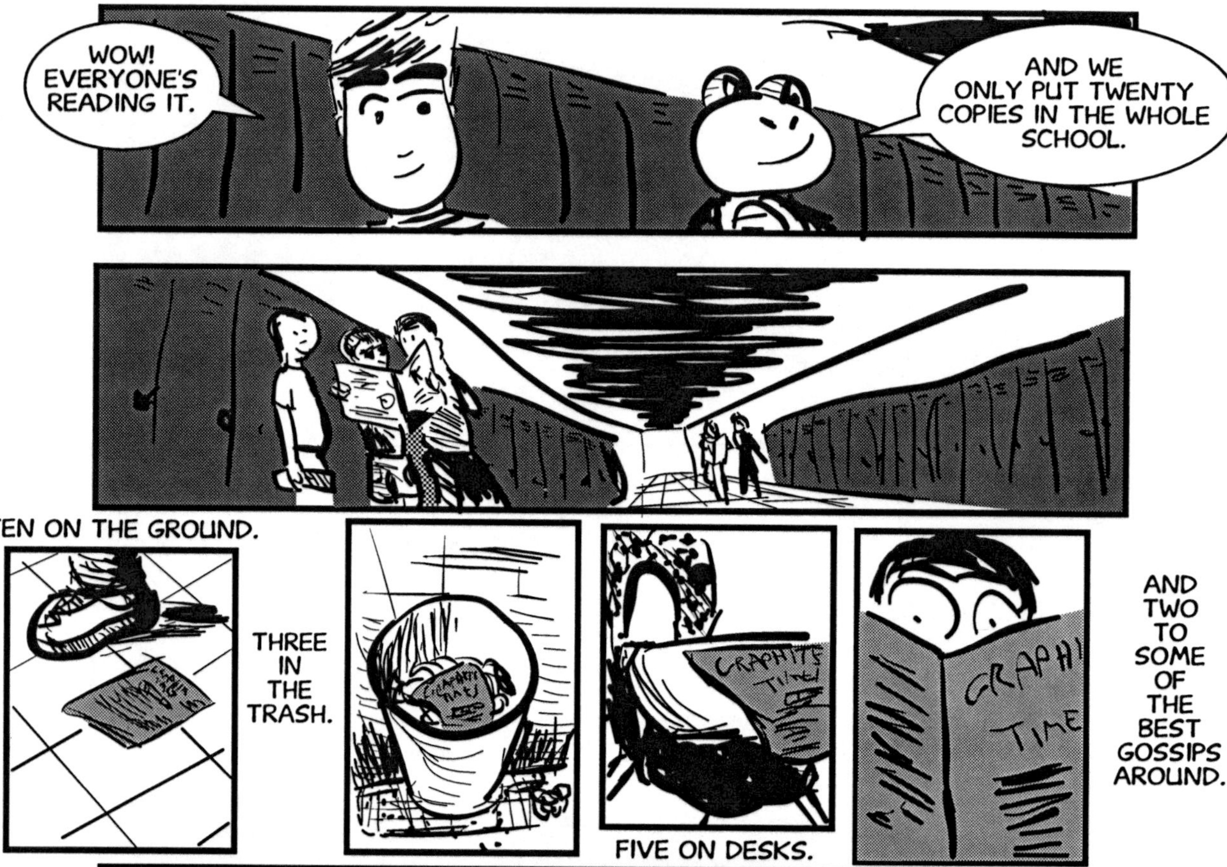
WOW! EVERYONE'S READING IT.
AND WE ONLY PUT TWENTY COPIES IN THE WHOLE SCHOOL.
TEN ON THE GROUND.
THREE IN THE TRASH.
FIVE ON DESKS.
AND TWO TO SOME OF THE BEST GOSSIPS AROUND.
GRAPHITE TIMES
GRAPHI TIME

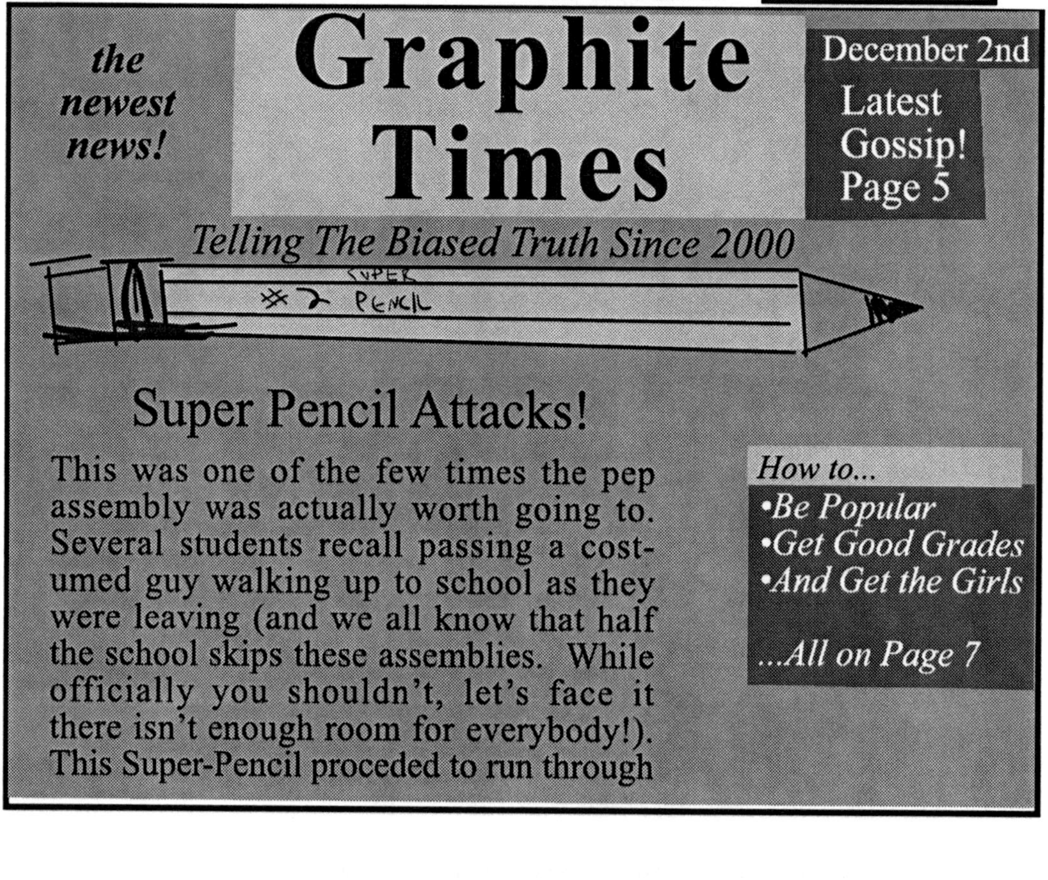

the newest news!

Graphite Times

December 2nd

Latest Gossip! Page 5

Telling The Biased Truth Since 2000

SUPER
#2 PENCIL

Super Pencil Attacks!

This was one of the few times the pep assembly was actually worth going to. Several students recall passing a costumed guy walking up to school as they were leaving (and we all know that half the school skips these assemblies. While officially you shouldn't, let's face it there isn't enough room for everybody!). This Super-Pencil proceeded to run through

How to...

- *Be Popular*
- *Get Good Grades*
- *And Get the Girls*

...All on Page 7

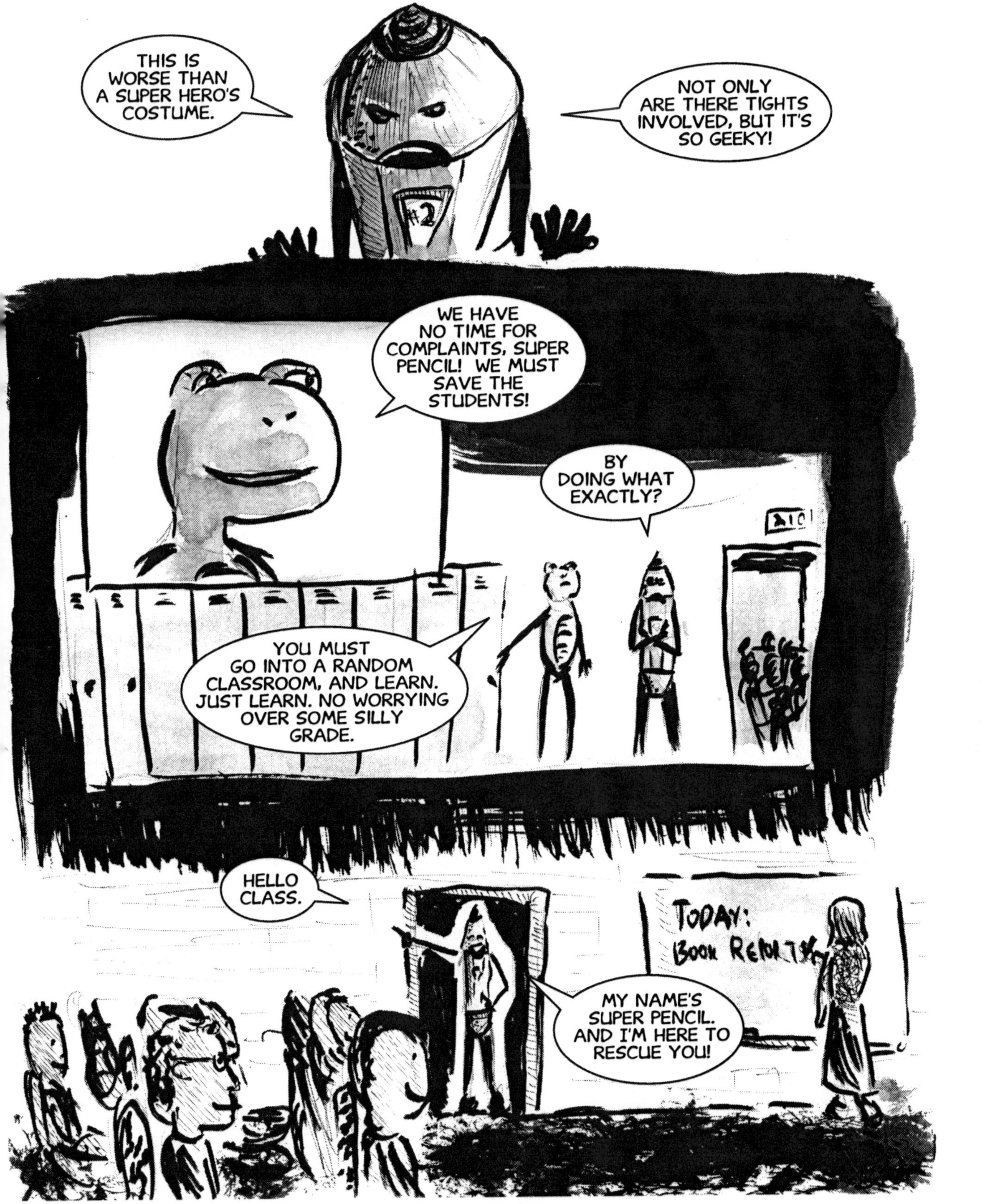
THIS IS WORSE THAN A SUPER HERO'S COSTUME.
NOT ONLY ARE THERE TIGHTS INVOLVED, BUT IT'S SO GEEKY!
#2
WE HAVE NO TIME FOR COMPLAINTS, SUPER PENCIL! WE MUST SAVE THE STUDENTS!
BY DOING WHAT EXACTLY?
YOU MUST GO INTO A RANDOM CLASSROOM, AND LEARN. JUST LEARN. NO WORRYING OVER SOME SILLY GRADE.
HELLO CLASS.
TODAY:
MY NAME'S SUPER PENCIL. AND I'M HERE TO RESCUE YOU!

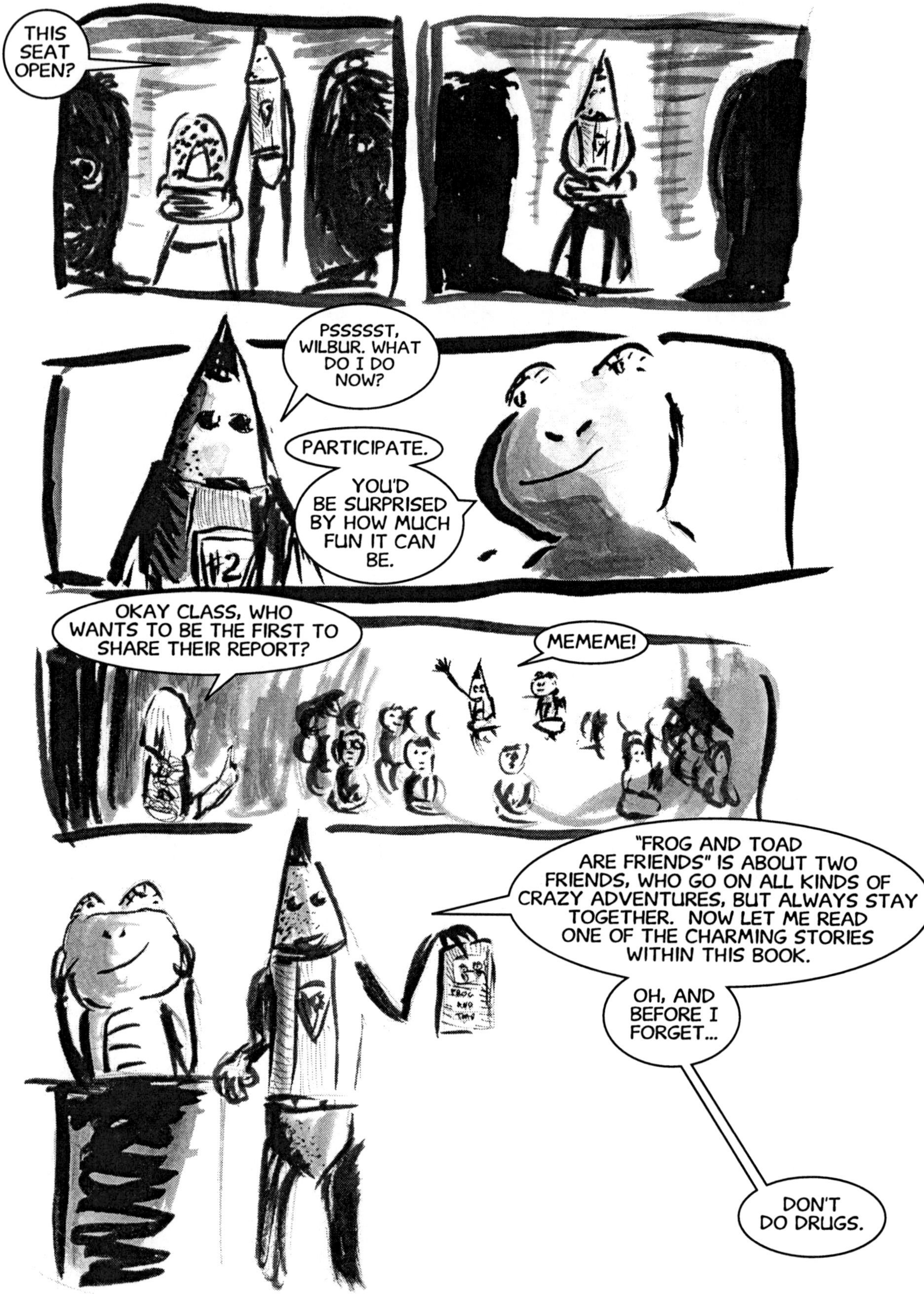
THIS SEAT OPEN?
PSSSSST, WILBUR. WHAT DO I DO NOW?
PARTICIPATE.
YOU'D BE SURPRISED BY HOW MUCH FUN IT CAN BE.
OKAY CLASS, WHO WANTS TO BE THE FIRST TO SHARE THEIR REPORT?
MEMEME!
"FROG AND TOAD ARE FRIENDS" IS ABOUT TWO FRIENDS, WHO GO ON ALL KINDS OF CRAZY ADVENTURES, BUT ALWAYS STAY TOGETHER. NOW LET ME READ ONE OF THE CHARMING STORIES WITHIN THIS BOOK.
OH, AND BEFORE I FORGET...
DON'T DO DRUGS.

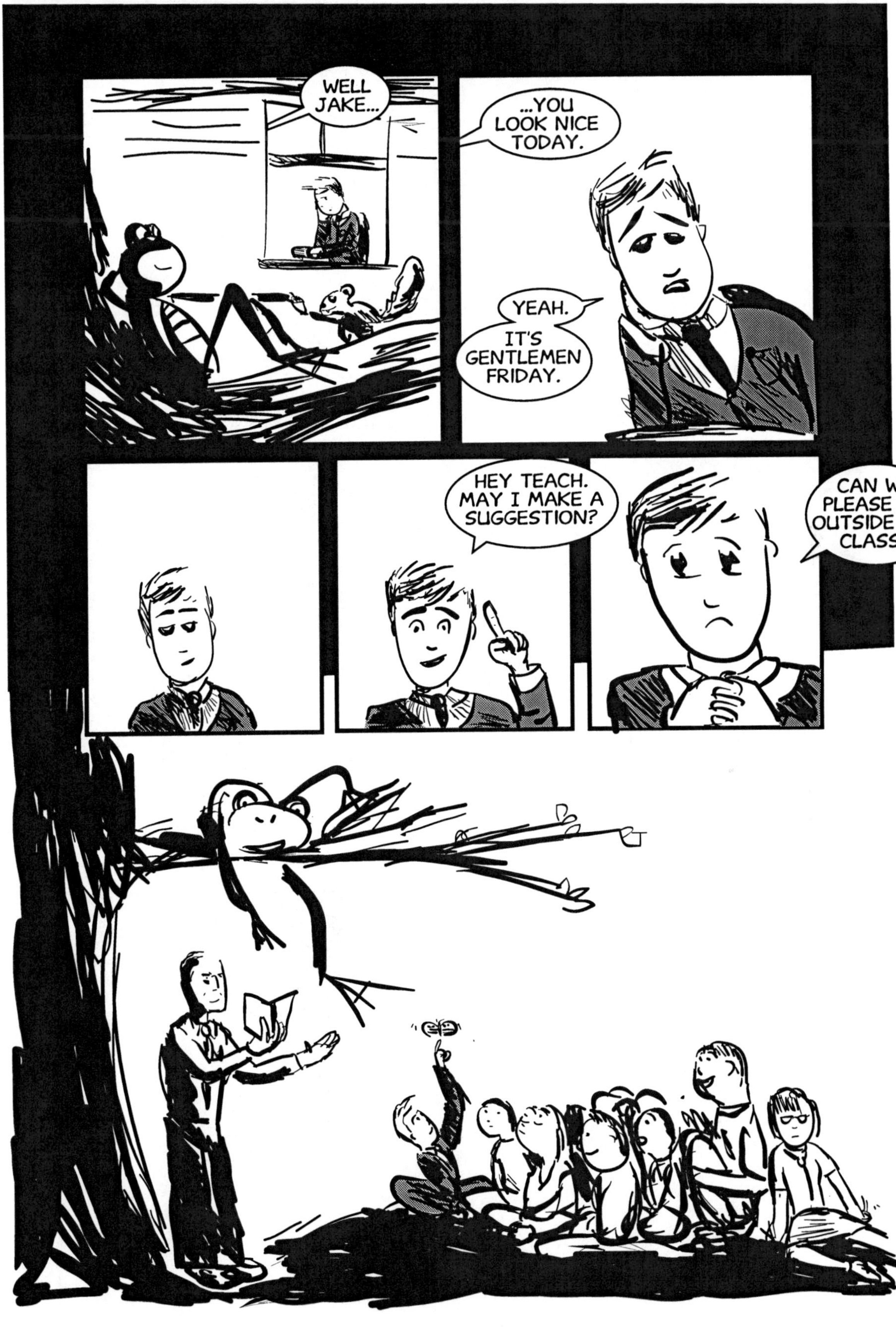
WELL JAKE...
...YOU LOOK NICE TODAY.
YEAH.
IT'S GENTLEMEN FRIDAY.
HEY TEACH. MAY I MAKE A SUGGESTION?
CAN WE PLEASE GO OUTSIDE FOR CLASS?

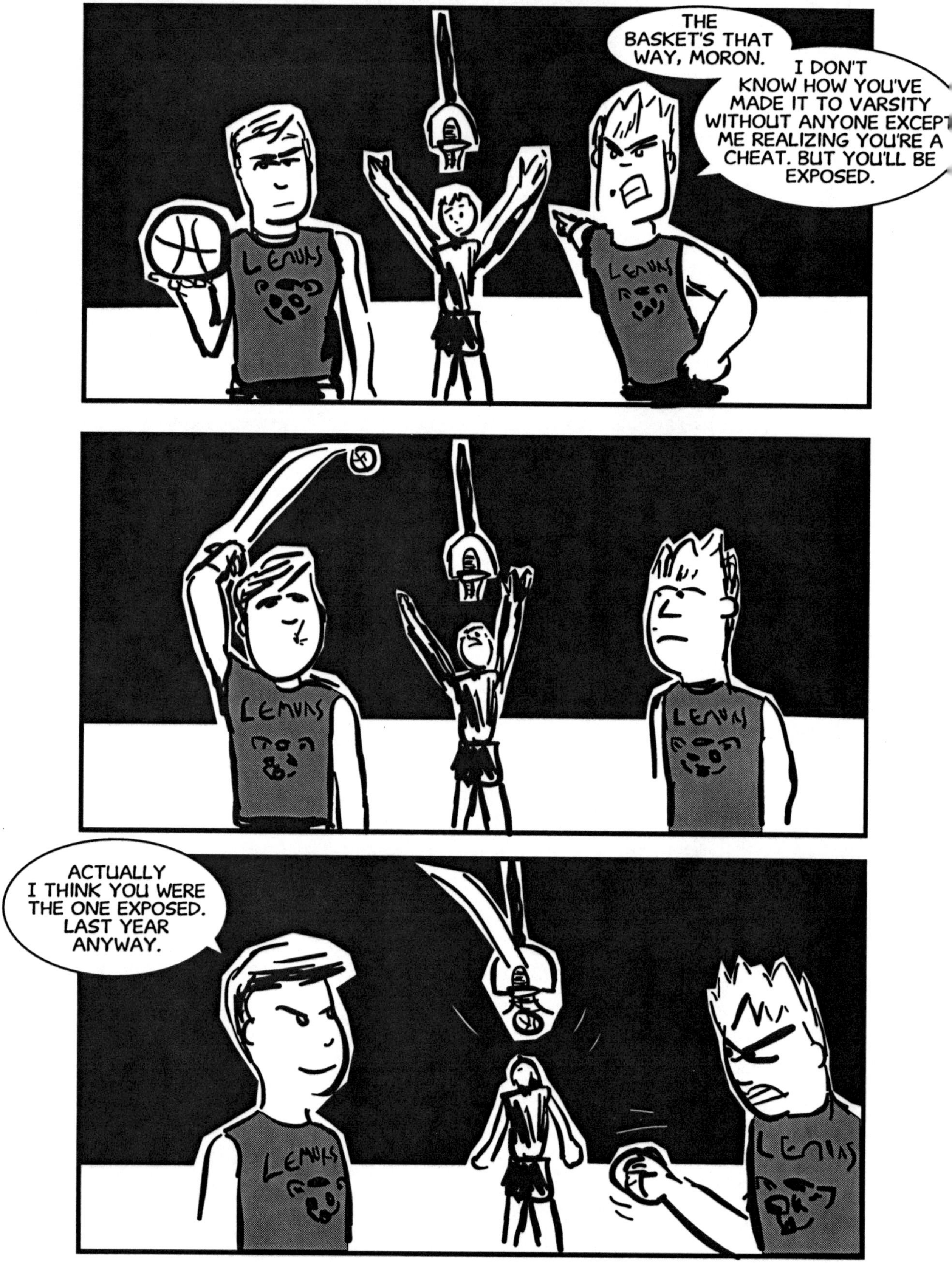
THE BASKET'S THAT WAY, MORON.
I DON'T KNOW HOW YOU'VE MADE IT TO VARSITY WITHOUT ANYONE EXCEPT ME REALIZING YOU'RE A CHEAT. BUT YOU'LL BE EXPOSED.
ACTUALLY I THINK YOU WERE THE ONE EXPOSED. LAST YEAR ANYWAY.

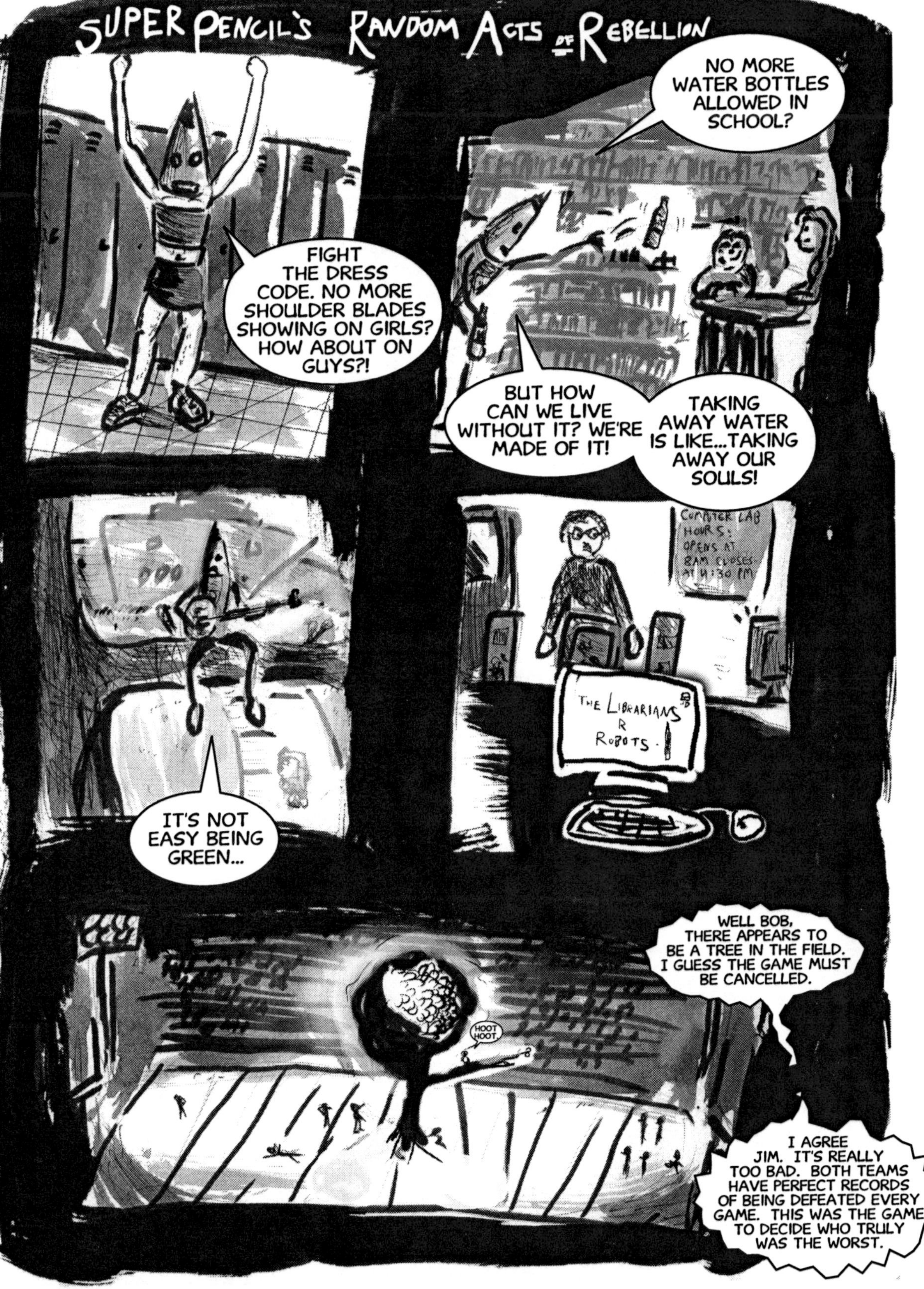
SUPER PENCIL'S RANDOM ACTS OF REBELLION
FIGHT THE DRESS CODE. NO MORE SHOULDER BLADES SHOWING ON GIRLS? HOW ABOUT ON GUYS?!
NO MORE WATER BOTTLES ALLOWED IN SCHOOL?
BUT HOW CAN WE LIVE WITHOUT IT? WE'RE MADE OF IT!
TAKING AWAY WATER IS LIKE...TAKING AWAY OUR SOULS!
IT'S NOT EASY BEING GREEN...
THE LIBRARIANS R ROBOTS.
WELL BOB, THERE APPEARS TO BE A TREE IN THE FIELD. I GUESS THE GAME MUST BE CANCELLED.
HOOT HOOT.
I AGREE JIM. IT'S REALLY TOO BAD. BOTH TEAMS HAVE PERFECT RECORDS OF BEING DEFEATED EVERY GAME. THIS WAS THE GAME TO DECIDE WHO TRULY WAS THE WORST.

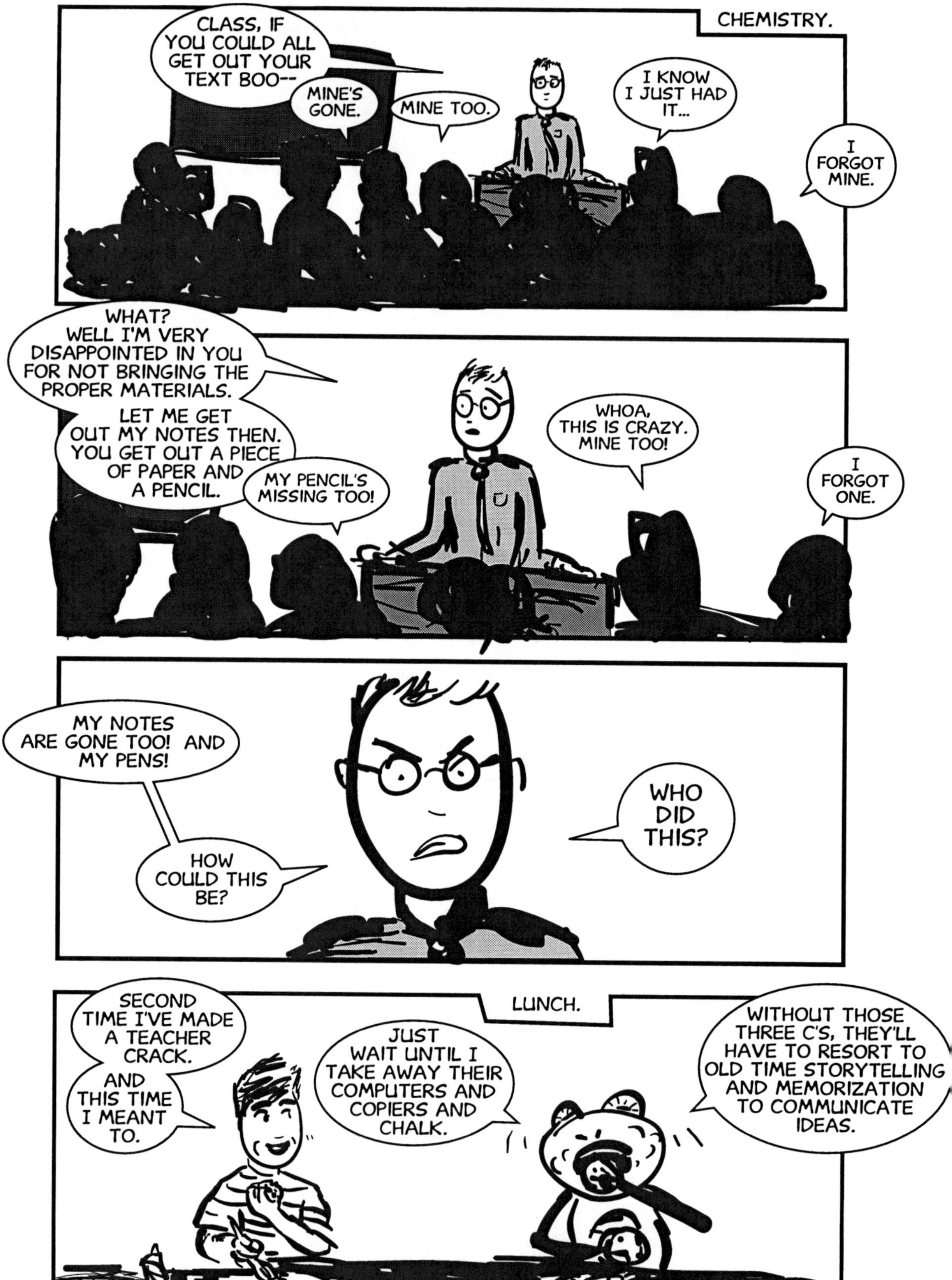
CHEMISTRY.
CLASS, IF YOU COULD ALL GET OUT YOUR TEXT BOO--
MINE'S GONE.
MINE TOO.
I KNOW I JUST HAD IT...
I FORGOT MINE.
WHAT? WELL I'M VERY DISAPPOINTED IN YOU FOR NOT BRINGING THE PROPER MATERIALS.
LET ME GET OUT MY NOTES THEN. YOU GET OUT A PIECE OF PAPER AND A PENCIL.
MY PENCIL'S MISSING TOO!
WHOA, THIS IS CRAZY. MINE TOO!
I FORGOT ONE.
MY NOTES ARE GONE TOO! AND MY PENS!
HOW COULD THIS BE?
WHO DID THIS?
LUNCH.
SECOND TIME I'VE MADE A TEACHER CRACK.
AND THIS TIME I MEANT TO.
JUST WAIT UNTIL I TAKE AWAY THEIR COMPUTERS AND COPIERS AND CHALK.
WITHOUT THOSE THREE C'S, THEY'LL HAVE TO RESORT TO OLD TIME STORYTELLING AND MEMORIZATION TO COMMUNICATE IDEAS.

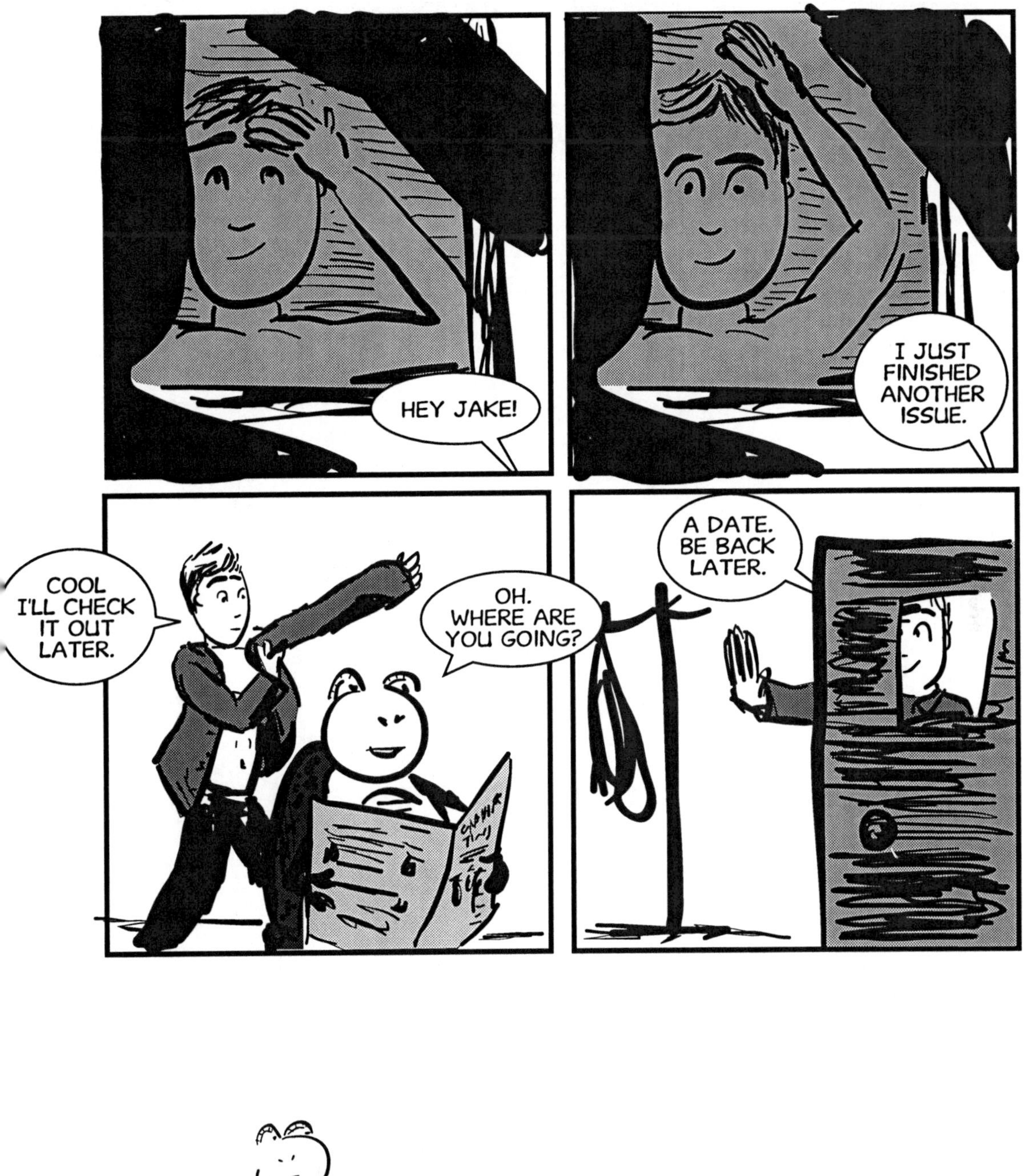
HEY JAKE!
I JUST FINISHED ANOTHER ISSUE.
COOL I'LL CHECK IT OUT LATER.
OH. WHERE ARE YOU GOING?
A DATE. BE BACK LATER.

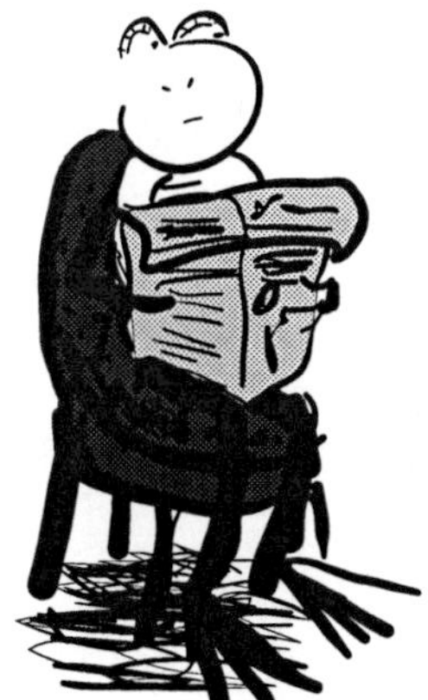

News that is hip. And very biased.

Graphite Times

January 12th

Interview with a Bully Page 25

Causing Lead Poisoning Since 2000

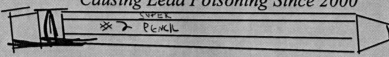

Vice Principal Student Affairs

When the new dress code, which tried to prevent any skin from showing (remind you of any other places?) was enforced, one of its enforcers had to be 2nd in command, Vice Principal Clink. But as it turns out, he was actually one of the biggest advocates of the old school dresses. Or maybe none at all. It seems that our Administrator Clink, responsiblefor all the disciplinary actions at the school, was seeing some more skin than he should have. *continued on page 3*

continued on page 3

How to...
- *Complete a Drug Deal*
- *Cheat on a Test*
- *Skip Class*

...and get away with it!

...All on Page 7

Super Pencil running away from the scene of a crime

photo by Edward Edification

Age and Apathy

With age people are given more and more powers and responsibilities. Yet the youth of today refuses to vote. So why is it that these young adults refuse to make a difference?

Page 16

Athletics over Academics

Without a doubt, this is a sport school, and the biggest sport at this school is Football. The cheerleaders, the fans, the band, the players, chances are you've been in one of these groups before. Now when you compare this school to any other, sure, academics will play a part in which you say is best, but let's face it, the number one football team is really what makes the school number one. Knowing how terrible the football teamwas this year, Super Pencil decided to help their record out...... Page 12

The tree that was planted in the football field right before the big rivalry game against Mad High.

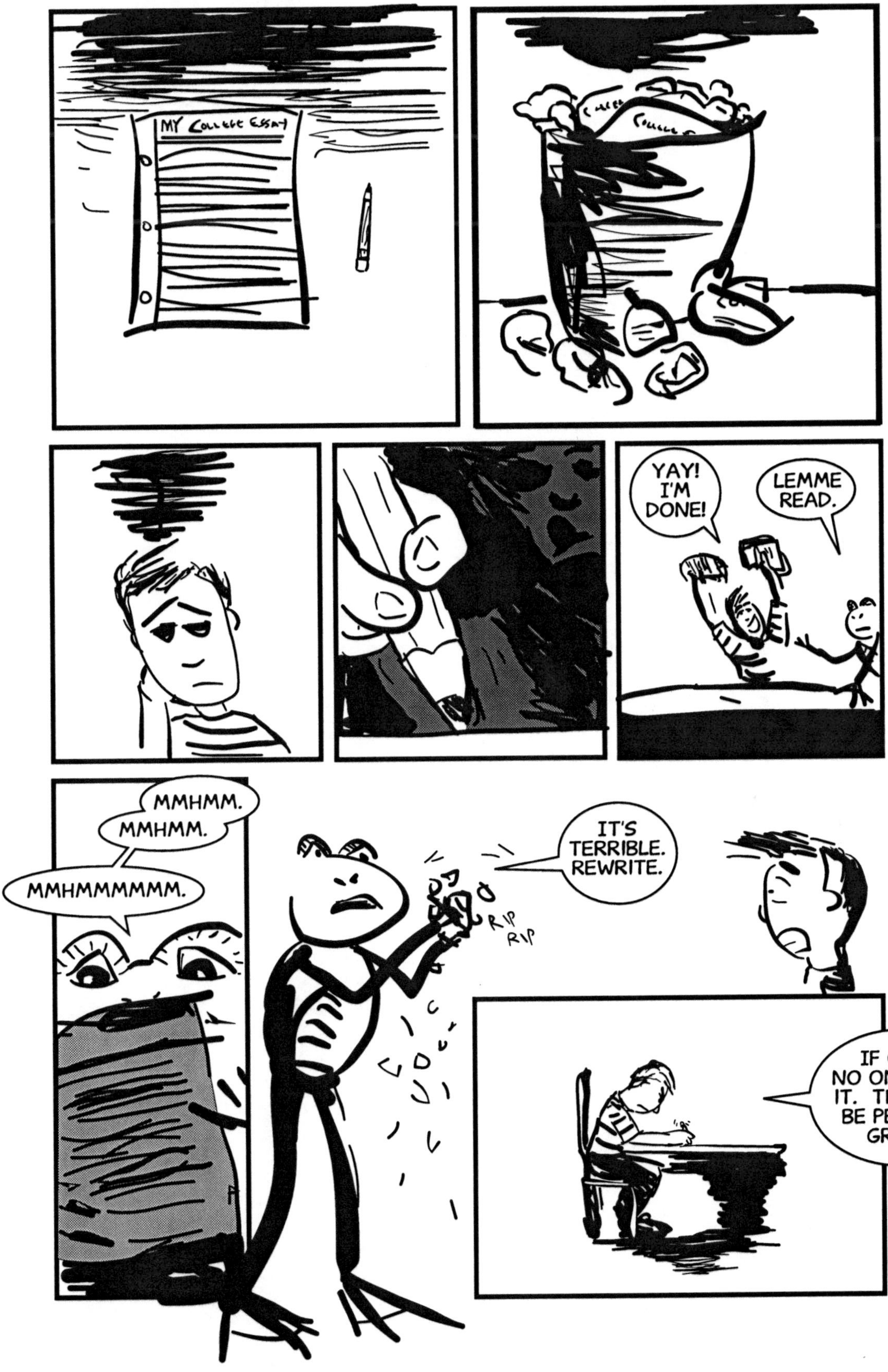
MY COLLEGE ESSAY
YAY! I'M DONE!
LEMME READ.
MMHMMMMMM.
MMHMM.
MMHMM.
RIP RIP
IT'S TERRIBLE. REWRITE.
IF ONLY NO ONE READ IT. THEN IT'D BE PERFECT. GRRRR.

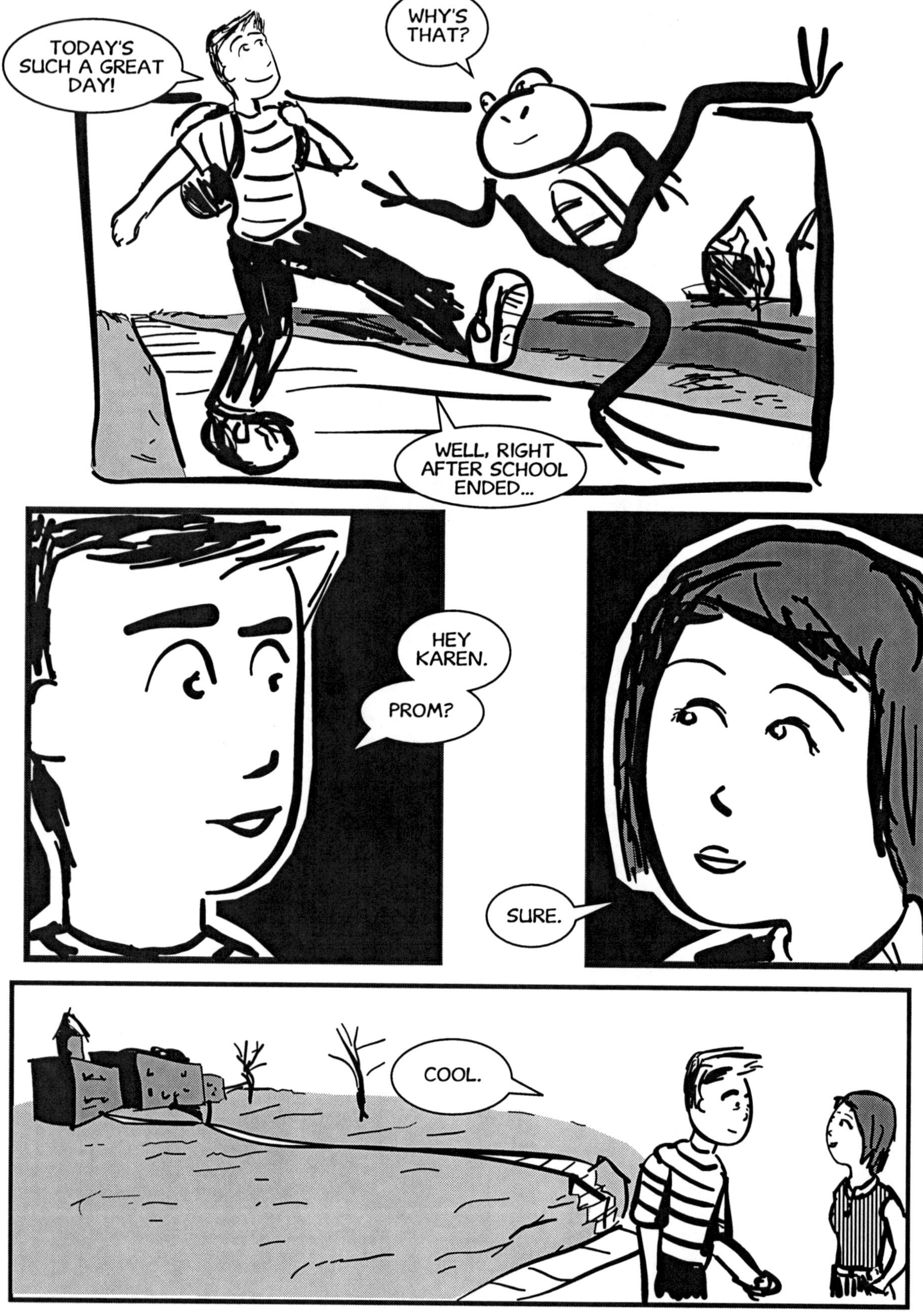
TODAY'S SUCH A GREAT DAY!
WHY'S THAT?
WELL, RIGHT AFTER SCHOOL ENDED...
HEY KAREN.
PROM?
SURE.
COOL.

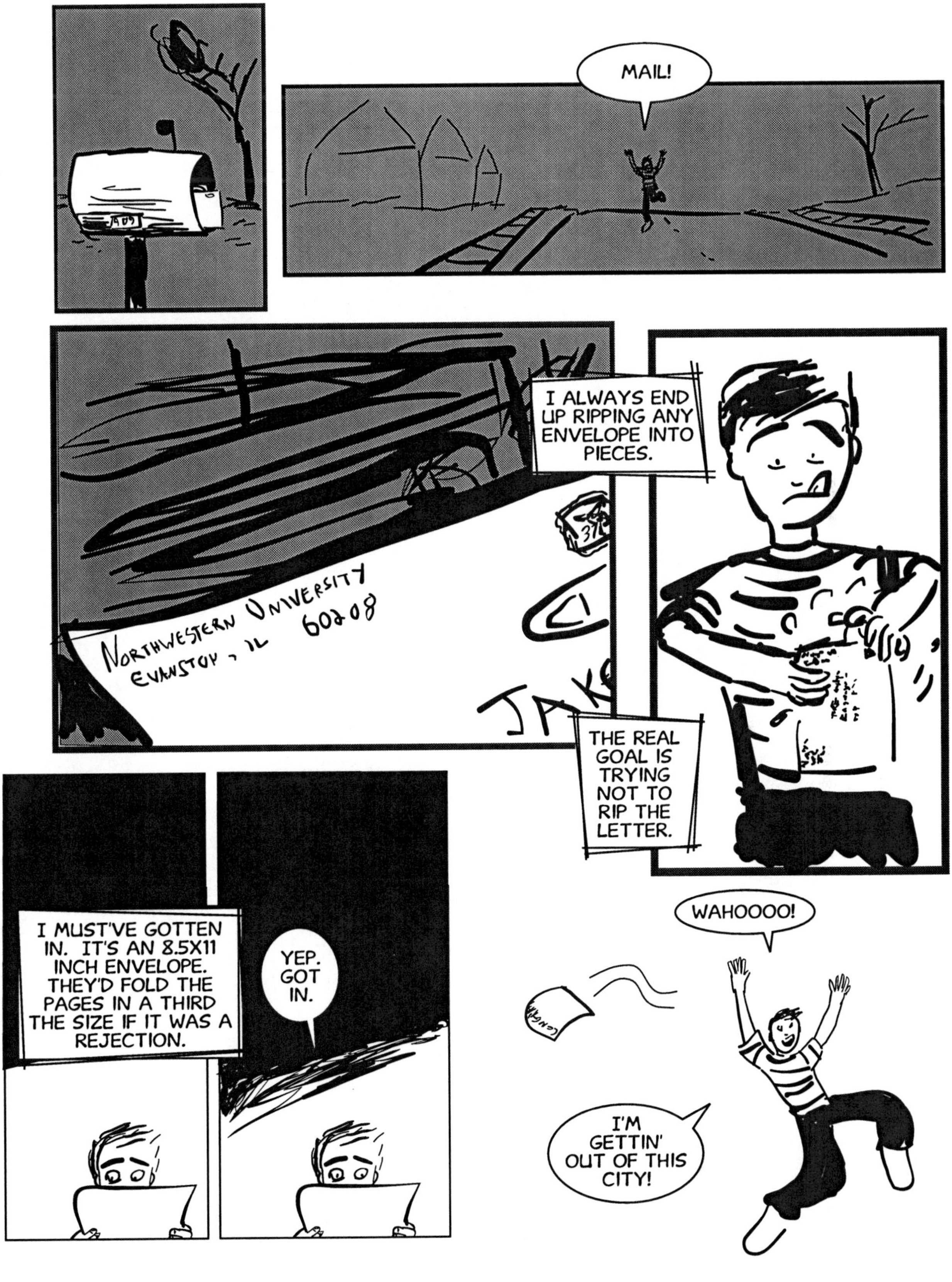
MAIL!
NORTHWESTERN UNIVERSITY
EVANSTON, IL 60208
I ALWAYS END UP RIPPING ANY ENVELOPE INTO PIECES.
THE REAL GOAL IS TRYING NOT TO RIP THE LETTER.
I MUST'VE GOTTEN IN. IT'S AN 8.5X11 INCH ENVELOPE. THEY'D FOLD THE PAGES IN A THIRD THE SIZE IF IT WAS A REJECTION.
YEP. GOT IN.
WAHOOOO!
I'M GETTIN' OUT OF THIS CITY!

News for the Illiterate.

Graphite Times

March 7th

Got news? Just yell it in the hallway. It'll get here eventually.

Making News Happen Since 2000

SUPER
#2 PENCIL

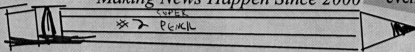

Teacher Report Cards

Every trimester every student gets a little piece of paper which lists the classes they took, the grade they got, and a little comment that was obviously some generic comment that the teachers choose to give by selecting a comment from a list of comments, like "Is good to have in class." (the best one I know has to be "Appears to need more sleep") Well anyway, it's long past time for the tables to be turned. Here they are, the grades. Not the student's grades, but the teacher's. And of course they get a little happy comment too.

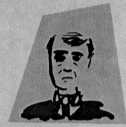

Principal Samson

D-

Needs to put the "pal" back in "Principal"

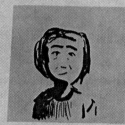

Miss Clark

B+

No comment..

Yeah, you'd rather have a bad comment than no comment at all.

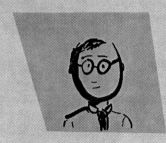

Mr. Yack

C-

Does not work well with others.

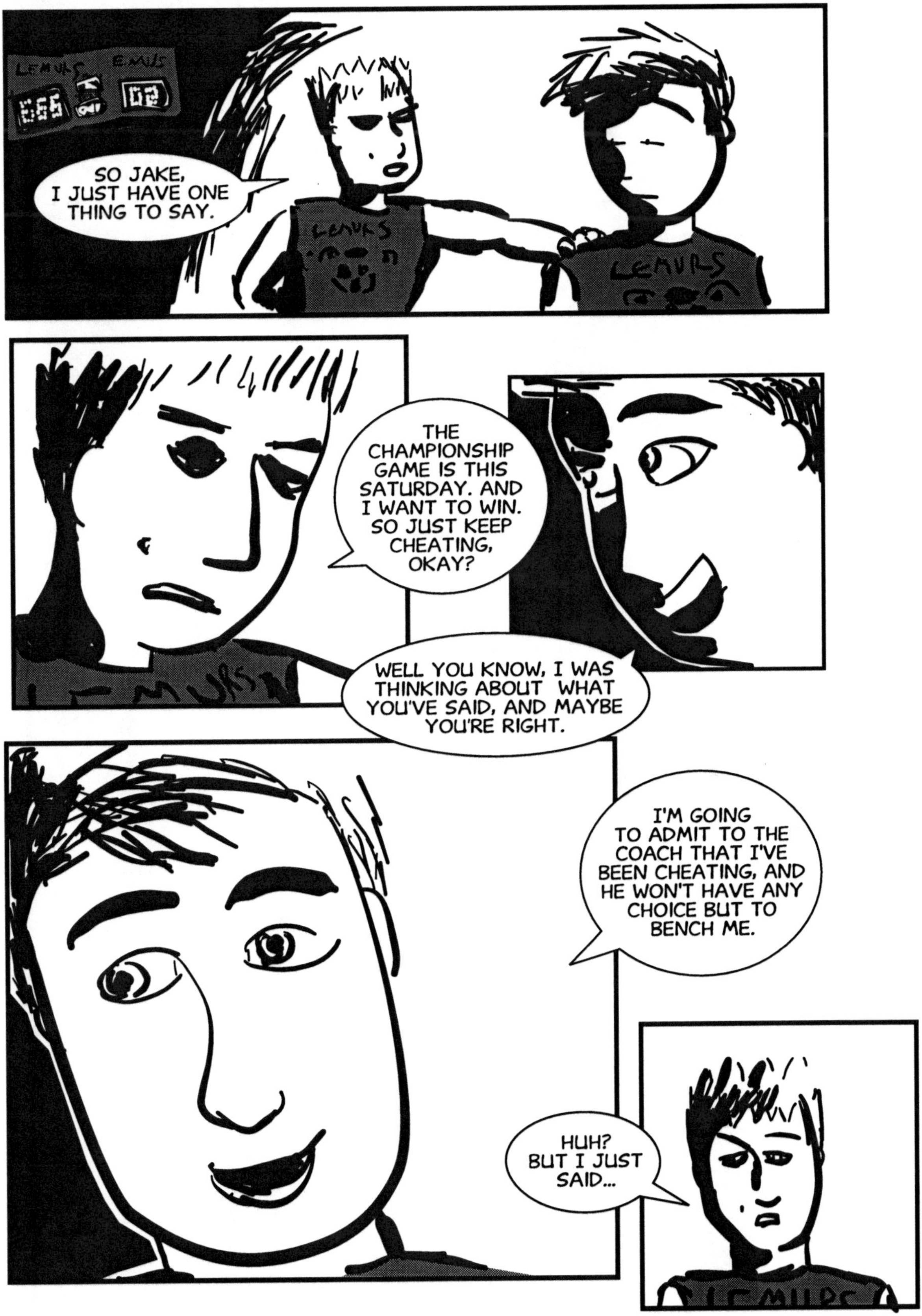
LEMURS EMUS
SO JAKE, I JUST HAVE ONE THING TO SAY.
LEMURS
LEMURS
THE CHAMPIONSHIP GAME IS THIS SATURDAY. AND I WANT TO WIN. SO JUST KEEP CHEATING, OKAY?
WELL YOU KNOW, I WAS THINKING ABOUT WHAT YOU'VE SAID, AND MAYBE YOU'RE RIGHT.
I'M GOING TO ADMIT TO THE COACH THAT I'VE BEEN CHEATING, AND HE WON'T HAVE ANY CHOICE BUT TO BENCH ME.
HUH? BUT I JUST SAID...

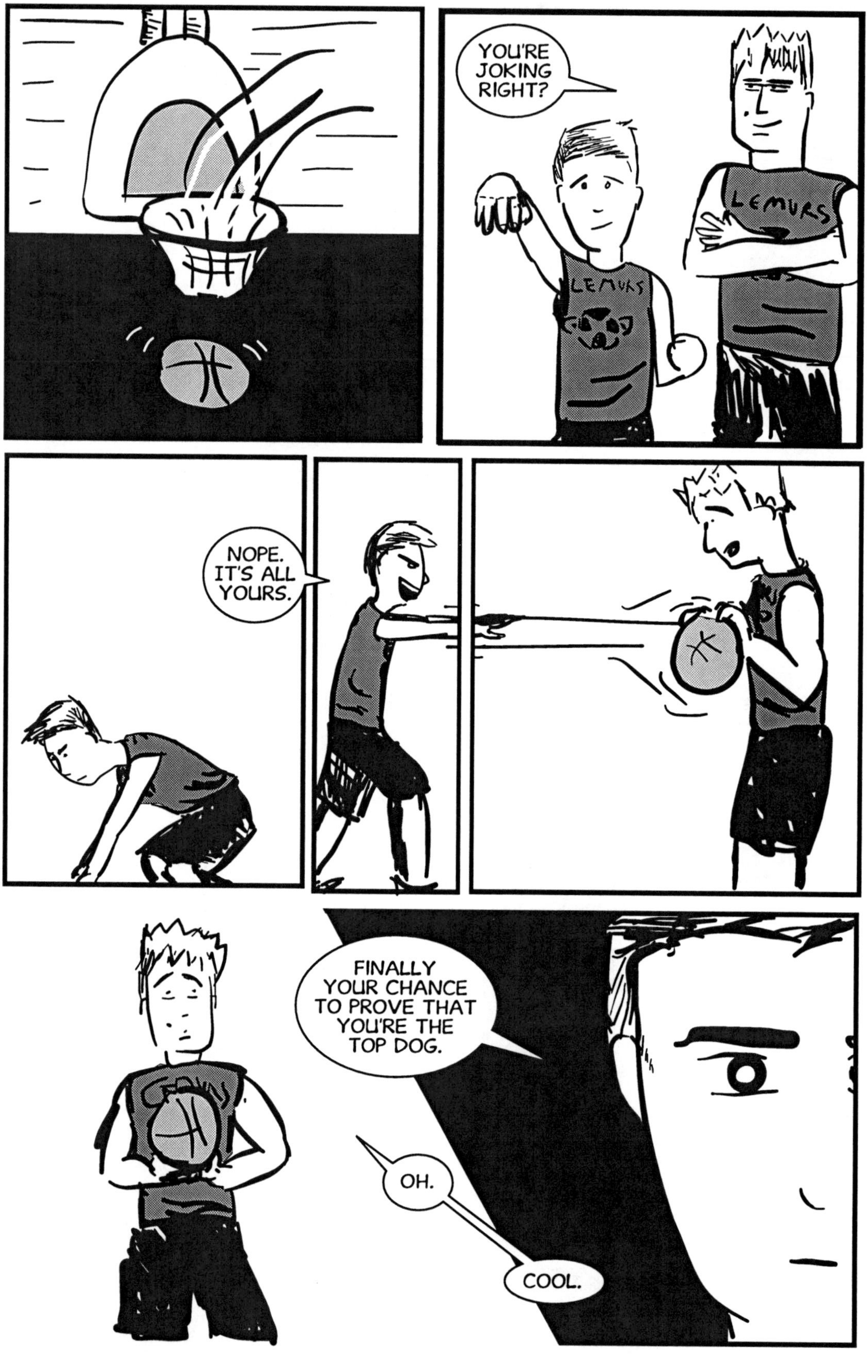
YOU'RE JOKING RIGHT?
LEMURS
NOPE. IT'S ALL YOURS.
FINALLY YOUR CHANCE TO PROVE THAT YOU'RE THE TOP DOG.
OH.
COOL.

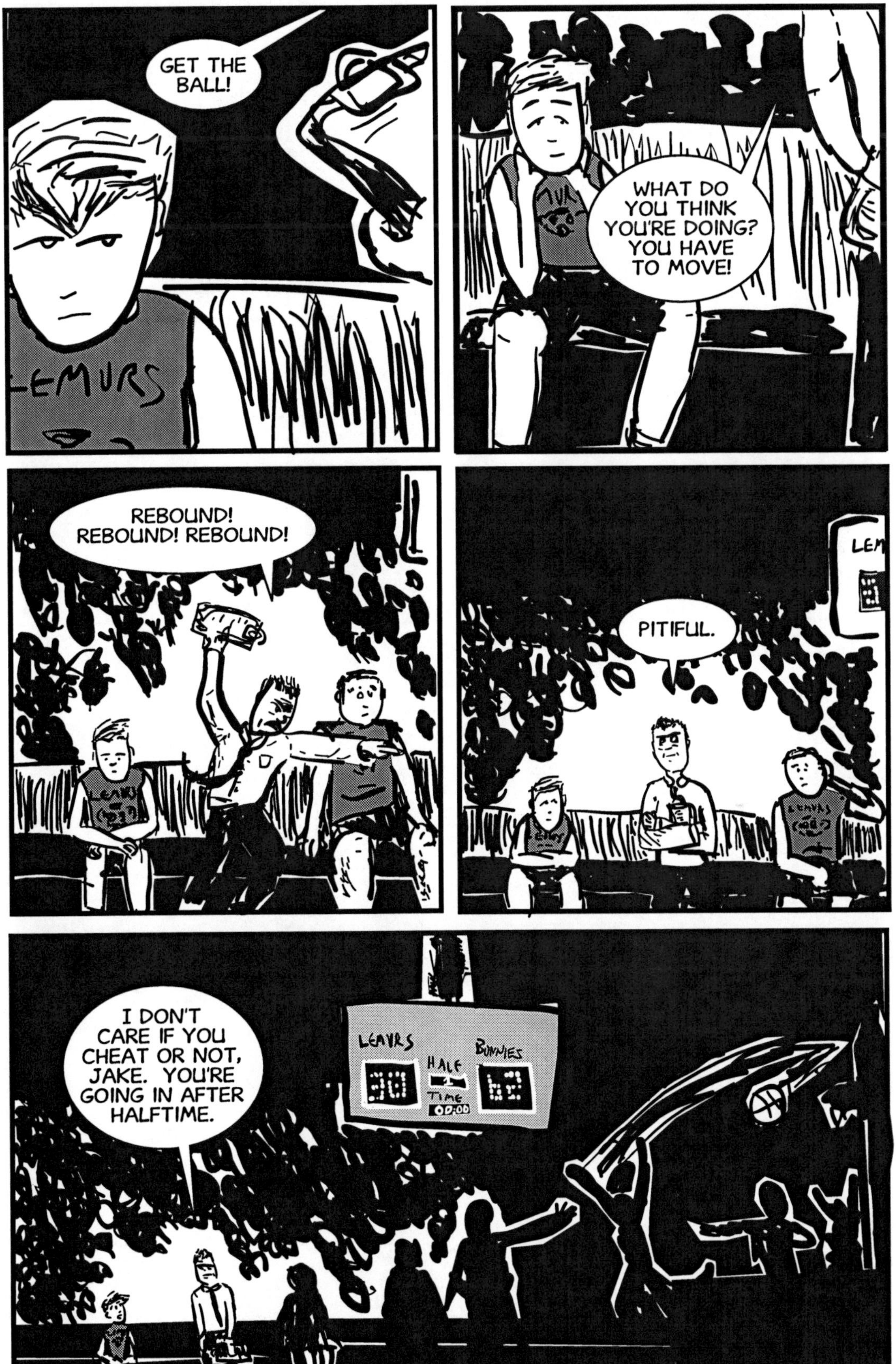
GET THE BALL!
WHAT DO YOU THINK YOU'RE DOING? YOU HAVE TO MOVE!
REBOUND! REBOUND! REBOUND!
PITIFUL.
LEMURS
BUNNIES
HALF
TIME
I DON'T CARE IF YOU CHEAT OR NOT, JAKE. YOU'RE GOING IN AFTER HALFTIME.

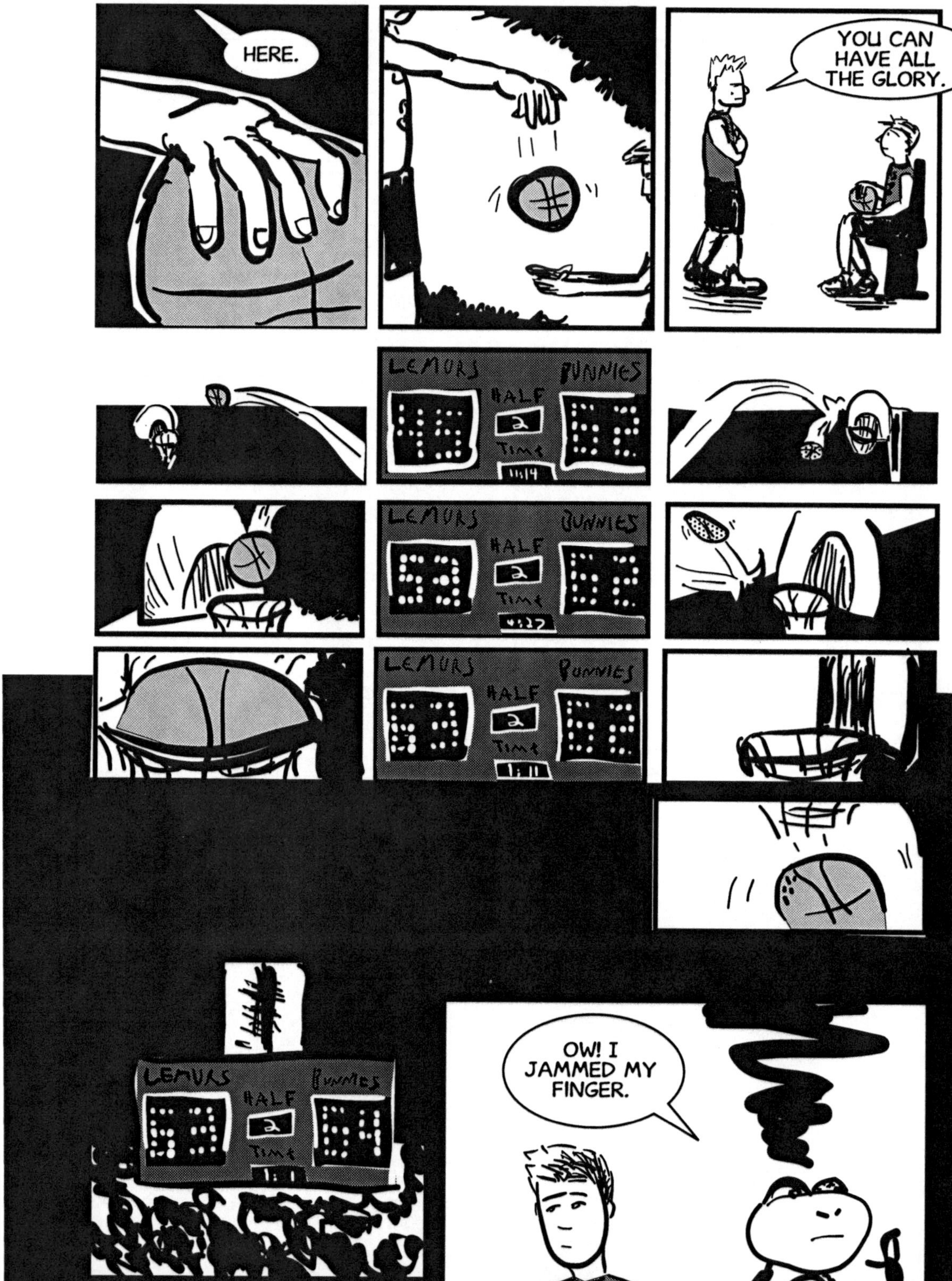
HERE.
YOU CAN HAVE ALL THE GLORY.
LEMURS
BUNNIES
HALF
OW! I JAMMED MY FINGER.
LEMURS

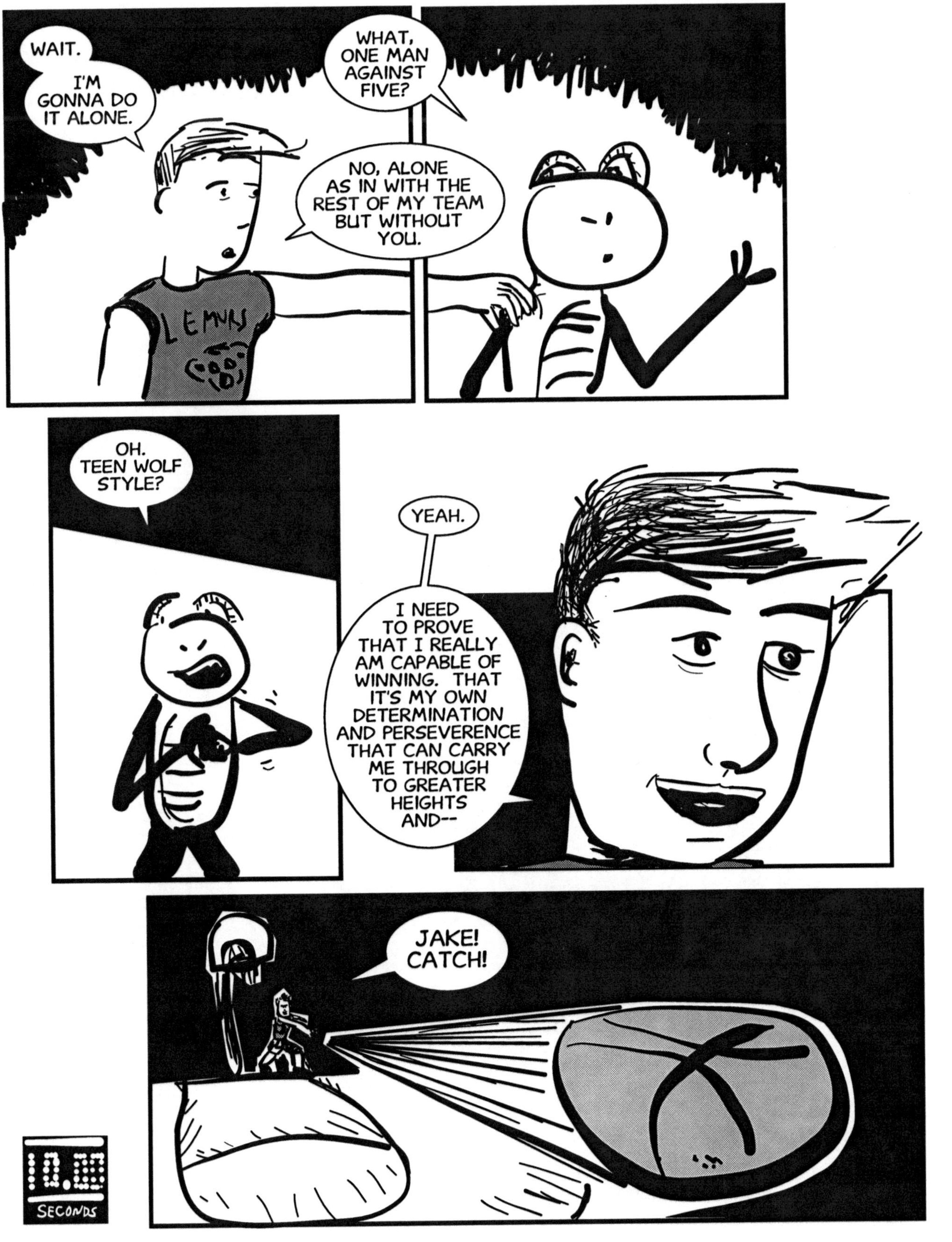
WAIT.
I'M GONNA DO IT ALONE.
WHAT, ONE MAN AGAINST FIVE?
NO, ALONE AS IN WITH THE REST OF MY TEAM BUT WITHOUT YOU.
OH. TEEN WOLF STYLE?
YEAH.
I NEED TO PROVE THAT I REALLY AM CAPABLE OF WINNING. THAT IT'S MY OWN DETERMINATION AND PERSEVERENCE THAT CAN CARRY ME THROUGH TO GREATER HEIGHTS AND--
JAKE! CATCH!
SECONDS

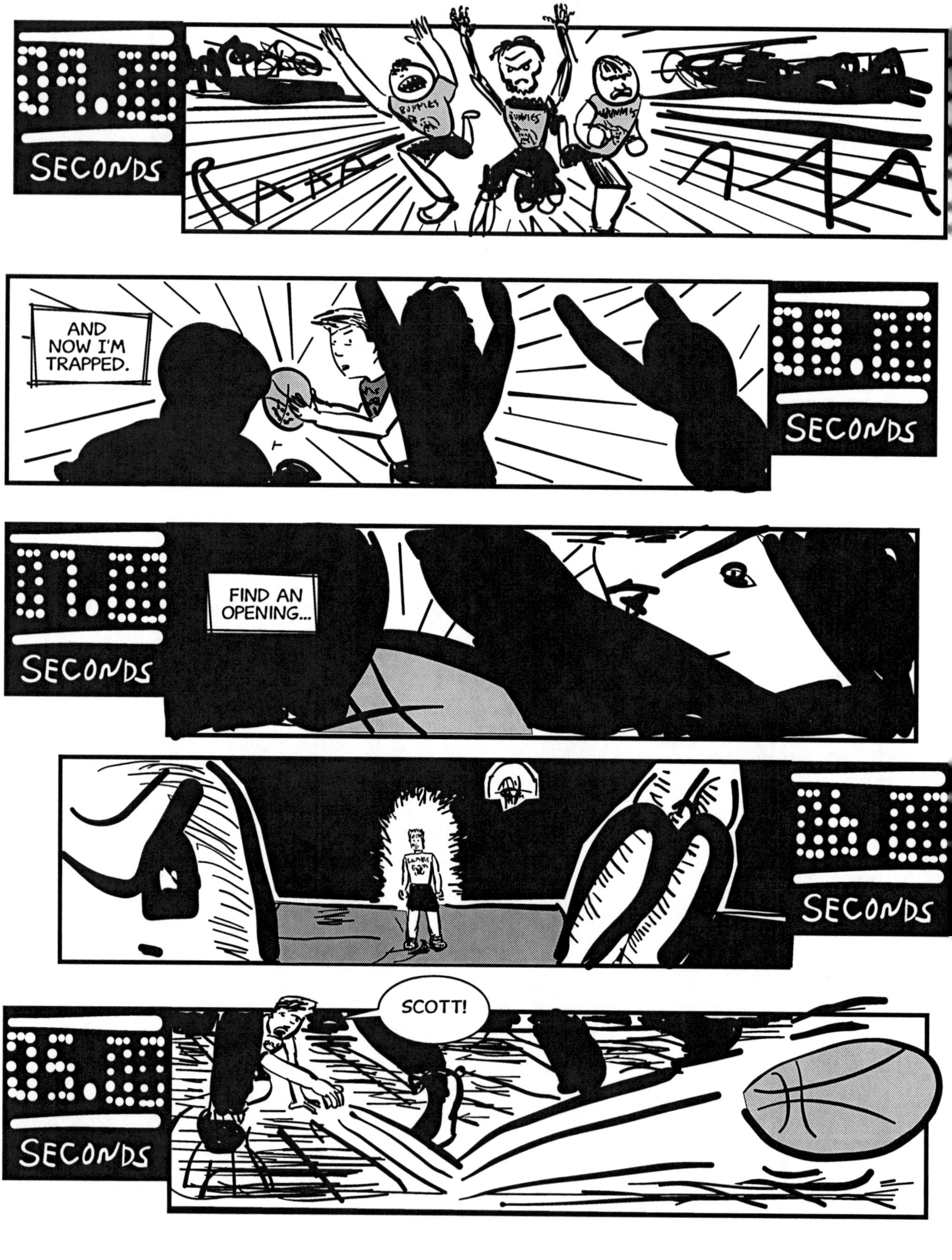
SECONDS
AND NOW I'M TRAPPED.
SECONDS
SECONDS
FIND AN OPENING...
SECONDS
SECONDS
SCOTT!

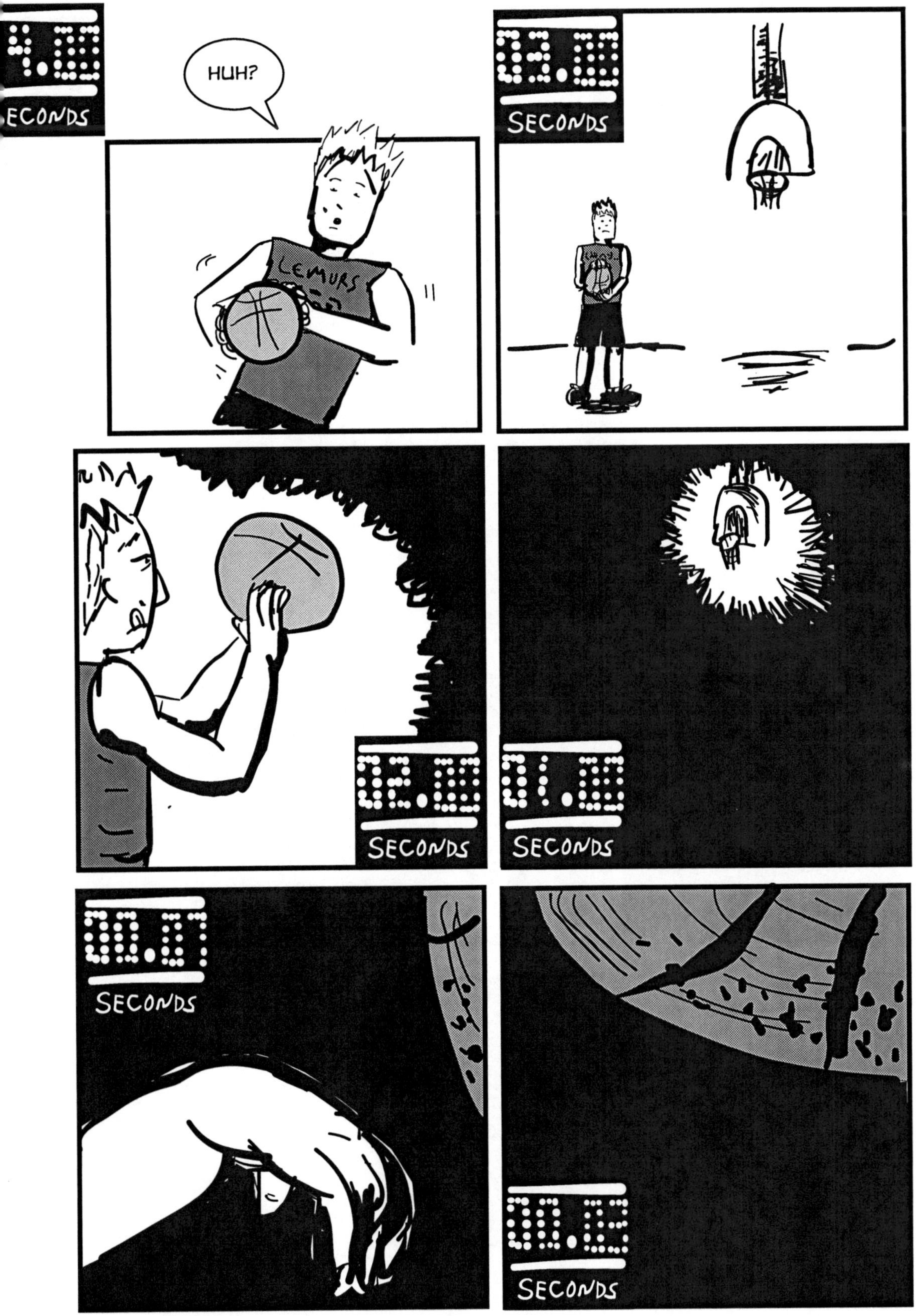
4.00
ECONDS
HUH?
LEMURS
03.00
SECONDS
02.00
SECONDS
01.00
SECONDS
00.07
SECONDS
00.03
SECONDS

SECONDS

BRRRING

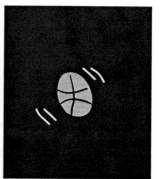

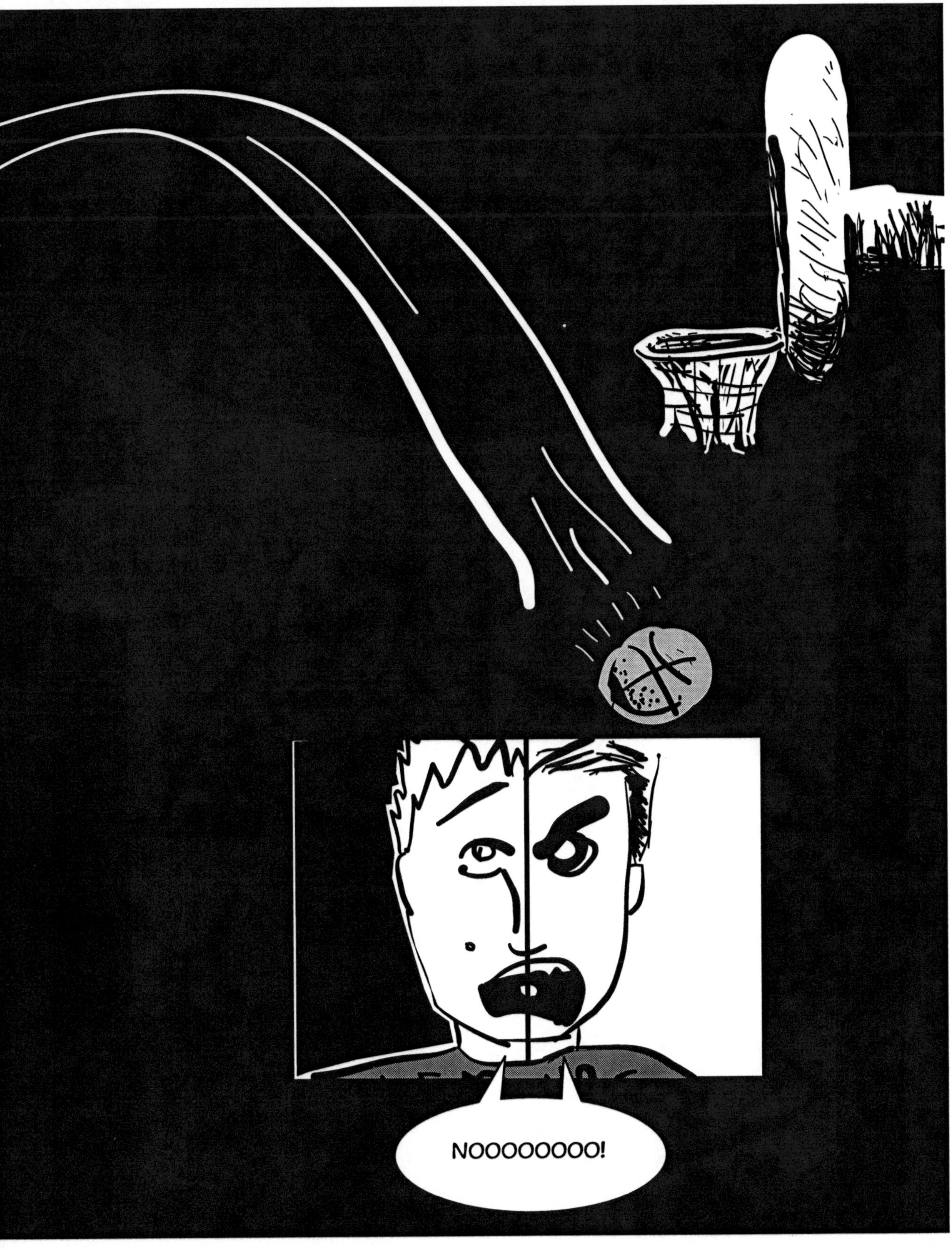
NOOOOOOOO!

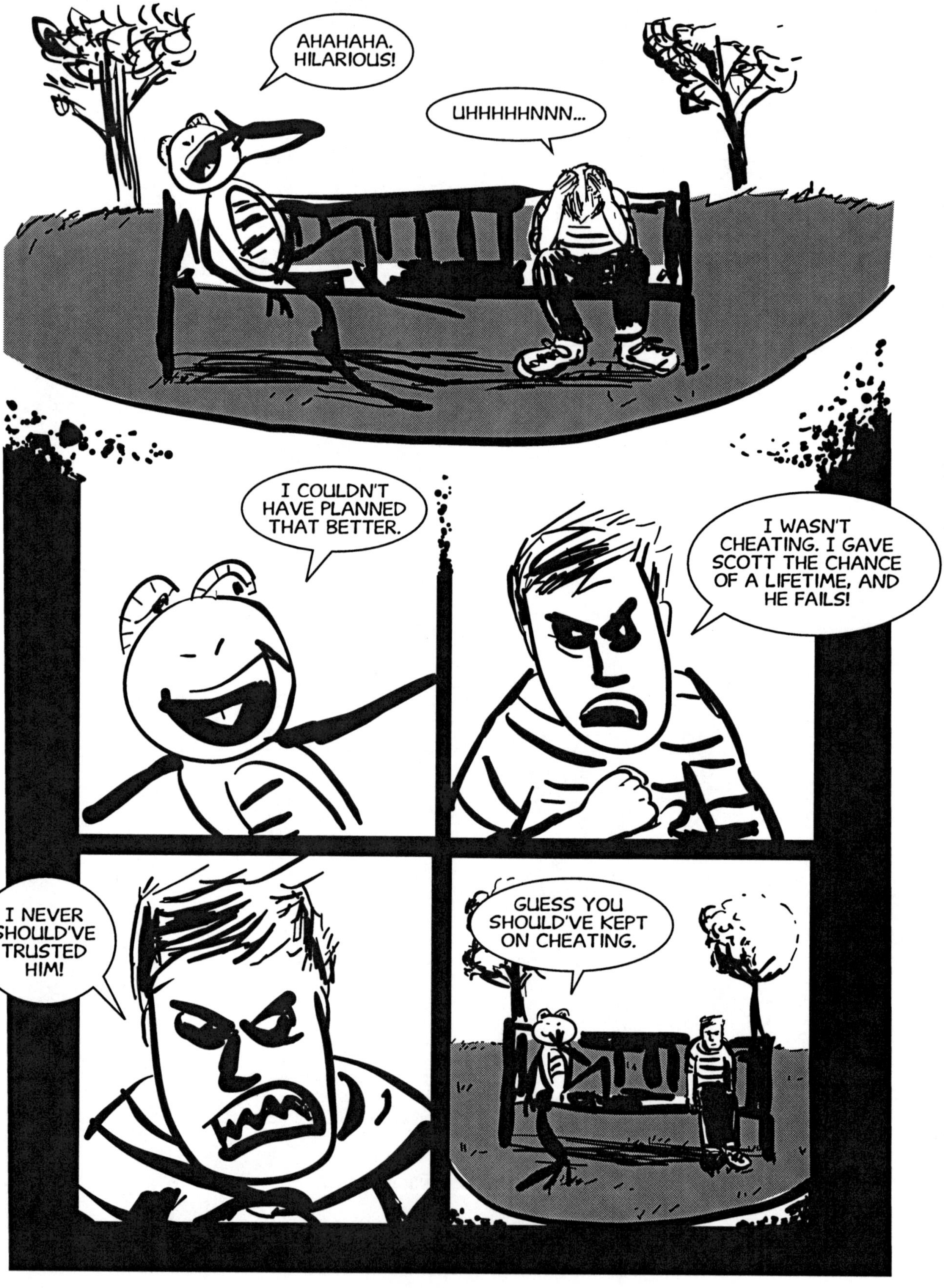
AHAHAHA. HILARIOUS!
UHHHHHNNN...
I COULDN'T HAVE PLANNED THAT BETTER.
I WASN'T CHEATING. I GAVE SCOTT THE CHANCE OF A LIFETIME, AND HE FAILS!
I NEVER SHOULD'VE TRUSTED HIM!
GUESS YOU SHOULD'VE KEPT ON CHEATING.

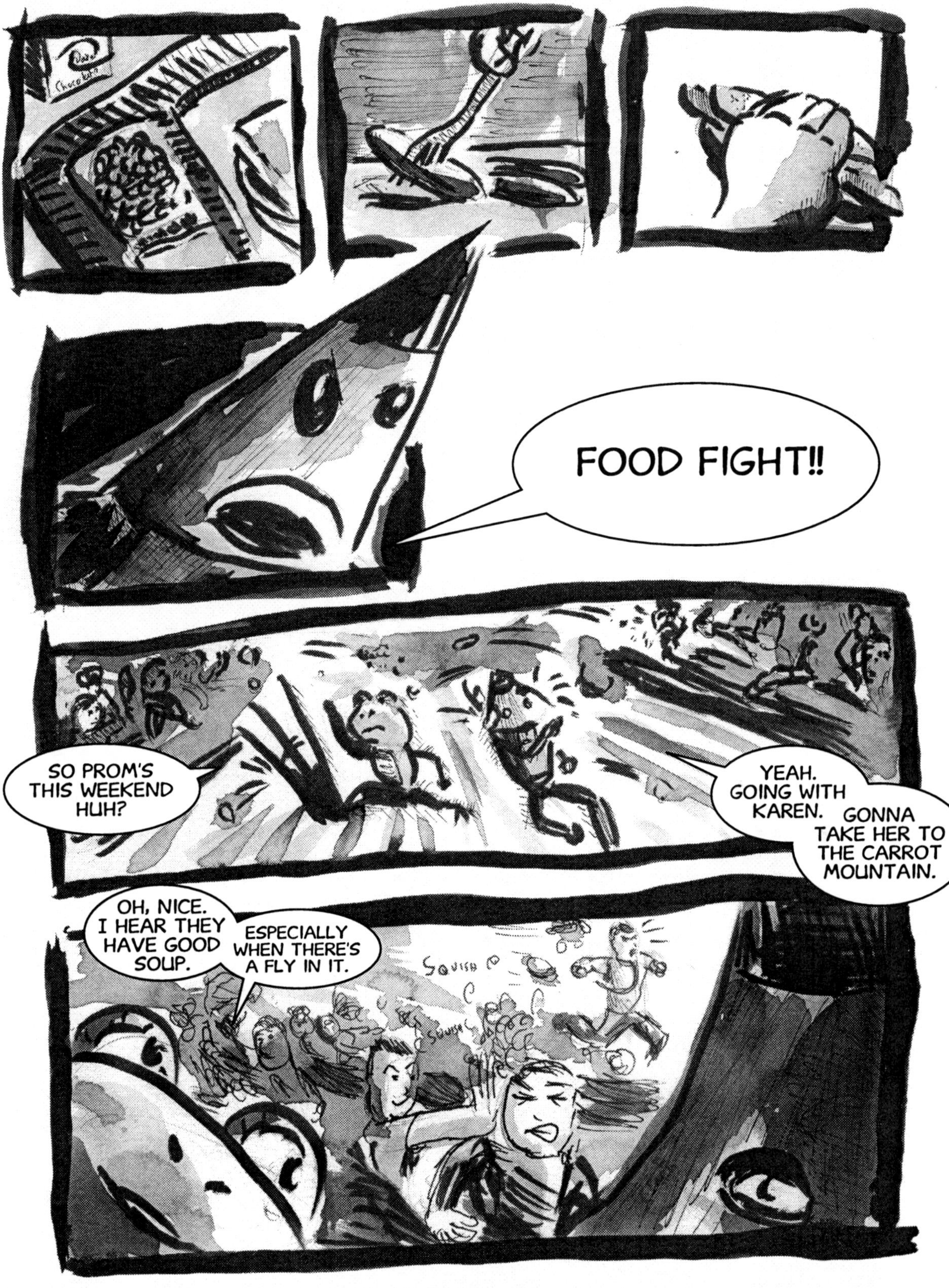
FOOD FIGHT!!
SO PROM'S THIS WEEKEND HUH?
YEAH. GOING WITH KAREN.
GONNA TAKE HER TO THE CARROT MOUNTAIN.
OH, NICE. I HEAR THEY HAVE GOOD SOUP.
ESPECIALLY WHEN THERE'S A FLY IN IT.

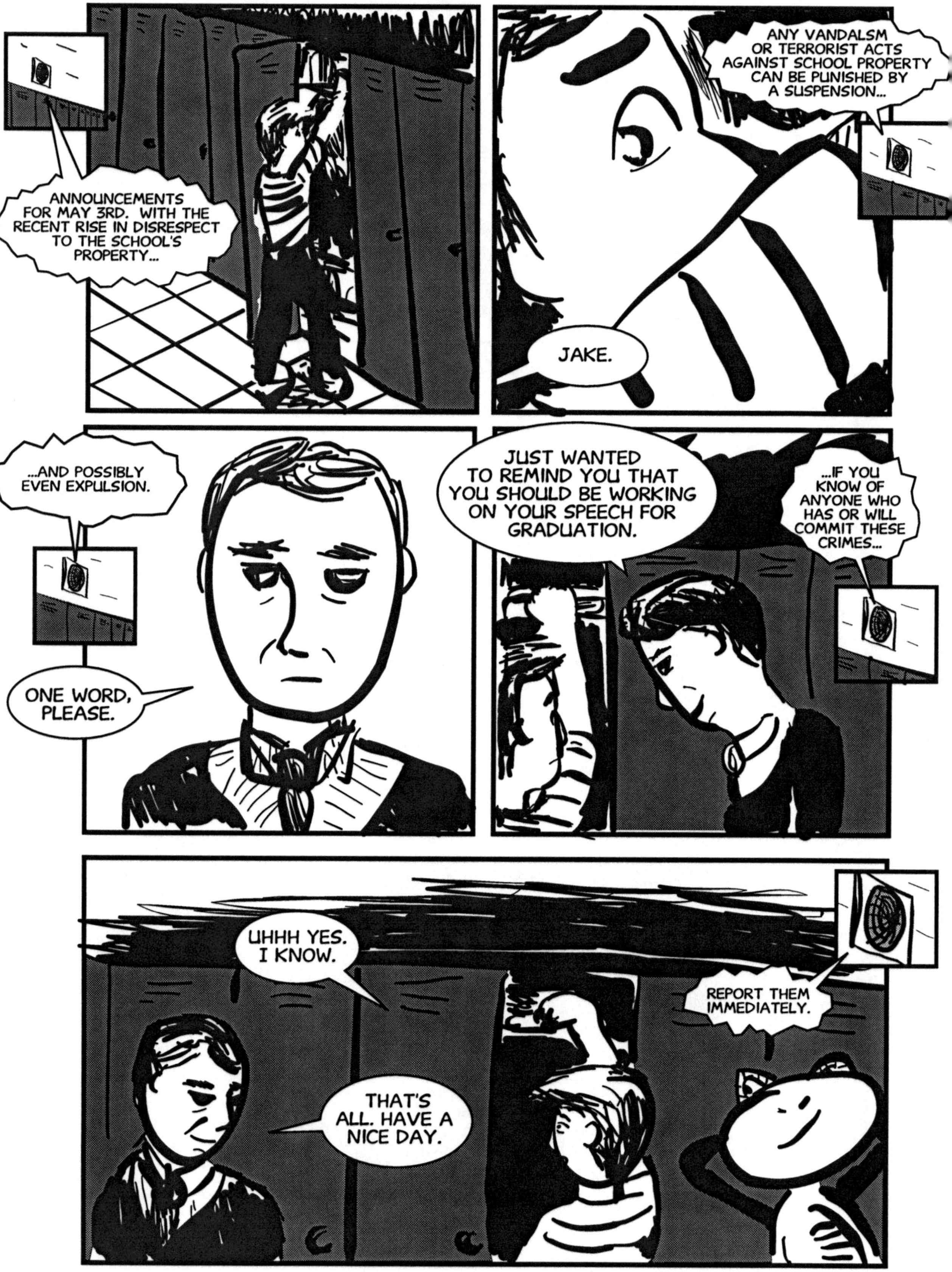
ANNOUNCEMENTS FOR MAY 3RD. WITH THE RECENT RISE IN DISRESPECT TO THE SCHOOL'S PROPERTY...
ANY VANDALSM OR TERRORIST ACTS AGAINST SCHOOL PROPERTY CAN BE PUNISHED BY A SUSPENSION...
JAKE.
...AND POSSIBLY EVEN EXPULSION.
ONE WORD, PLEASE.
JUST WANTED TO REMIND YOU THAT YOU SHOULD BE WORKING ON YOUR SPEECH FOR GRADUATION.
...IF YOU KNOW OF ANYONE WHO HAS OR WILL COMMIT THESE CRIMES...
UHHH YES. I KNOW.
REPORT THEM IMMEDIATELY.
THAT'S ALL. HAVE A NICE DAY.

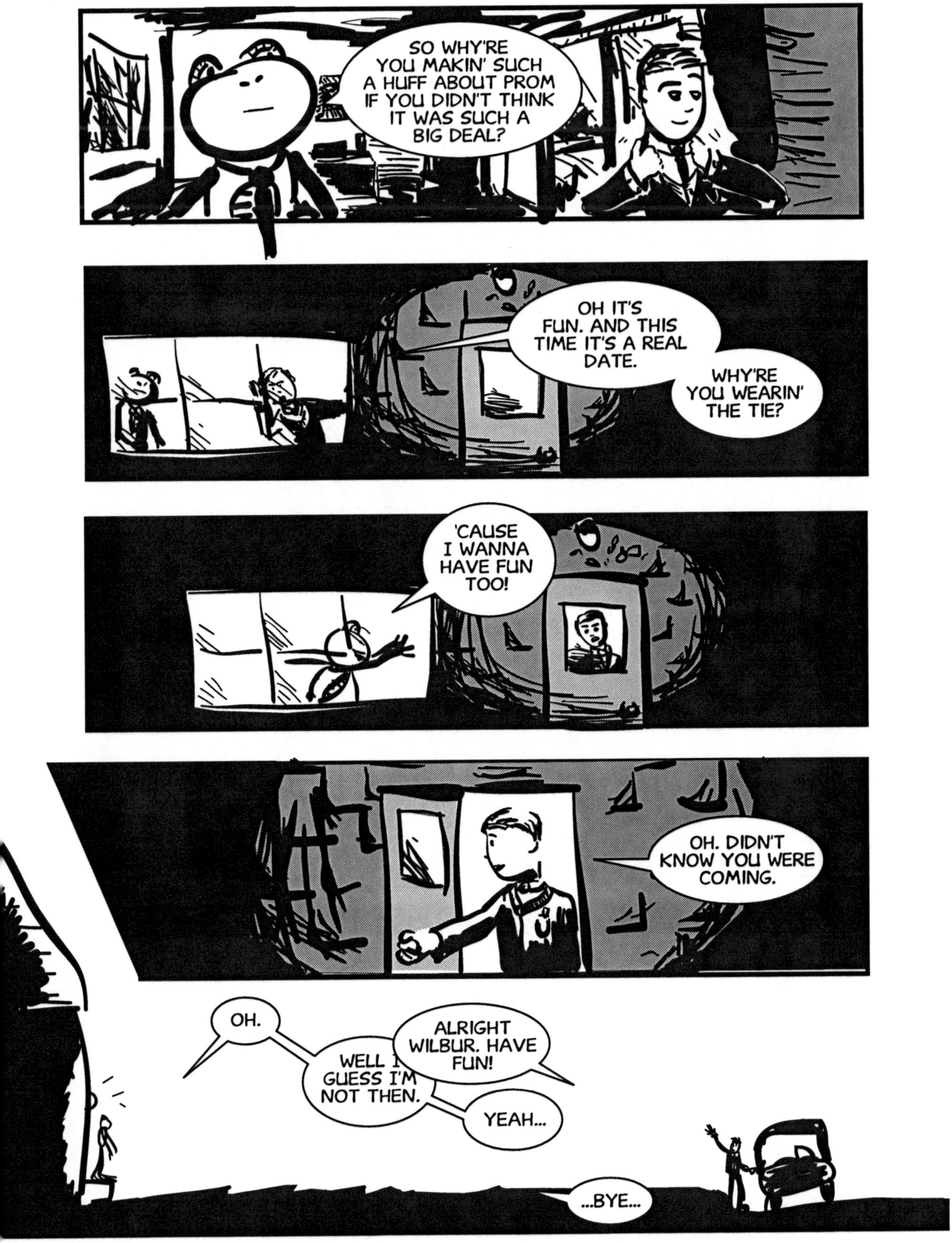
SO WHY'RE YOU MAKIN' SUCH A HUFF ABOUT PROM IF YOU DIDN'T THINK IT WAS SUCH A BIG DEAL?
OH IT'S FUN. AND THIS TIME IT'S A REAL DATE.
WHY'RE YOU WEARIN' THE TIE?
'CAUSE I WANNA HAVE FUN TOO!
OH. DIDN'T KNOW YOU WERE COMING.
OH.
WELL I GUESS I'M NOT THEN.
ALRIGHT WILBUR. HAVE FUN!
YEAH...
...BYE...

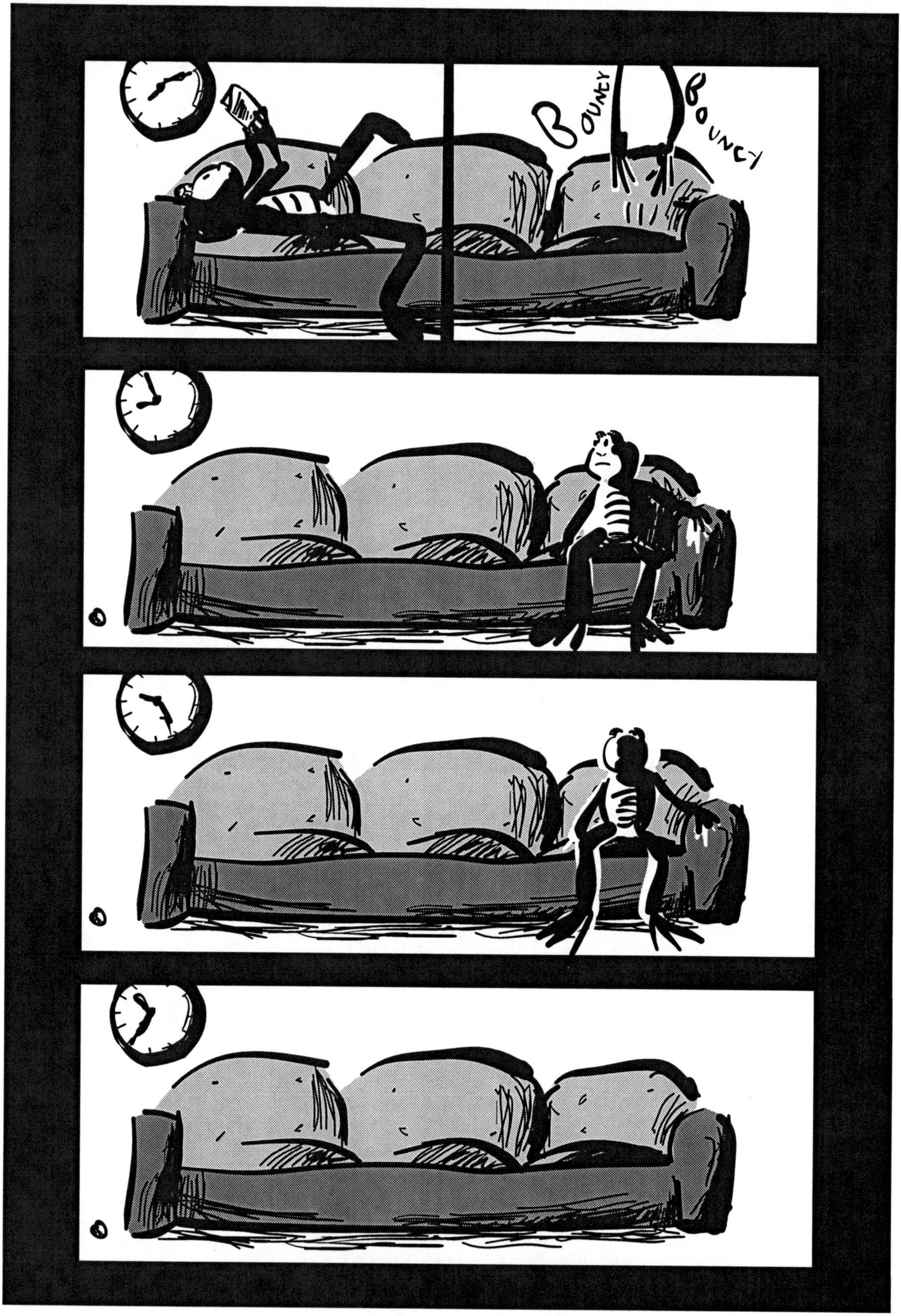
BOUNCY
BOUNCY

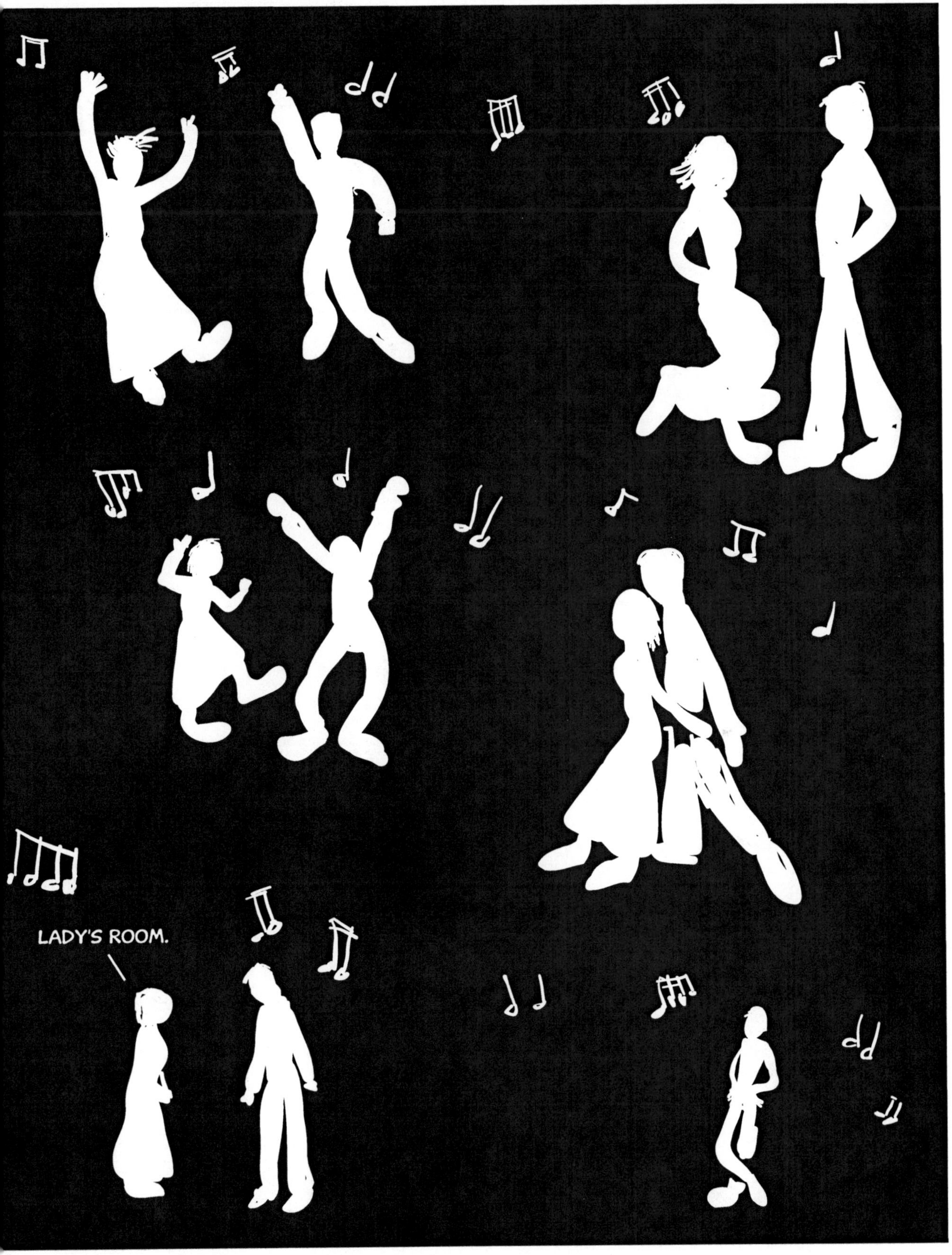
LADY'S ROOM.

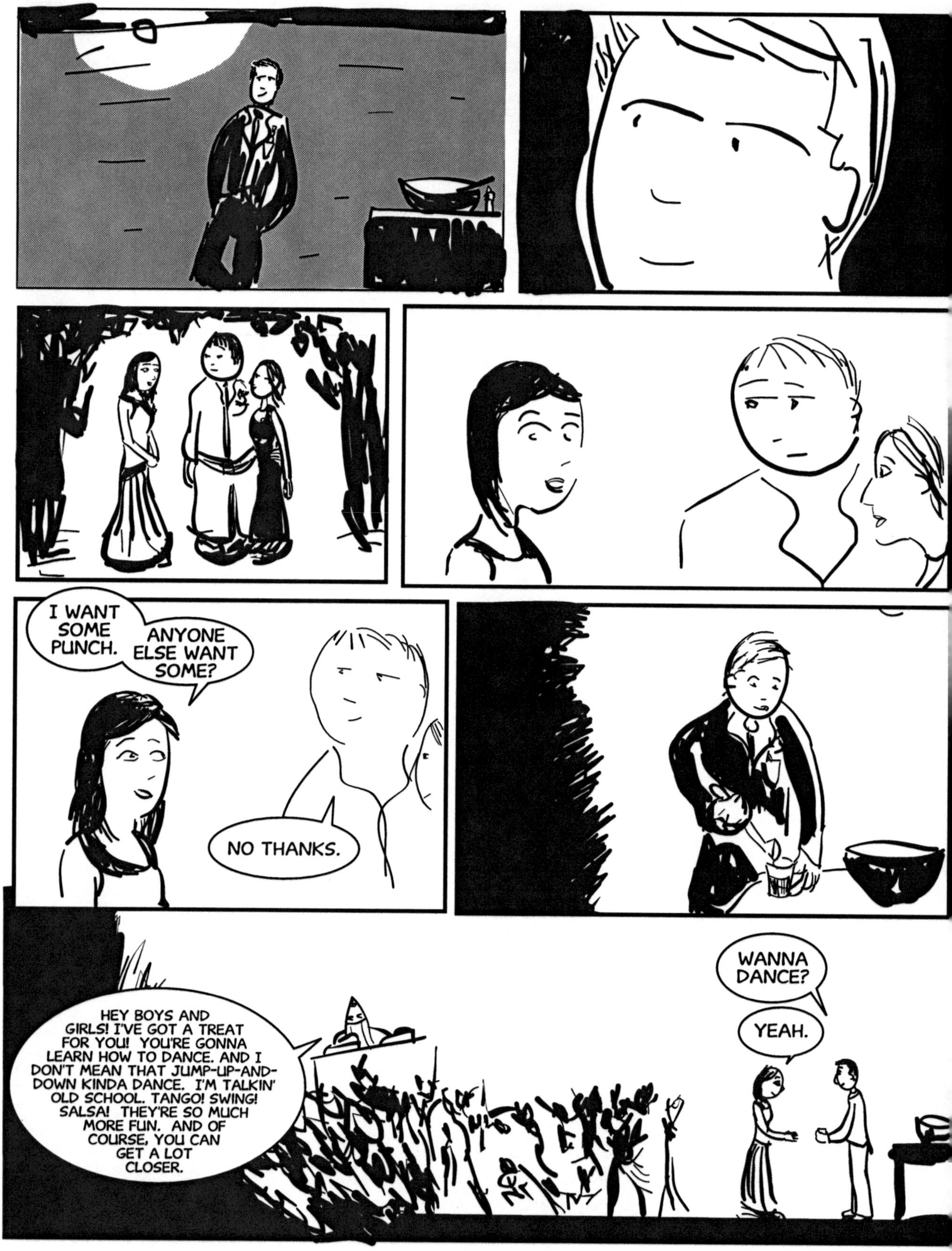
I WANT SOME PUNCH.
ANYONE ELSE WANT SOME?
NO THANKS.
HEY BOYS AND GIRLS! I'VE GOT A TREAT FOR YOU! YOU'RE GONNA LEARN HOW TO DANCE. AND I DON'T MEAN THAT JUMP-UP-AND-DOWN KINDA DANCE. I'M TALKIN' OLD SCHOOL. TANGO! SWING! SALSA! THEY'RE SO MUCH MORE FUN. AND OF COURSE, YOU CAN GET A LOT CLOSER.
WANNA DANCE?
YEAH.

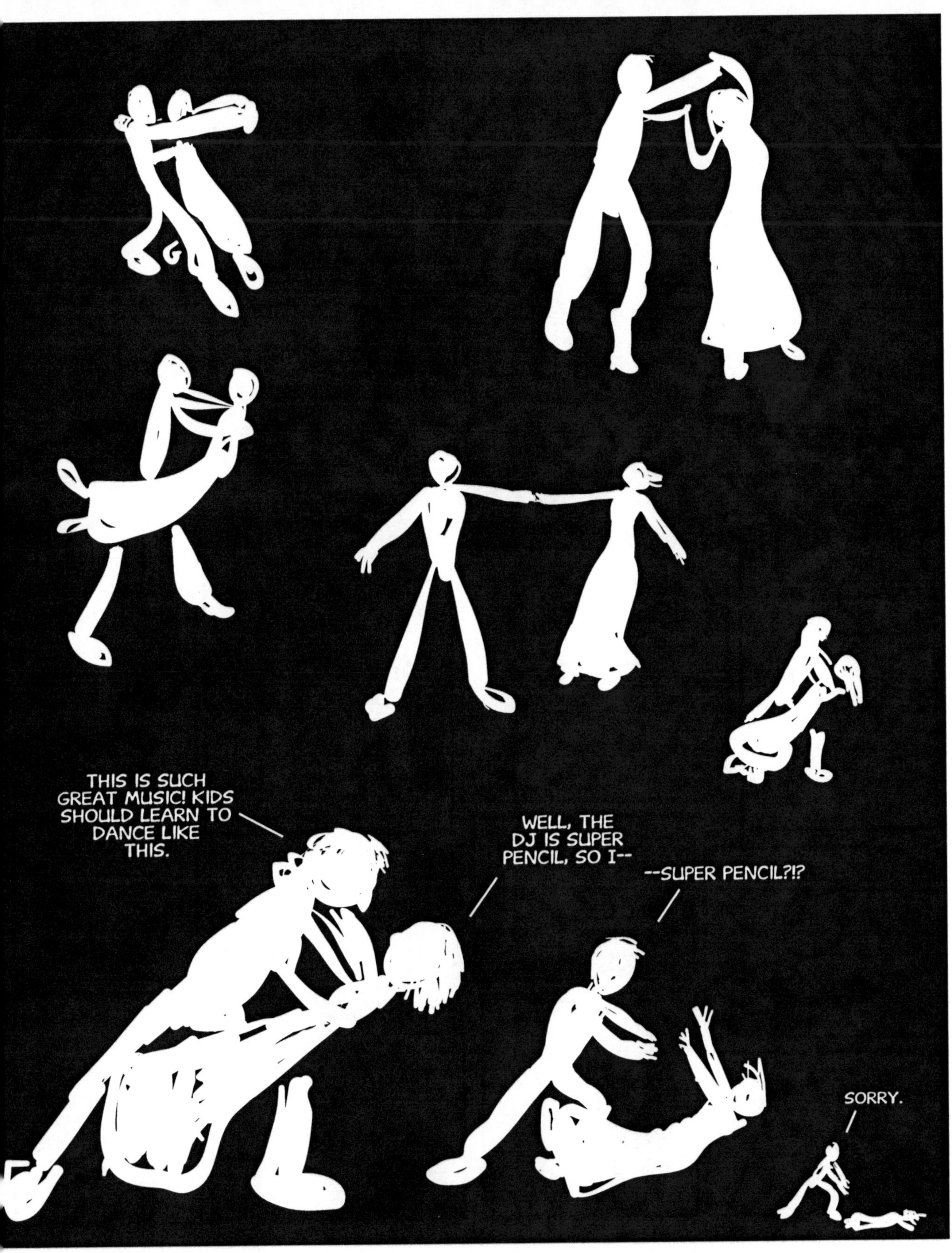
THIS IS SUCH GREAT MUSIC! KIDS SHOULD LEARN TO DANCE LIKE THIS.
WELL, THE DJ IS SUPER PENCIL, SO I--
--SUPER PENCIL?!?
SORRY.

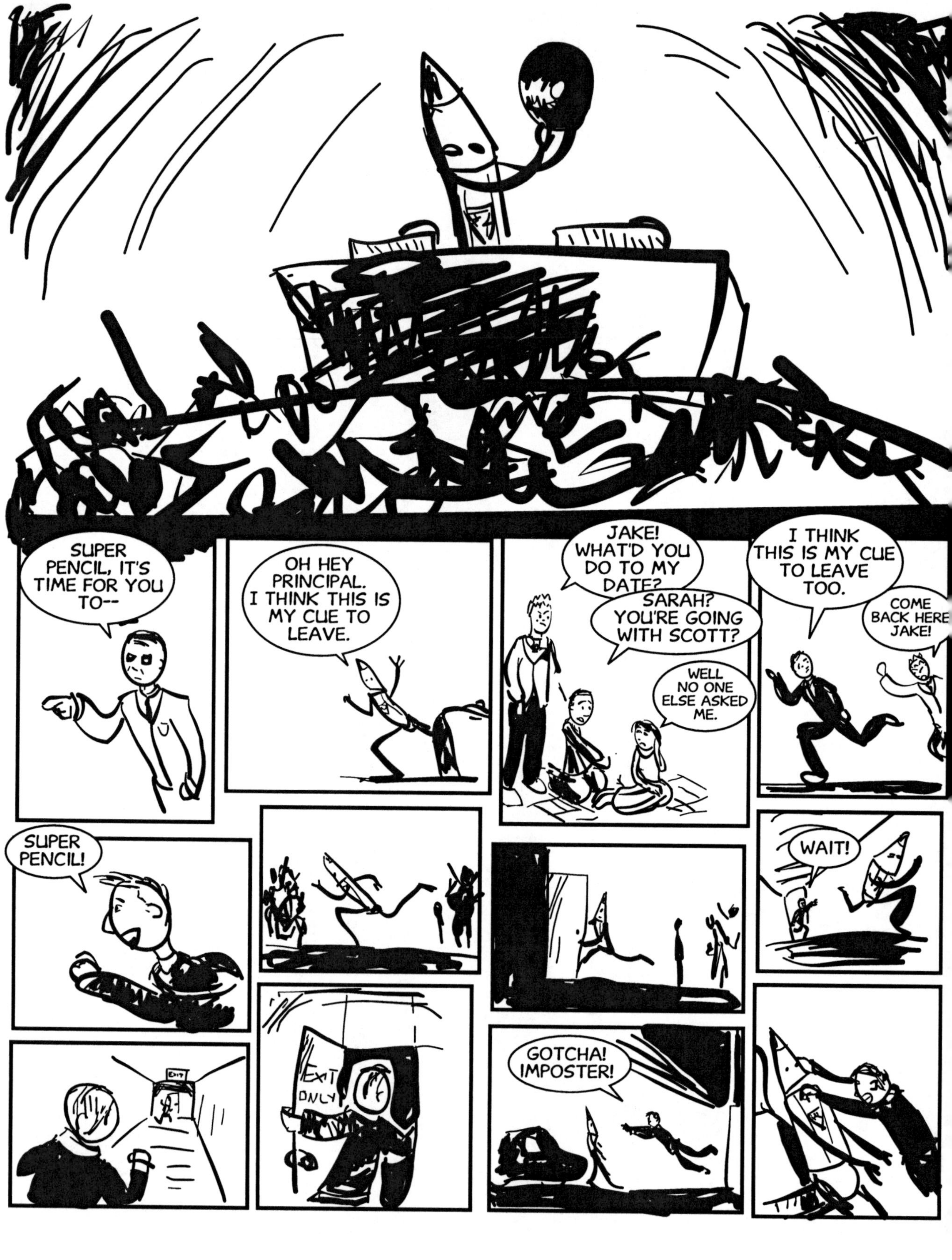
SUPER PENCIL, IT'S TIME FOR YOU TO--
OH HEY PRINCIPAL. I THINK THIS IS MY CUE TO LEAVE.
JAKE! WHAT'D YOU DO TO MY DATE?
SARAH? YOU'RE GOING WITH SCOTT?
WELL NO ONE ELSE ASKED ME.
I THINK THIS IS MY CUE TO LEAVE TOO.
COME BACK HERE JAKE!
SUPER PENCIL!
WAIT!
EXIT
EXIT ONLY
GOTCHA! IMPOSTER!

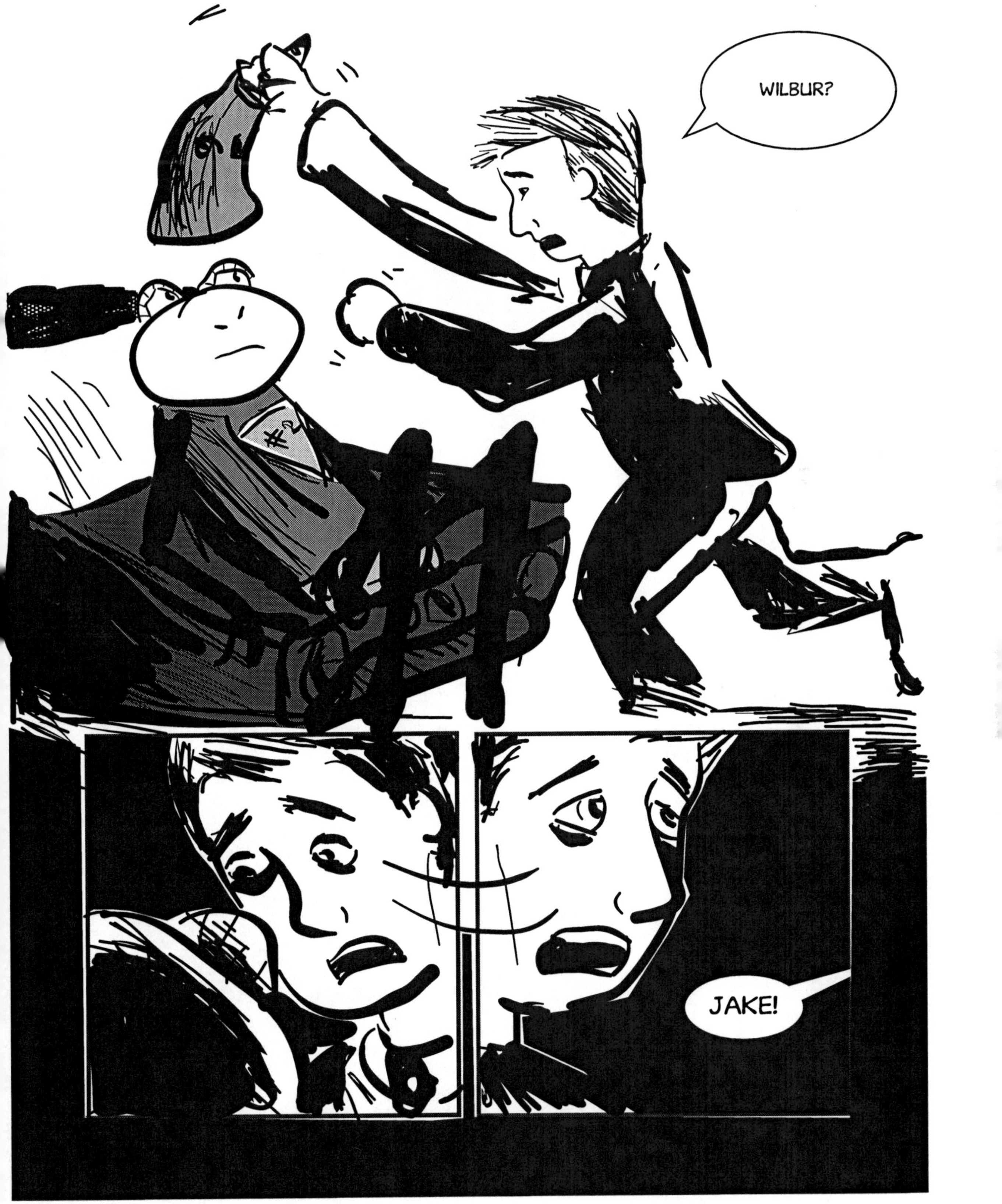
WILBUR?
JAKE!

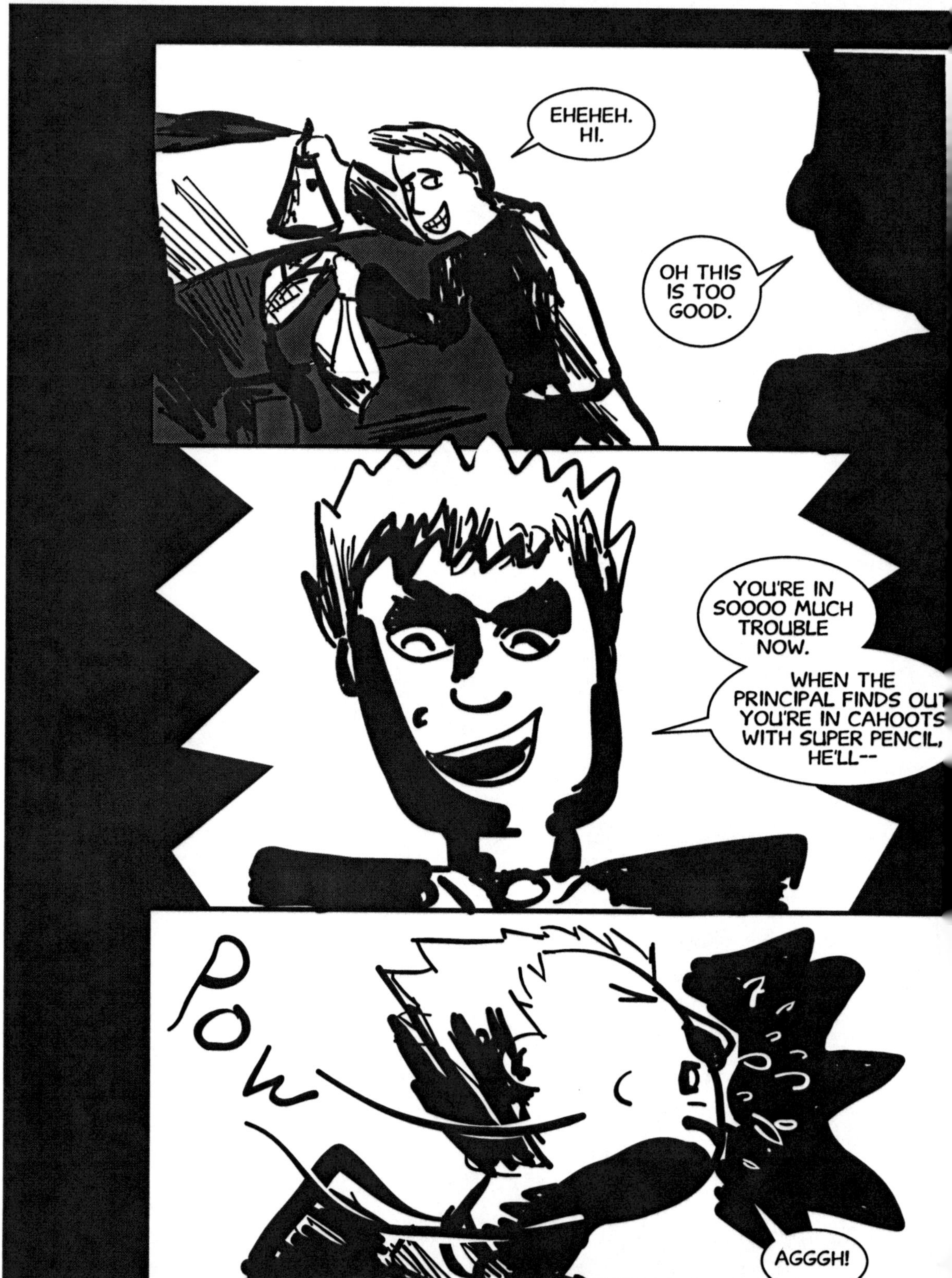

EHEHEH. HI.
OH THIS IS TOO GOOD.
YOU'RE IN SOOOO MUCH TROUBLE NOW.
WHEN THE PRINCIPAL FINDS OUT YOU'RE IN CAHOOTS WITH SUPER PENCIL, HE'LL--
POW
AGGGH!

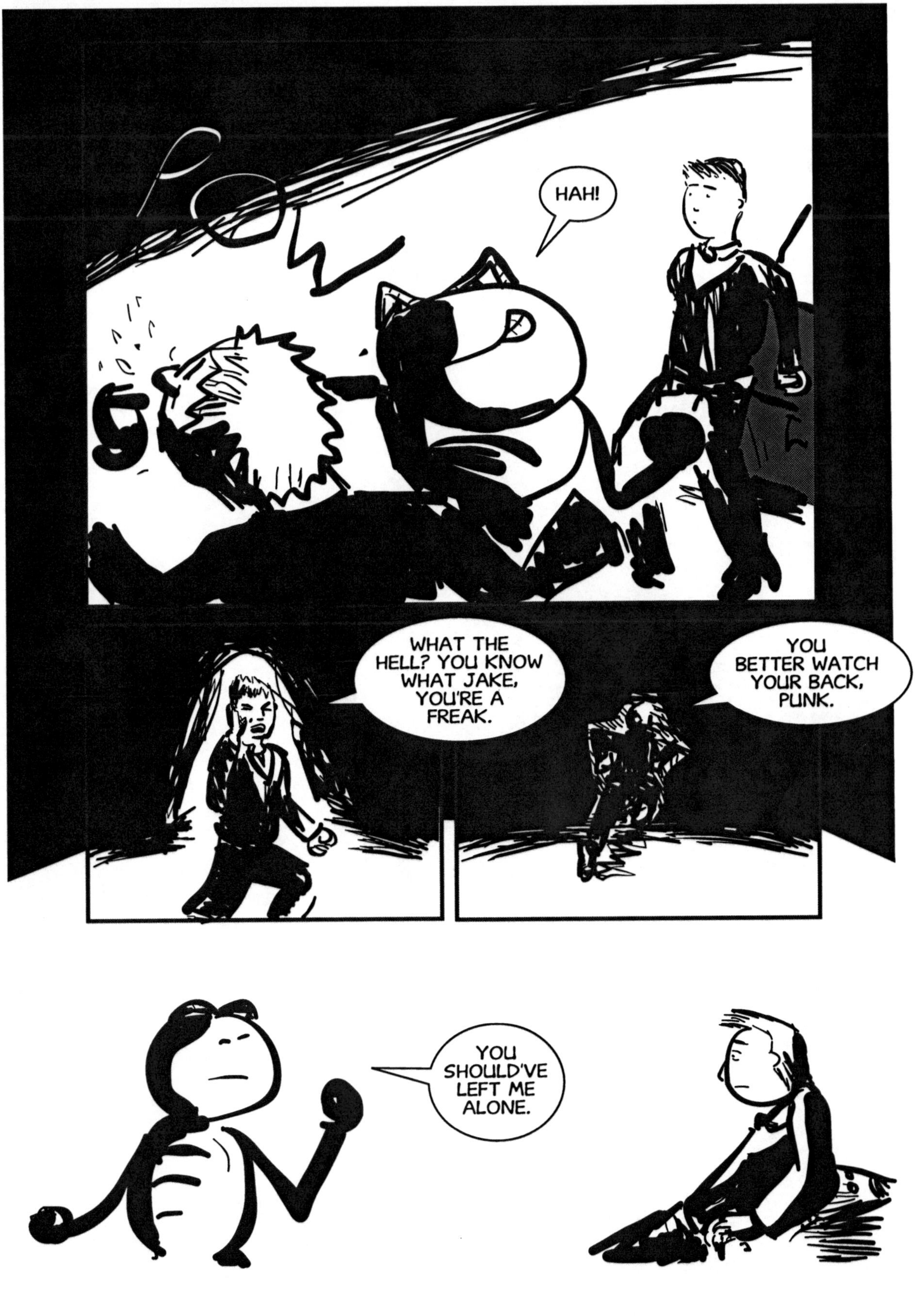
POW
HAH!
WHAT THE HELL? YOU KNOW WHAT JAKE, YOU'RE A FREAK.
YOU BETTER WATCH YOUR BACK, PUNK.
YOU SHOULD'VE LEFT ME ALONE.

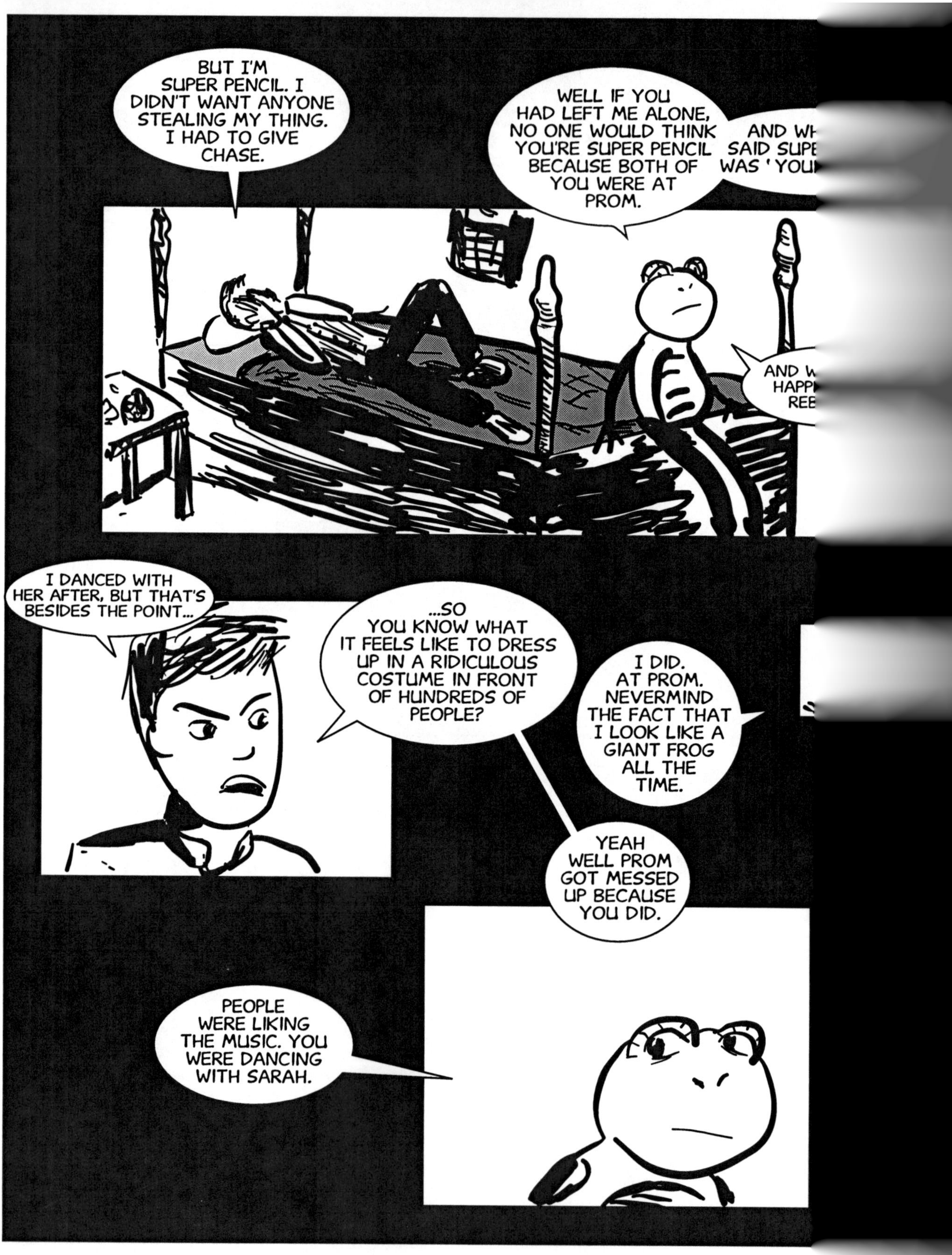
BUT I'M SUPER PENCIL. I DIDN'T WANT ANYONE STEALING MY THING. I HAD TO GIVE CHASE.
WELL IF YOU HAD LEFT ME ALONE, NO ONE WOULD THINK YOU'RE SUPER PENCIL BECAUSE BOTH OF YOU WERE AT PROM.
I DANCED WITH HER AFTER, BUT THAT'S BESIDES THE POINT...
...SO YOU KNOW WHAT IT FEELS LIKE TO DRESS UP IN A RIDICULOUS COSTUME IN FRONT OF HUNDREDS OF PEOPLE?
I DID. AT PROM. NEVERMIND THE FACT THAT I LOOK LIKE A GIANT FROG ALL THE TIME.
YEAH WELL PROM GOT MESSED UP BECAUSE YOU DID.
PEOPLE WERE LIKING THE MUSIC. YOU WERE DANCING WITH SARAH.

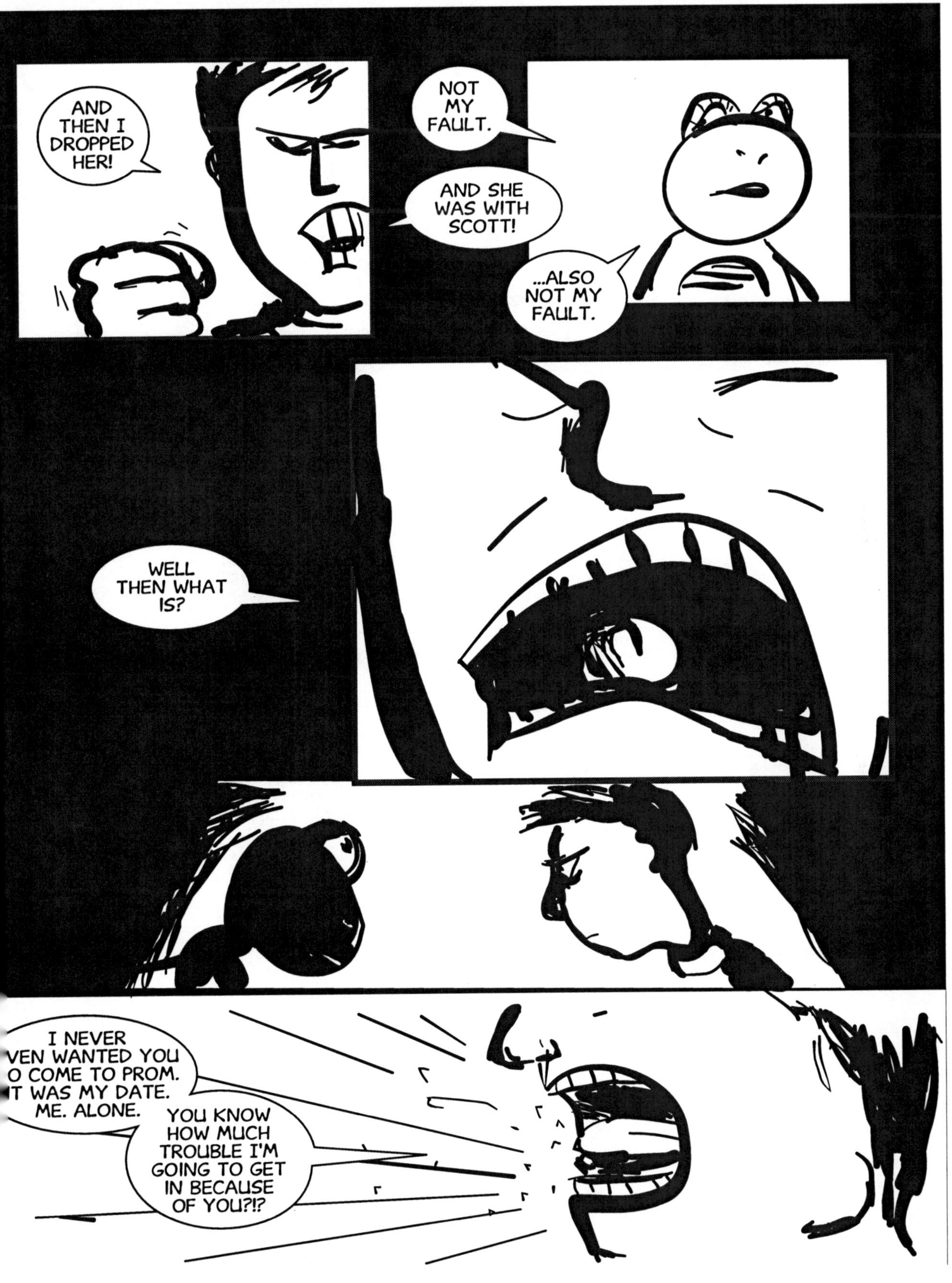

AND THEN I DROPPED HER!
NOT MY FAULT.
AND SHE WAS WITH SCOTT!
...ALSO NOT MY FAULT.
WELL THEN WHAT IS?
I NEVER
VEN WANTED YOU
O COME TO PROM.
T WAS MY DATE.
ME. ALONE.
YOU KNOW HOW MUCH TROUBLE I'M GOING TO GET IN BECAUSE OF YOU?!?

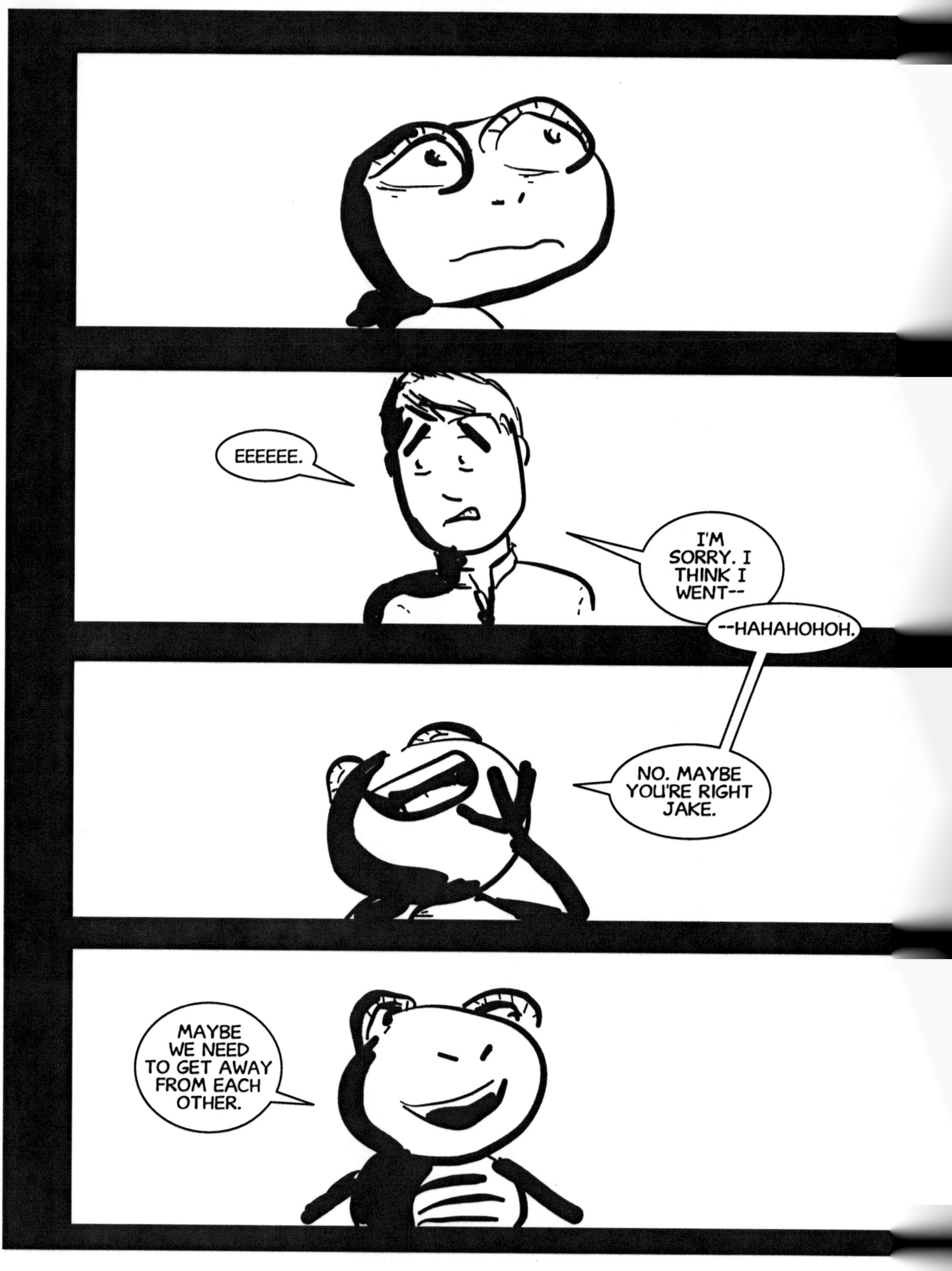
EEEEEE.
I'M SORRY. I THINK I WENT--
--HAHAHOHOH.
NO. MAYBE YOU'RE RIGHT JAKE.
MAYBE WE NEED TO GET AWAY FROM EACH OTHER.

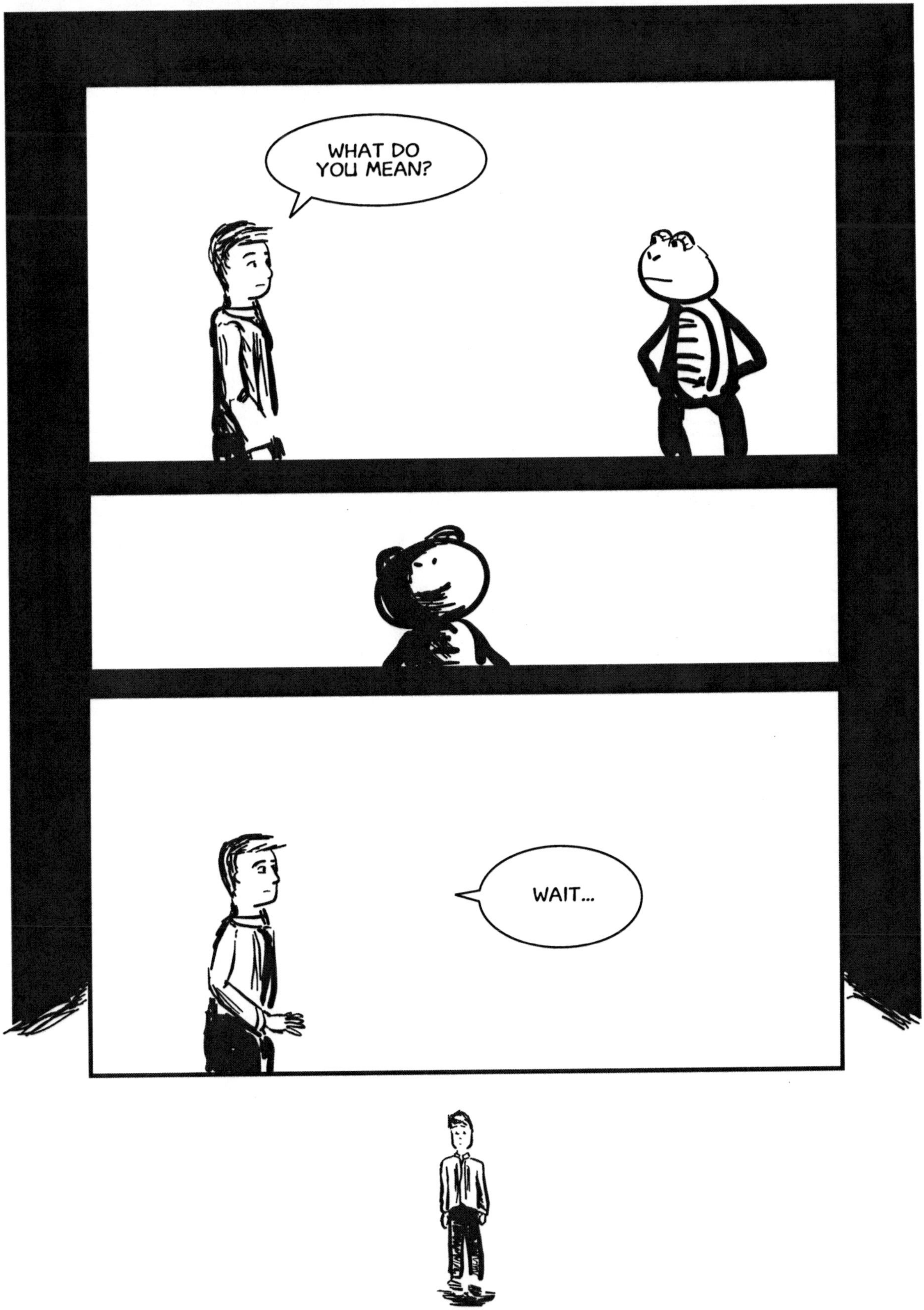
WHAT DO YOU MEAN?
WAIT...

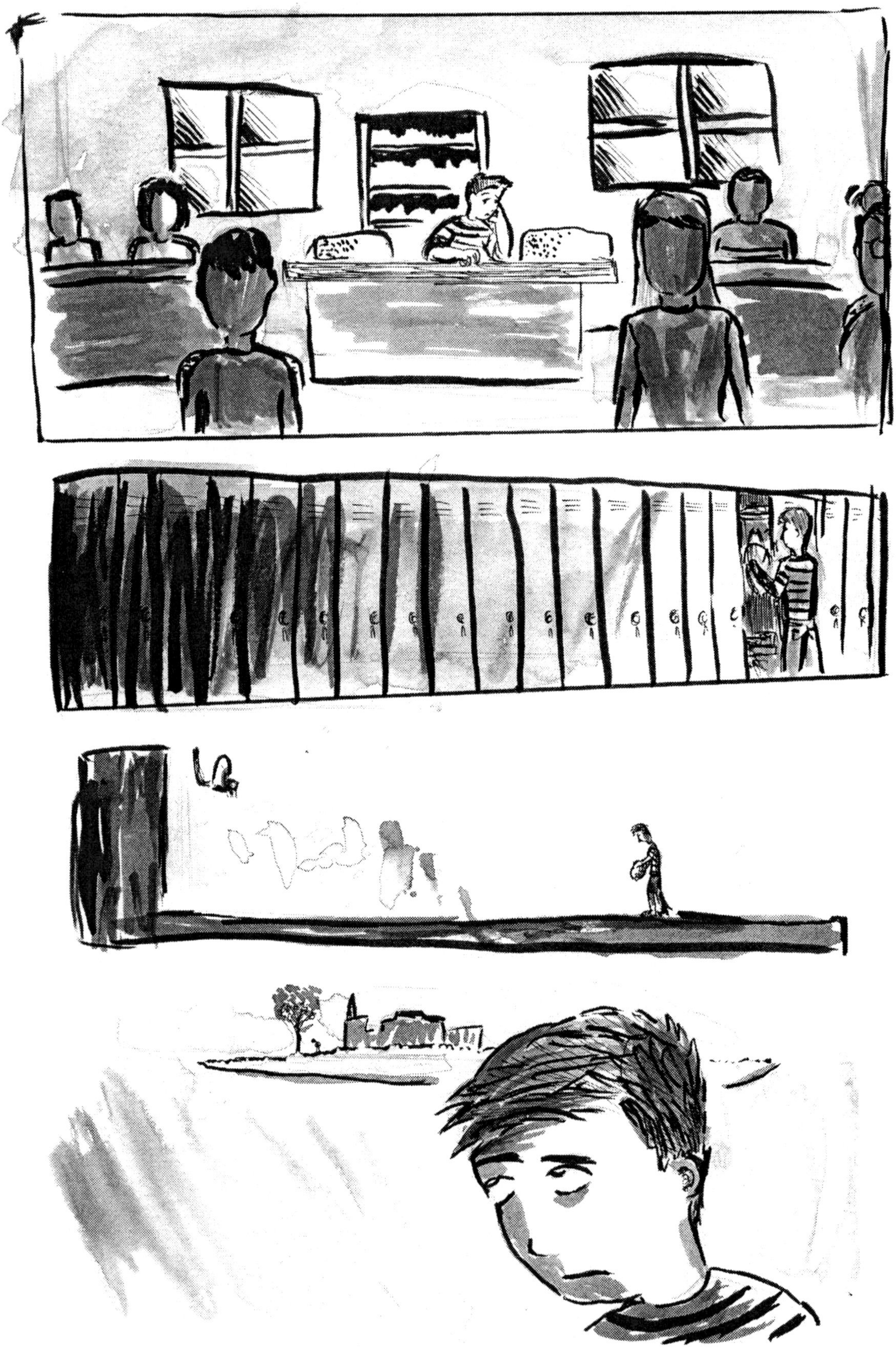

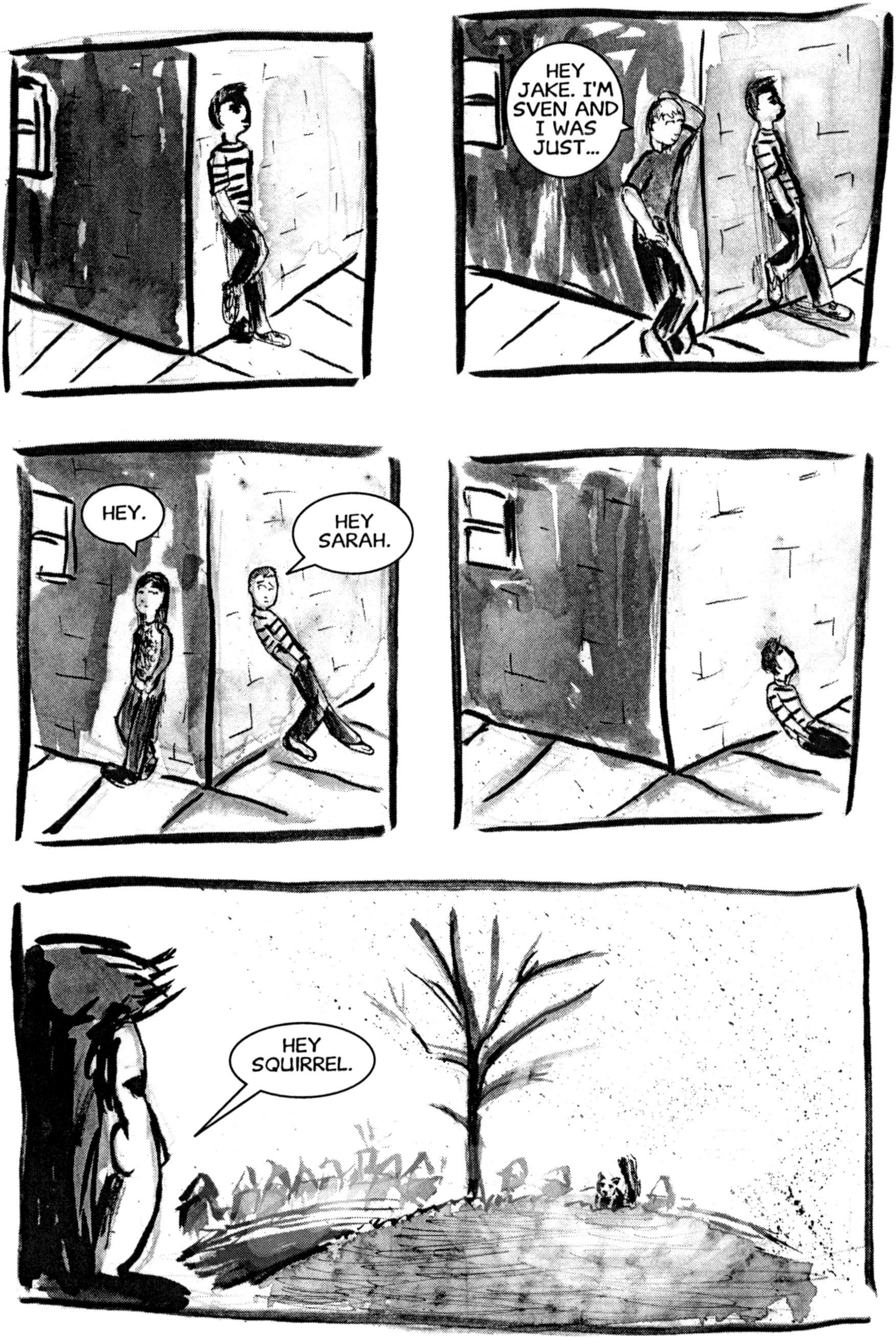
HEY JAKE. I'M SVEN AND I WAS JUST...
HEY.
HEY SARAH.
HEY SQUIRREL.

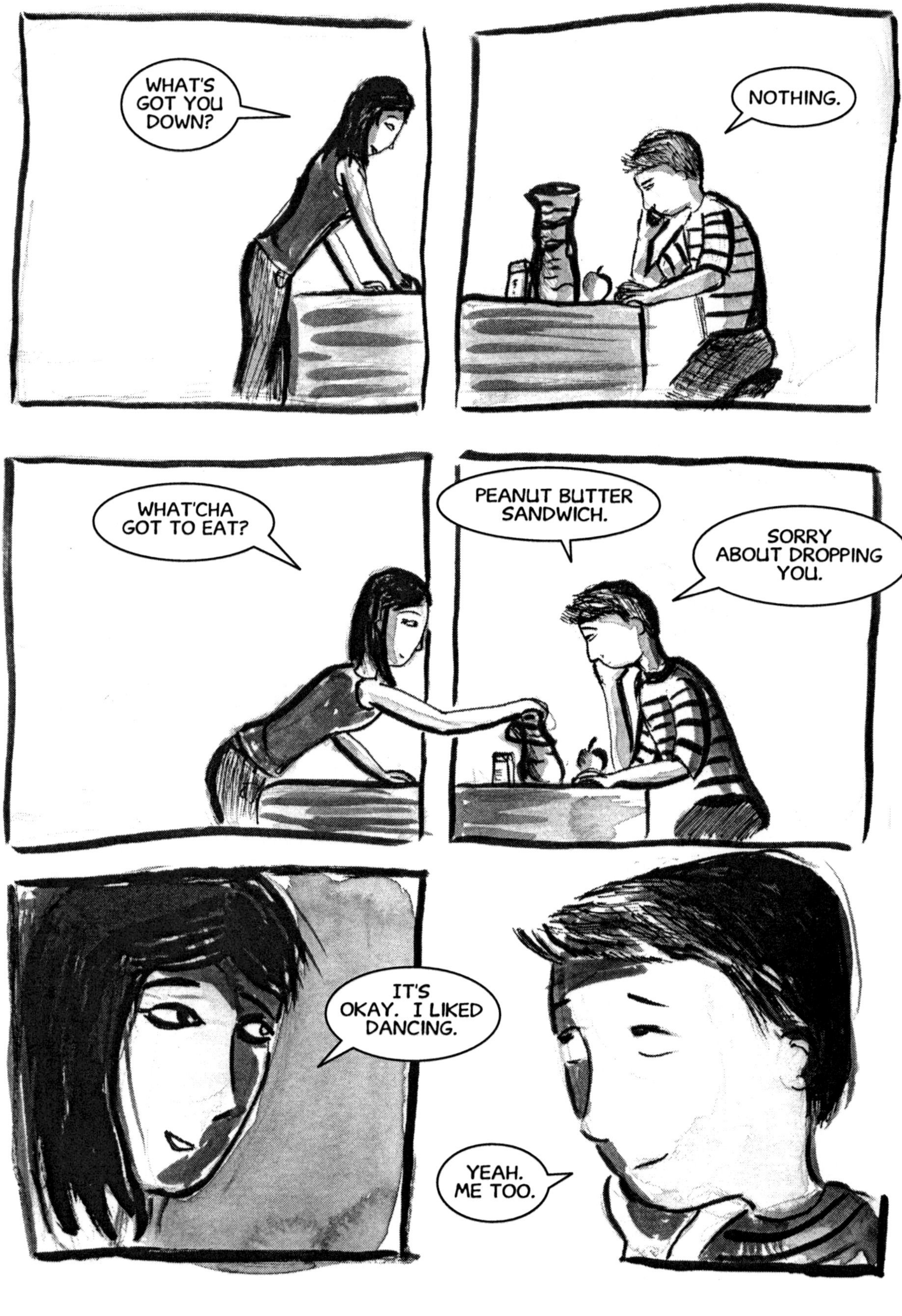
WHAT'S GOT YOU DOWN?
NOTHING.
WHAT'CHA GOT TO EAT?
PEANUT BUTTER SANDWICH.
SORRY ABOUT DROPPING YOU.
IT'S OKAY. I LIKED DANCING.
YEAH. ME TOO.

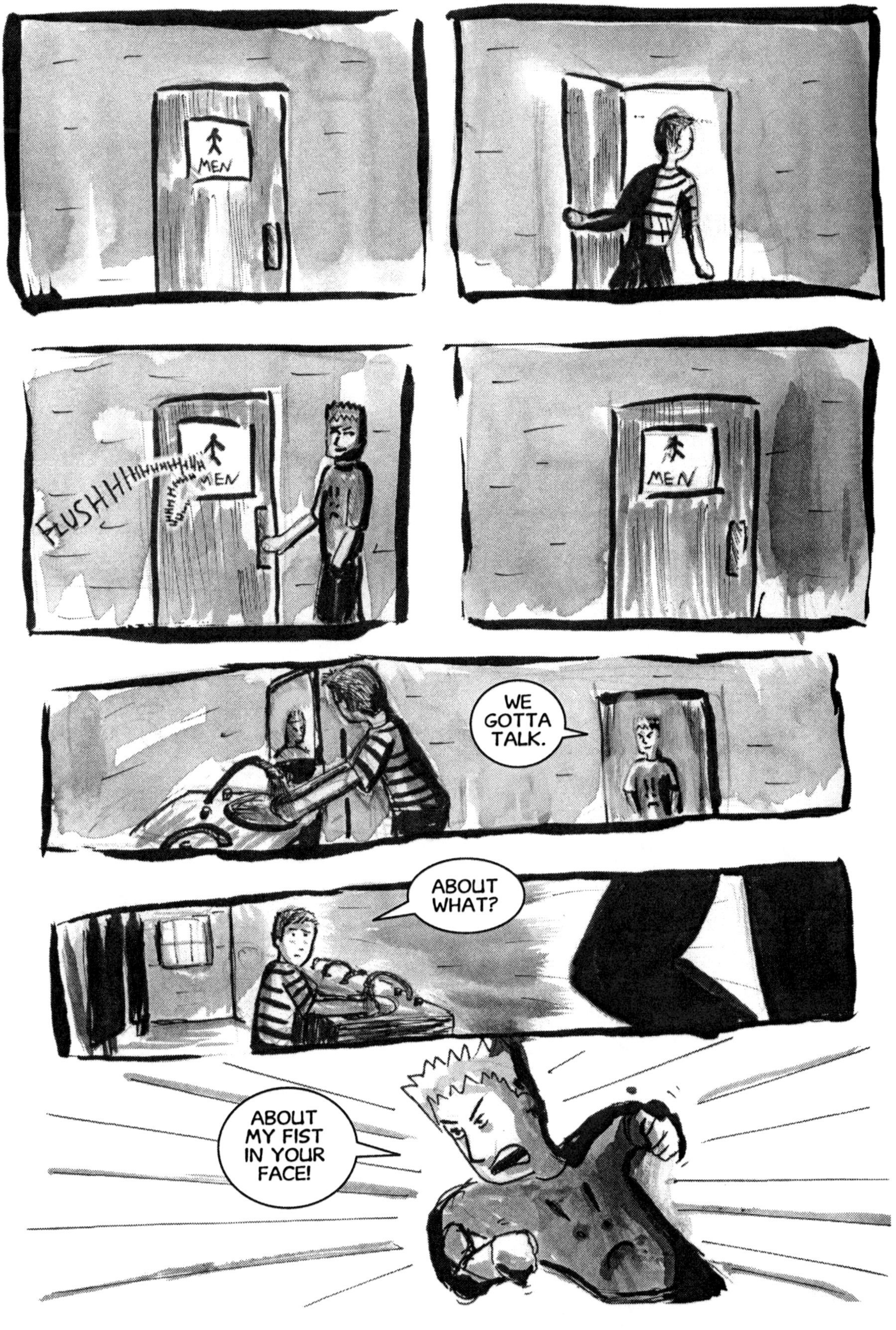
MEN
MEN
FLUSHHHHHHHHHHH
MEN
WE GOTTA TALK.
ABOUT WHAT?
ABOUT MY FIST IN YOUR FACE!

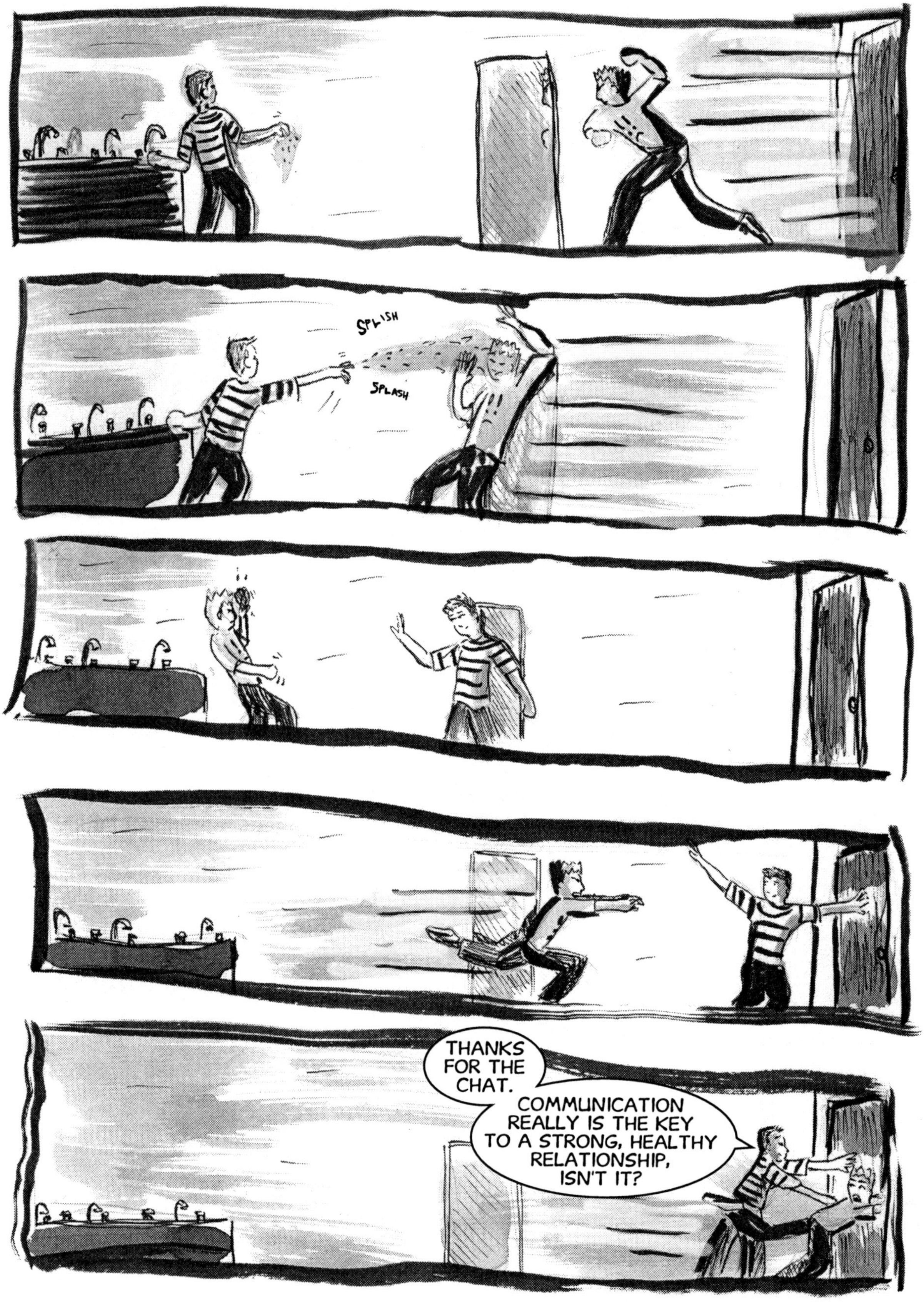
SPLISH
SPLASH
THANKS FOR THE CHAT.
COMMUNICATION REALLY IS THE KEY TO A STRONG, HEALTHY RELATIONSHIP, ISN'T IT?

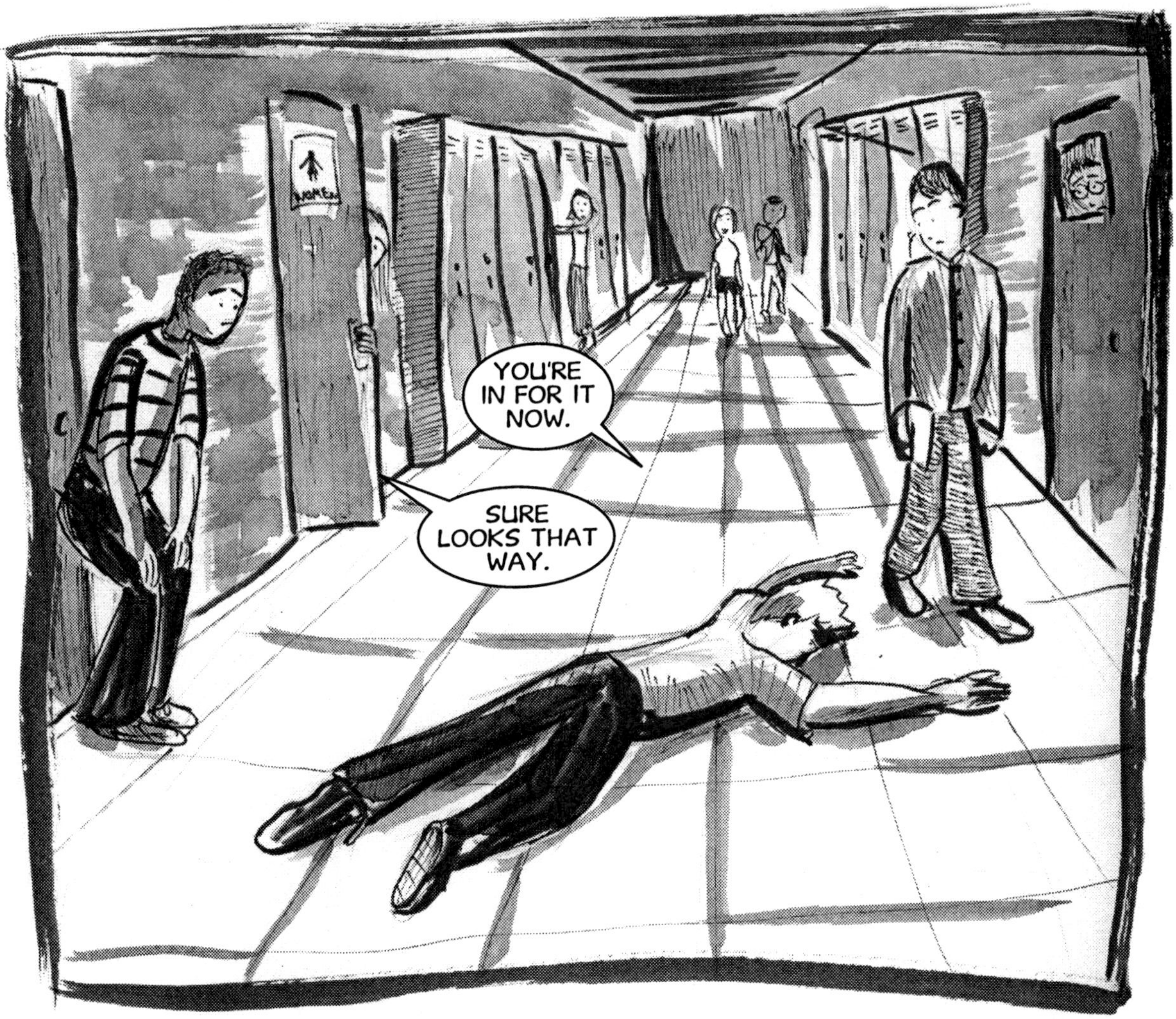
YOU'RE IN FOR IT NOW.
SURE LOOKS THAT WAY.

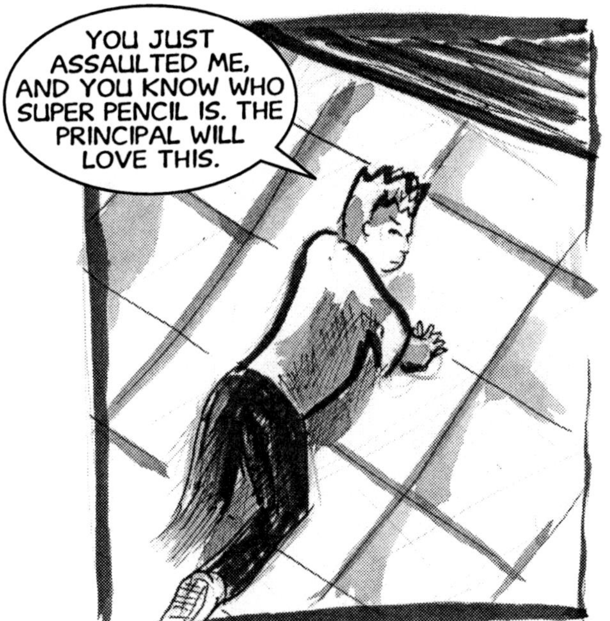
YOU JUST ASSAULTED ME, AND YOU KNOW WHO SUPER PENCIL IS. THE PRINCIPAL WILL LOVE THIS.

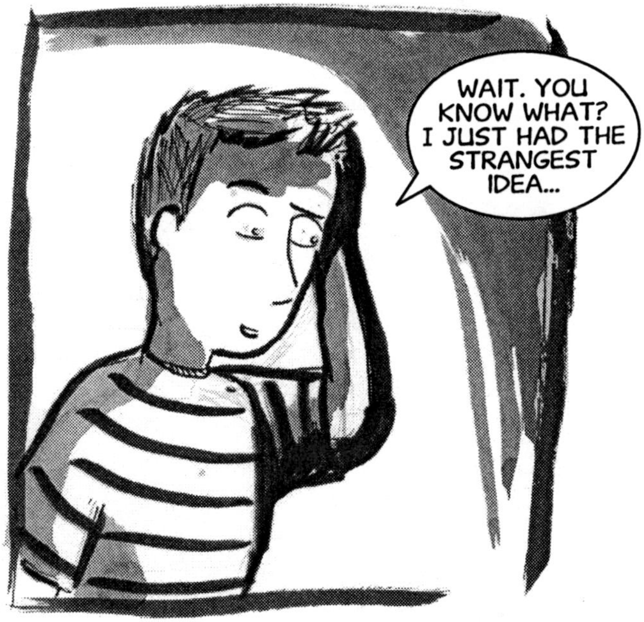
WAIT. YOU KNOW WHAT? I JUST HAD THE STRANGEST IDEA...

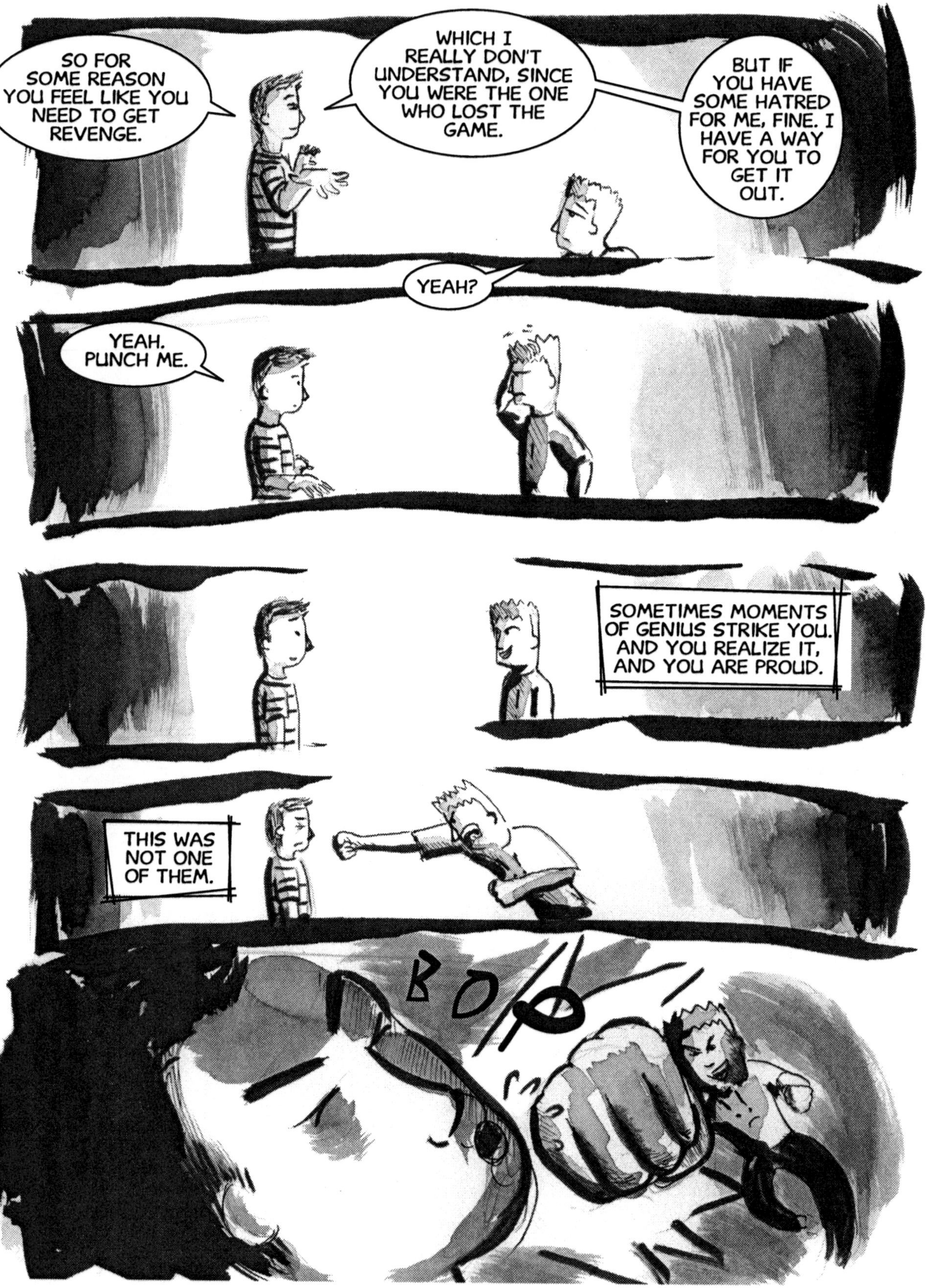
SO FOR SOME REASON YOU FEEL LIKE YOU NEED TO GET REVENGE.
WHICH I REALLY DON'T UNDERSTAND, SINCE YOU WERE THE ONE WHO LOST THE GAME.
BUT IF YOU HAVE SOME HATRED FOR ME, FINE. I HAVE A WAY FOR YOU TO GET IT OUT.
YEAH?
YEAH. PUNCH ME.
SOMETIMES MOMENTS OF GENIUS STRIKE YOU. AND YOU REALIZE IT, AND YOU ARE PROUD.
THIS WAS NOT ONE OF THEM.
BOP

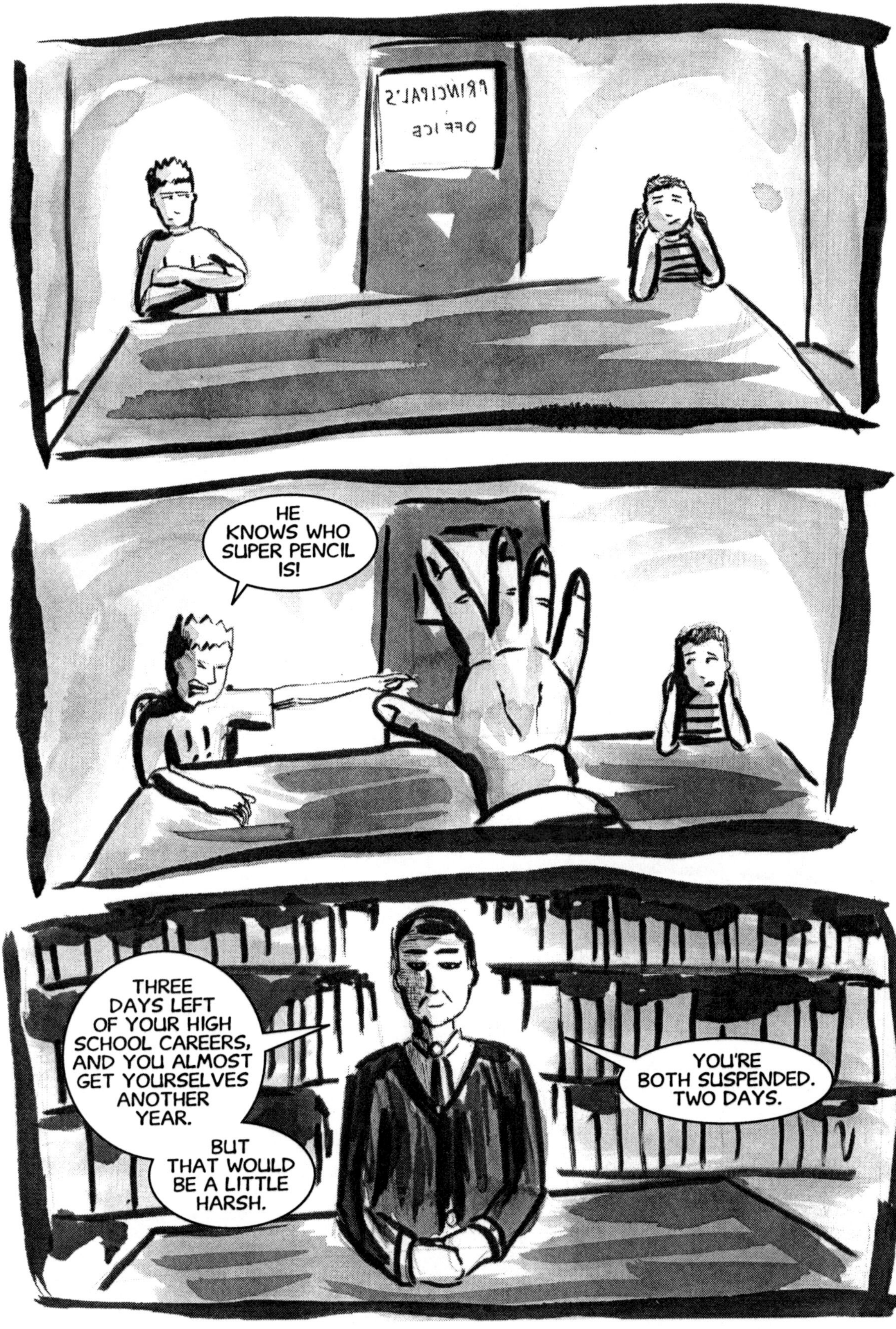
PRINCIPAL'S OFFICE
HE KNOWS WHO SUPER PENCIL IS!
THREE DAYS LEFT OF YOUR HIGH SCHOOL CAREERS, AND YOU ALMOST GET YOURSELVES ANOTHER YEAR.
BUT THAT WOULD BE A LITTLE HARSH.
YOU'RE BOTH SUSPENDED. TWO DAYS.

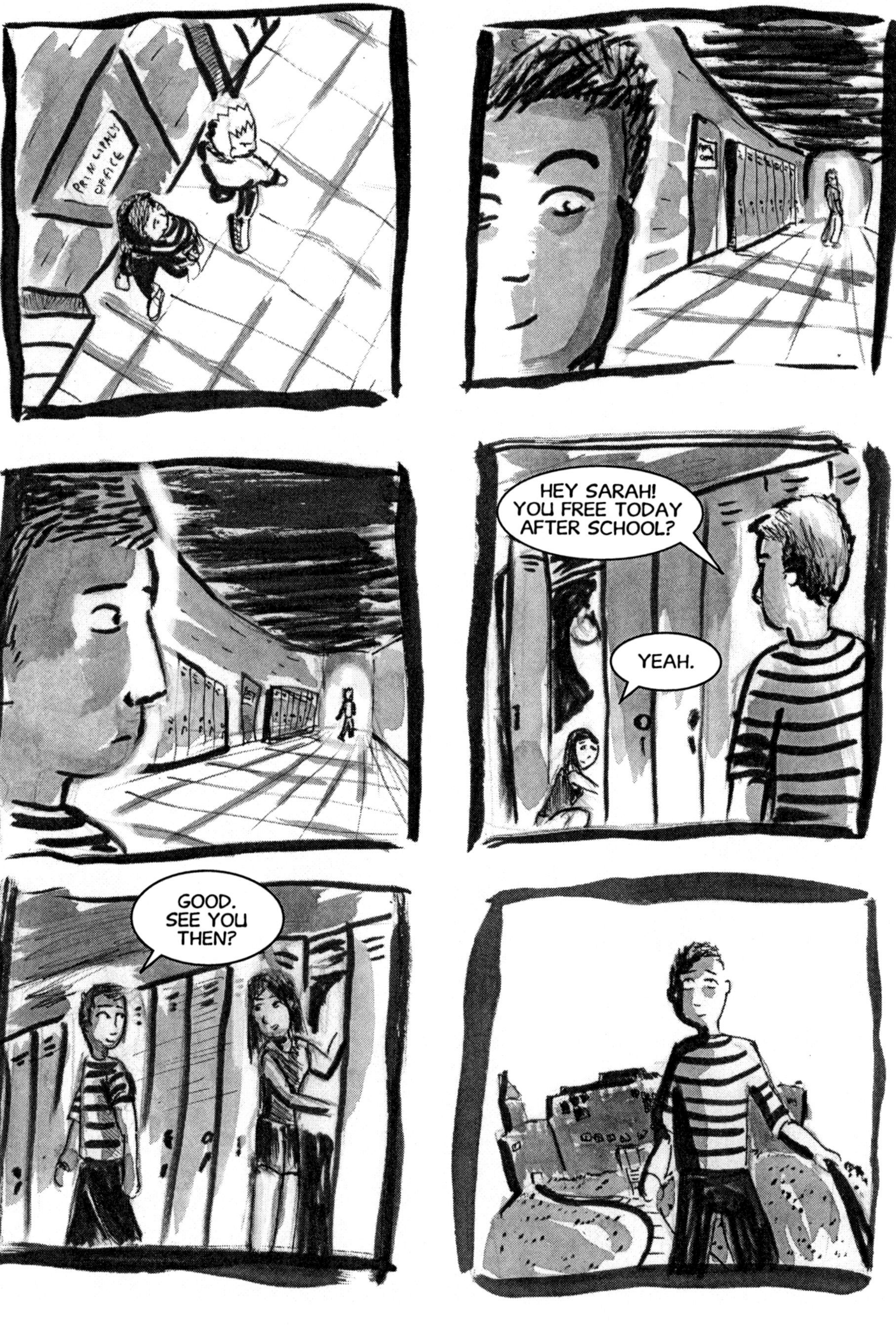
HEY SARAH! YOU FREE TODAY AFTER SCHOOL?
YEAH.
GOOD. SEE YOU THEN?

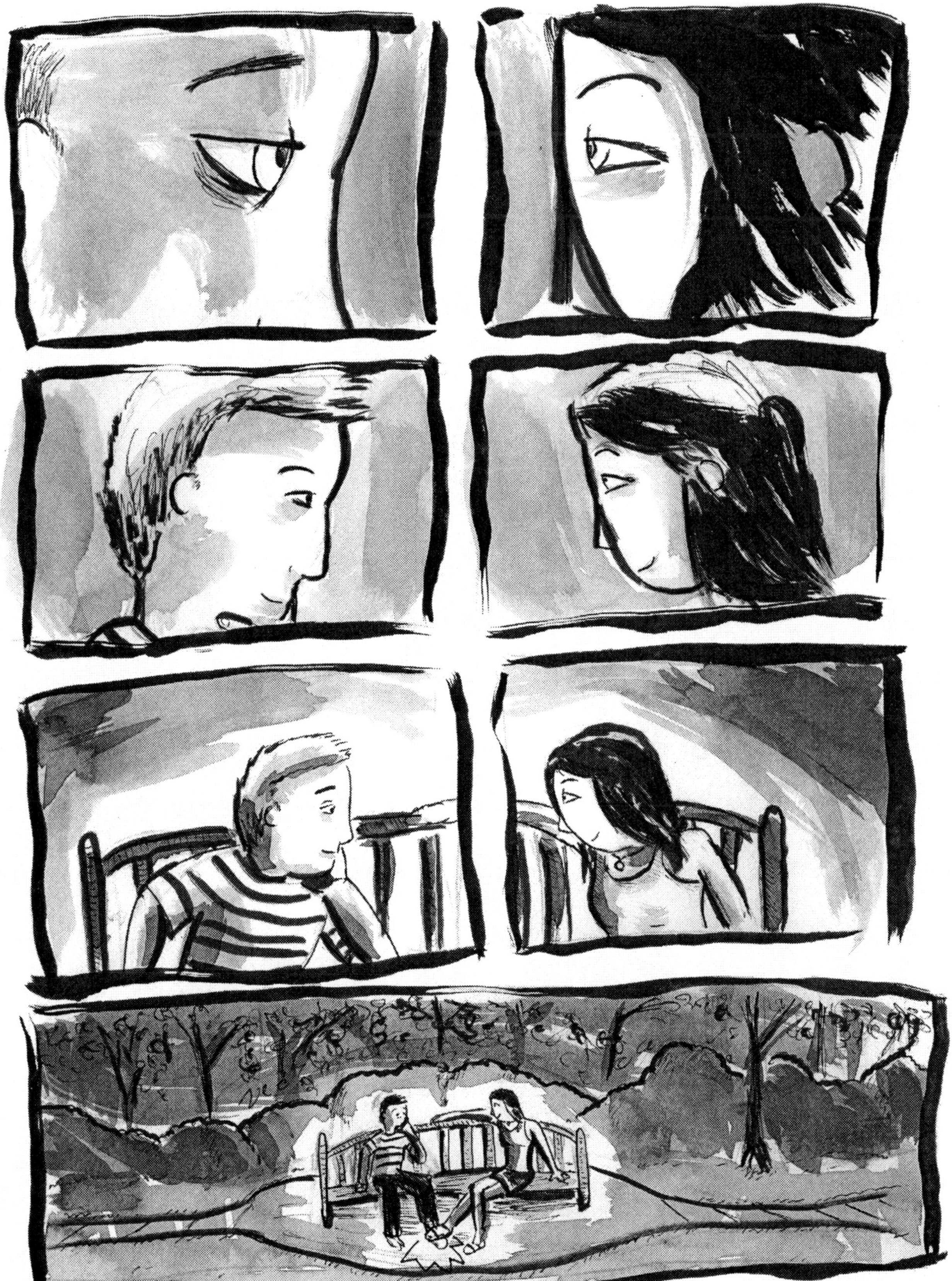

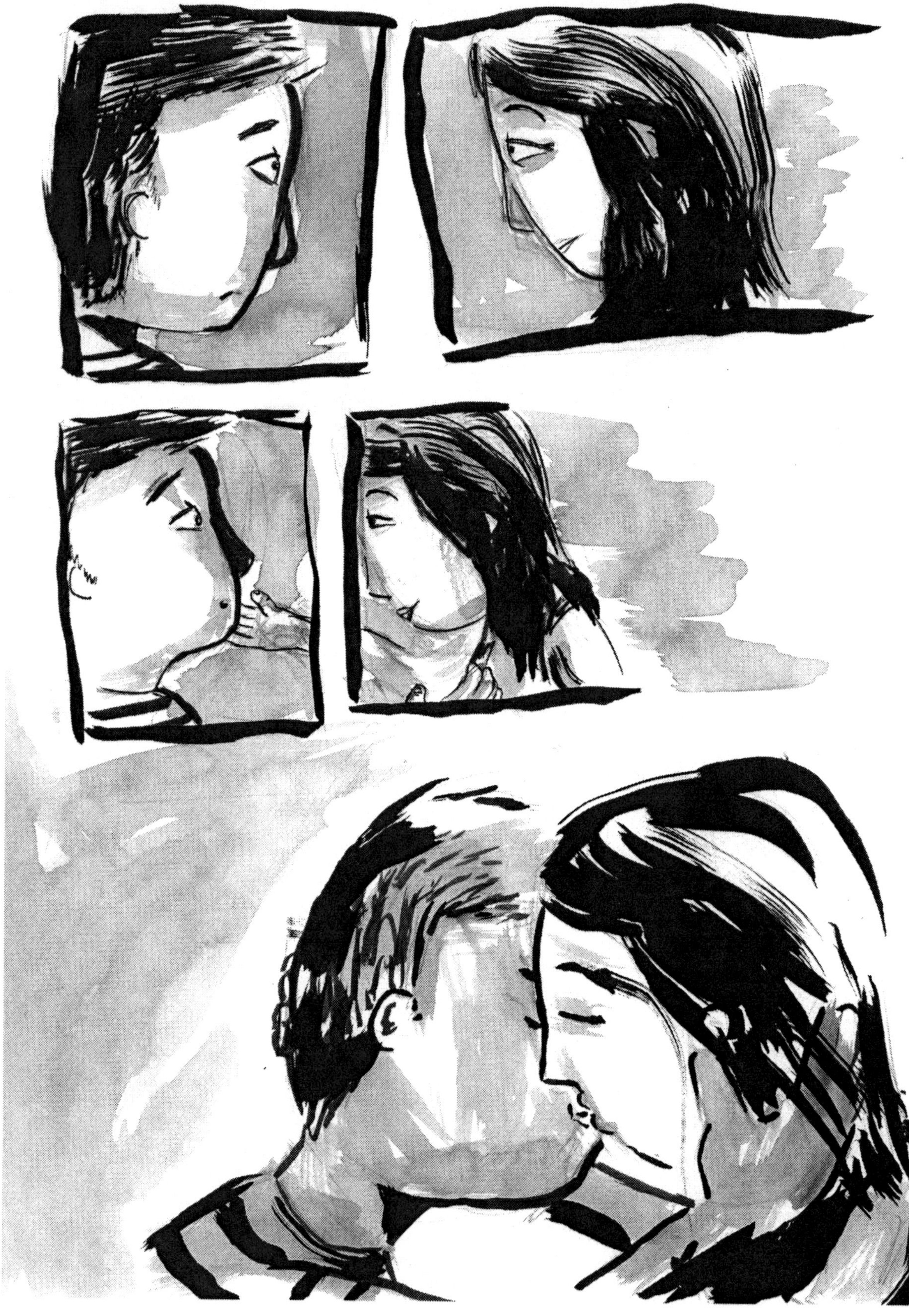

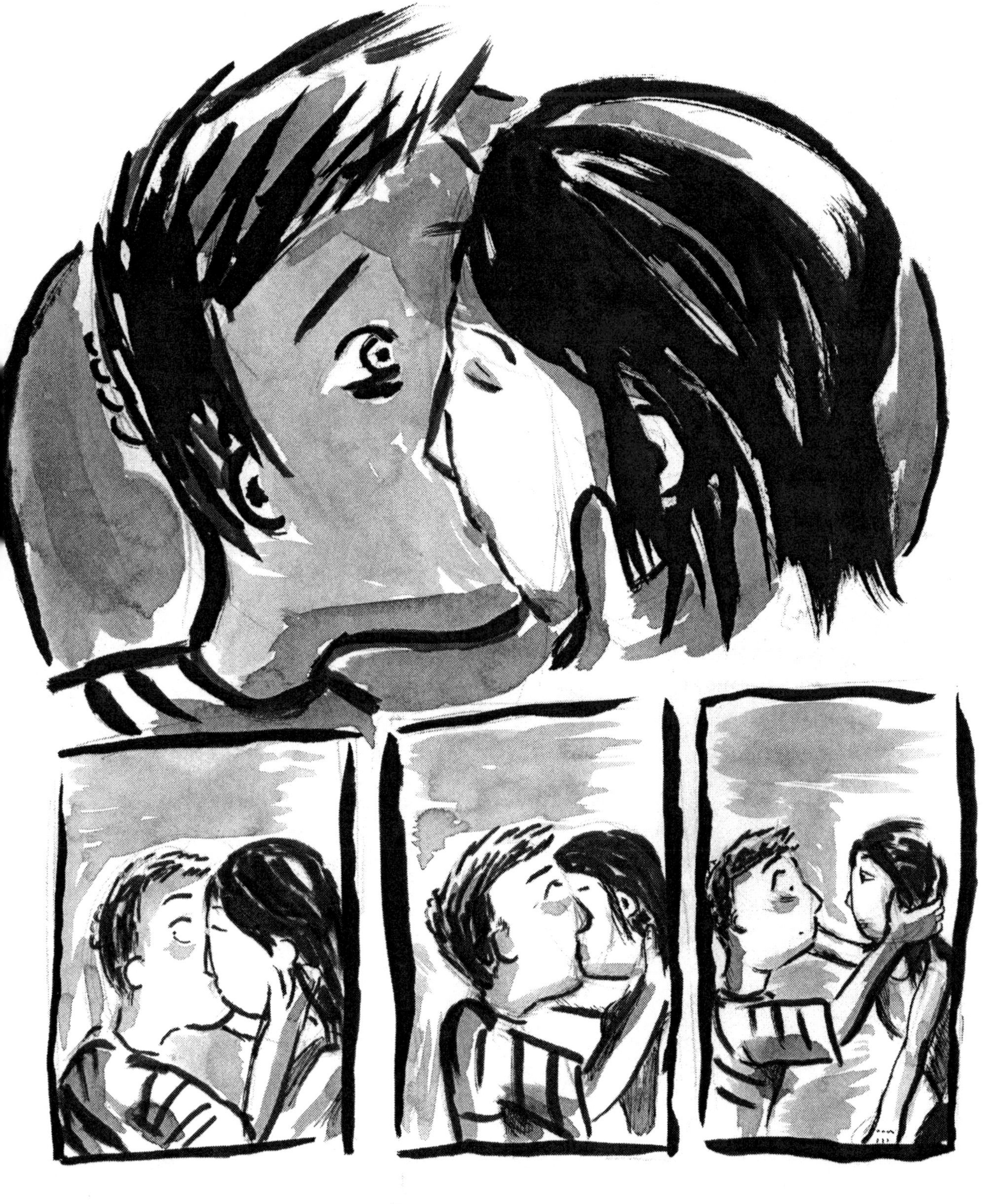

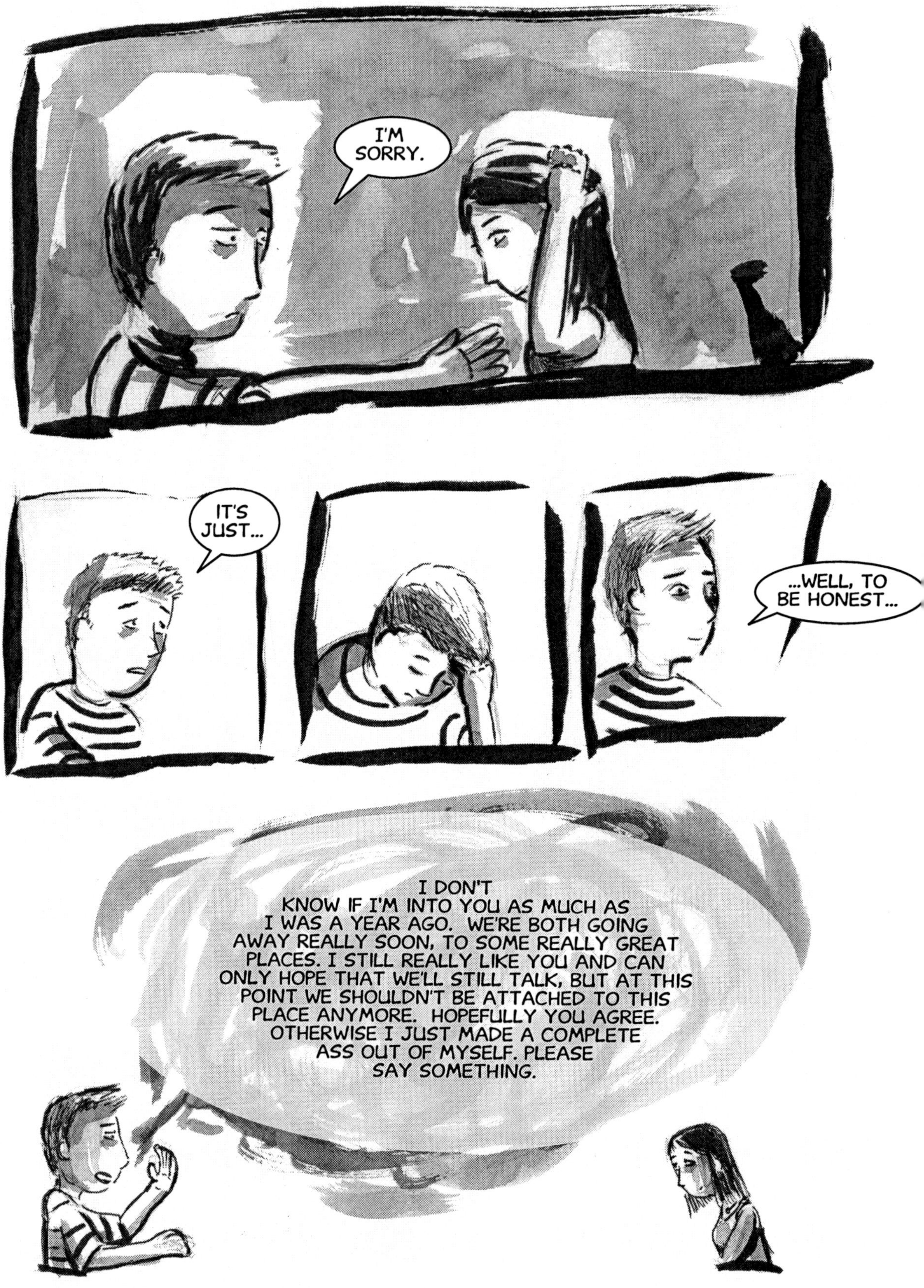
I'M SORRY.
IT'S JUST...
...WELL, TO BE HONEST...
I DON'T KNOW IF I'M INTO YOU AS MUCH AS I WAS A YEAR AGO. WE'RE BOTH GOING AWAY REALLY SOON, TO SOME REALLY GREAT PLACES. I STILL REALLY LIKE YOU AND CAN ONLY HOPE THAT WE'LL STILL TALK, BUT AT THIS POINT WE SHOULDN'T BE ATTACHED TO THIS PLACE ANYMORE. HOPEFULLY YOU AGREE. OTHERWISE I JUST MADE A COMPLETE ASS OUT OF MYSELF. PLEASE SAY SOMETHING.

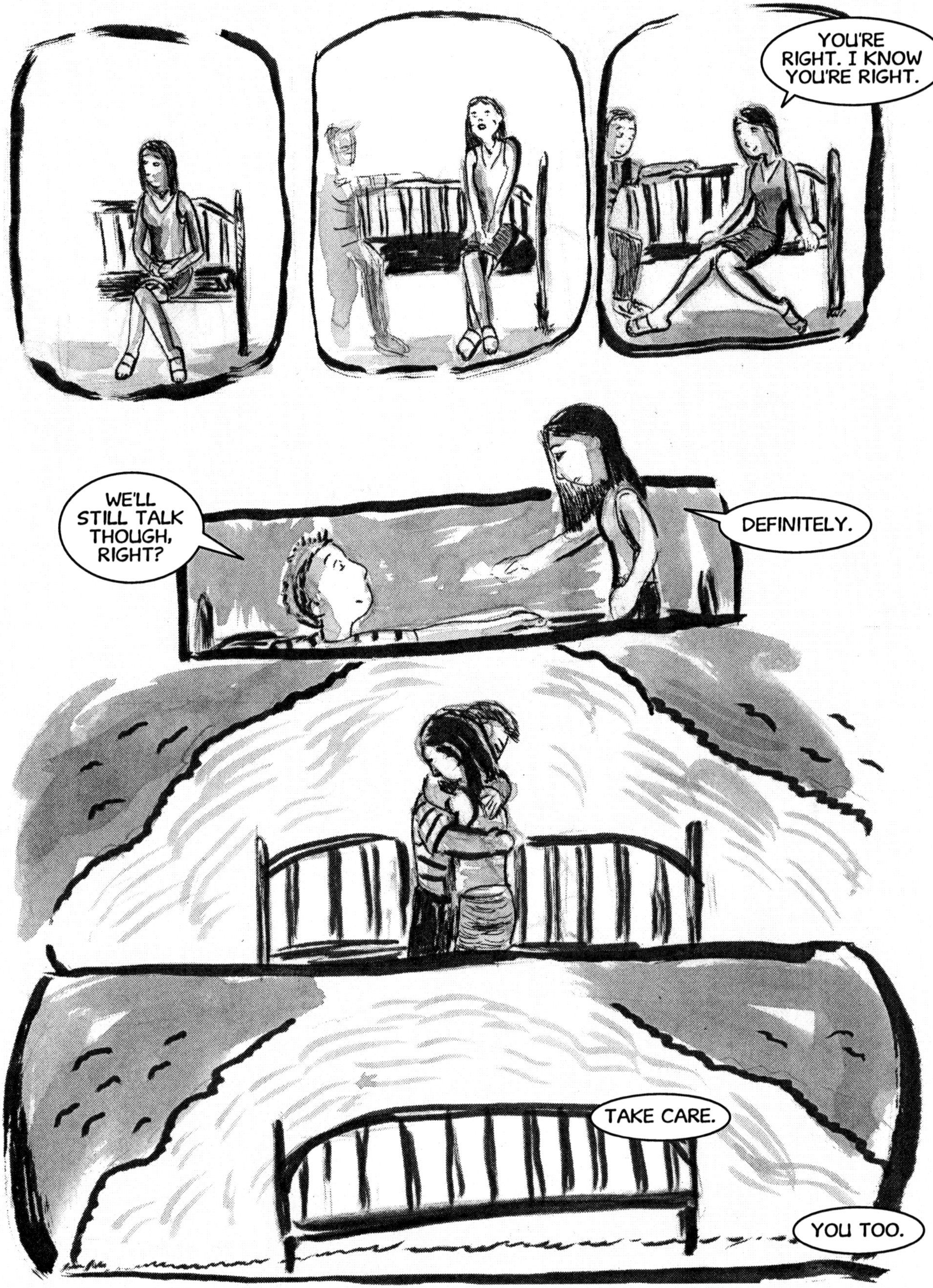
YOU'RE RIGHT. I KNOW YOU'RE RIGHT.
WE'LL STILL TALK THOUGH, RIGHT?
DEFINITELY.
TAKE CARE.
YOU TOO.

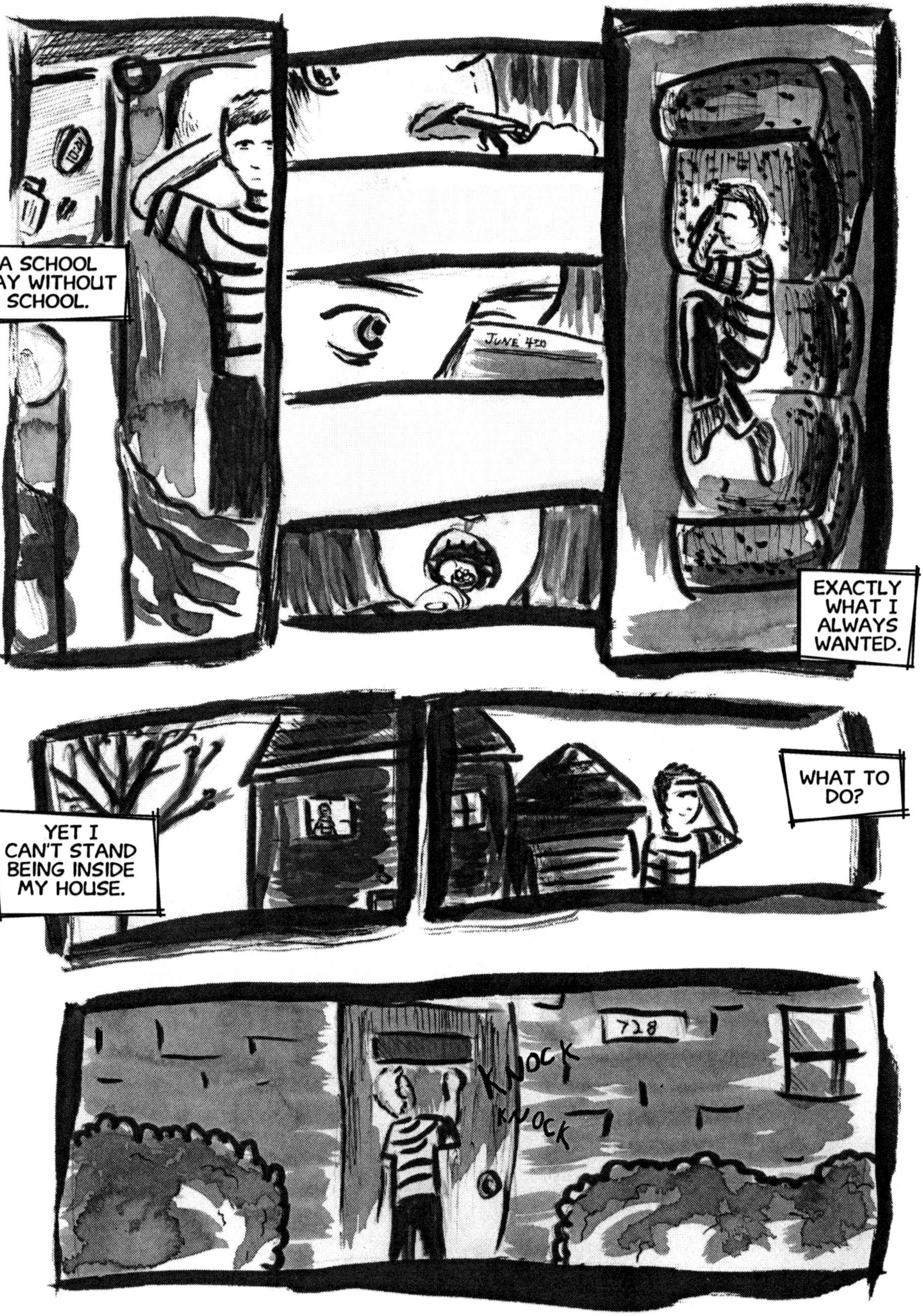
A SCHOOL DAY WITHOUT SCHOOL.
JUNE 4TH
EXACTLY WHAT I ALWAYS WANTED.
YET I CAN'T STAND BEING INSIDE MY HOUSE.
WHAT TO DO?
728
KNOCK
KNOCK

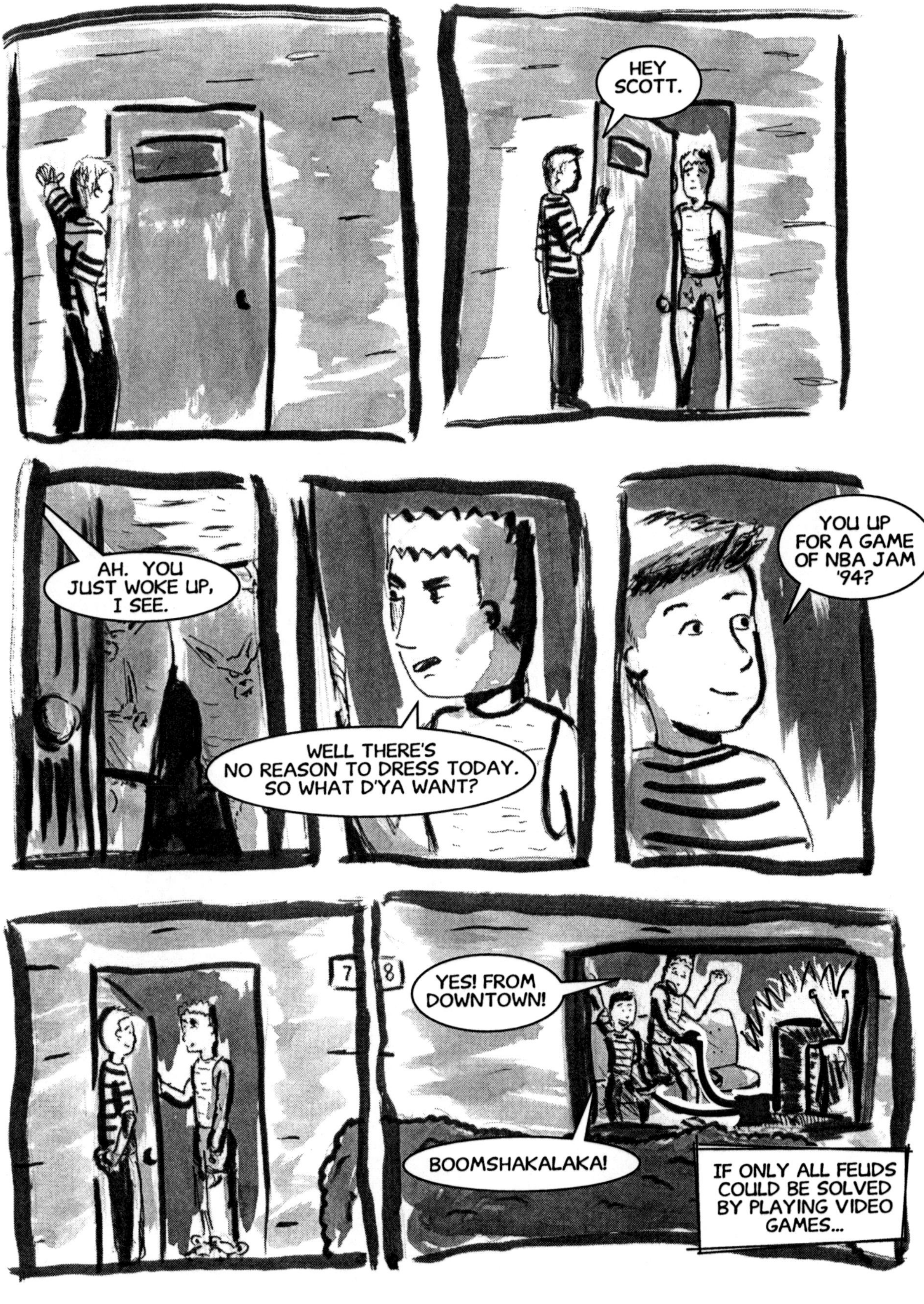
HEY SCOTT.
AH. YOU JUST WOKE UP, I SEE.
WELL THERE'S NO REASON TO DRESS TODAY. SO WHAT D'YA WANT?
YOU UP FOR A GAME OF NBA JAM '94?
7
8
YES! FROM DOWNTOWN!
BOOMSHAKALAKA!
IF ONLY ALL FEUDS COULD BE SOLVED BY PLAYING VIDEO GAMES...

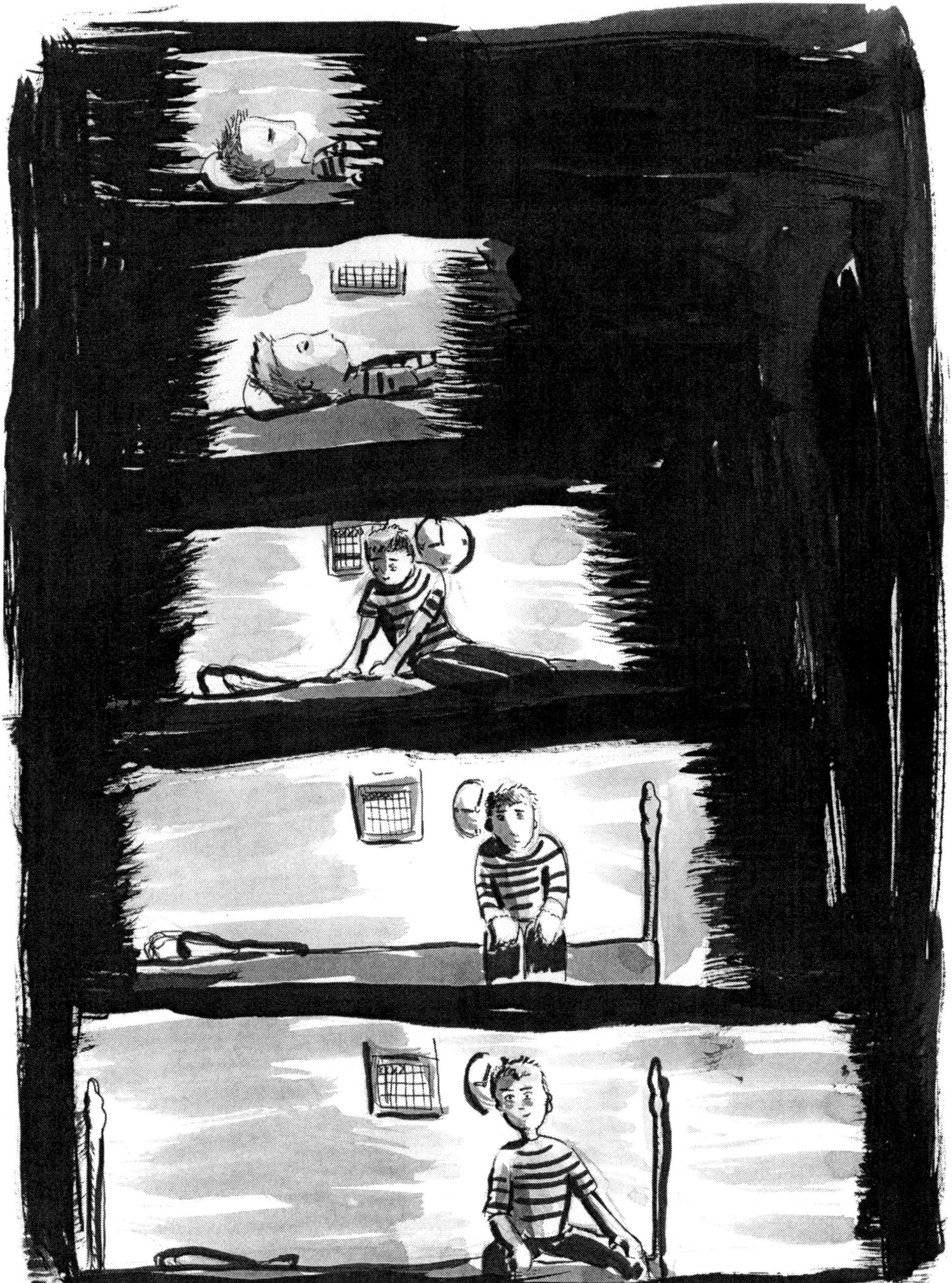

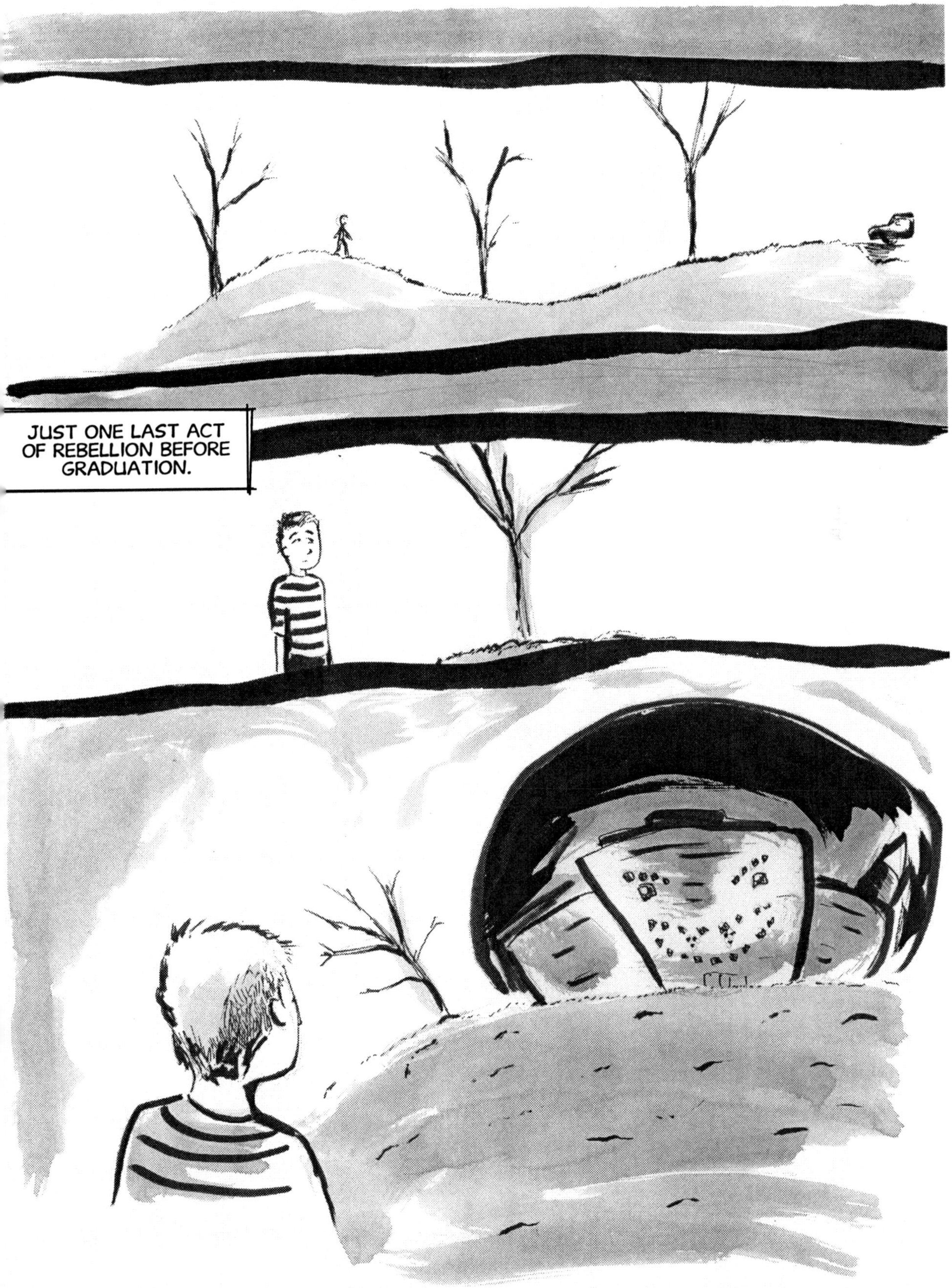
JUST ONE LAST ACT OF REBELLION BEFORE GRADUATION.

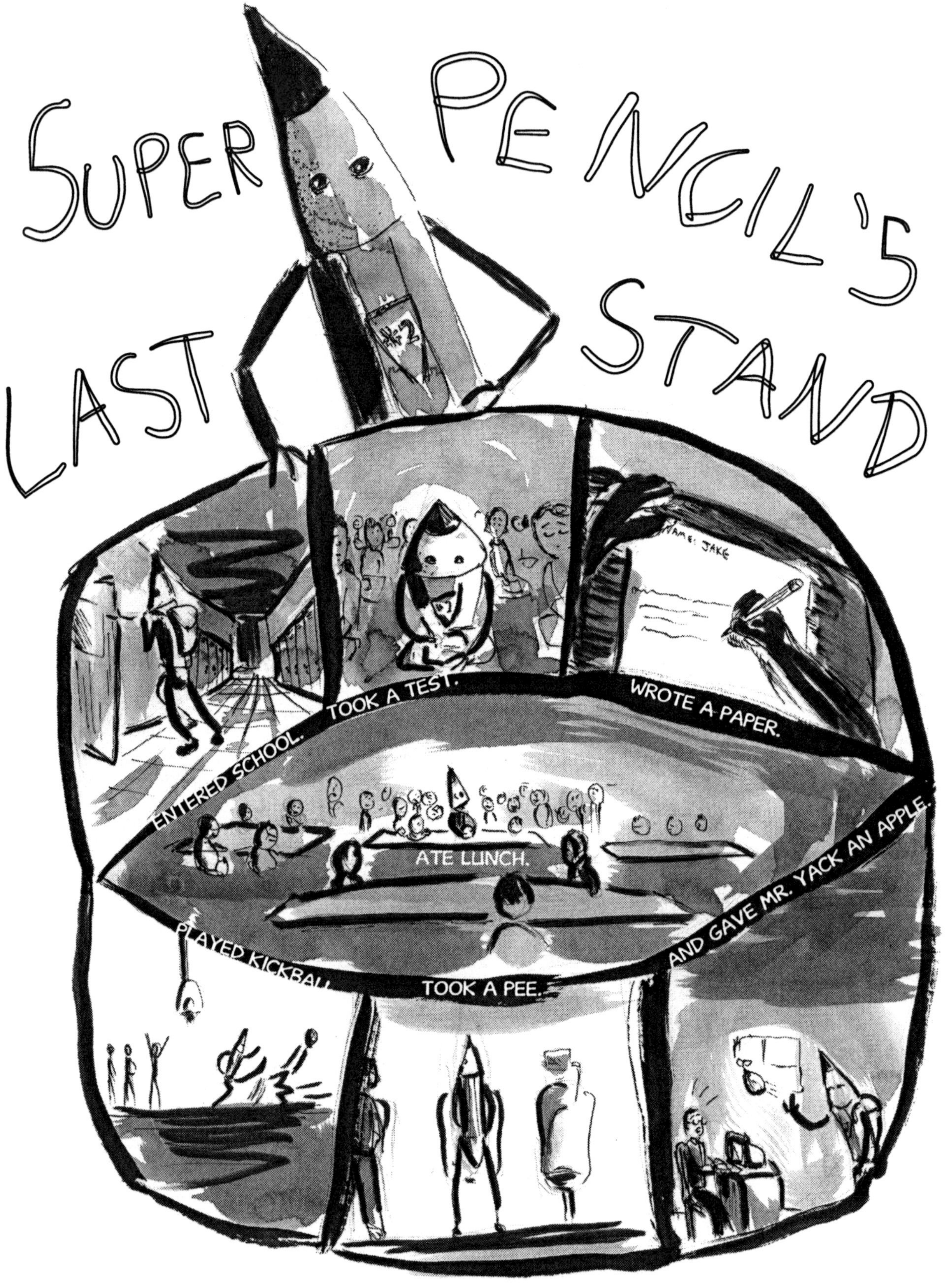
SUPER PENCIL'S LAST STAND
NAME: JAKE
ENTERED SCHOOL.
TOOK A TEST.
WROTE A PAPER.
ATE LUNCH.
PLAYED KICKBALL
TOOK A PEE.
AND GAVE MR. YACK AN APPLE.

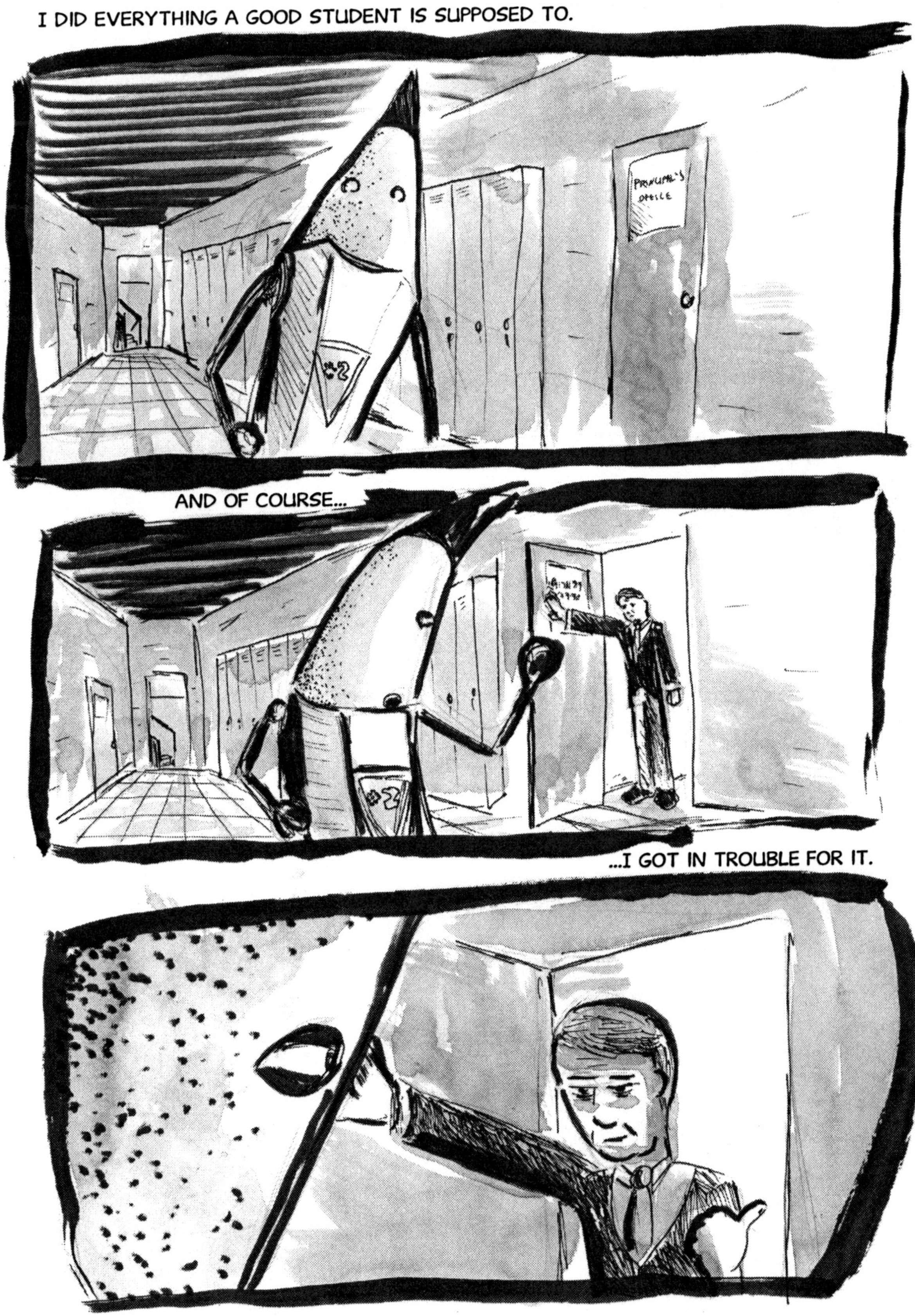
I DID EVERYTHING A GOOD STUDENT IS SUPPOSED TO.
PRINCIPAL'S OFFICE
AND OF COURSE...
...I GOT IN TROUBLE FOR IT.

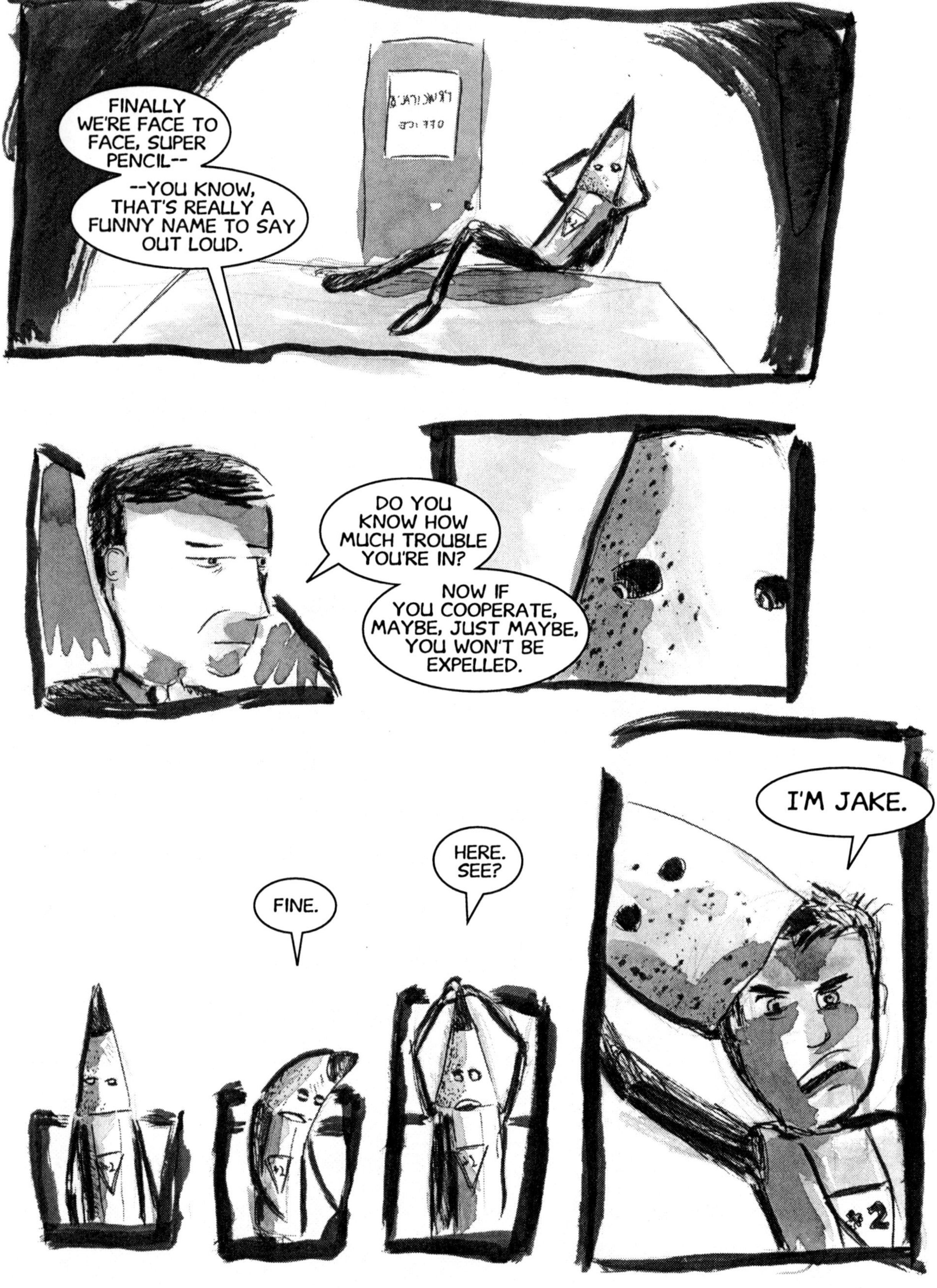
FINALLY WE'RE FACE TO FACE, SUPER PENCIL--
--YOU KNOW, THAT'S REALLY A FUNNY NAME TO SAY OUT LOUD.
DO YOU KNOW HOW MUCH TROUBLE YOU'RE IN?
NOW IF YOU COOPERATE, MAYBE, JUST MAYBE, YOU WON'T BE EXPELLED.
FINE.
HERE. SEE?
I'M JAKE.
#2

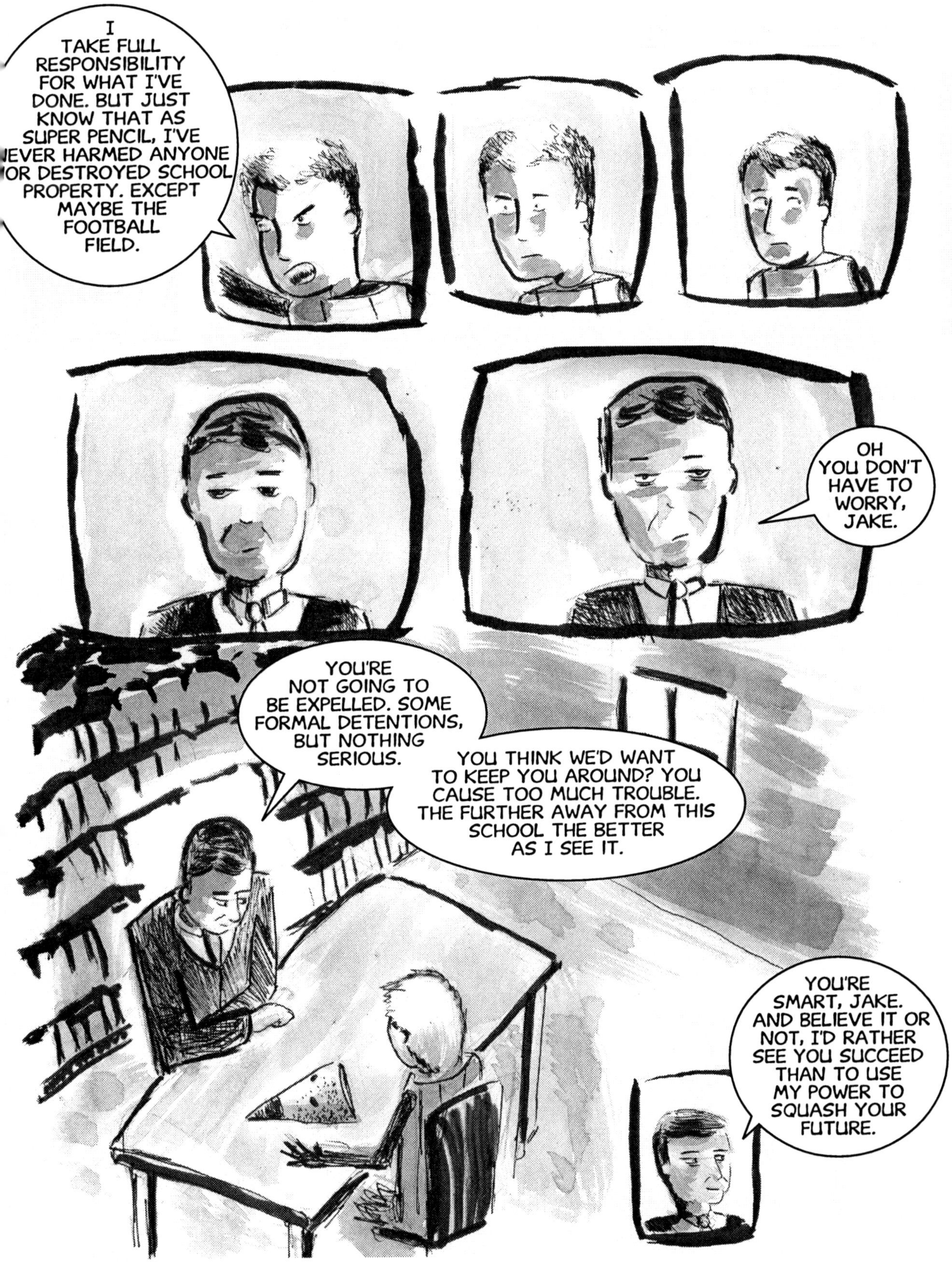
I TAKE FULL RESPONSIBILITY FOR WHAT I'VE DONE. BUT JUST KNOW THAT AS SUPER PENCIL, I'VE NEVER HARMED ANYONE OR DESTROYED SCHOOL PROPERTY. EXCEPT MAYBE THE FOOTBALL FIELD.
OH YOU DON'T HAVE TO WORRY, JAKE.
YOU'RE NOT GOING TO BE EXPELLED. SOME FORMAL DETENTIONS, BUT NOTHING SERIOUS.
YOU THINK WE'D WANT TO KEEP YOU AROUND? YOU CAUSE TOO MUCH TROUBLE. THE FURTHER AWAY FROM THIS SCHOOL THE BETTER AS I SEE IT.
YOU'RE SMART, JAKE. AND BELIEVE IT OR NOT, I'D RATHER SEE YOU SUCCEED THAN TO USE MY POWER TO SQUASH YOUR FUTURE.

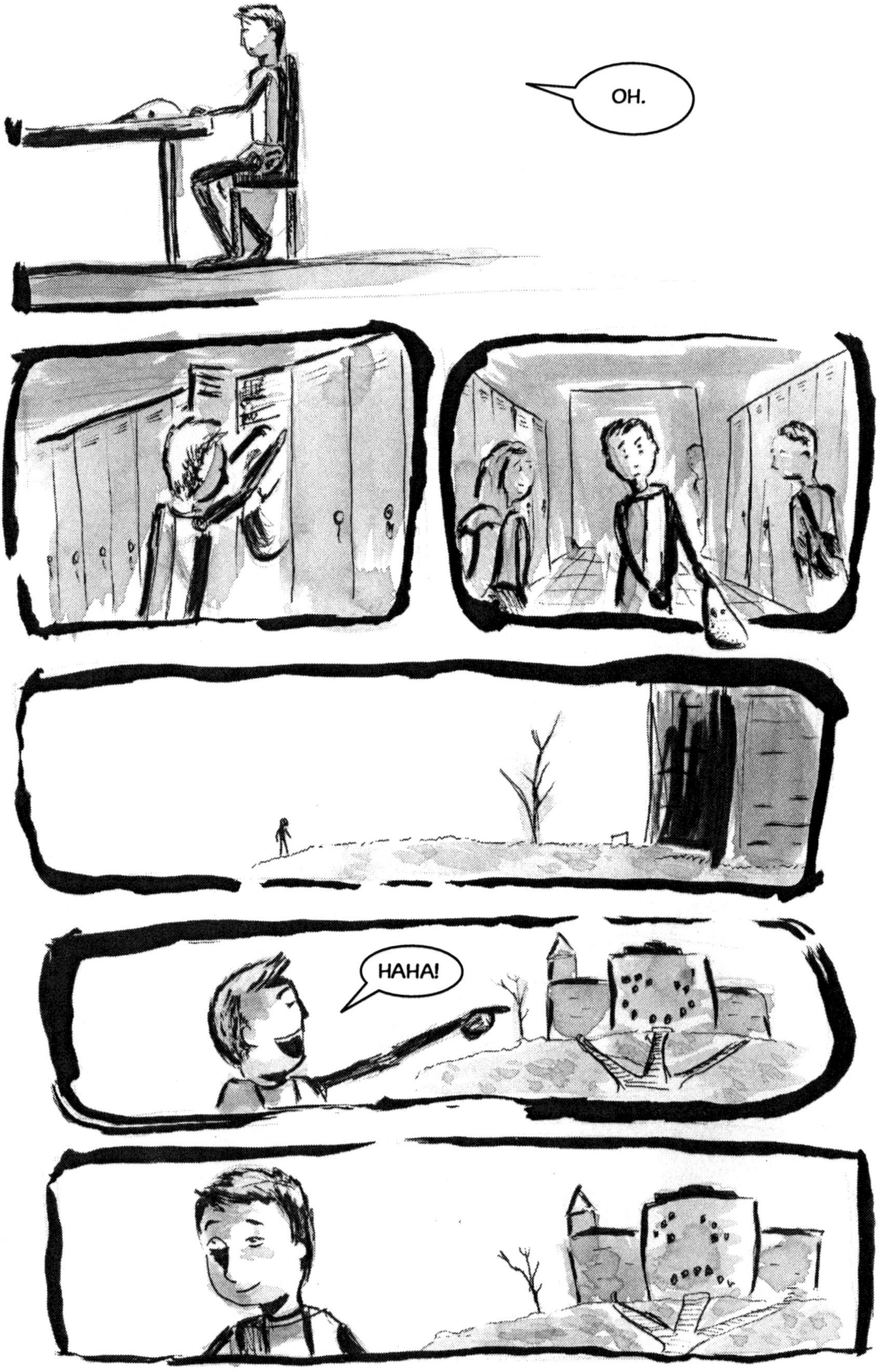
OH.
HAHA!

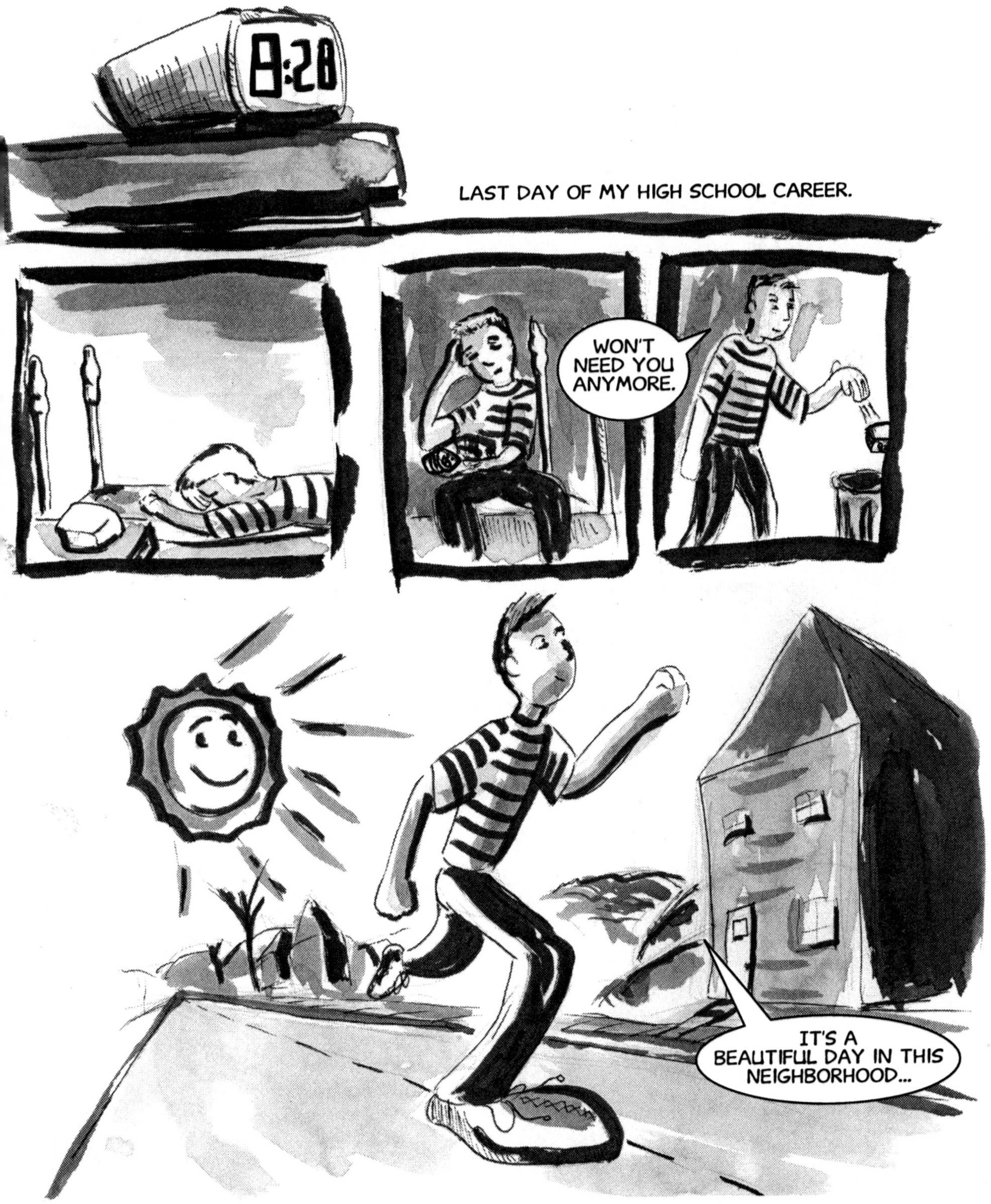
8:28
LAST DAY OF MY HIGH SCHOOL CAREER.
WON'T NEED YOU ANYMORE.
IT'S A BEAUTIFUL DAY IN THIS NEIGHBORHOOD...

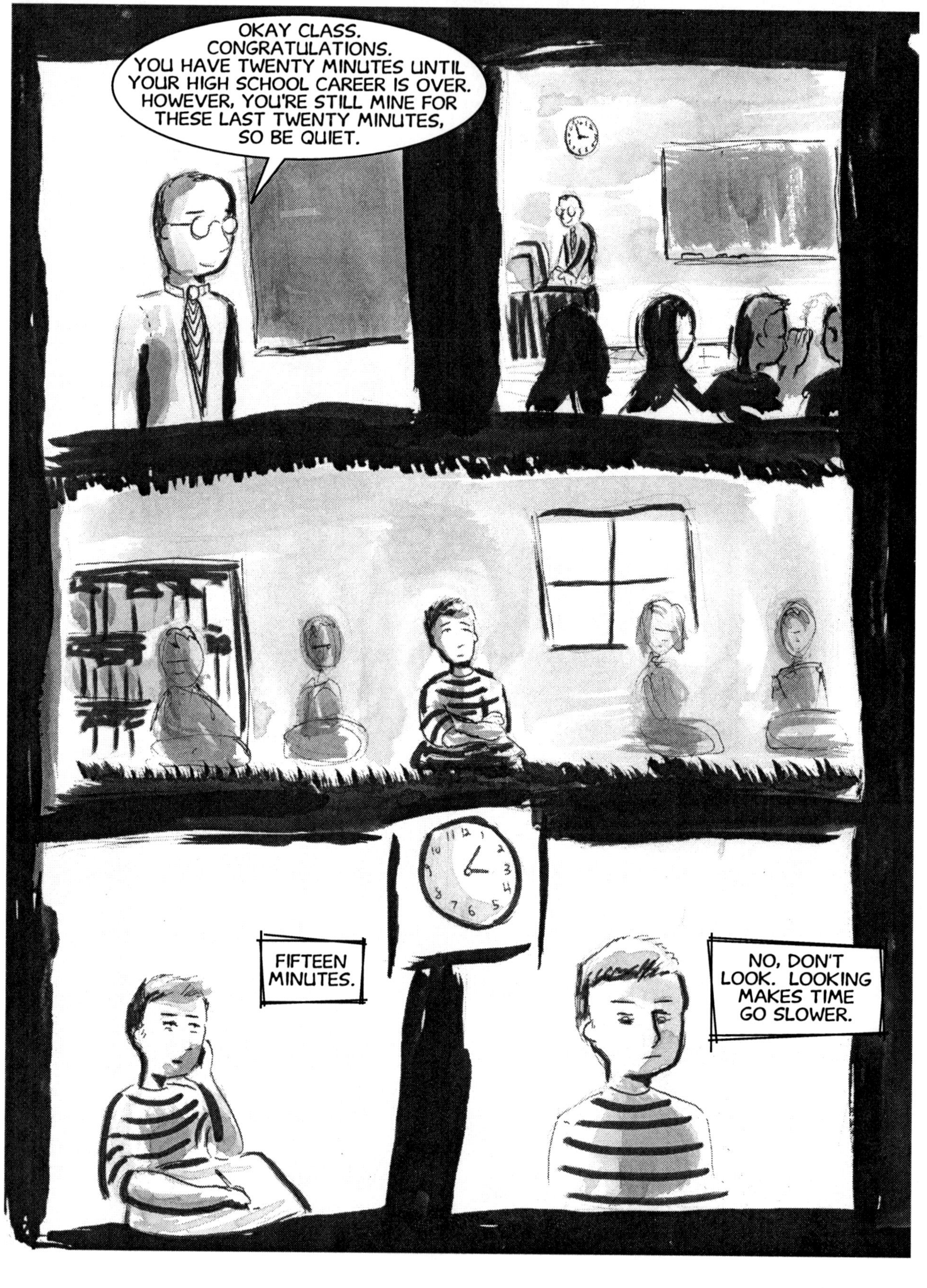
OKAY CLASS. CONGRATULATIONS. YOU HAVE TWENTY MINUTES UNTIL YOUR HIGH SCHOOL CAREER IS OVER. HOWEVER, YOU'RE STILL MINE FOR THESE LAST TWENTY MINUTES, SO BE QUIET.
FIFTEEN MINUTES.
NO, DON'T LOOK. LOOKING MAKES TIME GO SLOWER.

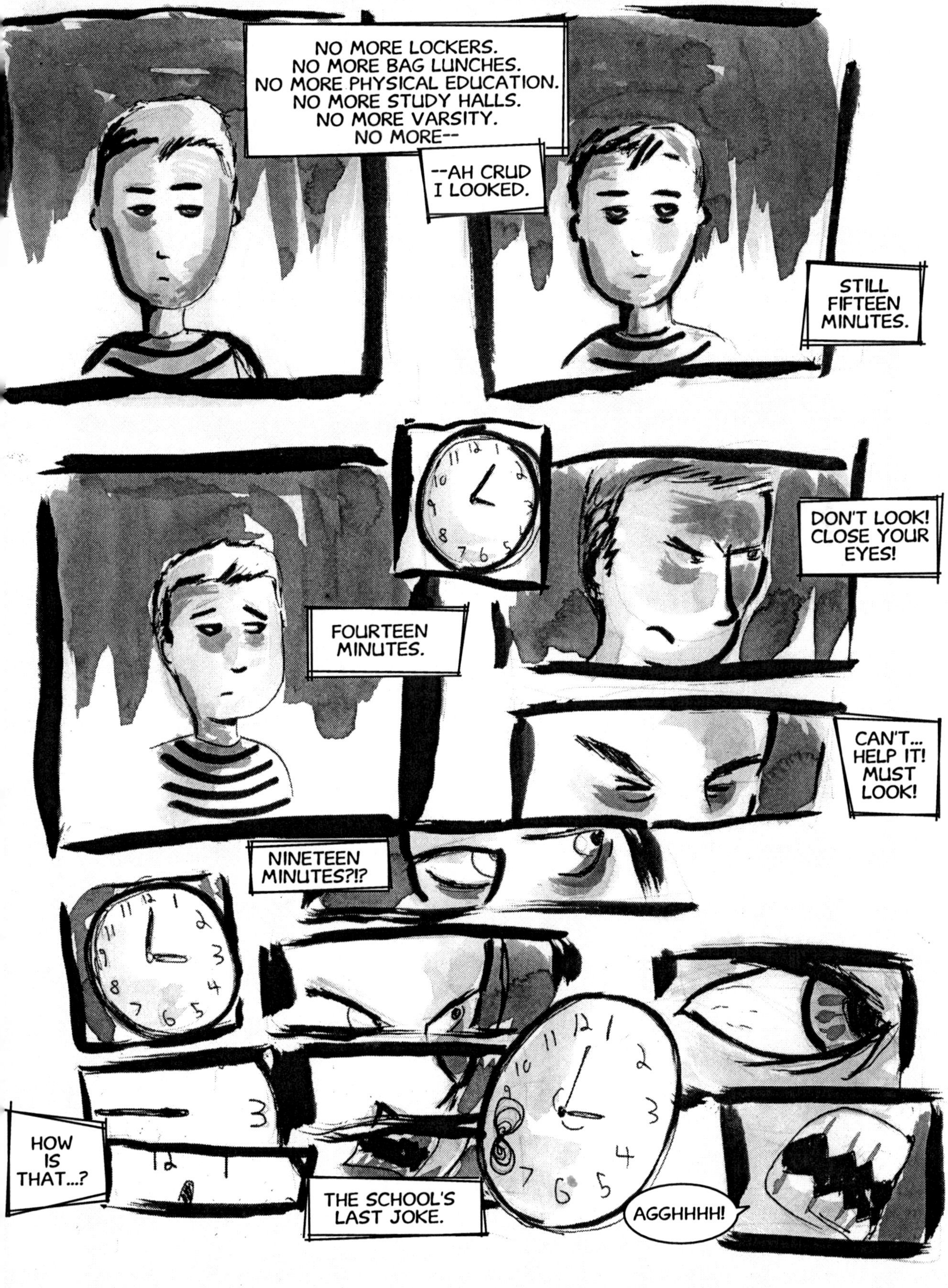
NO MORE LOCKERS.
NO MORE BAG LUNCHES.
NO MORE PHYSICAL EDUCATION.
NO MORE STUDY HALLS.
NO MORE VARSITY.
NO MORE--
--AH CRUD I LOOKED.
STILL FIFTEEN MINUTES.
FOURTEEN MINUTES.
DON'T LOOK! CLOSE YOUR EYES!
CAN'T... HELP IT! MUST LOOK!
NINETEEN MINUTES?!?
HOW IS THAT...?
THE SCHOOL'S LAST JOKE.
AGGHHHH!

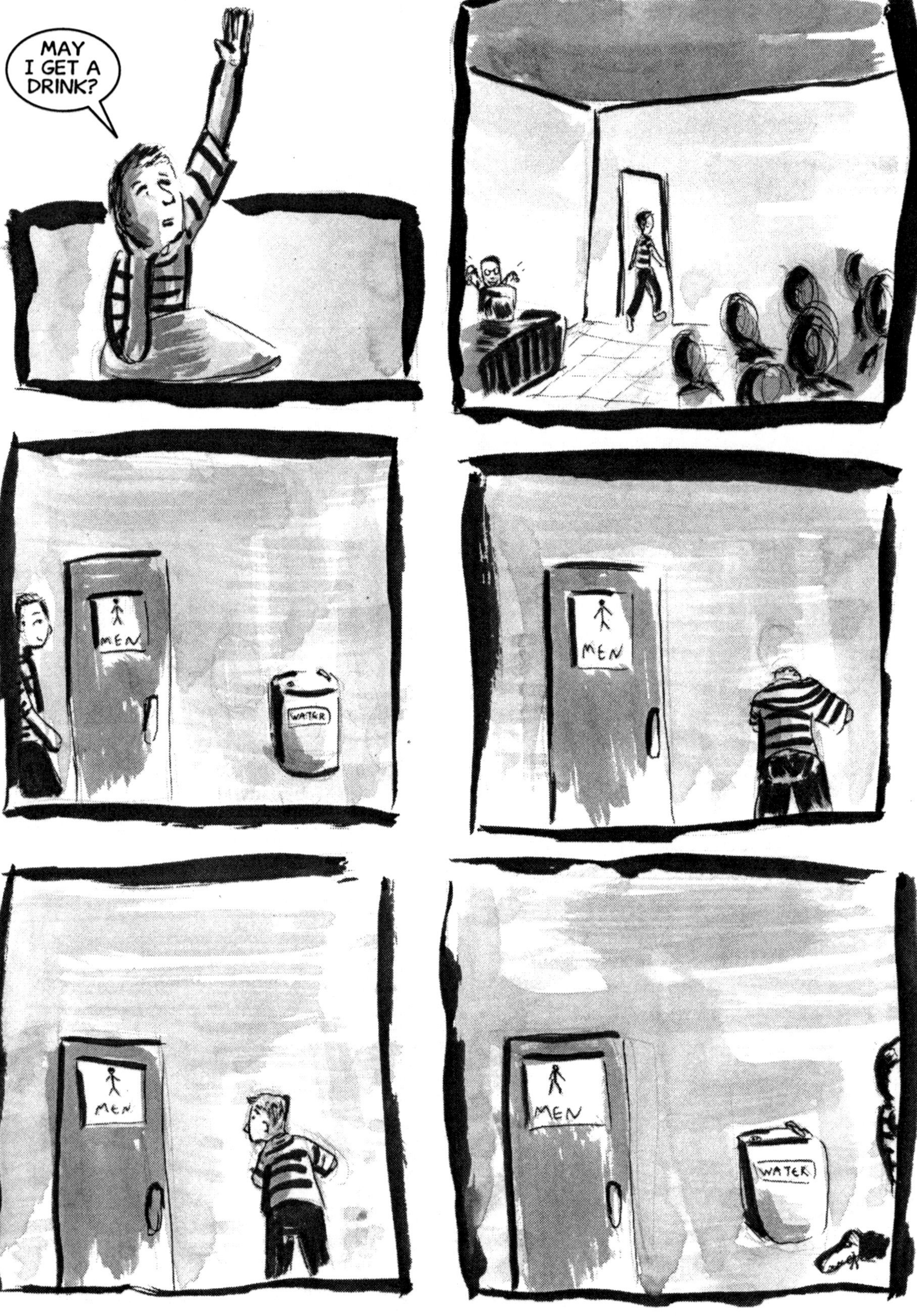
MAY I GET A DRINK?
MEN
WATER
MEN
MEN
MEN
WATER

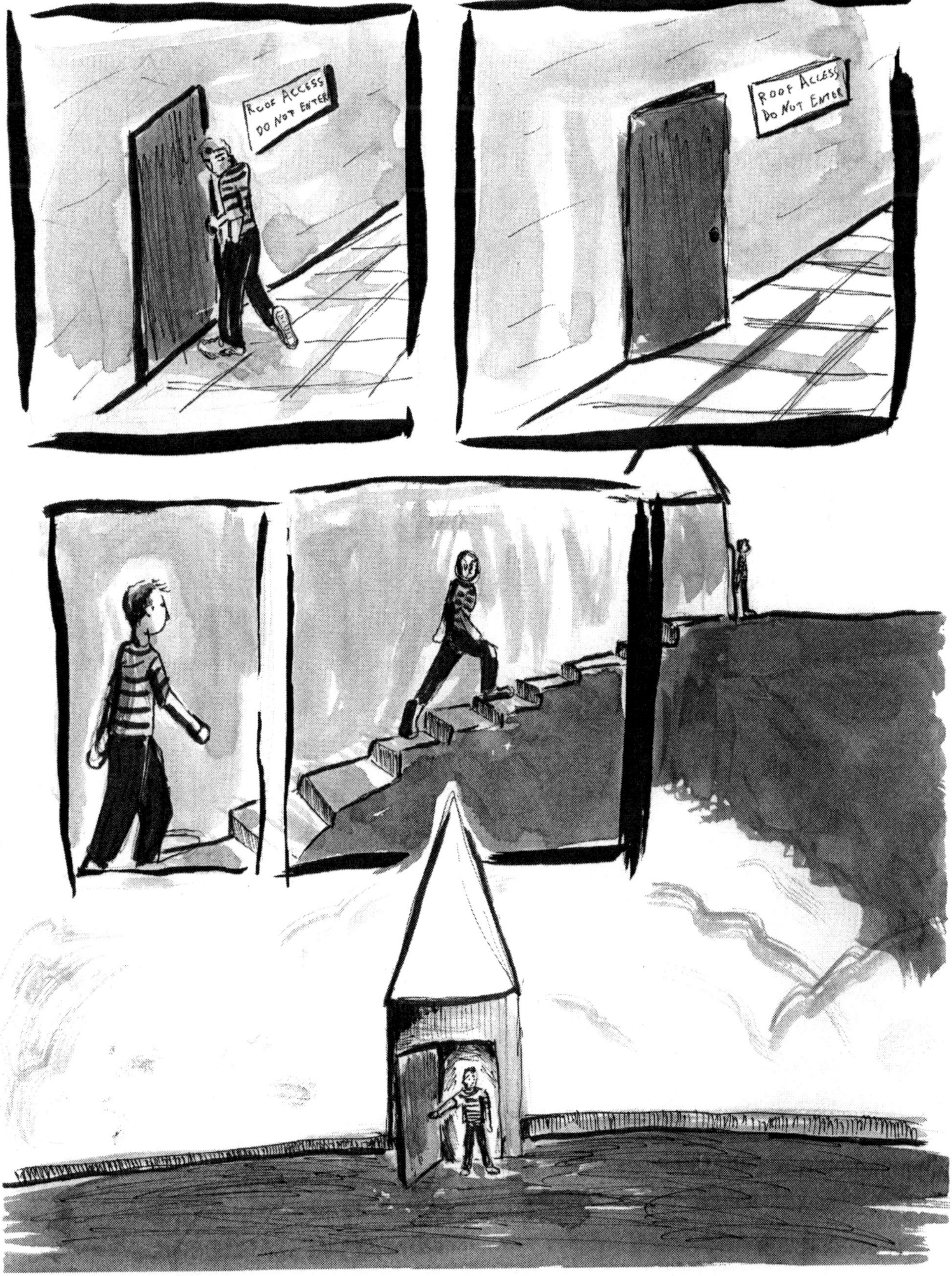
ROOF ACCESS
DO NOT ENTER
ROOF ACCESS
DO NOT ENTER

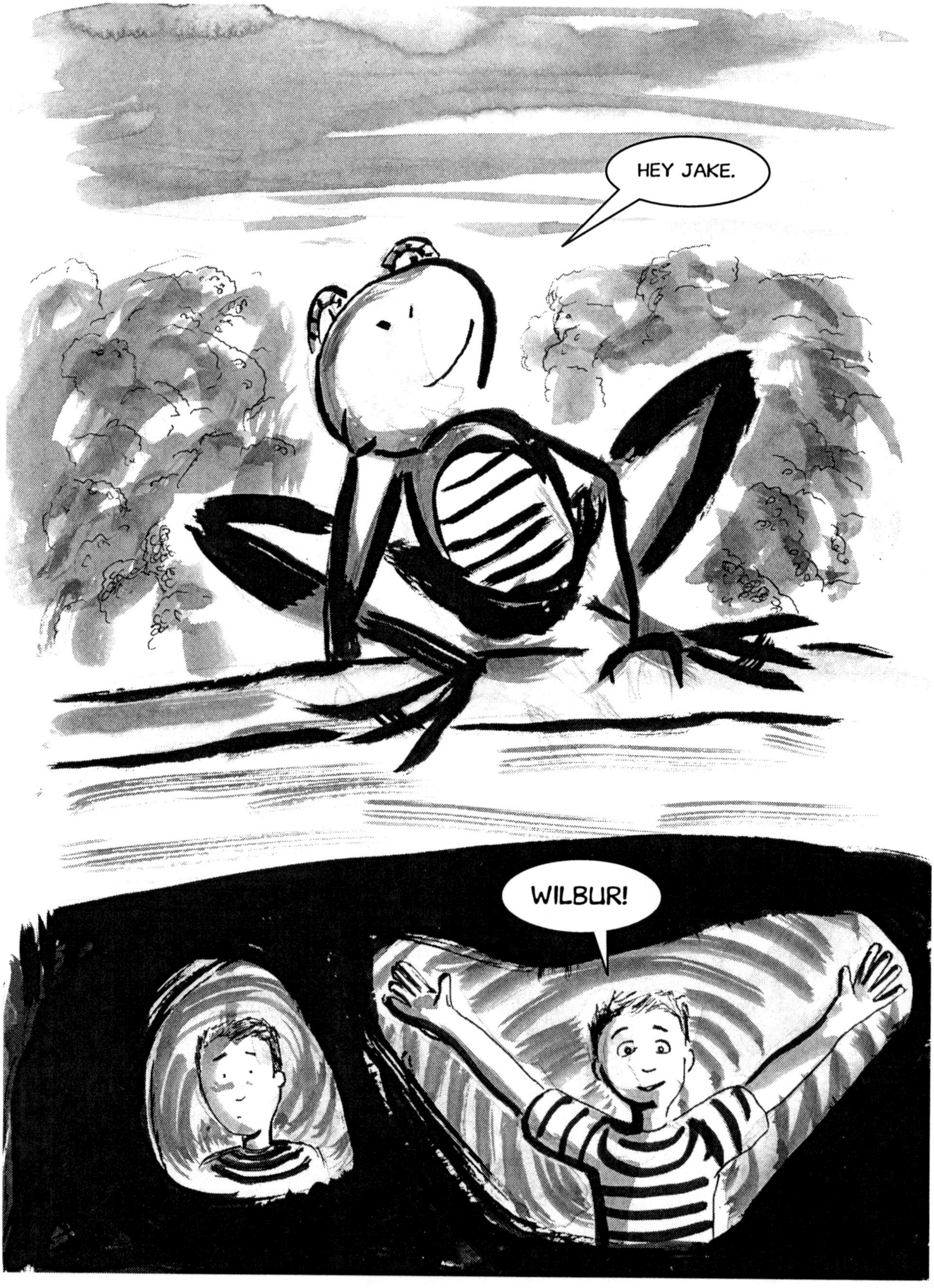
HEY JAKE.
WILBUR!

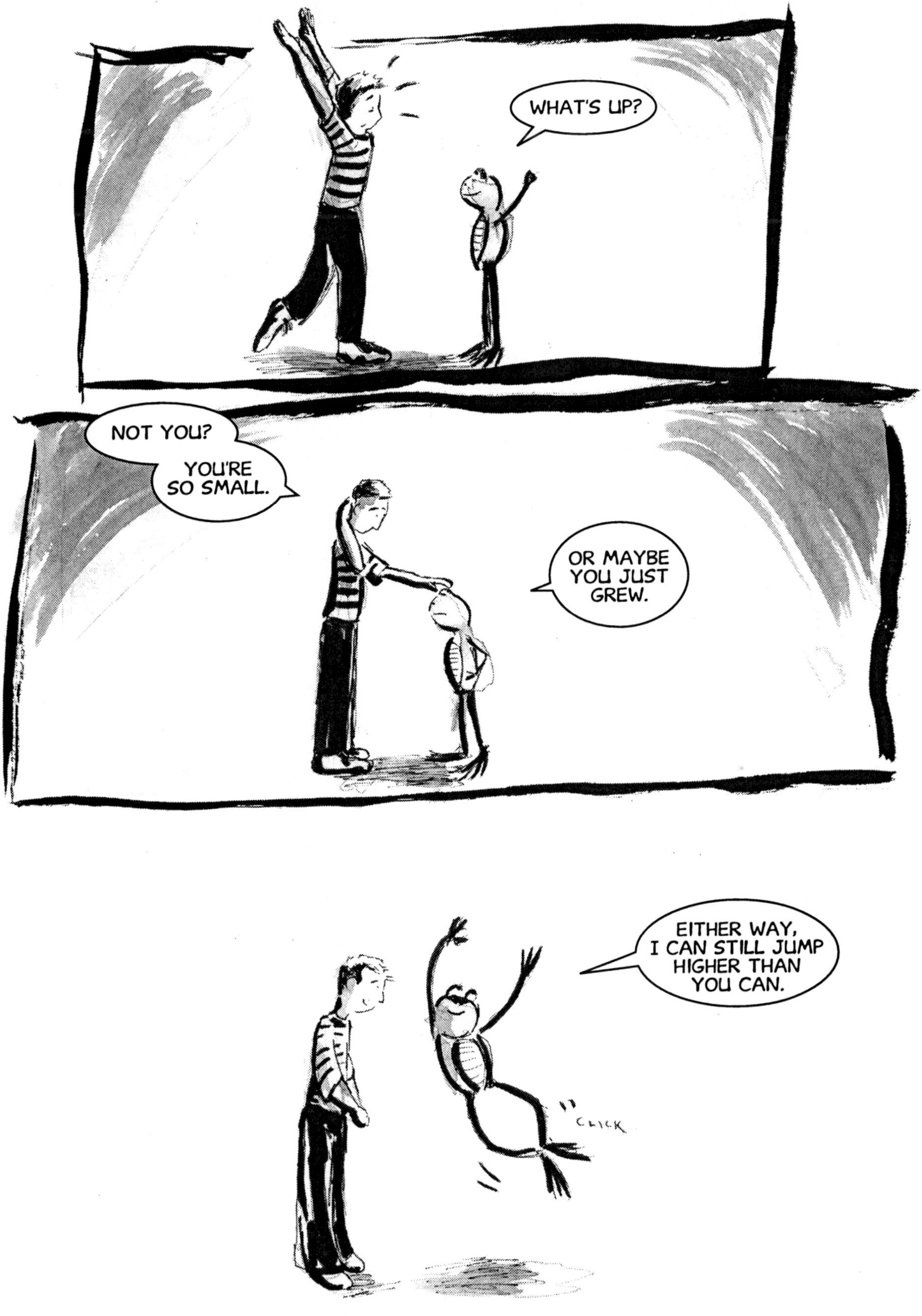
WHAT'S UP?
NOT YOU?
YOU'RE SO SMALL.
OR MAYBE YOU JUST GREW.
EITHER WAY, I CAN STILL JUMP HIGHER THAN YOU CAN.
CLICK

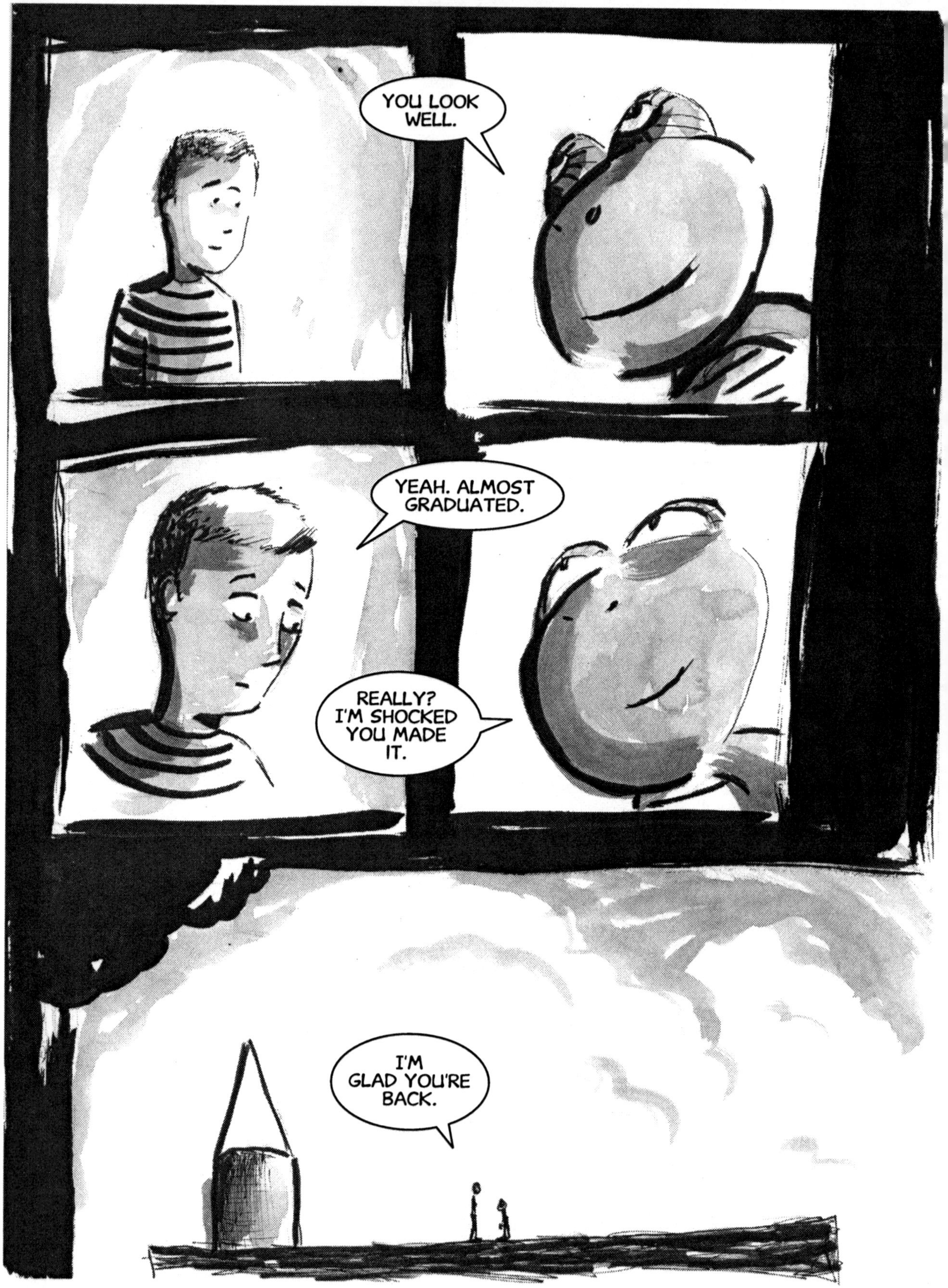
YOU LOOK WELL.
YEAH. ALMOST GRADUATED.
REALLY? I'M SHOCKED YOU MADE IT.
I'M GLAD YOU'RE BACK.

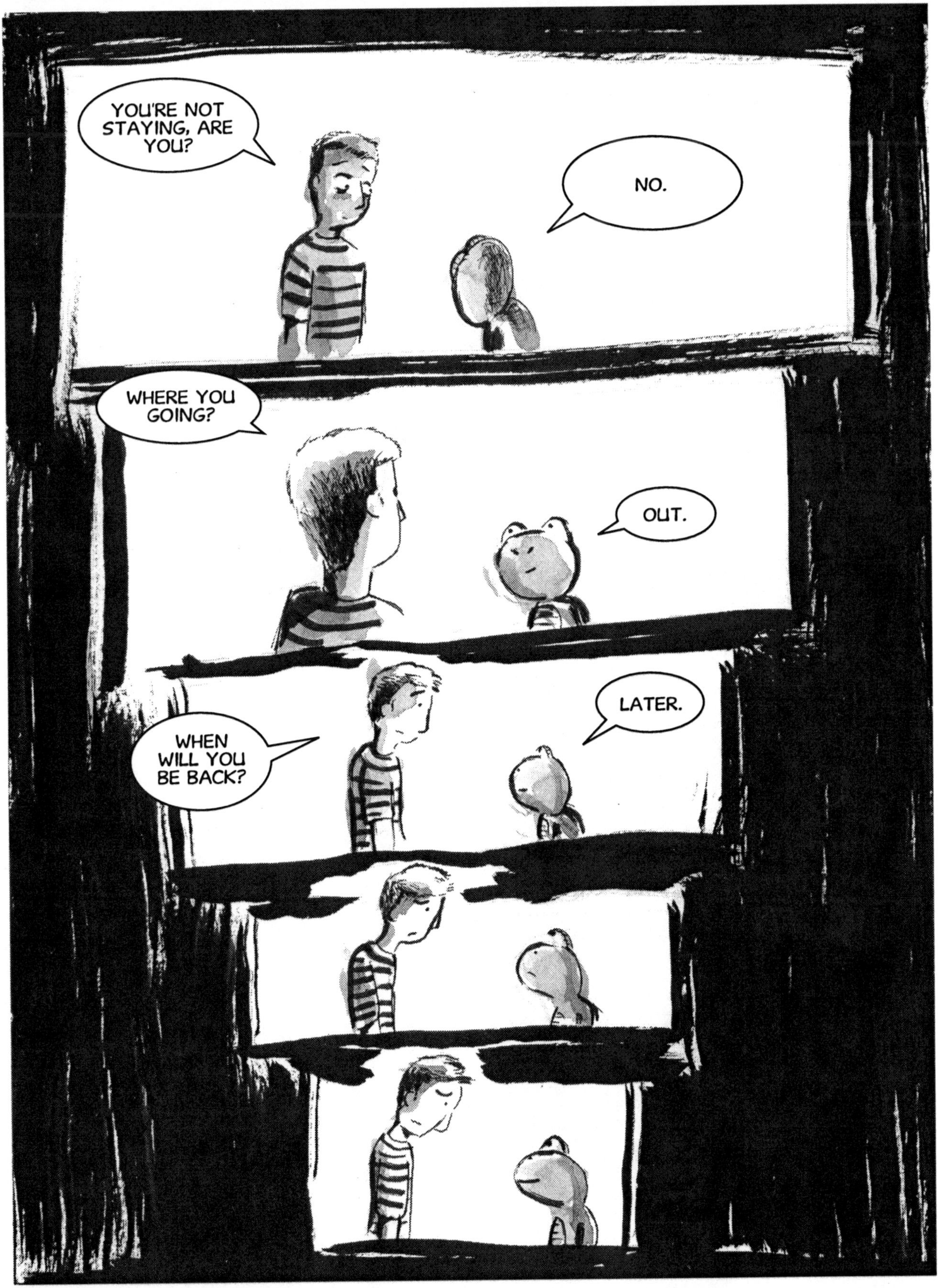
YOU'RE NOT STAYING, ARE YOU?
NO.
WHERE YOU GOING?
OUT.
WHEN WILL YOU BE BACK?
LATER.

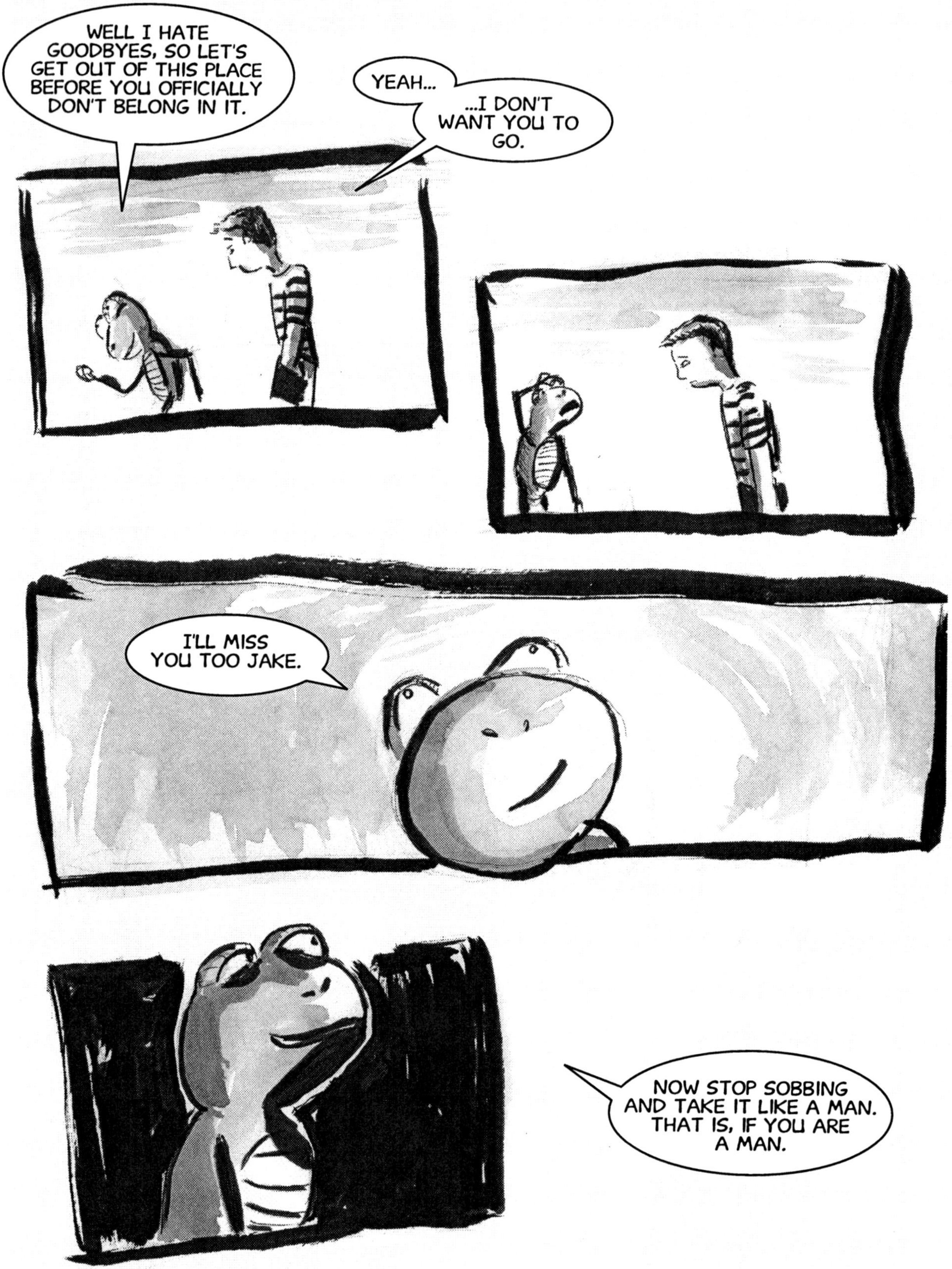
WELL I HATE GOODBYES, SO LET'S GET OUT OF THIS PLACE BEFORE YOU OFFICIALLY DON'T BELONG IN IT.
YEAH...
...I DON'T WANT YOU TO GO.
I'LL MISS YOU TOO JAKE.
NOW STOP SOBBING AND TAKE IT LIKE A MAN. THAT IS, IF YOU ARE A MAN.

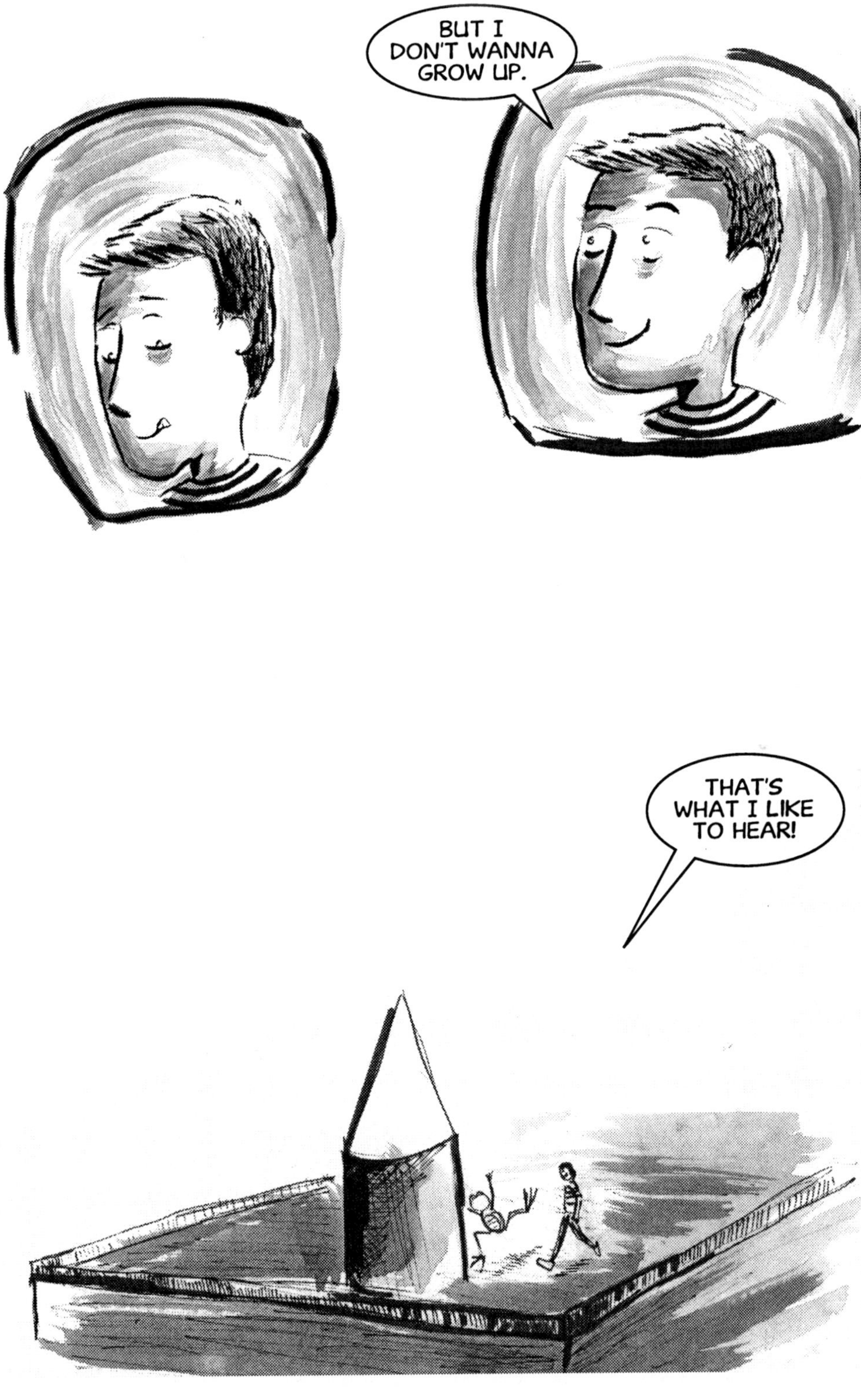
BUT I DON'T WANNA GROW UP.
THAT'S WHAT I LIKE TO HEAR!

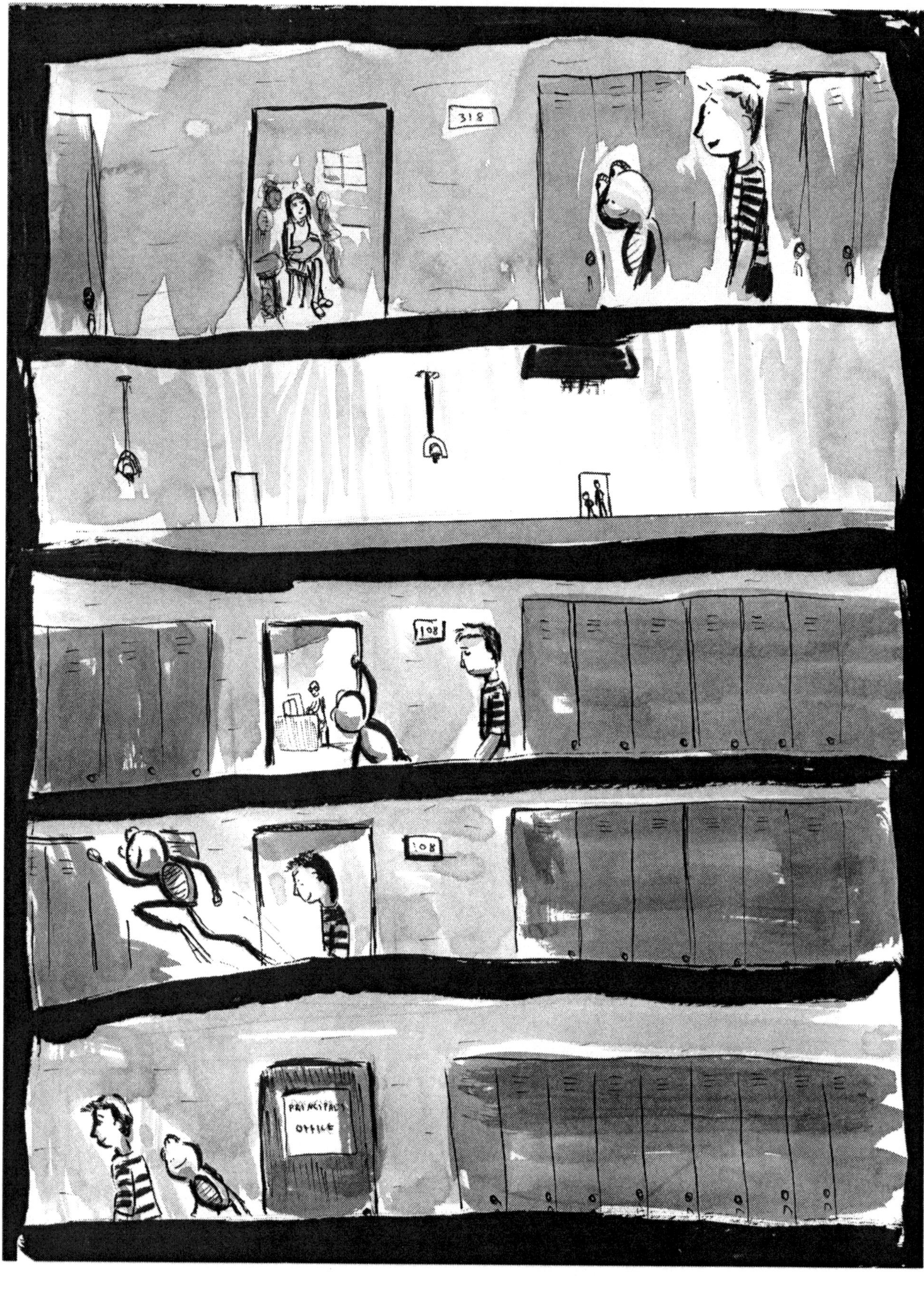
318
108
108
PRINCIPAL'S
OFFICE

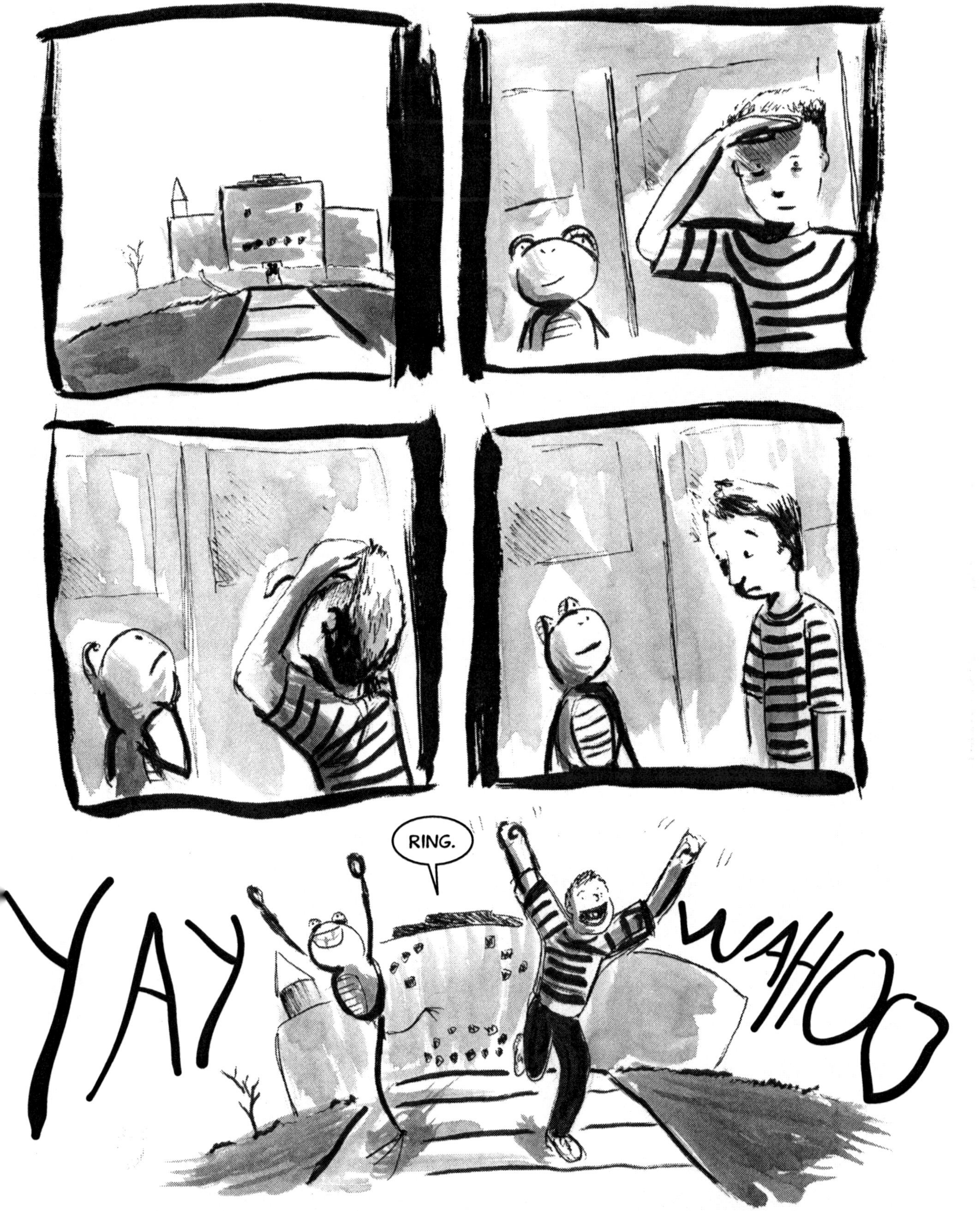
RING.
YAY
WAHOO

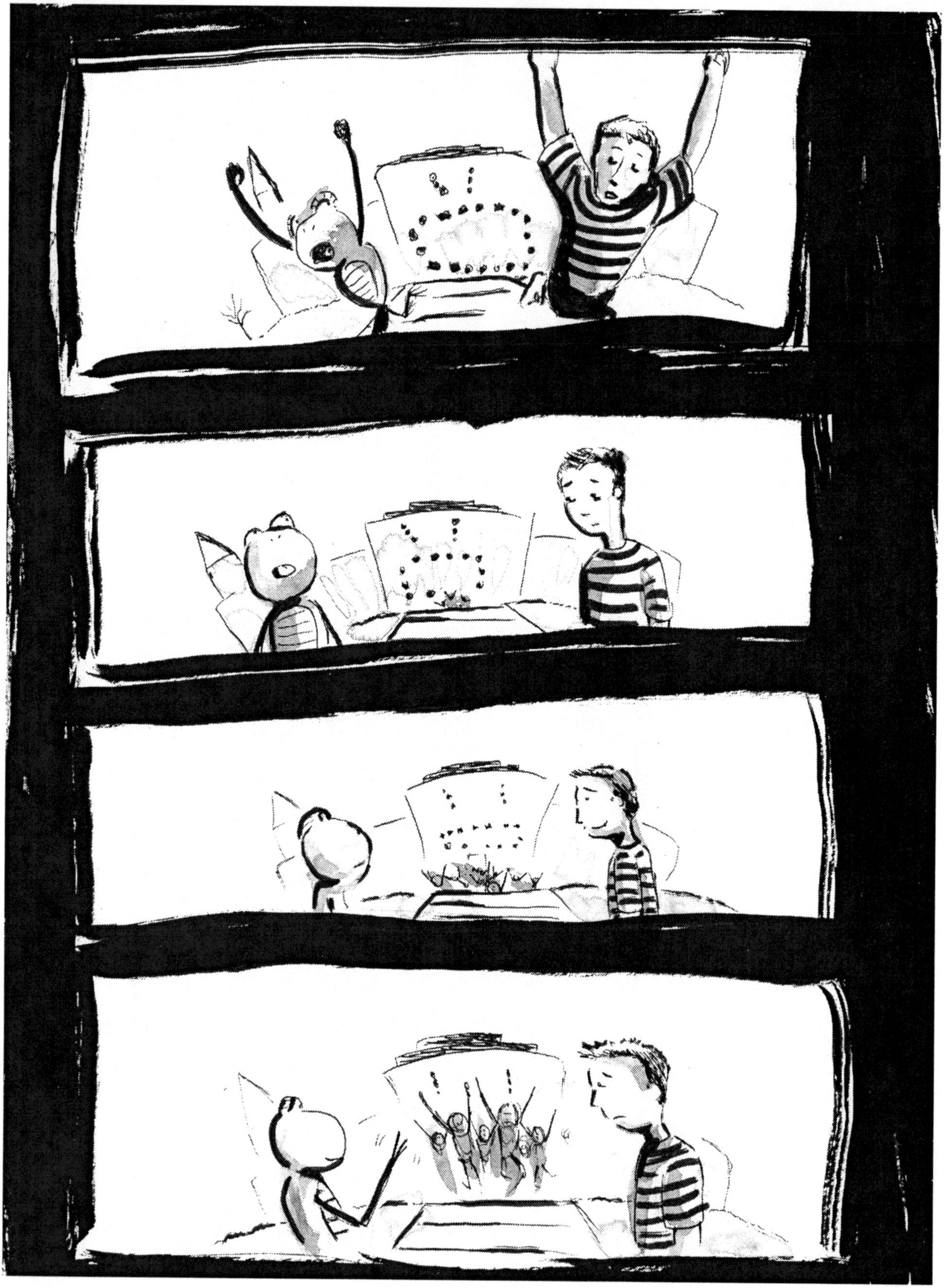

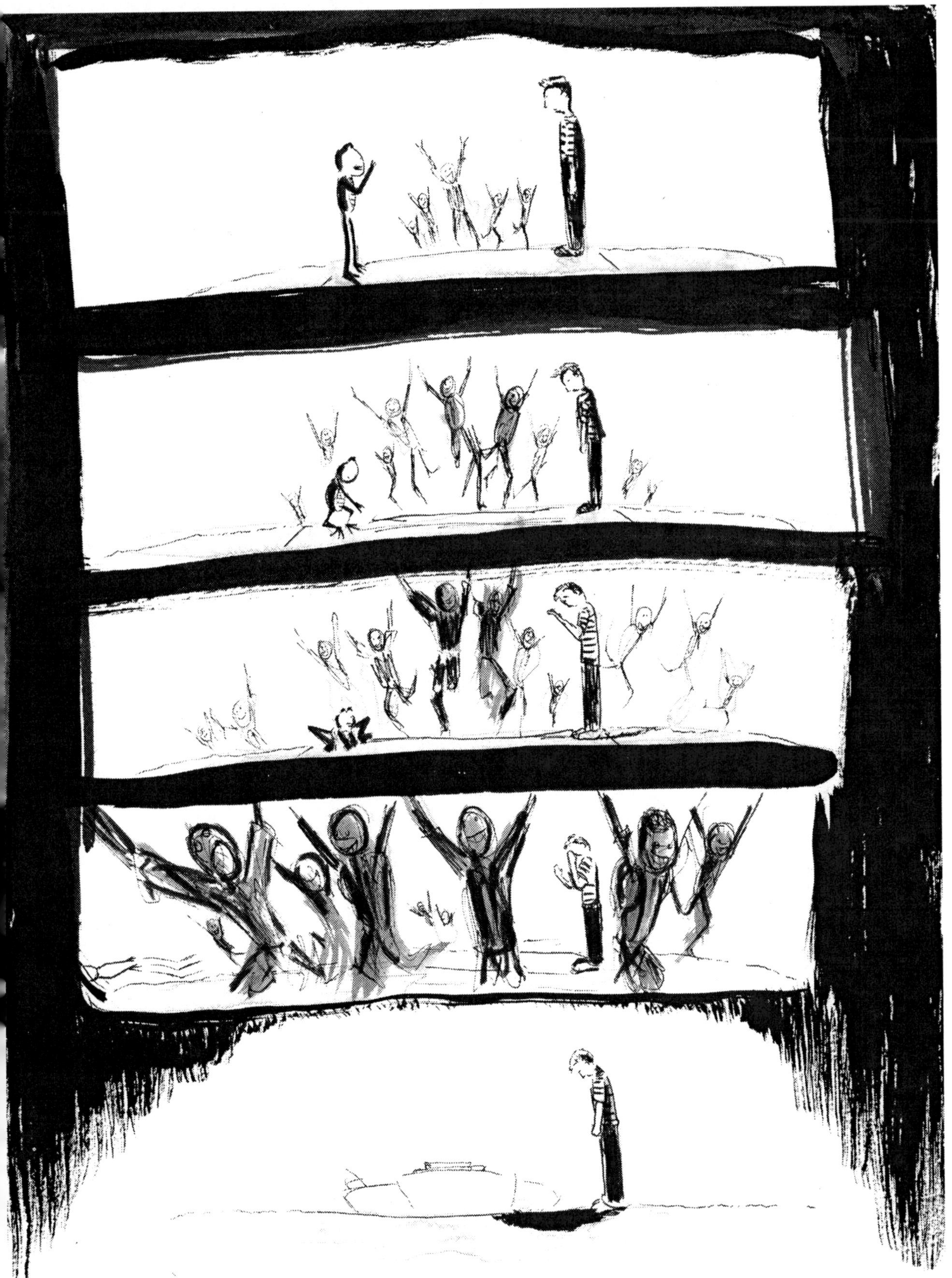

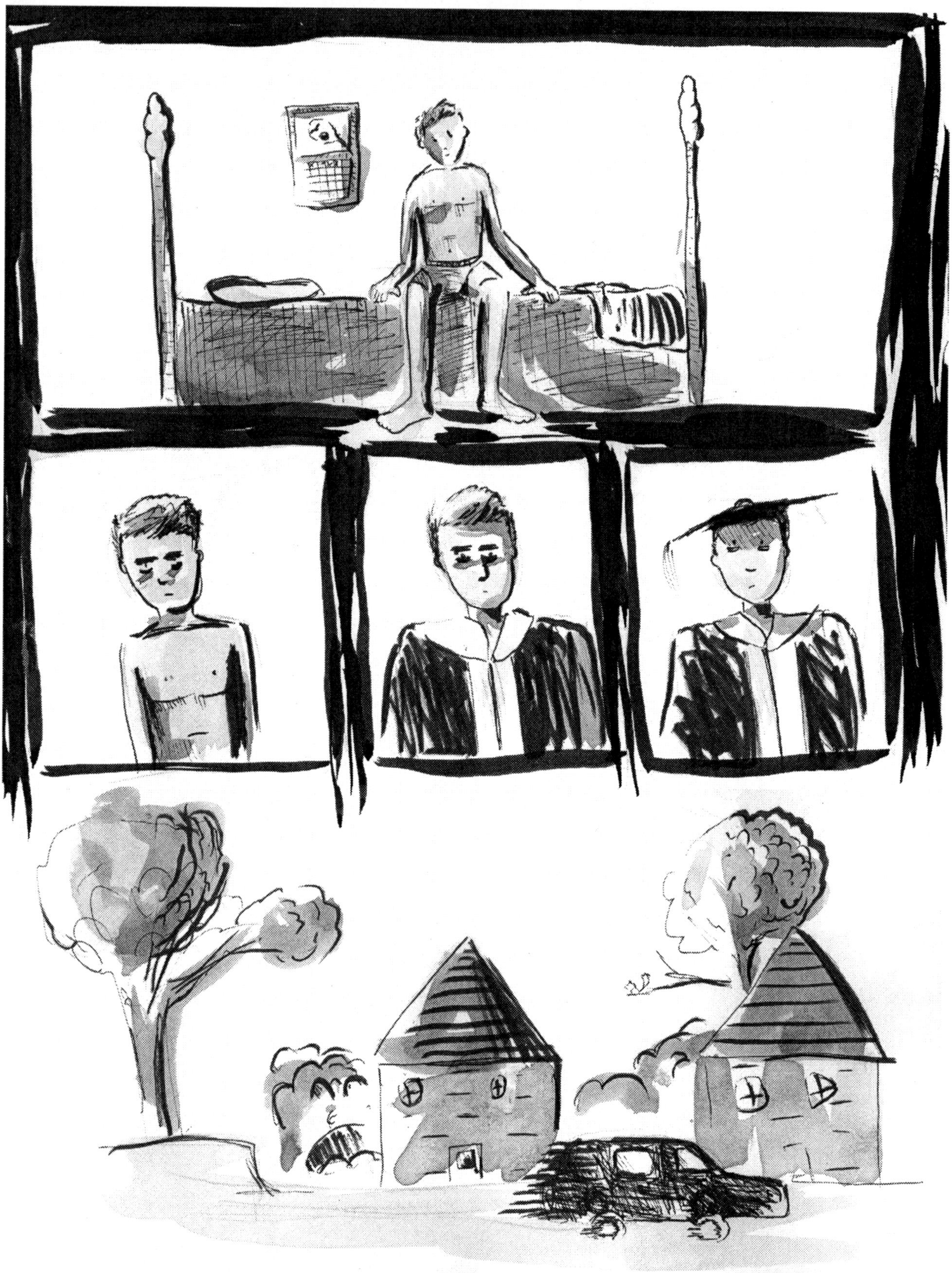

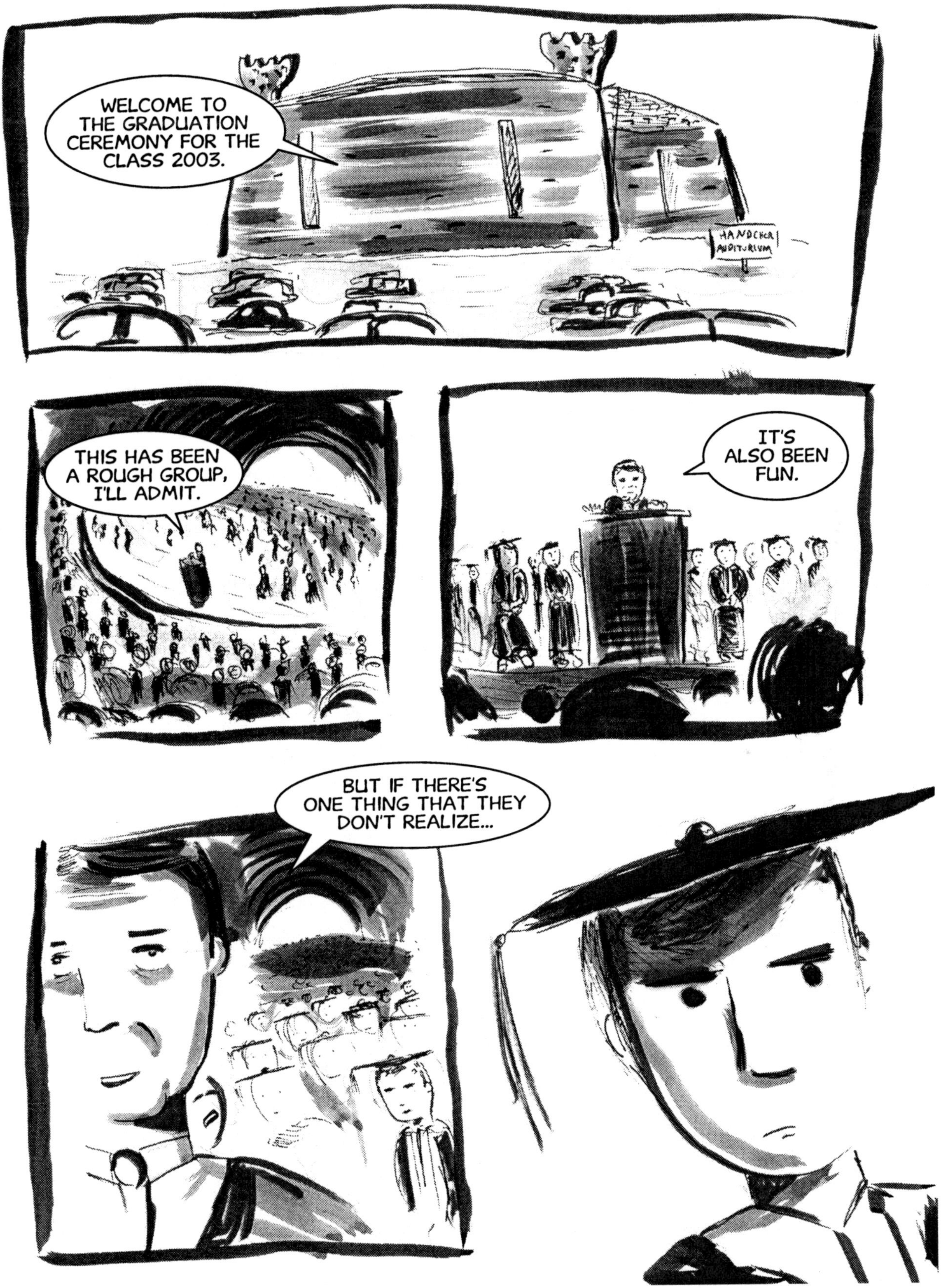
WELCOME TO THE GRADUATION CEREMONY FOR THE CLASS 2003.
HANDCHER AUDITORIUM
THIS HAS BEEN A ROUGH GROUP, I'LL ADMIT.
IT'S ALSO BEEN FUN.
BUT IF THERE'S ONE THING THAT THEY DON'T REALIZE...

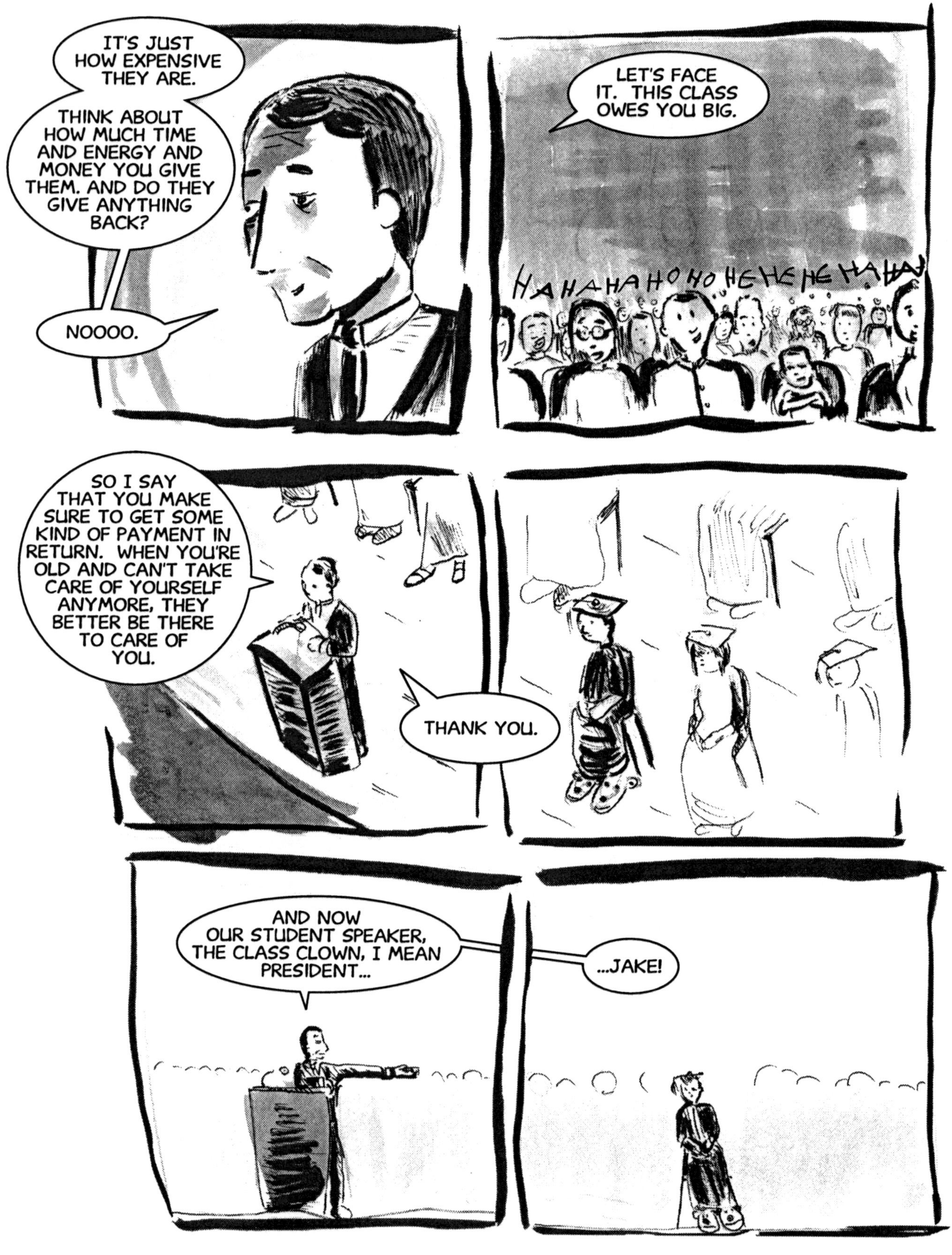
IT'S JUST HOW EXPENSIVE THEY ARE.
THINK ABOUT HOW MUCH TIME AND ENERGY AND MONEY YOU GIVE THEM. AND DO THEY GIVE ANYTHING BACK?
NOOOO.
LET'S FACE IT. THIS CLASS OWES YOU BIG.
HAHAHAHOHOHOHEHEHEHEHAHA
SO I SAY THAT YOU MAKE SURE TO GET SOME KIND OF PAYMENT IN RETURN. WHEN YOU'RE OLD AND CAN'T TAKE CARE OF YOURSELF ANYMORE, THEY BETTER BE THERE TO CARE OF YOU.
THANK YOU.
AND NOW OUR STUDENT SPEAKER, THE CLASS CLOWN, I MEAN PRESIDENT...
...JAKE!

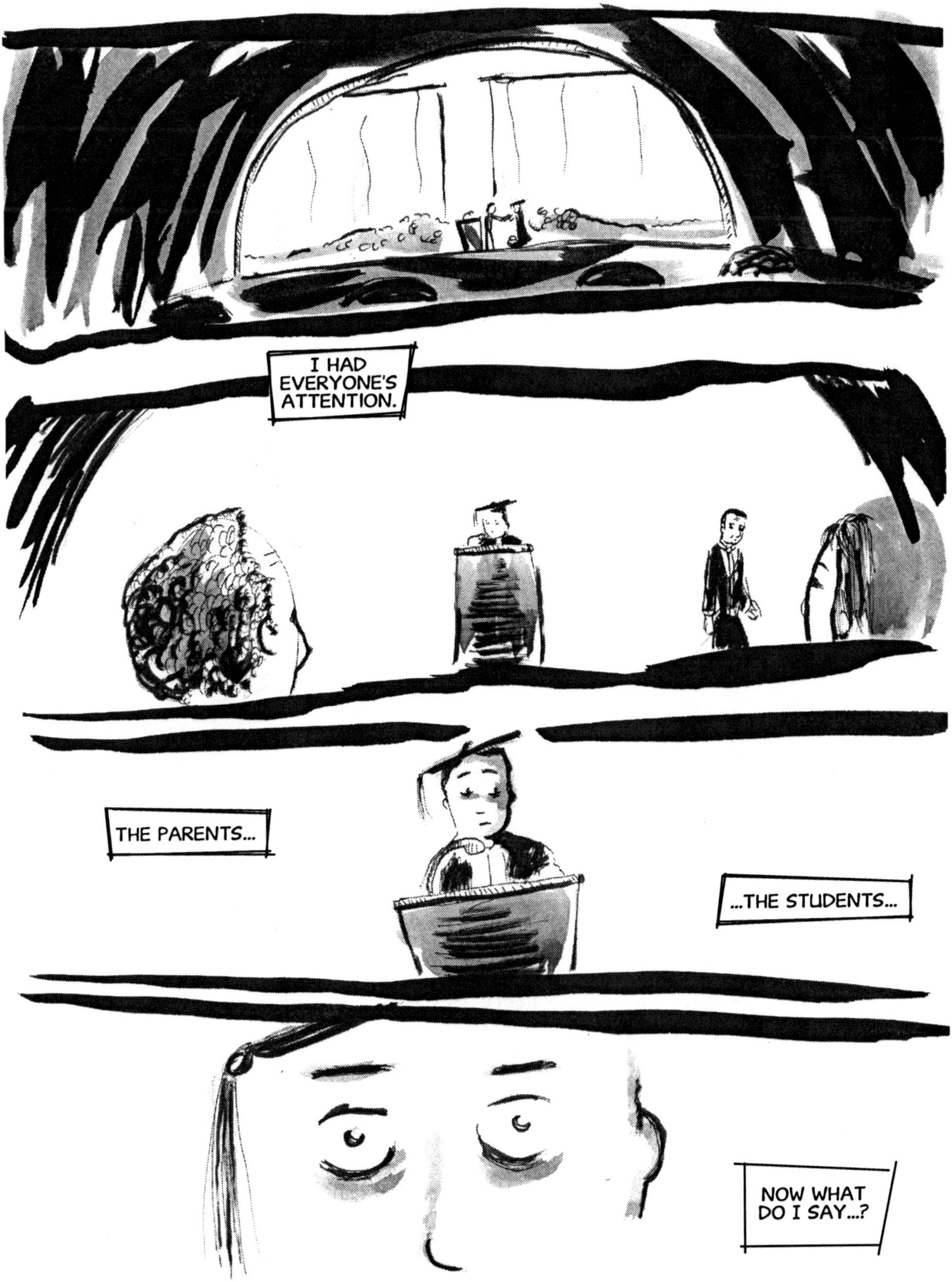
I HAD EVERYONE'S ATTENTION.
THE PARENTS...
...THE STUDENTS...
NOW WHAT DO I SAY...?

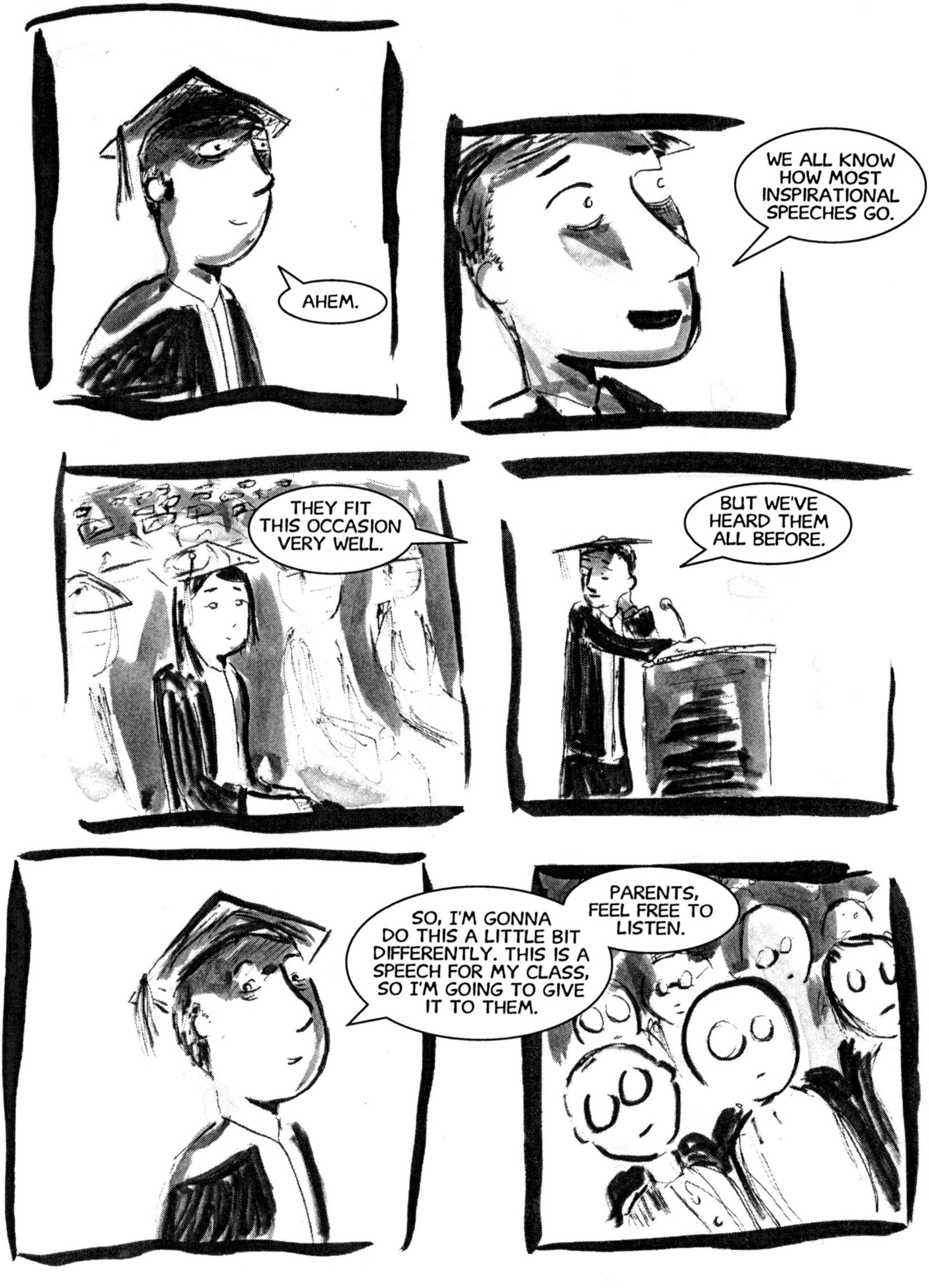
AHEM.
WE ALL KNOW HOW MOST INSPIRATIONAL SPEECHES GO.
THEY FIT THIS OCCASION VERY WELL.
BUT WE'VE HEARD THEM ALL BEFORE.
SO, I'M GONNA DO THIS A LITTLE BIT DIFFERENTLY. THIS IS A SPEECH FOR MY CLASS, SO I'M GOING TO GIVE IT TO THEM.
PARENTS, FEEL FREE TO LISTEN.

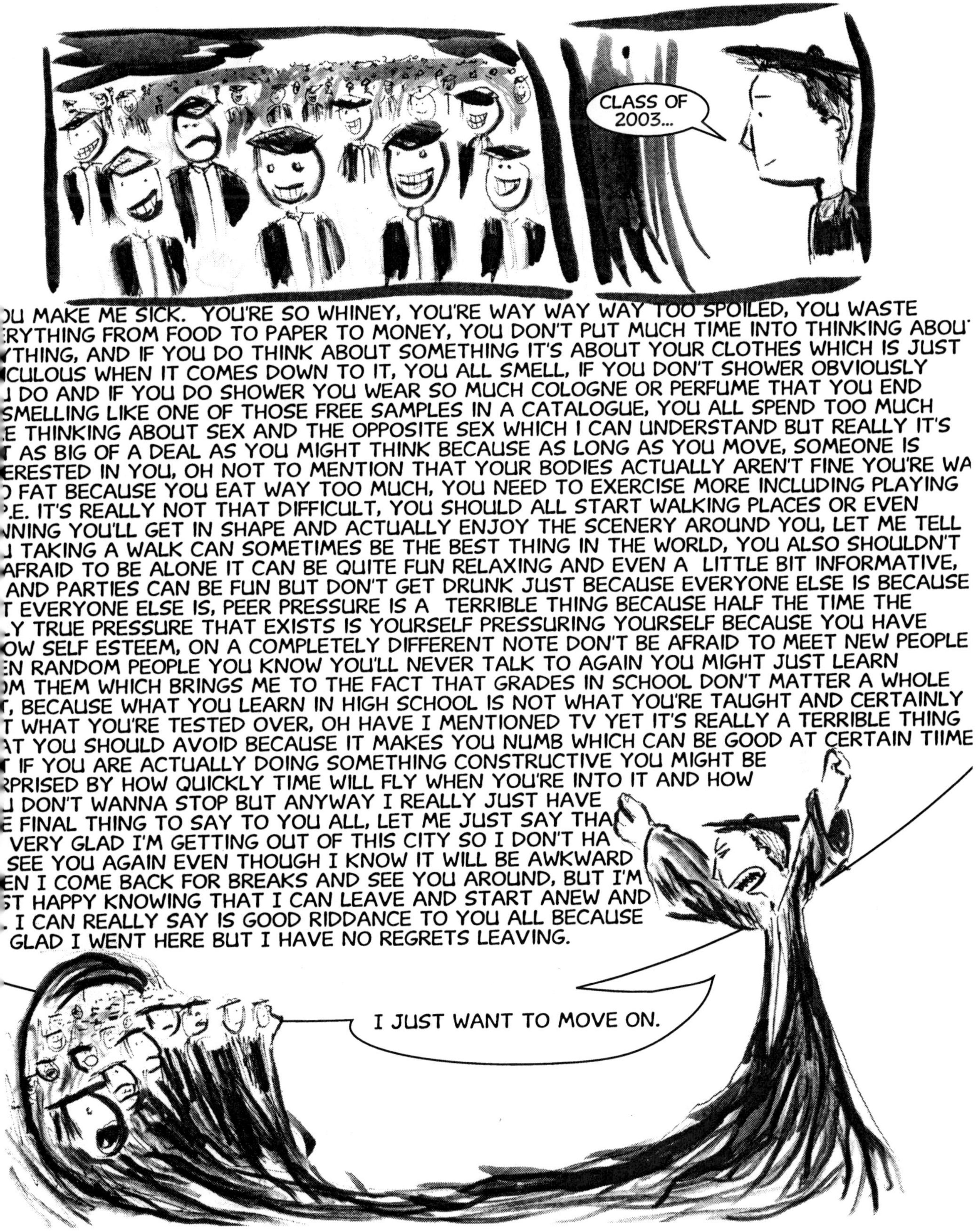
CLASS OF 2003...
OU MAKE ME SICK. YOU'RE SO WHINEY, YOU'RE WAY WAY WAY TOO SPOILED, YOU WASTE ERYTHING FROM FOOD TO PAPER TO MONEY, YOU DON'T PUT MUCH TIME INTO THINKING ABOU YTHING, AND IF YOU DO THINK ABOUT SOMETHING IT'S ABOUT YOUR CLOTHES WHICH IS JUST ICULOUS WHEN IT COMES DOWN TO IT, YOU ALL SMELL, IF YOU DON'T SHOWER OBVIOUSLY U DO AND IF YOU DO SHOWER YOU WEAR SO MUCH COLOGNE OR PERFUME THAT YOU END SMELLING LIKE ONE OF THOSE FREE SAMPLES IN A CATALOGUE, YOU ALL SPEND TOO MUCH E THINKING ABOUT SEX AND THE OPPOSITE SEX WHICH I CAN UNDERSTAND BUT REALLY IT'S T AS BIG OF A DEAL AS YOU MIGHT THINK BECAUSE AS LONG AS YOU MOVE, SOMEONE IS ERESTED IN YOU, OH NOT TO MENTION THAT YOUR BODIES ACTUALLY AREN'T FINE YOU'RE WA O FAT BECAUSE YOU EAT WAY TOO MUCH, YOU NEED TO EXERCISE MORE INCLUDING PLAYING P.E. IT'S REALLY NOT THAT DIFFICULT, YOU SHOULD ALL START WALKING PLACES OR EVEN NNING YOU'LL GET IN SHAPE AND ACTUALLY ENJOY THE SCENERY AROUND YOU, LET ME TELL U TAKING A WALK CAN SOMETIMES BE THE BEST THING IN THE WORLD, YOU ALSO SHOULDN'T AFRAID TO BE ALONE IT CAN BE QUITE FUN RELAXING AND EVEN A LITTLE BIT INFORMATIVE, AND PARTIES CAN BE FUN BUT DON'T GET DRUNK JUST BECAUSE EVERYONE ELSE IS BECAUSE T EVERYONE ELSE IS, PEER PRESSURE IS A TERRIBLE THING BECAUSE HALF THE TIME THE LY TRUE PRESSURE THAT EXISTS IS YOURSELF PRESSURING YOURSELF BECAUSE YOU HAVE OW SELF ESTEEM, ON A COMPLETELY DIFFERENT NOTE DON'T BE AFRAID TO MEET NEW PEOPLE EN RANDOM PEOPLE YOU KNOW YOU'LL NEVER TALK TO AGAIN YOU MIGHT JUST LEARN OM THEM WHICH BRINGS ME TO THE FACT THAT GRADES IN SCHOOL DON'T MATTER A WHOLE T, BECAUSE WHAT YOU LEARN IN HIGH SCHOOL IS NOT WHAT YOU'RE TAUGHT AND CERTAINLY T WHAT YOU'RE TESTED OVER, OH HAVE I MENTIONED TV YET IT'S REALLY A TERRIBLE THING AT YOU SHOULD AVOID BECAUSE IT MAKES YOU NUMB WHICH CAN BE GOOD AT CERTAIN TIIME T IF YOU ARE ACTUALLY DOING SOMETHING CONSTRUCTIVE YOU MIGHT BE RPRISED BY HOW QUICKLY TIME WILL FLY WHEN YOU'RE INTO IT AND HOW U DON'T WANNA STOP BUT ANYWAY I REALLY JUST HAVE E FINAL THING TO SAY TO YOU ALL, LET ME JUST SAY THA VERY GLAD I'M GETTING OUT OF THIS CITY SO I DON'T HA SEE YOU AGAIN EVEN THOUGH I KNOW IT WILL BE AWKWARD EN I COME BACK FOR BREAKS AND SEE YOU AROUND, BUT I'M ST HAPPY KNOWING THAT I CAN LEAVE AND START ANEW AND I CAN REALLY SAY IS GOOD RIDDANCE TO YOU ALL BECAUSE GLAD I WENT HERE BUT I HAVE NO REGRETS LEAVING.
I JUST WANT TO MOVE ON.

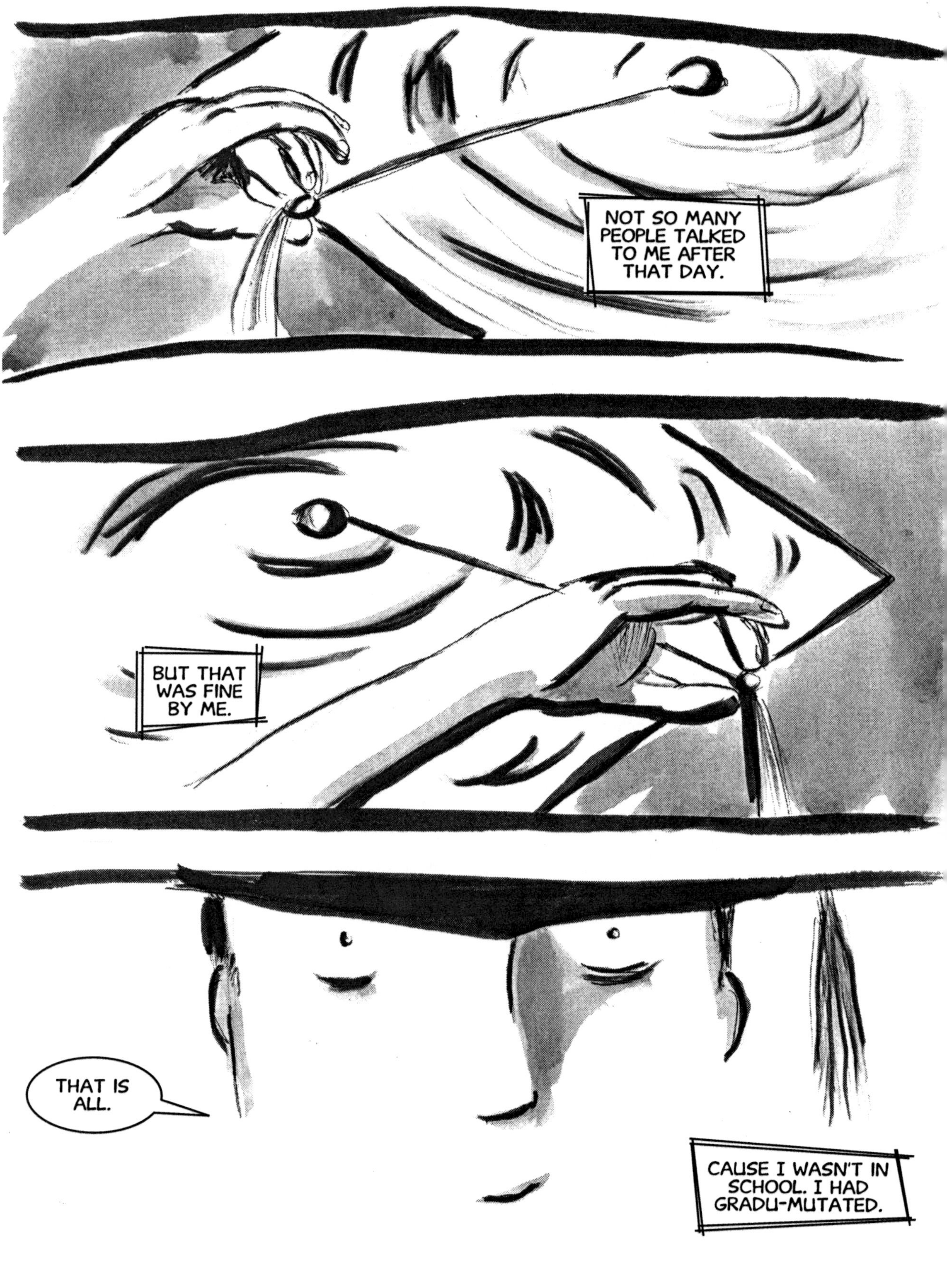
NOT SO MANY PEOPLE TALKED TO ME AFTER THAT DAY.
BUT THAT WAS FINE BY ME.
THAT IS ALL.
CAUSE I WASN'T IN SCHOOL. I HAD GRADU-MUTATED.

SUMMER

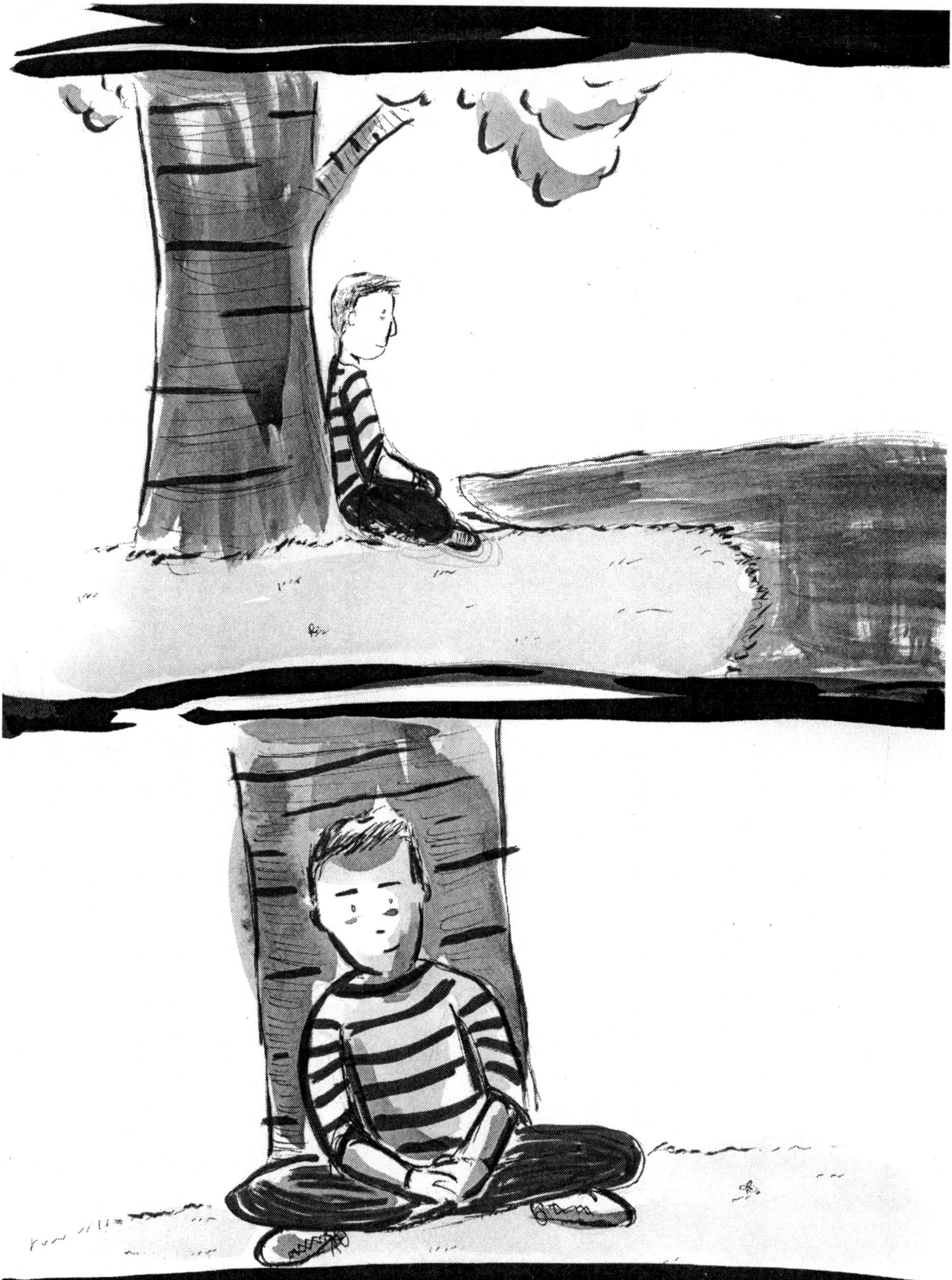

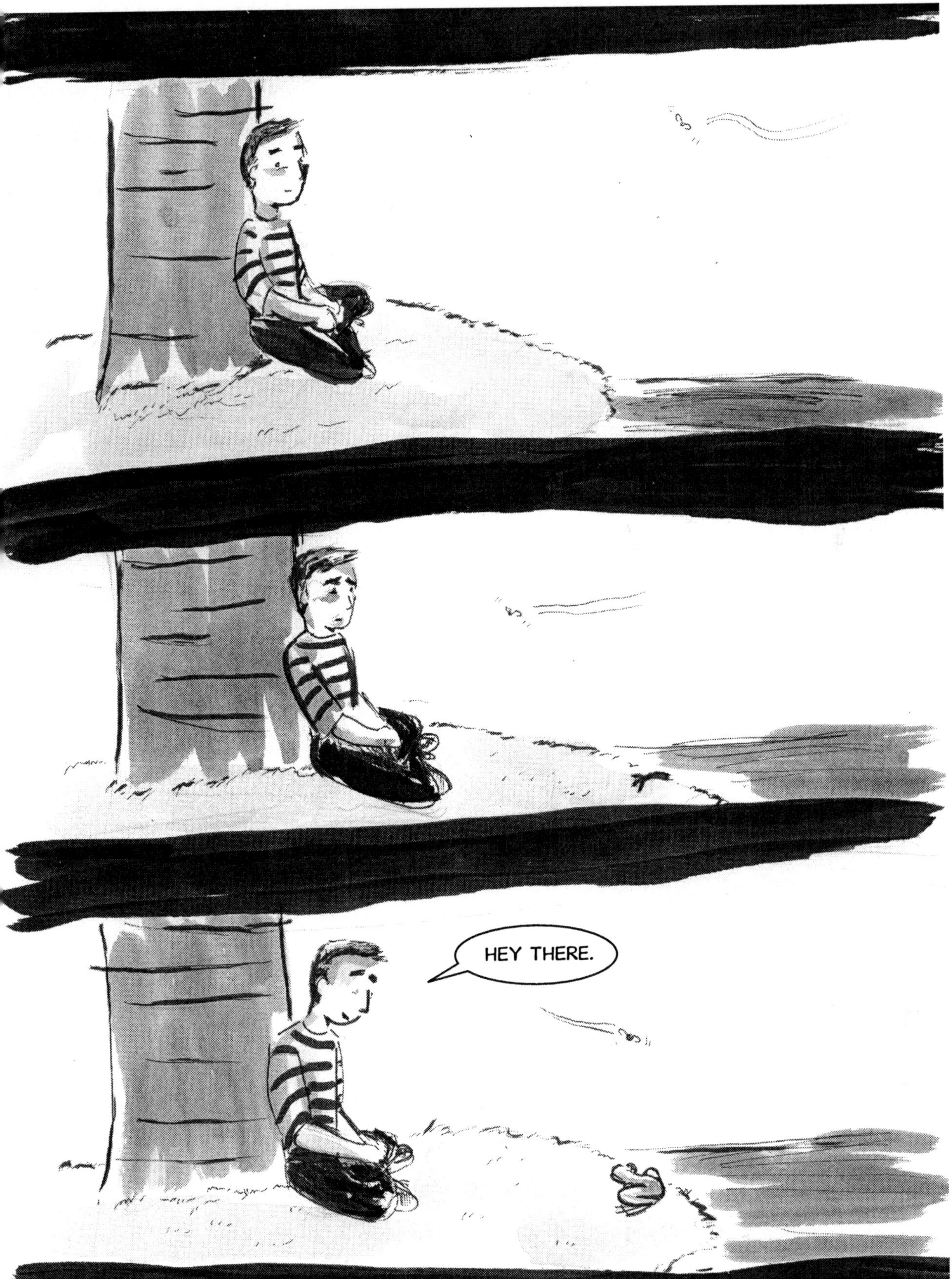
HEY THERE.

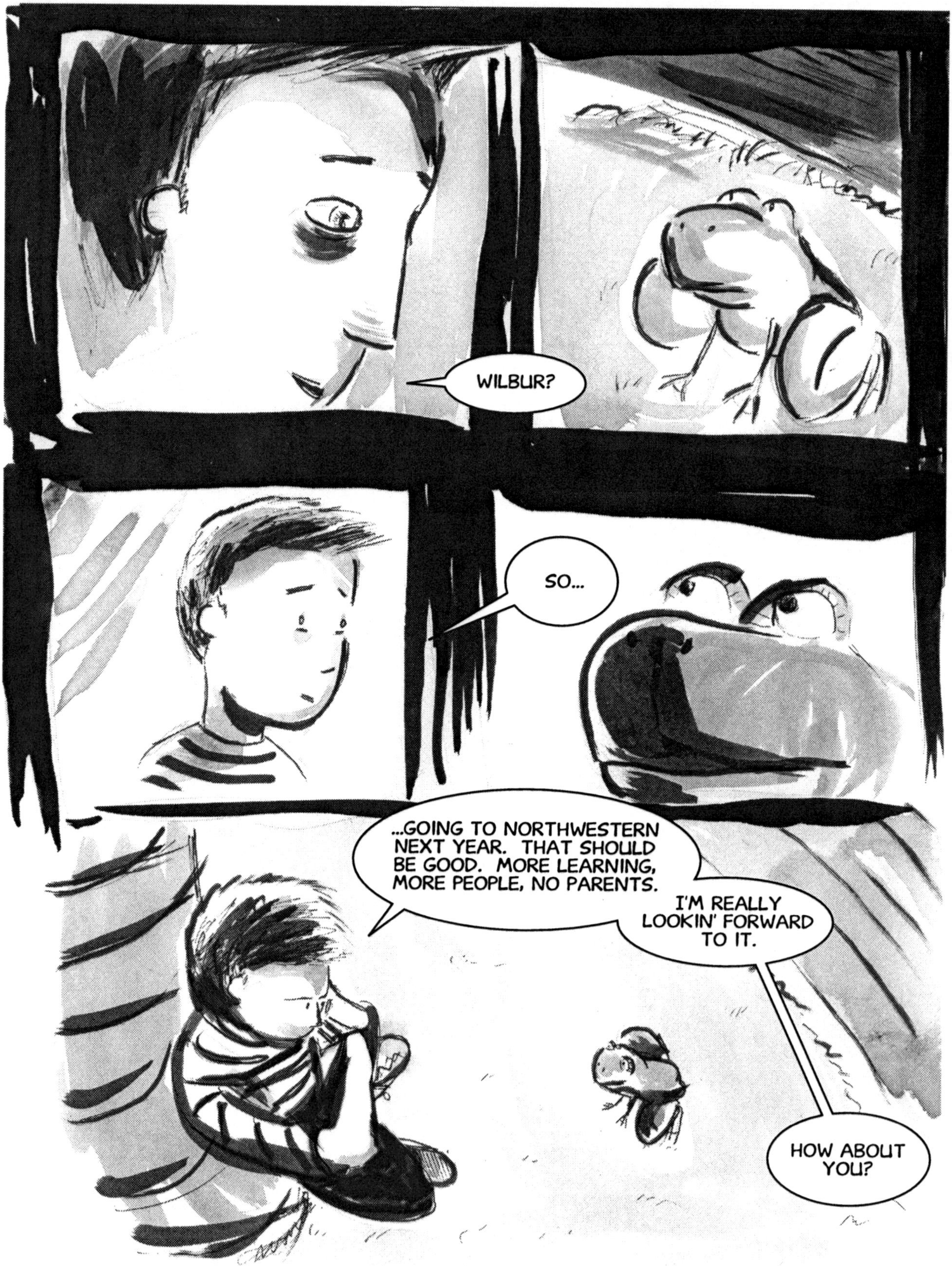
WILBUR?
SO...
...GOING TO NORTHWESTERN NEXT YEAR. THAT SHOULD BE GOOD. MORE LEARNING, MORE PEOPLE, NO PARENTS.
I'M REALLY LOOKIN' FORWARD TO IT.
HOW ABOUT YOU?

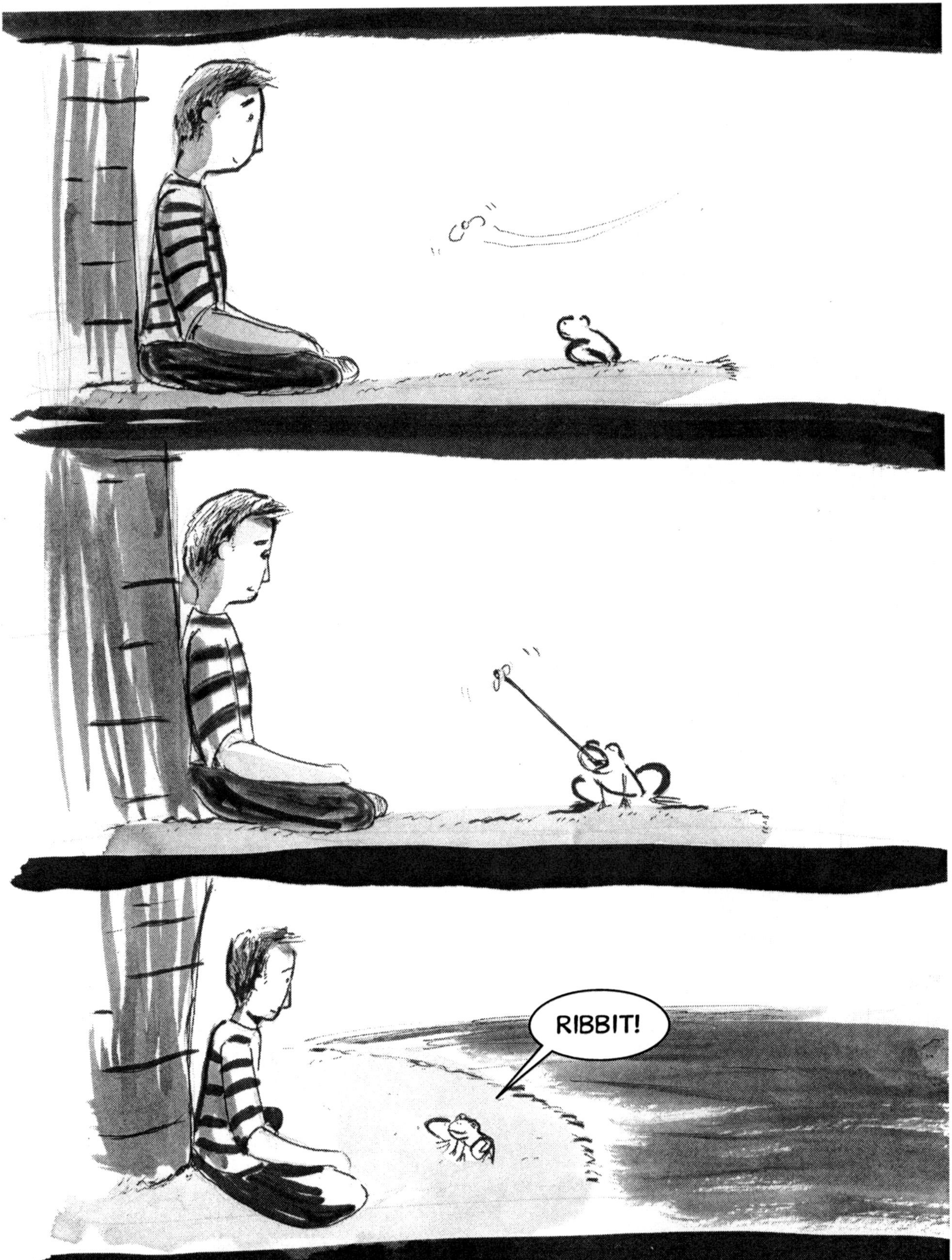
RIBBIT!

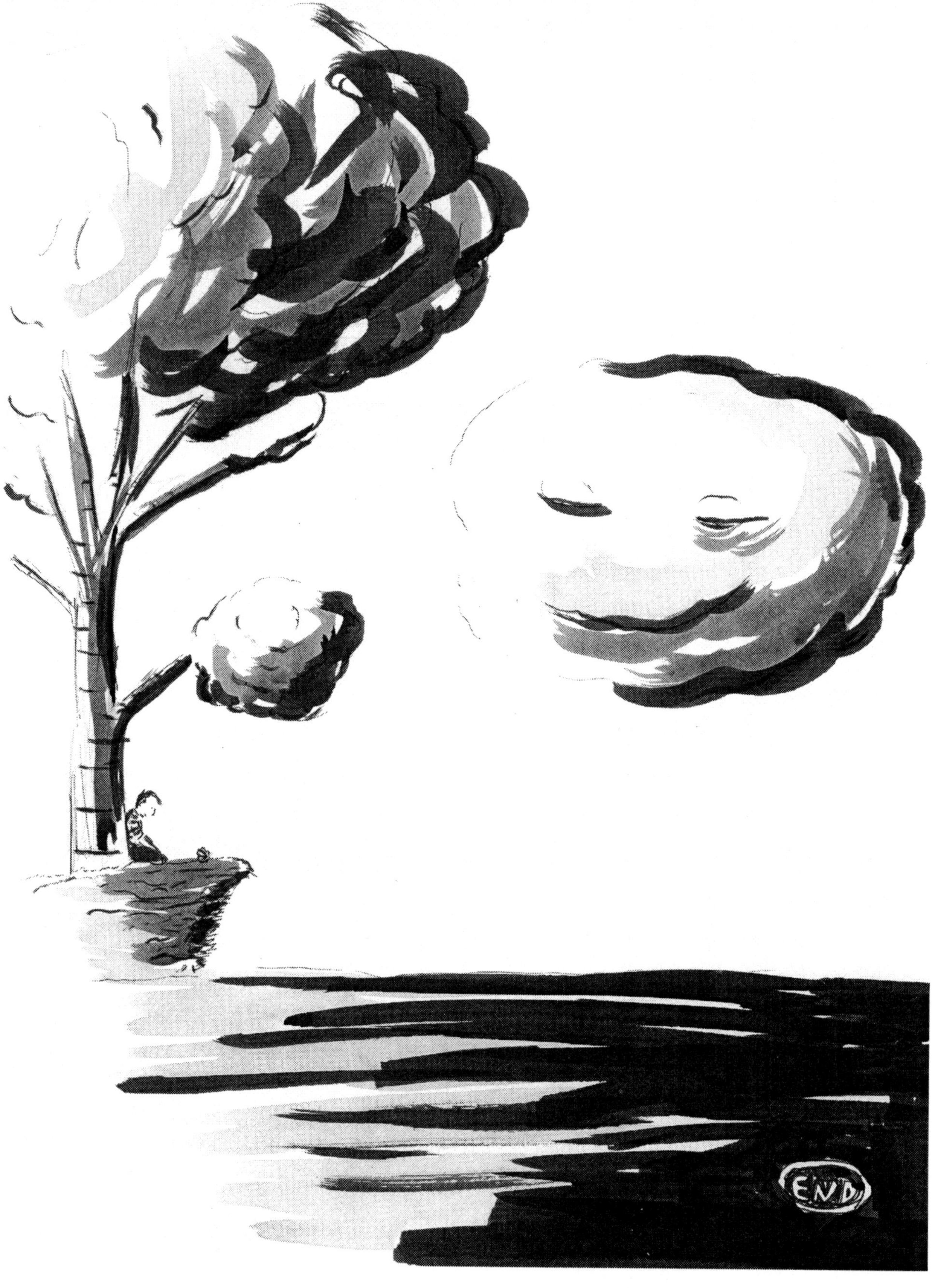
END

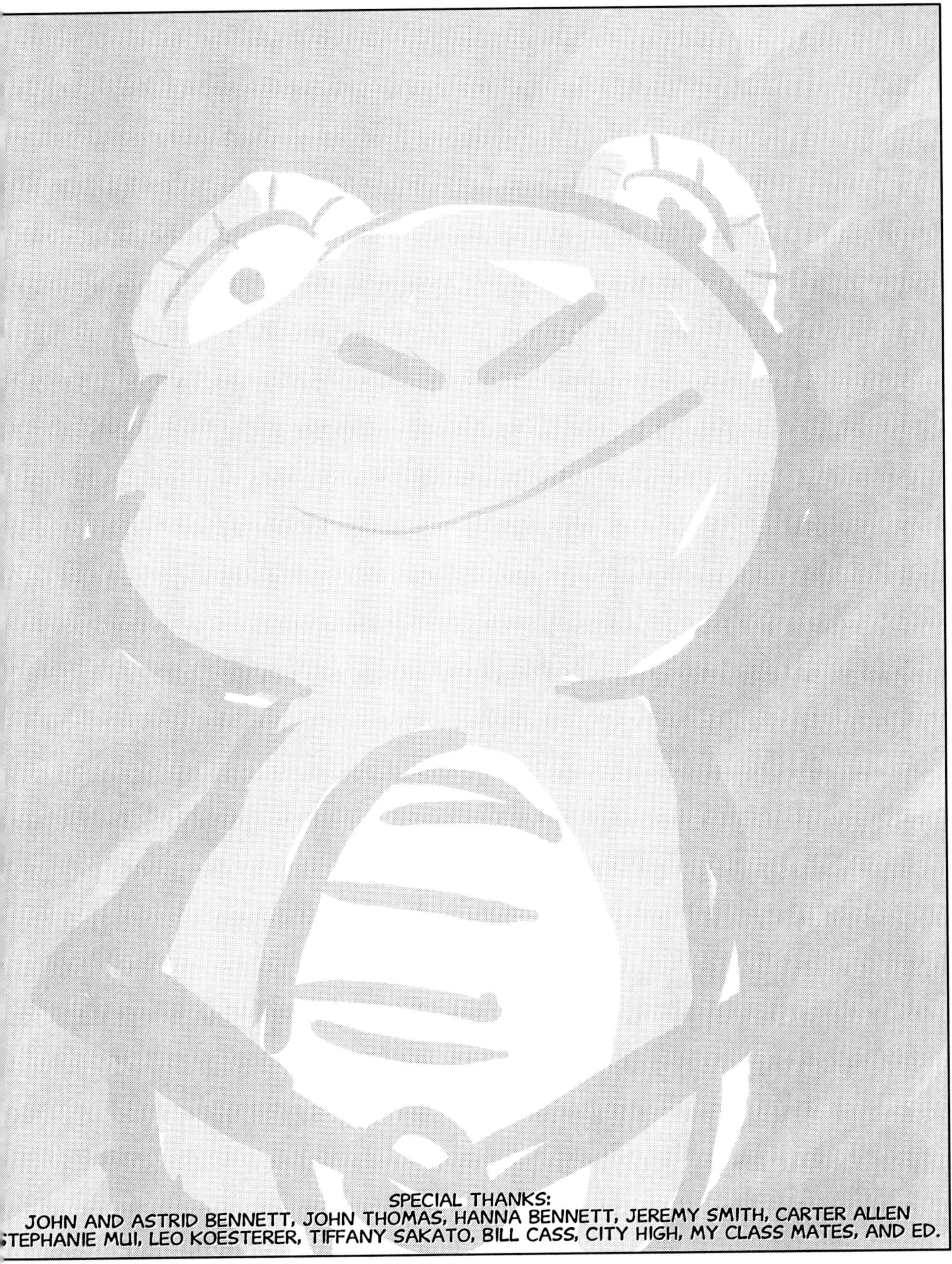

SPECIAL THANKS:
JOHN AND ASTRID BENNETT, JOHN THOMAS, HANNA BENNETT, JEREMY SMITH, CARTER ALLEN
STEPHANIE MUI, LEO KOESTERER, TIFFANY SAKATO, BILL CASS, CITY HIGH, MY CLASS MATES, AND ED.

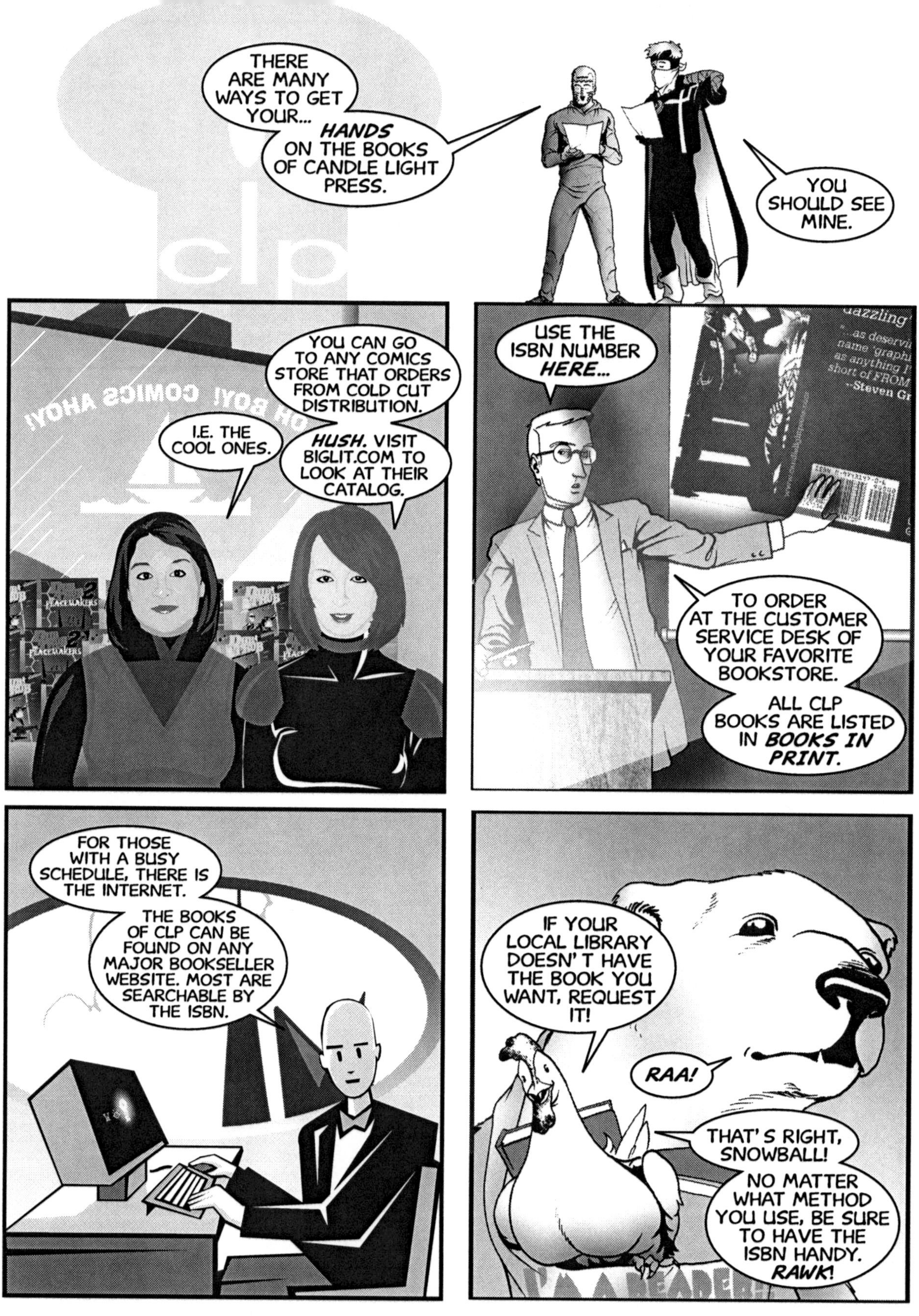

THERE ARE MANY WAYS TO GET YOUR... HANDS ON THE BOOKS OF CANDLE LIGHT PRESS.
YOU SHOULD SEE MINE.
YOU CAN GO TO ANY COMICS STORE THAT ORDERS FROM COLD CUT DISTRIBUTION.
I.E. THE COOL ONES.
HUSH. VISIT BIGLIT.COM TO LOOK AT THEIR CATALOG.
USE THE ISBN NUMBER HERE...
TO ORDER AT THE CUSTOMER SERVICE DESK OF YOUR FAVORITE BOOKSTORE.
ALL CLP BOOKS ARE LISTED IN BOOKS IN PRINT.
FOR THOSE WITH A BUSY SCHEDULE, THERE IS THE INTERNET.
THE BOOKS OF CLP CAN BE FOUND ON ANY MAJOR BOOKSELLER WEBSITE. MOST ARE SEARCHABLE BY THE ISBN.
IF YOUR LOCAL LIBRARY DOESN'T HAVE THE BOOK YOU WANT, REQUEST IT!
RAA!
THAT'S RIGHT, SNOWBALL!
NO MATTER WHAT METHOD YOU USE, BE SURE TO HAVE THE ISBN HANDY. RAWK!

From Our Family To Yours...

The creators of Candle Light Press are committed to making unique graphic literature available to the widest audience possible. Our books are available through a wide variety of outlets, including your local bookstore. Just have the ISBN handy and in short order you can be enjoying one of our fine books in the privacy of your own home. Whether you shop on the net, at the mall, or at your local comics retailer, the books of Candle Light Press are never far away. From our head office in spacious, scenic Iowa, we are constantly working to expand our library of novels and novellas. Our books are hand-crafted, machine-finished volumes that will compliment any home and provide hours of fun for comics readers expecting something different. It is our pleasure to bring these books from our family to yours.

CANDLE LIGHT PRESS MINI-CATALOG
Check 'em if ya got 'em!

clp

LaVergne, TN USA
29 September 2009
159376LV00003B/110/A